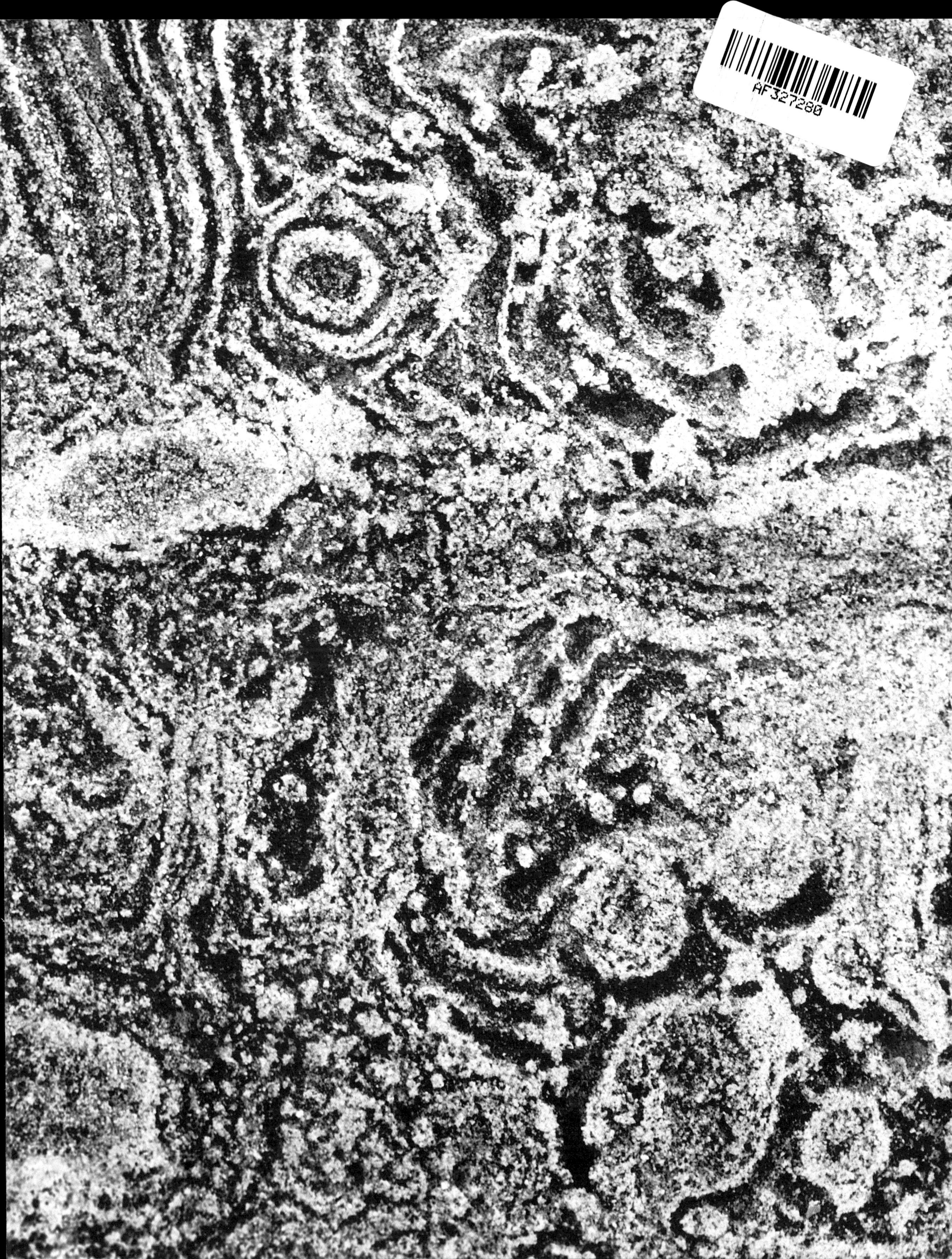

AF327280

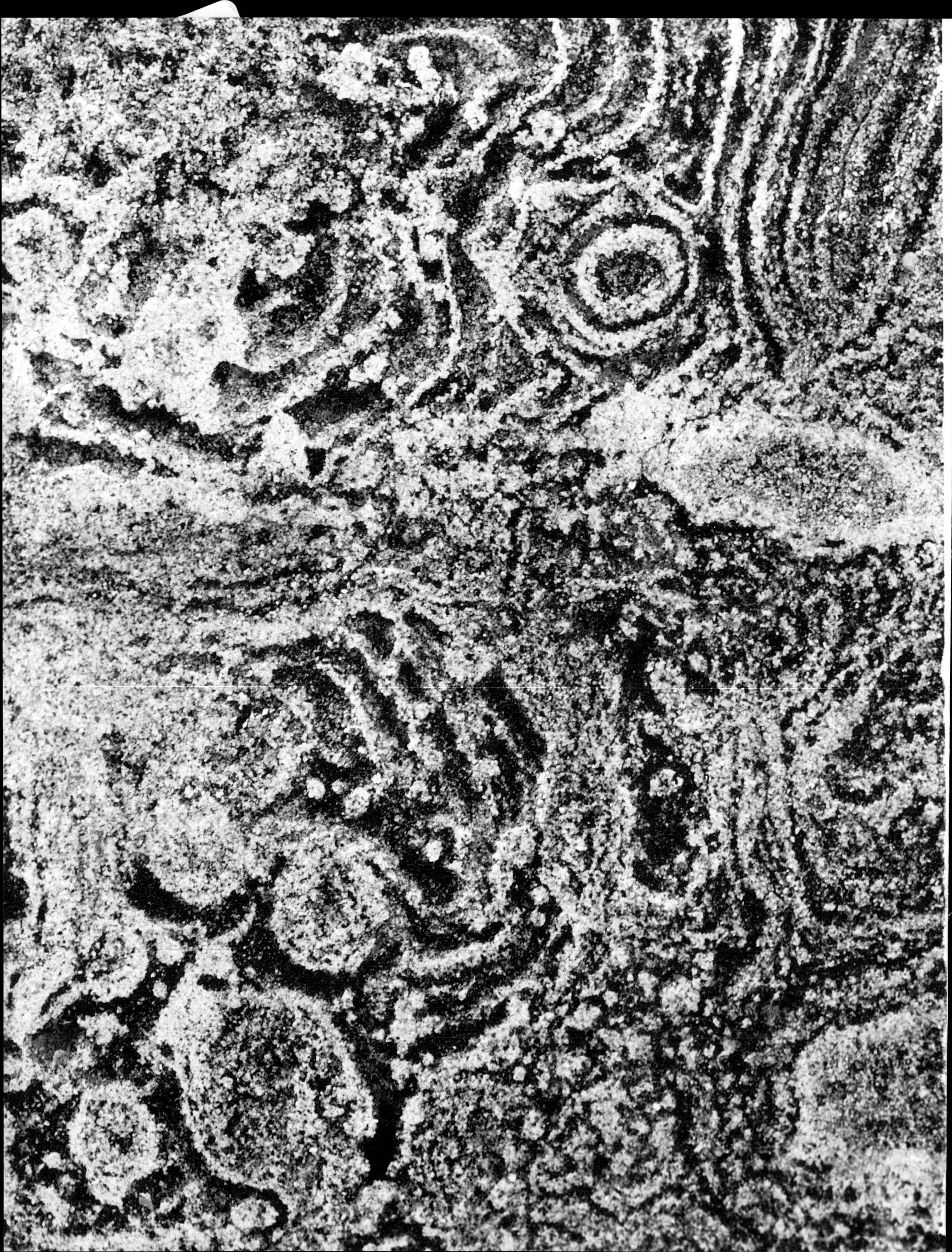

PRESENCE PASSING

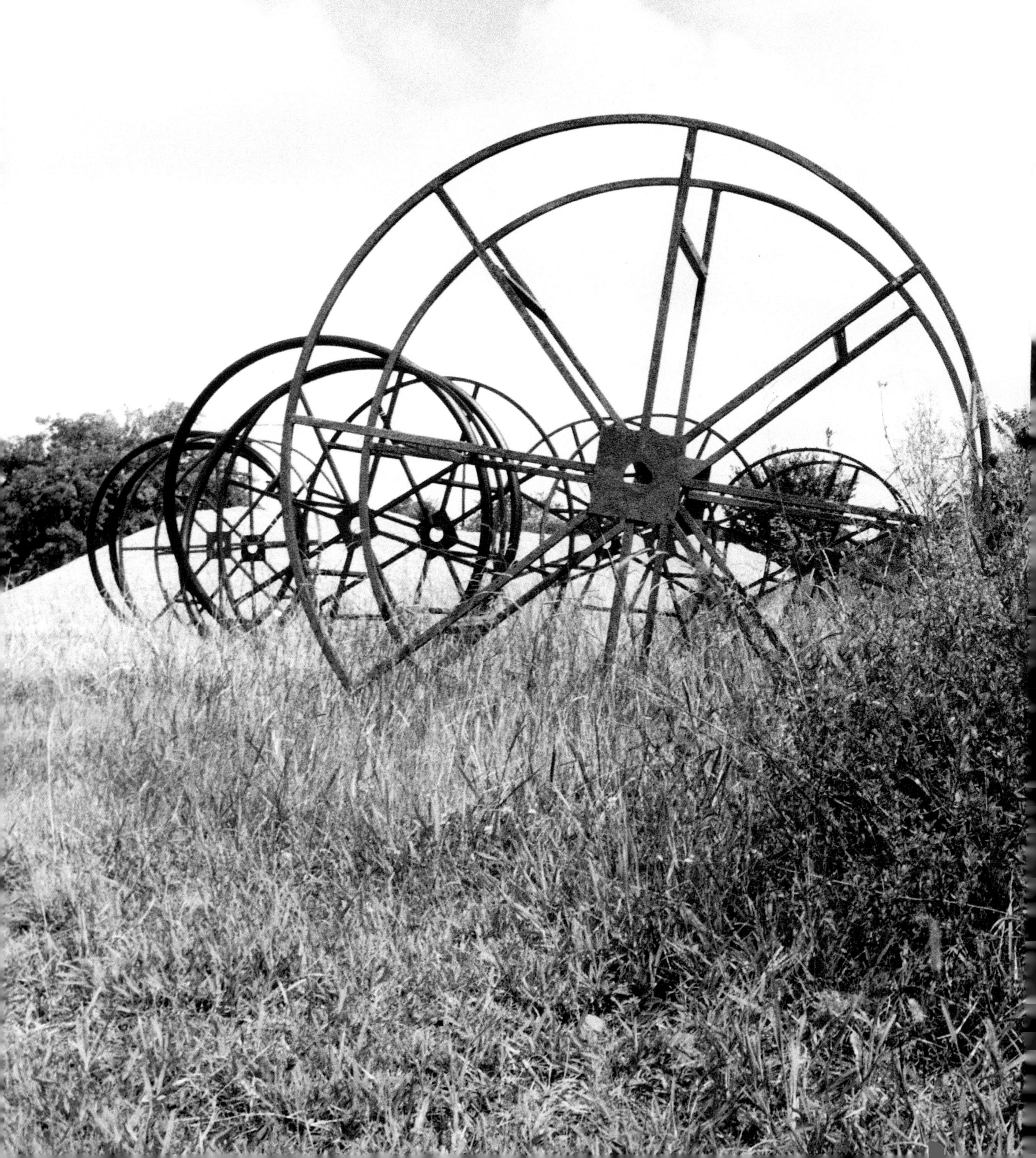

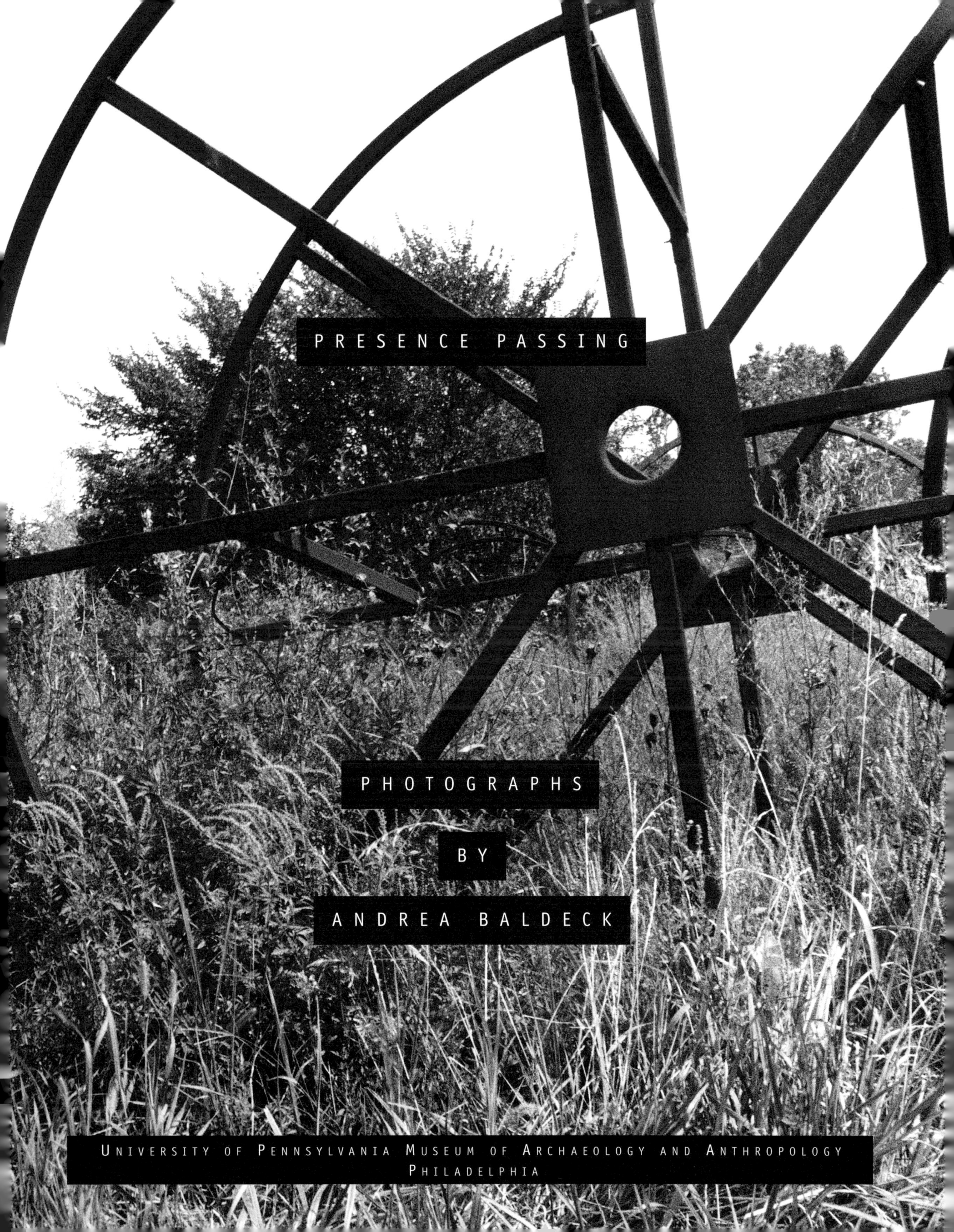

PRESENCE PASSING

PHOTOGRAPHS

BY

ANDREA BALDECK

UNIVERSITY OF PENNSYLVANIA MUSEUM OF ARCHAEOLOGY AND ANTHROPOLOGY
PHILADELPHIA

ISBN 978-1-934536-00-1

Cataloging in Publication Data available from
the U.S. Library of Congress, Washington, DC

Other Books by Andrea Baldeck:

Rudolf Staffel: Searching for Light, 1996

Hollis: Sonata Sonnets & Las Espinas, 1998

Breon O'Casey: In Honor of His Seventieth Birthday, 1998

Talismanic, 1998

Venice a personal View, 1999

Touching the Mekong, 2003

Hollis: Dark Encounter in Mid Air, 2004

The Heart of Haiti, 2006

Closely Observed, 2006

Printed in the USA on acid-free paper

CONTENTS

A small road diverges from the national nervous system of interstate highways, branching off in dendritic fashion, weaving through a land's peripheral tissue. Far beyond tangled ganglia enveloping urban centers, this slender fiber connects villages, hamlets, and settlements, small nodes marked by no more than a weathered sign, a widened pavement, a post office.

Paralleling rusted railroad tracks, where ties molder and weeds burgeon in unused roadbeds, the route passes a collapsing warehouse, empty of coal once shoveled into steam locomotives. Sloughing its distempered zinc siding, shedding asbestos shingles, it slumps beside a platform deserted of freight and passengers, where the last train left a shuttered station decades before.

In roadside junkyards cast-off vehicles sink into earth like felled pachyderms: accretions of steel designed for speed but rendered immobile, they surrender to the elements, one molecule at a time. Unruly grasses, tenacious vines, and implacable kudzu overtake and camouflage the remains in a haphazard burial mound.

Up and over a hummocked railway crossing, the road becomes Main Street. Stilled by the flight of commerce to a sprawling mall, this stretch of vacant shops — cobwebbed, untrafficked, moribund — stands like a gap-toothed row of decayed teeth in the landscape, its grip lost on a small town's custom. A faint flicker of life appears in the form of an elderly shopkeeper, moving falteringly among her muddled merchandise and memories. Sole living proprietor of the family store, she dwells in the previous century and finds comfort in the fulsome voice of a radio preacher. Feral cats prowl and poke amid detritus and devalued treasures, hoarded over an eccentric's lifetime, wordless testament to an uncontained magpie sensibility. Equally silent stands the deserted supper club, where nostalgia and naugahyde keep lonely company in the settled dust of desuetude. Defying the air of time arrested, a local diner extends its chrome-and-formica welcome: vehicles sleek and battered nose up close outside like steeds at a watering trough, while within sputters conversation born of the need for coffee and connection.

Quiet side streets lead to shells of houses, built, bought, or borrowed. Carapaces for frail flesh and fallible personas, their façades reflect the lives and fortunes of those sheltered within. Expedience trumps elegance when moldings crumble, rooflines buckle, and strength and wallets fail. Scars, patches, breaks, and mends befall both houses and bodies, age and rot assault flesh and timber. When forsaken, foreclosed, or emptied by fire, the remaining husks gape and yaw under the pull of gravity and push of weather. Dusty windows turn glaucous eyes to the street; torn curtains stir as winds breach broken panes. Doors, no longer welcoming, sport curled tongues of sprung and rusted screen. Walls sag, buckle, shed stucco and paint like scabrous skin, leaving palimpsests of stains and textures. Behind these walls, windows, and doors lie odd clues to tantalize the voyeur: an unmade bed, a single boot, a steamer trunk, a doll's carriage. In dwellings touched by fire, scorched clapboards bear blisters; a tangle of melted plumbing, unmoored, speaks of the crucible that annealed it, eerily creaking as it sways in a gusting wind.

Set back from the warren of streets, holding itself apart like a superior dowager, sits the house on the hill, emblem of past prosperity and social ascendance. Built with a fortune now spent and lost to memory, it broods in mildew and lace curtains. Faltering clocks keep company with empty chairs. Doors stand ajar, wallpaper peels, and a forgotten forebear stares out from his framed portrait at an empty room. Long gone are echoes of footfalls, clatter of silver on china, chatter of caged birds and dinner guests. Vanished with them is memory of the rifle-shot report which rent the reception hall mirror and left it fractured in its constricting frame.

Beyond dwellings languish gardens where order slides into entropy, randomness supplants deliberate design, and boundaries blur as borders encroach. Open space surrenders to a thicket, the triumph of botanical opportunism. Fruit falls from untended trees, a sticky, savory lure for scavenging insects. Nature thwarts the plan imposed upon it, which survives only in disjointed remnants — a chair, a pot, a broken birdbath — of a vanished intent.

Leaving town, two lanes of macadam bisect fields of soybeans and corn, carpet squares of cropland bordered by trees, where plantings edge up to the foundations of empty, abandoned barns. Gaping doors soundlessly tell of harvests and cattle gone; naked rafters span empty haylofts, vacant dovecotes bear witness to the vanished husbandry of a family farm, subsumed by agribusiness.

In a caesura between plantings slumbers an amusement park, shuttered against approaching winter, its whir and buzz stilled. Trampled weeds and packed earth mark the deserted fairway, folded in on itself in hibernation. Cartoon-ferocious grins transform vintage cockpits into imaginary rockets awaiting the next generation of captivated toddlers. Carousel horses, ridden hard, halt in mid-stride, anticipating a new coat of paint and swaddling tarpaulins. The bare skeleton of the Ferris wheel, shorn of its pendant chairs, pokes its steel into the hazy sky, as if beckoning for companionship to long-armed mechanical irrigators in adjacent fields.

At crossroads, churches stand like sentinels, rising above the fields in white-clapboard rectitude, triangulation points in a sea of green. Whether humble storefronts or Grant Wood-gothic icons, these are lodestones for sparse and scattered congregations, some still drawing the compass needles of shared belief, continuity, community. Close by stands the cemetery, repository of collective memory. Plastic flowers, tattered flags, votive statuary individualize a handful of headstones while others, eroded into illegibility, careen oddly, heaved by seasons of earth's freezes and thaws. Leaning conversationally toward each other, they suggest a posthumous reunion in progress. When the buried denizens of the churchyard outnumber the living congregation, when the center of the community does not hold, the church itself, vacated, deconsecrated, becomes a marker, a cenotaph. Decay's destruction sounds the final dirge.

Where land runs out, the road stops at water's edge. Wharves and fish-houses stand empty of the last big catch, now a destination for weekend crabbers with a cooler of ice and a bucket of bait. Fish traps teeter in uneven ranks, beards of gray seaweed clinging to their wire walls. Mounds of bleached oyster shells attest to the wealth of subaqueous life that once sustained watermen and filled plates in candle-lit restaurants. Seabirds vie for roosts on weathered pilings, barnacles moor themselves securely at the tide line, and marine worms burrow, consuming their home from within. Close to shore, their seaworthiness forsaken, disembodied boats settle on their timbers in permanent dry dock, worn bearers of dreams postponed, forgotten, unrealized.

A small road meanders countless miles through the landscape, unspooling images which ensnare the eye, breathe an air of mystery, and provoke unanswerable questions. Who built these structures, filled these empty rooms, tended orchard and garden, here pursued a life?

What is left behind serves as a metaphor for vanished lives and spent ambition. Tantalizing, incomplete clues beckon the voyeur and call up memories — distinct or inchoate, complex or spectral — that shape us. A world partly seen, partly imagined, encourages speculation, contemplation, storytelling.

Our built world is no bulwark against forces of change, but bears witness to human necessity, inventiveness, and creativity. The sequenced photographs that follow invite the viewer on a visual journey, to sense the passage of time. Culled from many locations, they are meant to suggest a mood rather than a region, using a vocabulary — vernacular architecture and castoff objects — accessible to the eye and common experience. The spirit of this collection is one of evocation, not documentation. It invites one to conjure meanings from the images, to wonder what each of us will leave behind, as presence passes and absence overtakes.

Andrea Baldeck

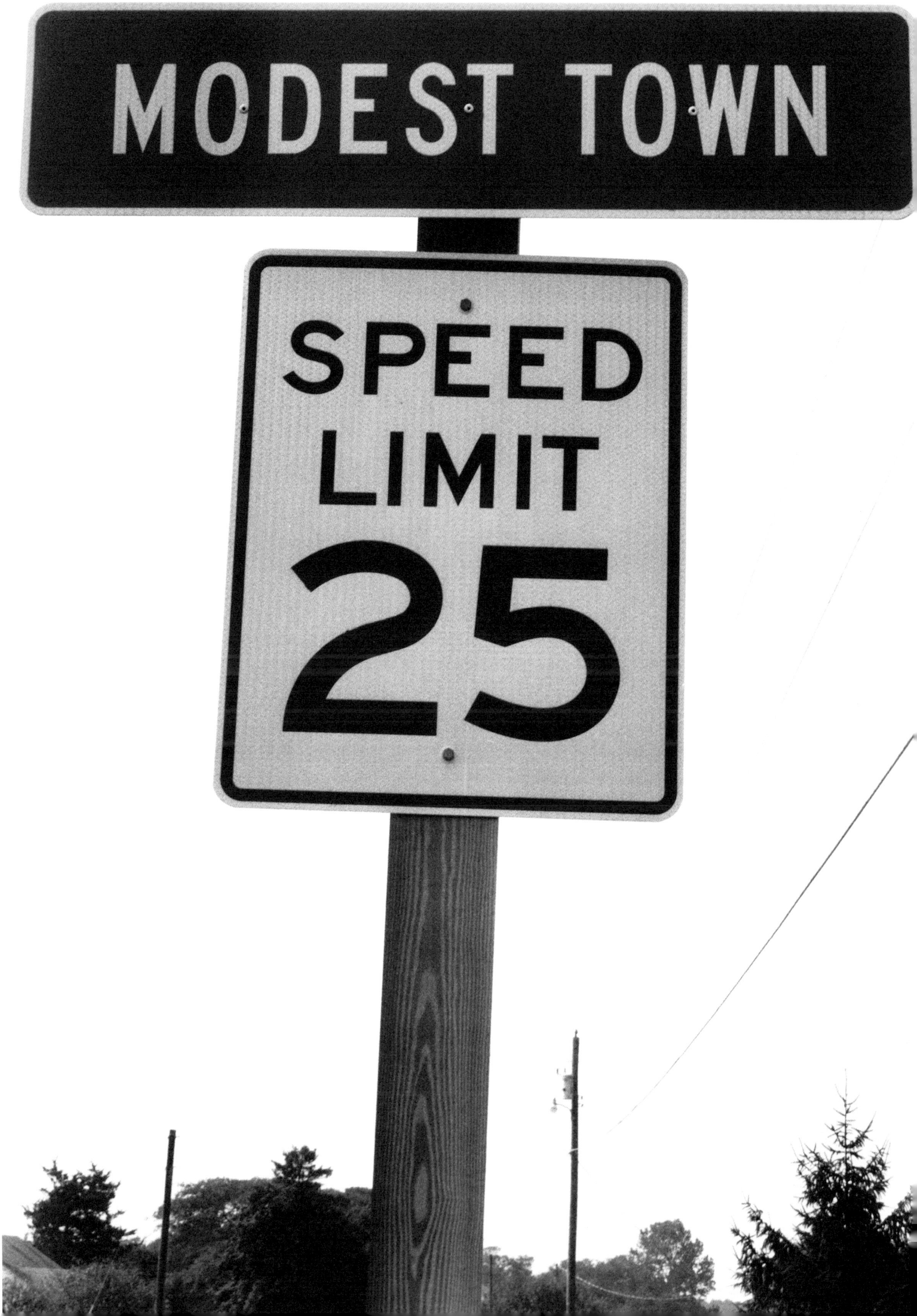

MODEST TOWN
SPEED
LIMIT
25

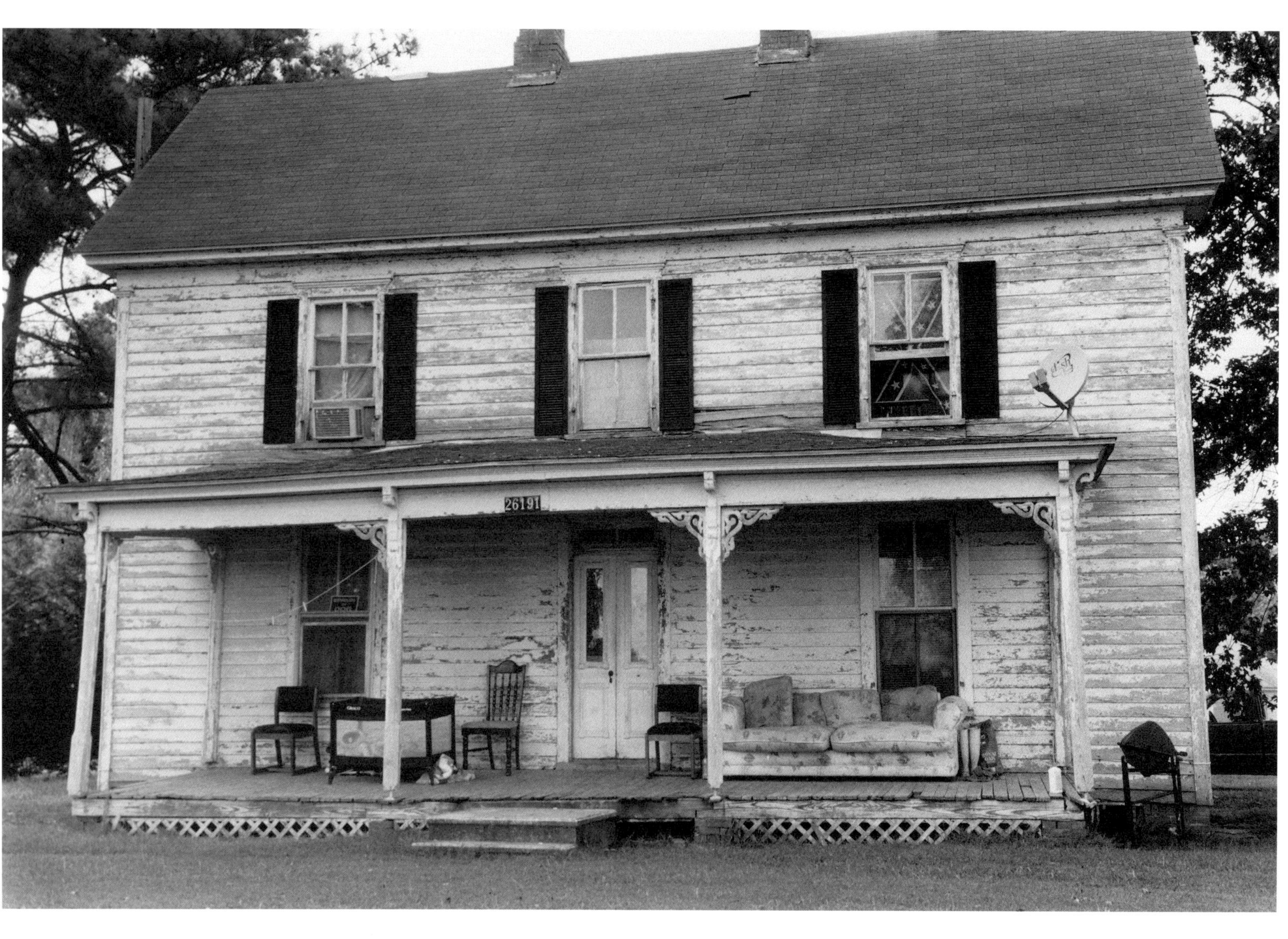

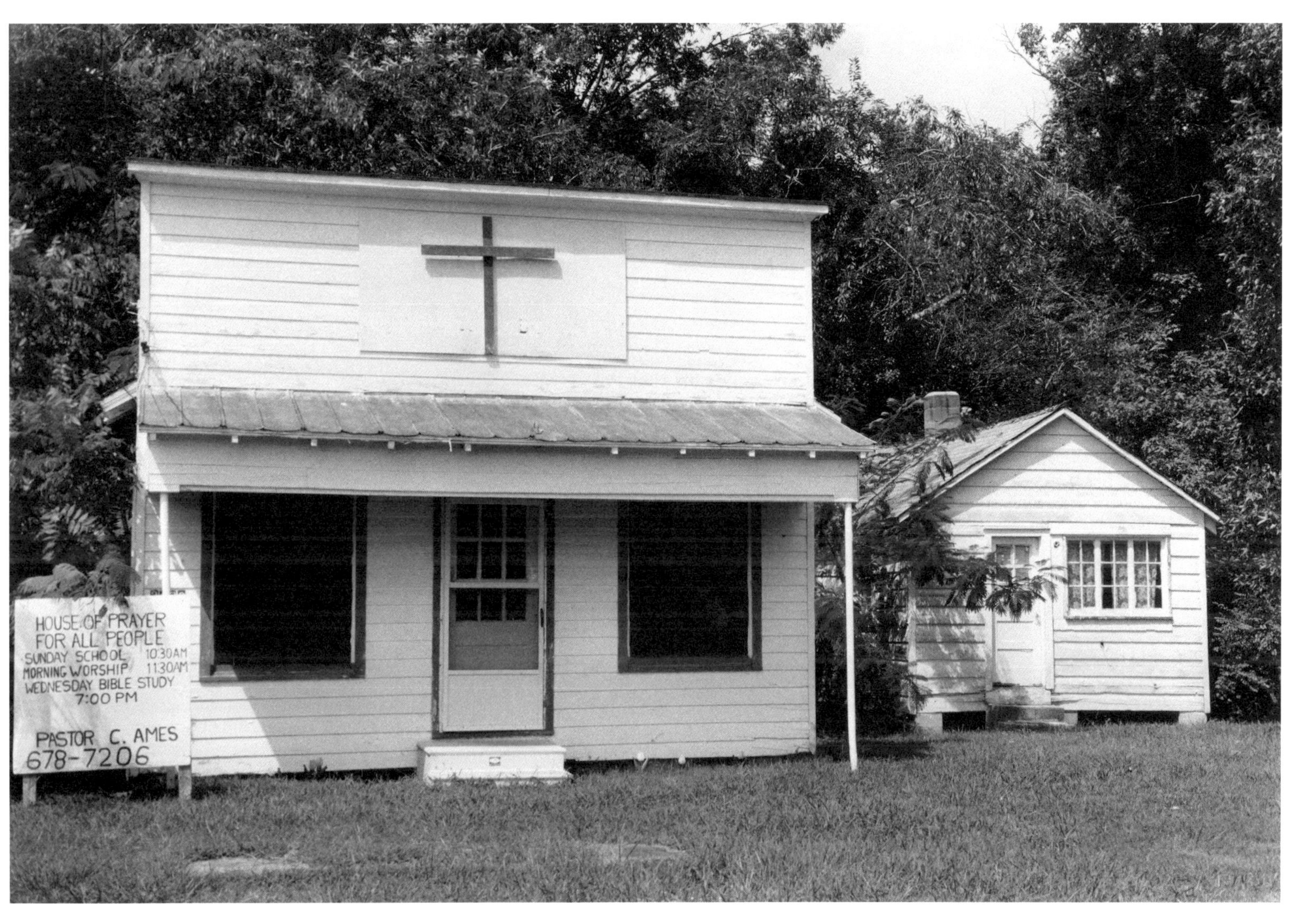
HOUSE OF PRAYER
FOR ALL PEOPLE
SUNDAY SCHOOL 10:30AM
MORNING WORSHIP 11:30AM
WEDNESDAY BIBLE STUDY
7:00 PM
PASTOR C. AMES
678-7206

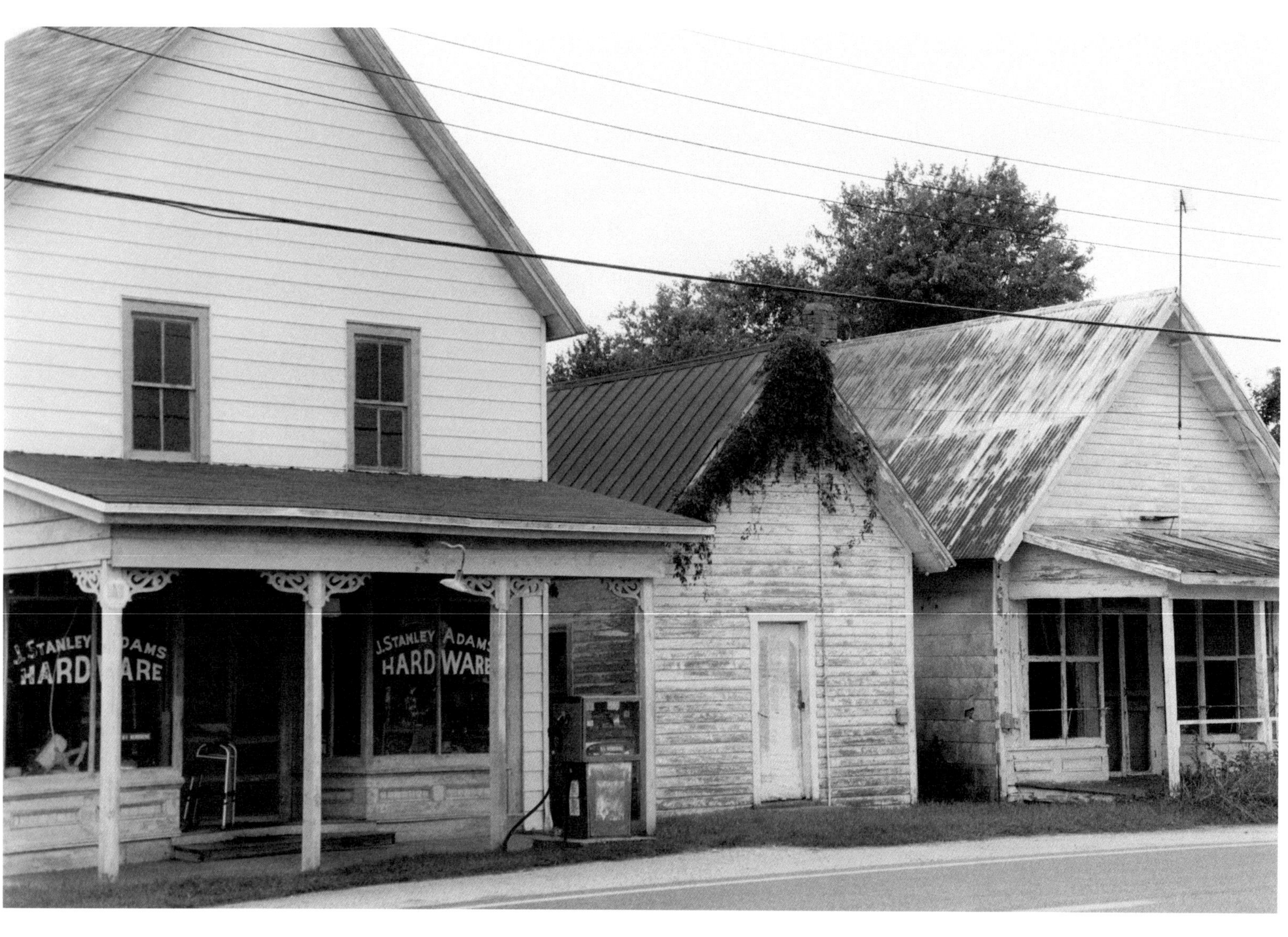
J. STANLEY ADAMS
HARDWARE
J. STANLEY ADAMS
HARDWARE

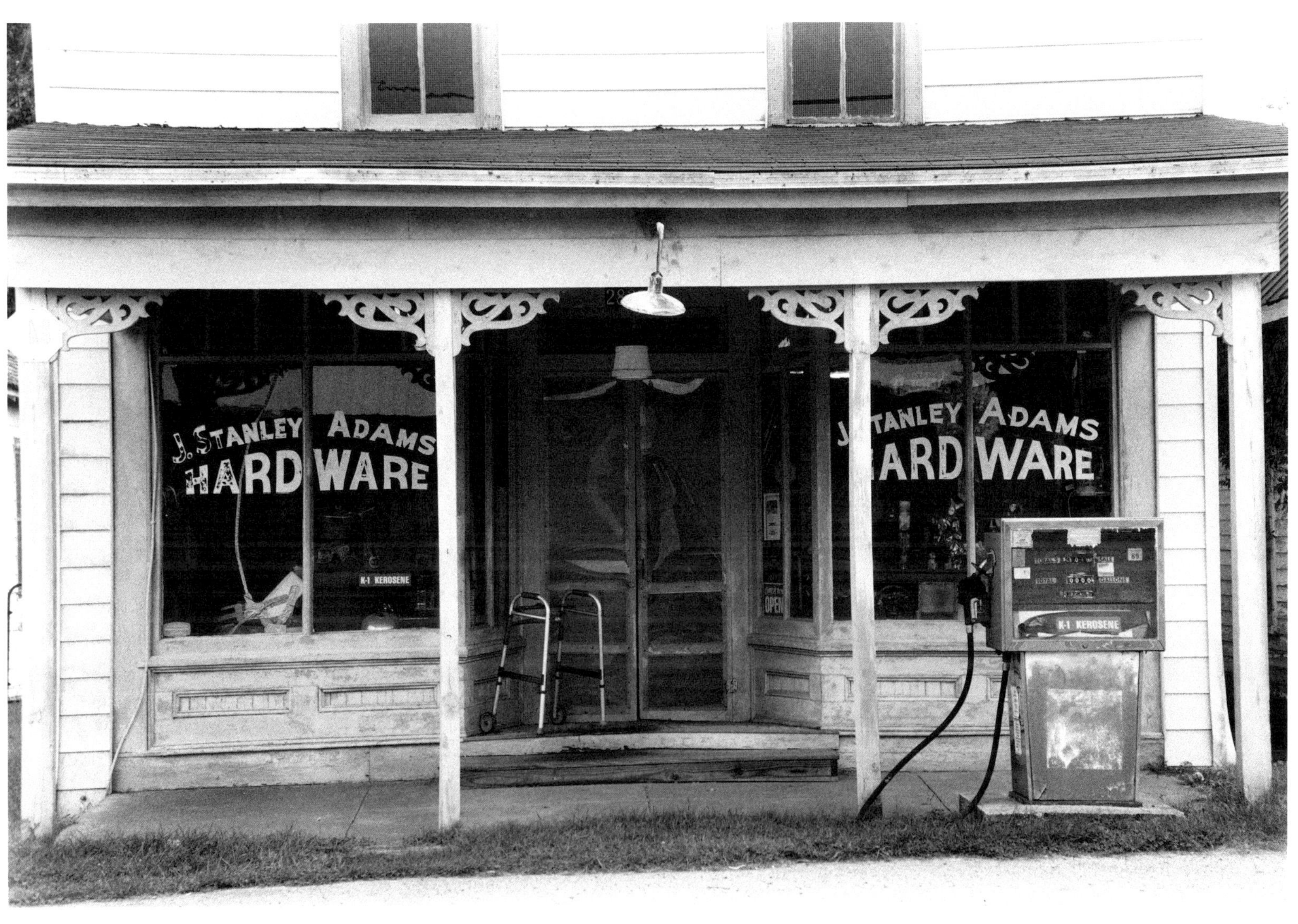

J. STANLEY ADAMS
HARDWARE
J. STANLEY ADAMS
HARDWARE
K-1 KEROSENE
K-1 KEROSENE
OPEN

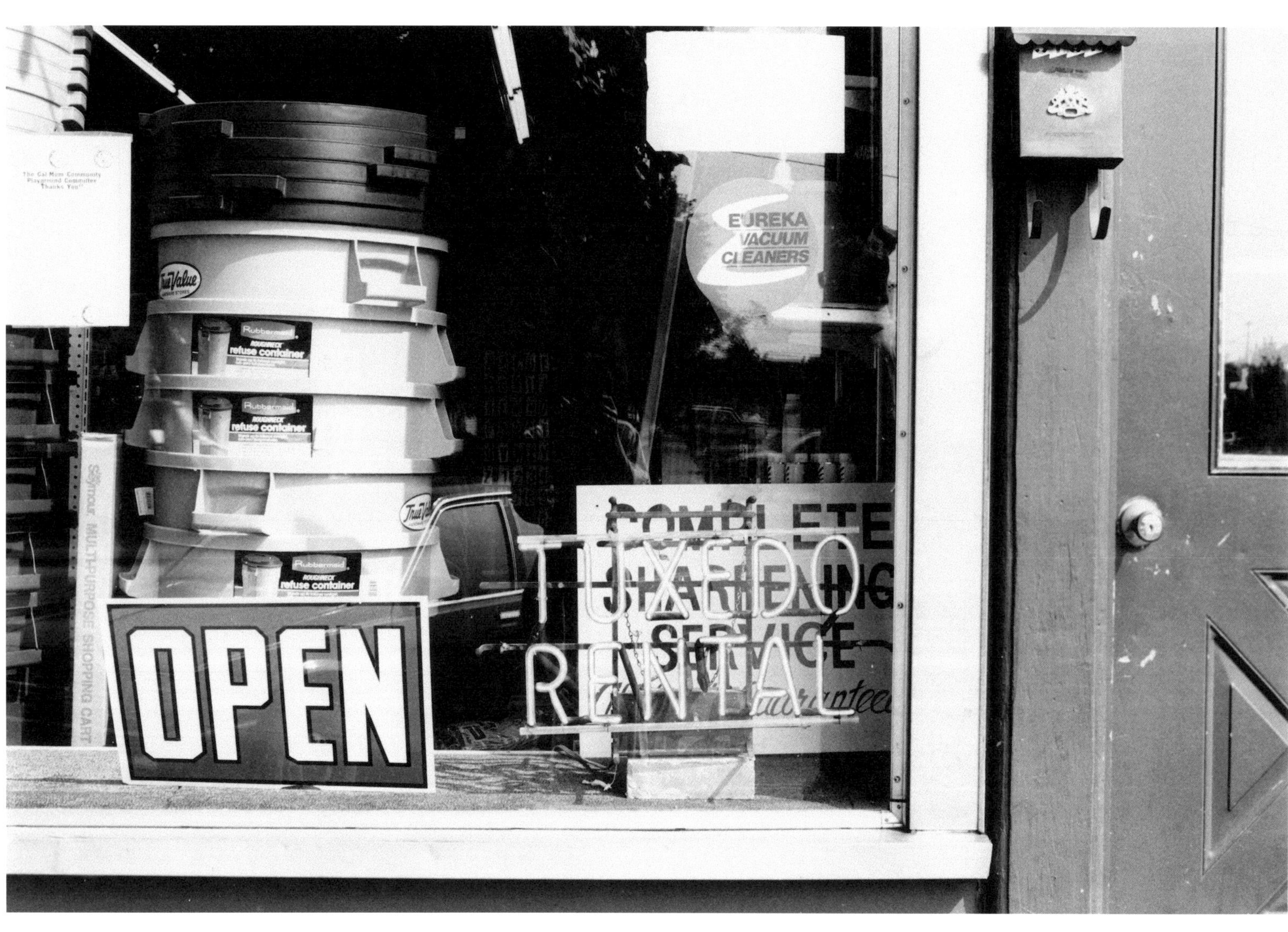
EUREKA
VACUUM
CLEANERS
True Value
Rubbermaid
refuse container
Rubbermaid
refuse container
Rubbermaid
refuse container
True Value
Seymour MULTI-PURPOSE SHOPPING CART
OPEN
COMPLETE
TUXEDO
SERVICE
RENTAL

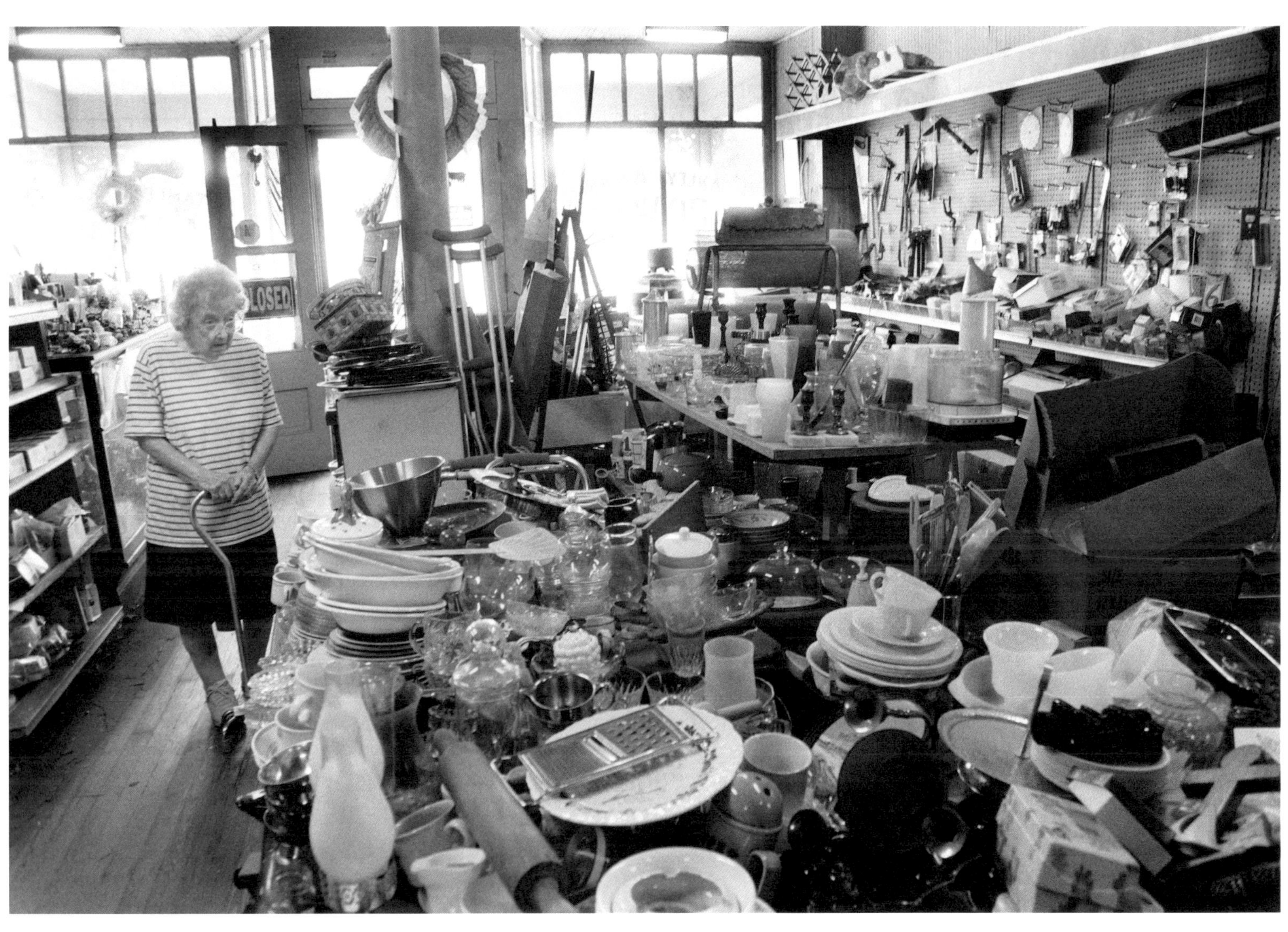

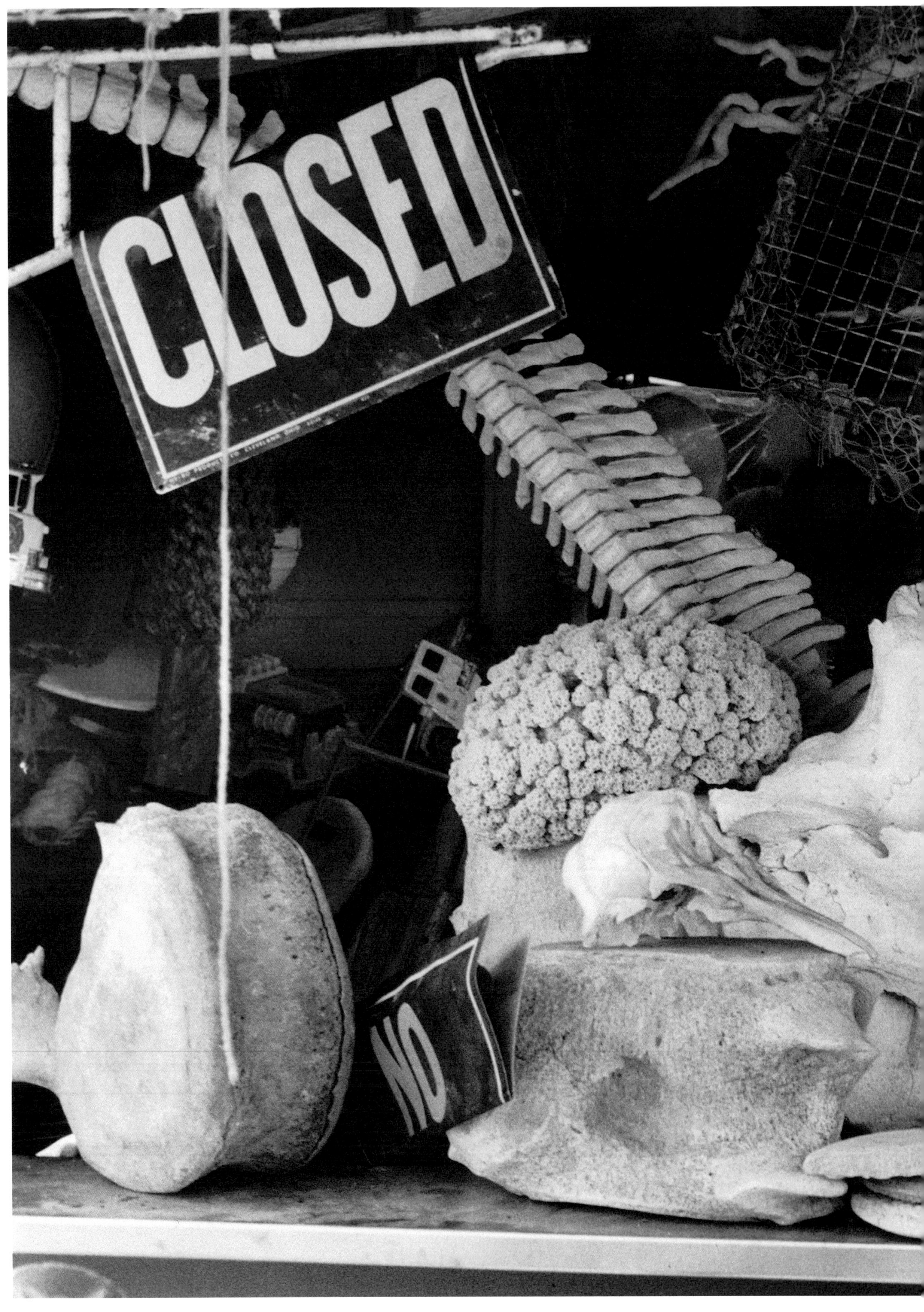
CLOSED
NO

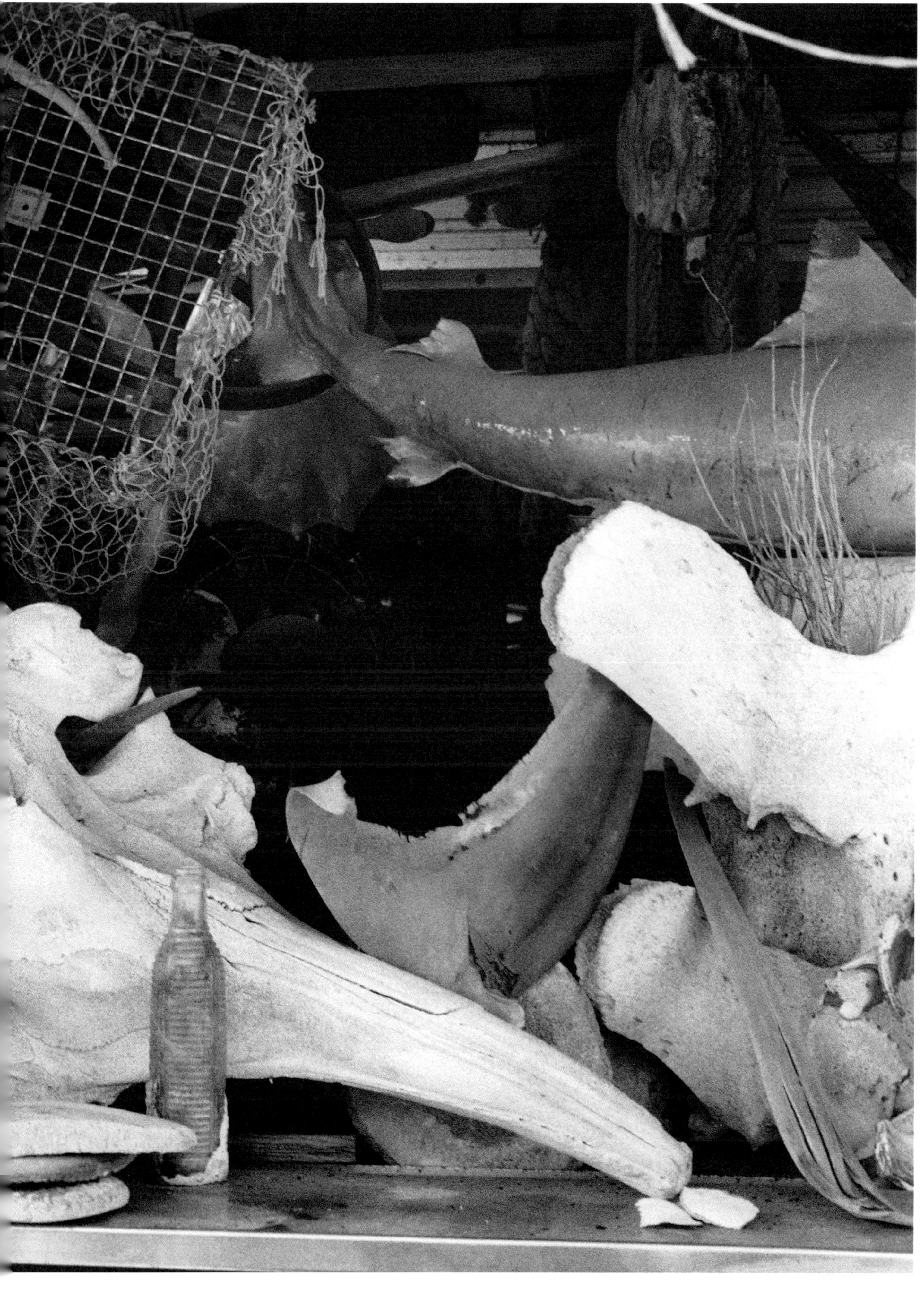

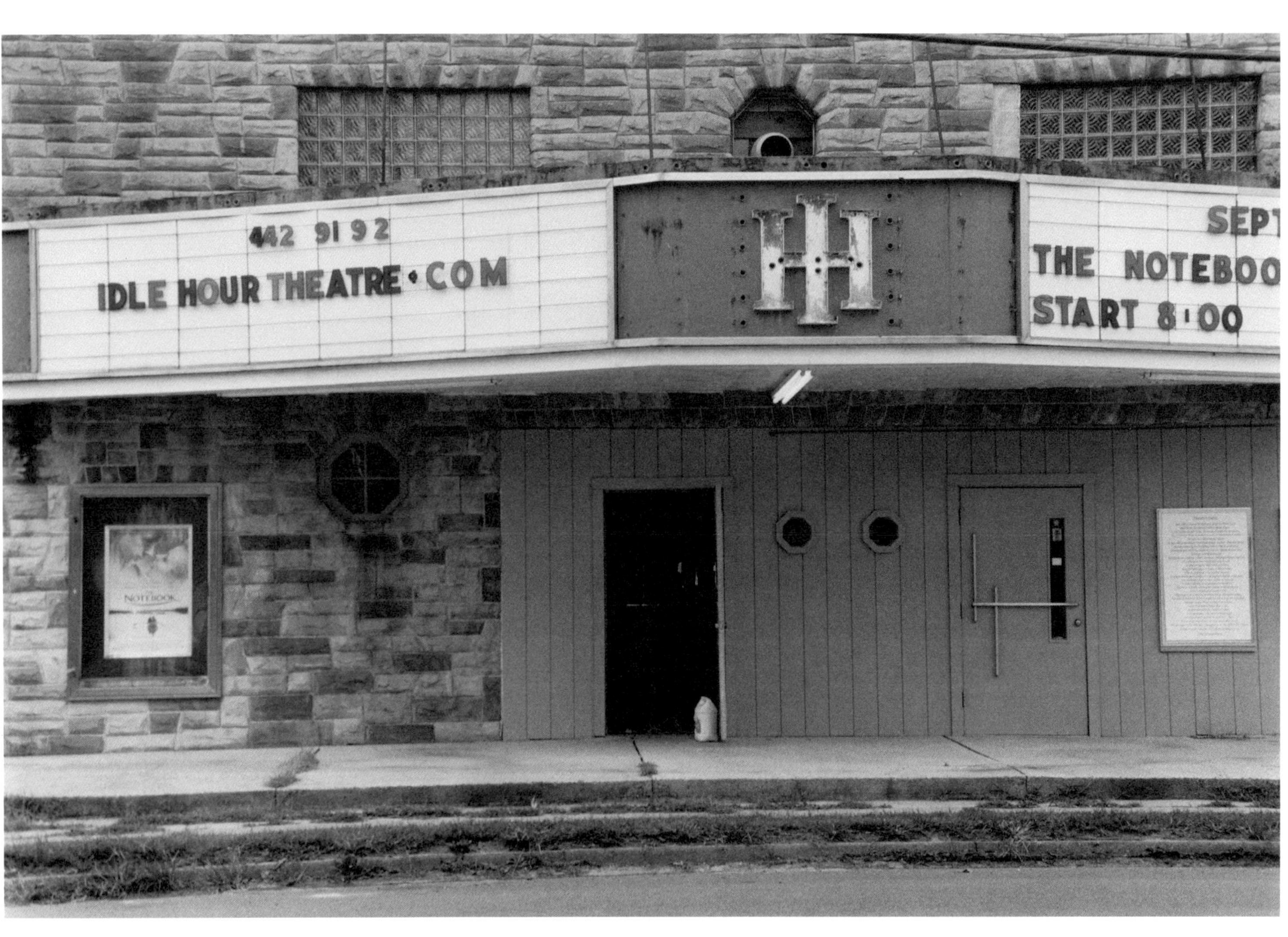
442 9192
IDLE HOUR THEATRE•COM
H
SEPT
THE NOTEBOO
START 8:00
NOTEBOOK

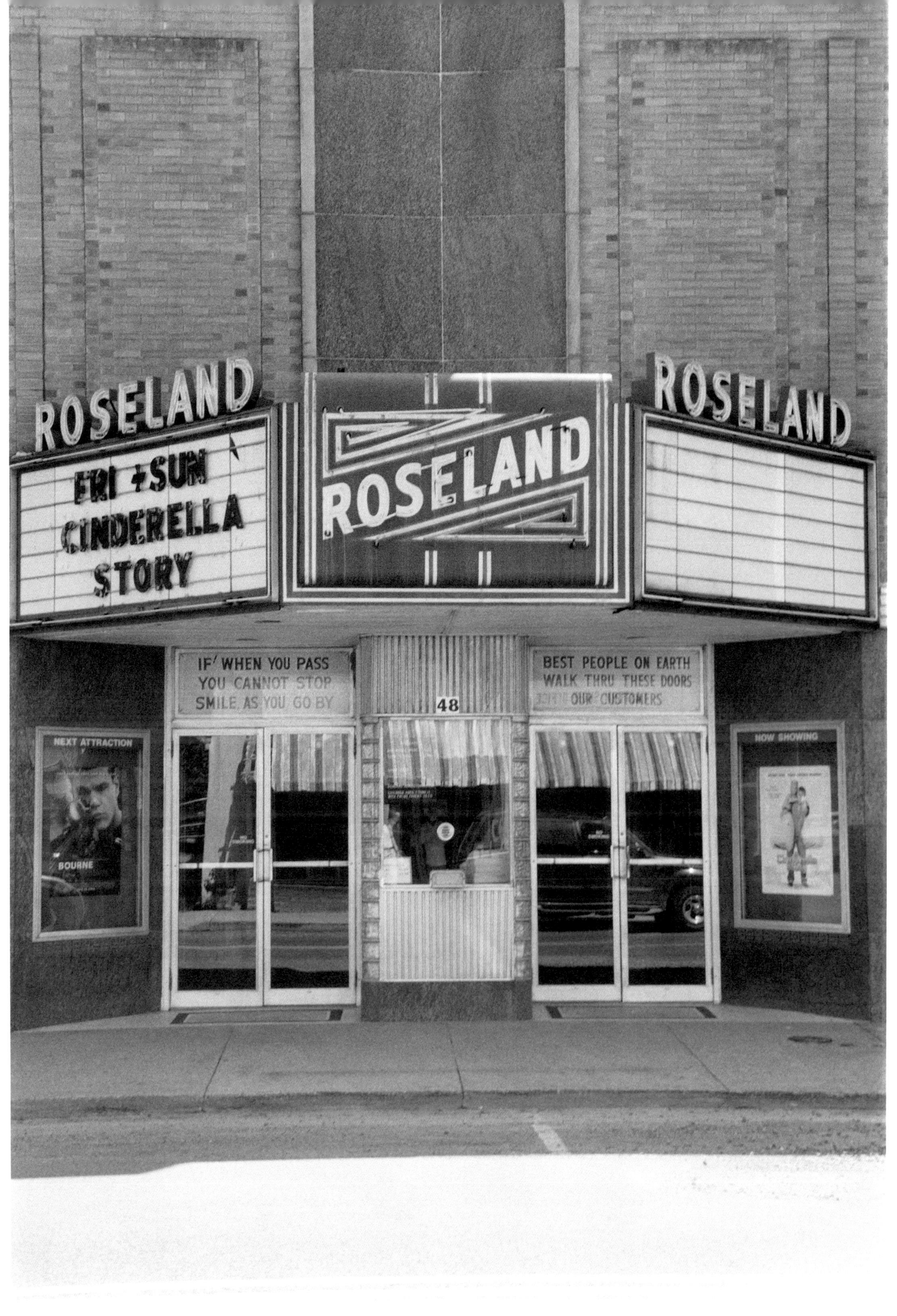

ROSELAND
ROSELAND
ROSELAND
FRI + SUN
CINDERELLA
STORY
IF WHEN YOU PASS
YOU CANNOT STOP
SMILE AS YOU GO BY
BEST PEOPLE ON EARTH
WALK THRU THESE DOORS
OUR CUSTOMERS
48
NEXT ATTRACTION
BOURNE
NOW SHOWING

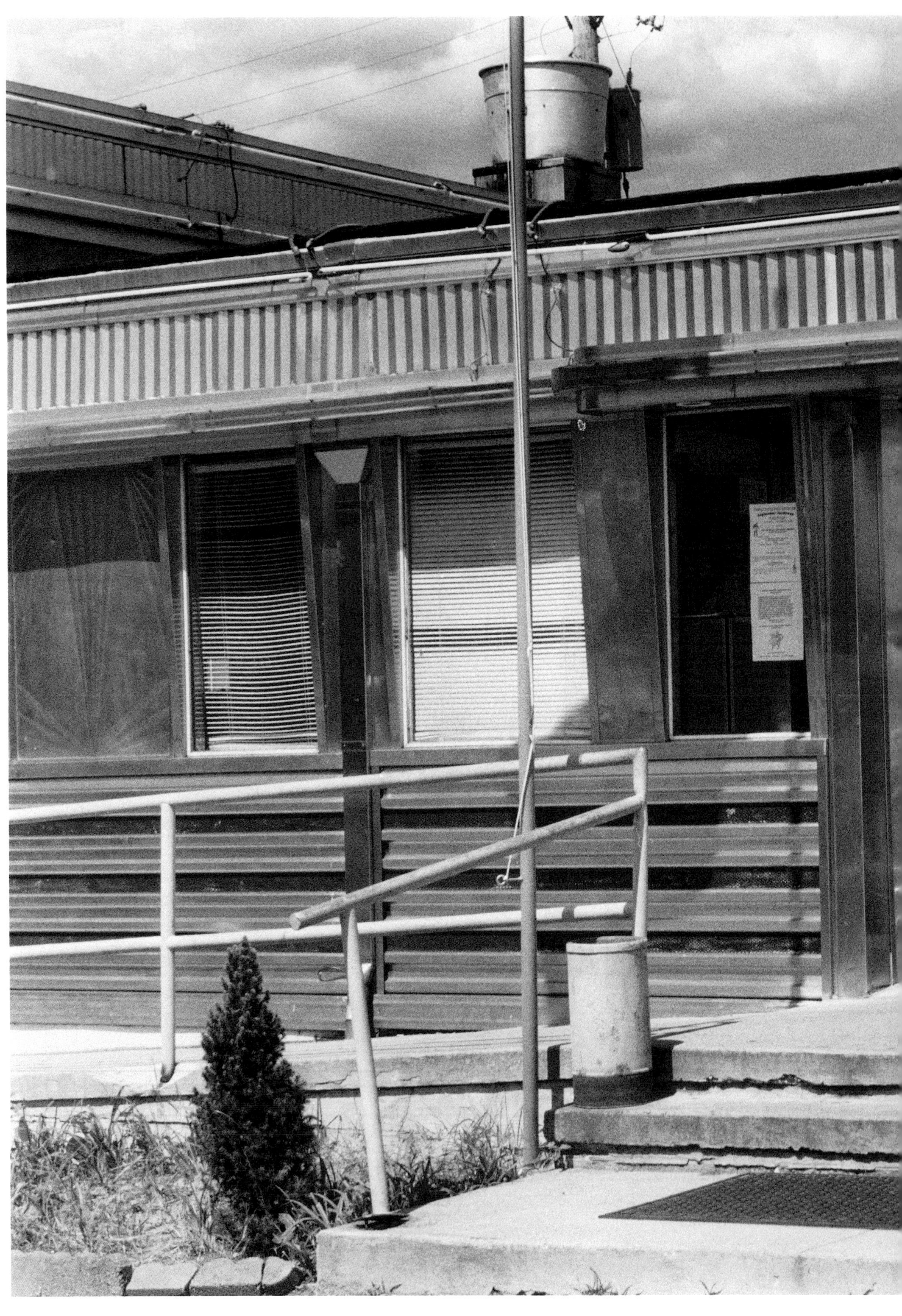

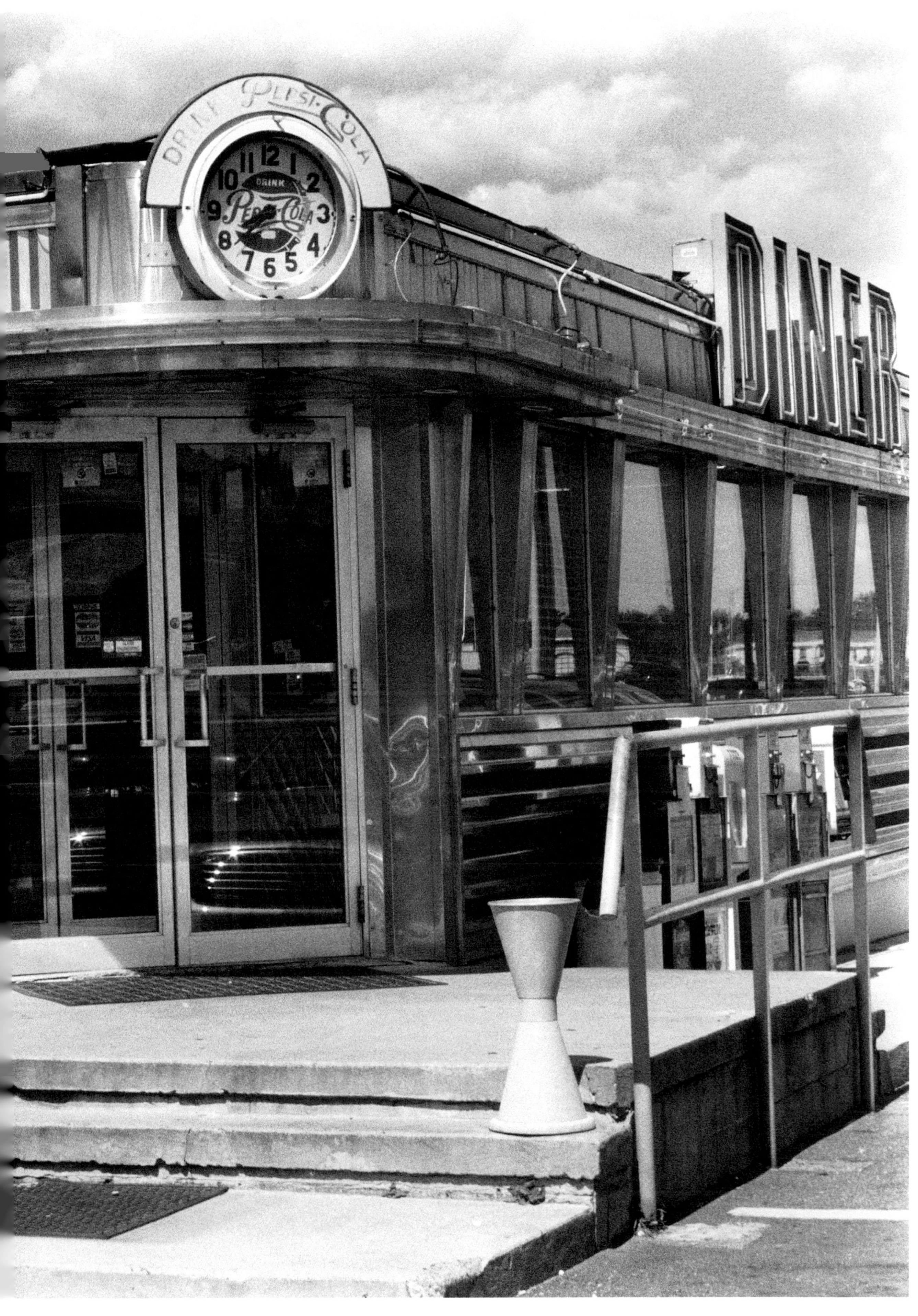
DRINK Pepsi-Cola
DRINK
Pepsi Cola
DINER

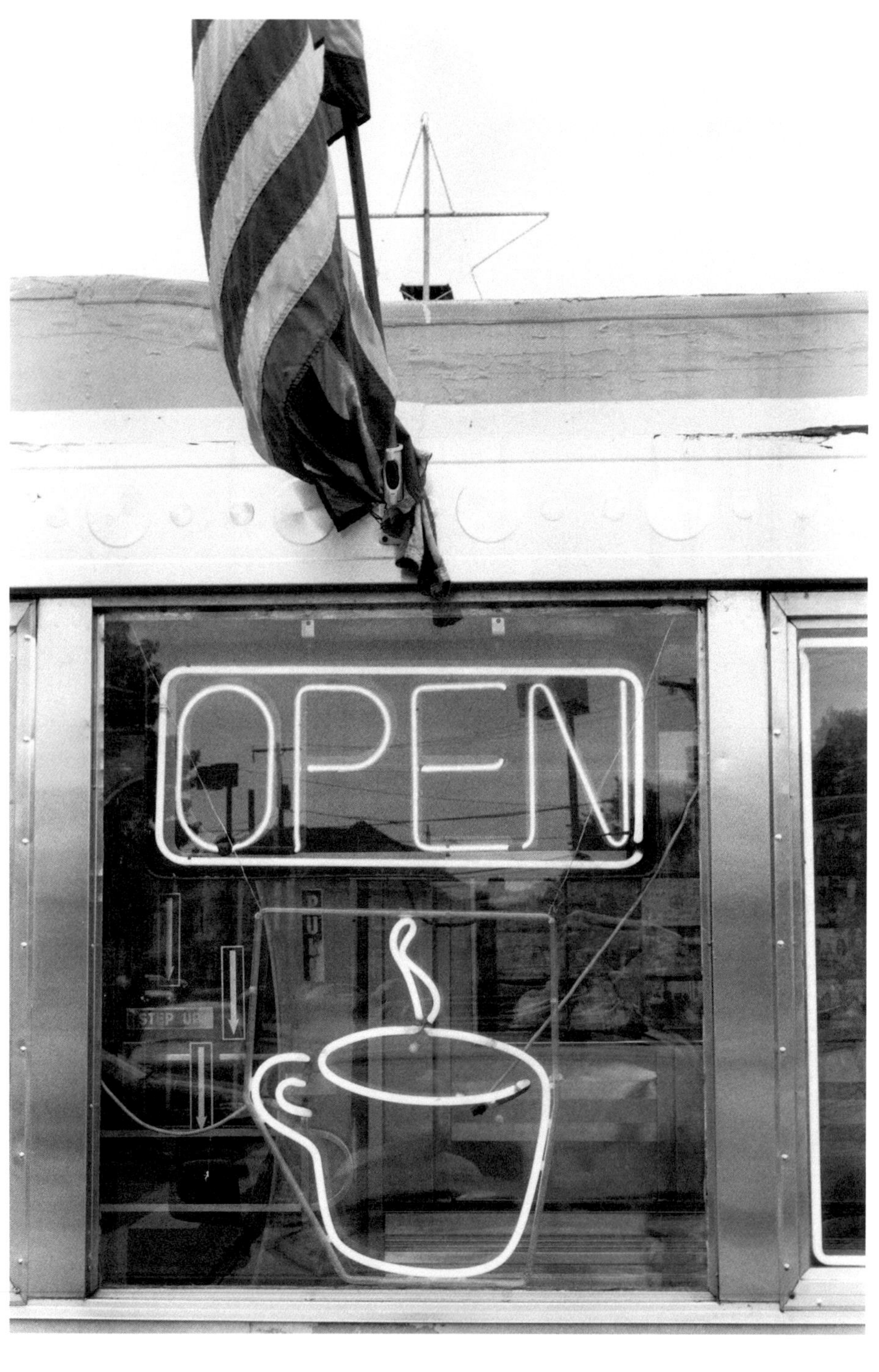
OPEN
STEP UP

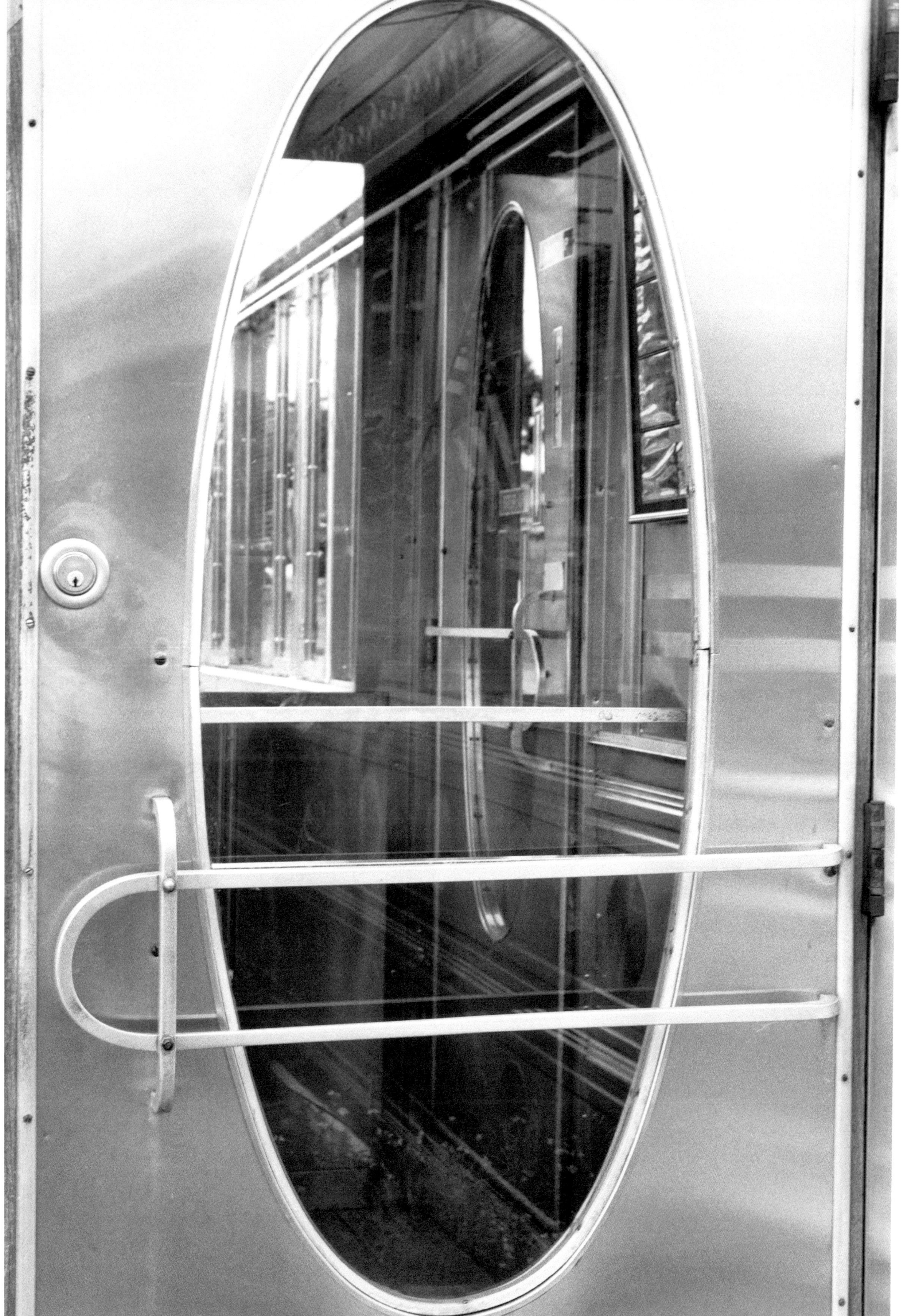

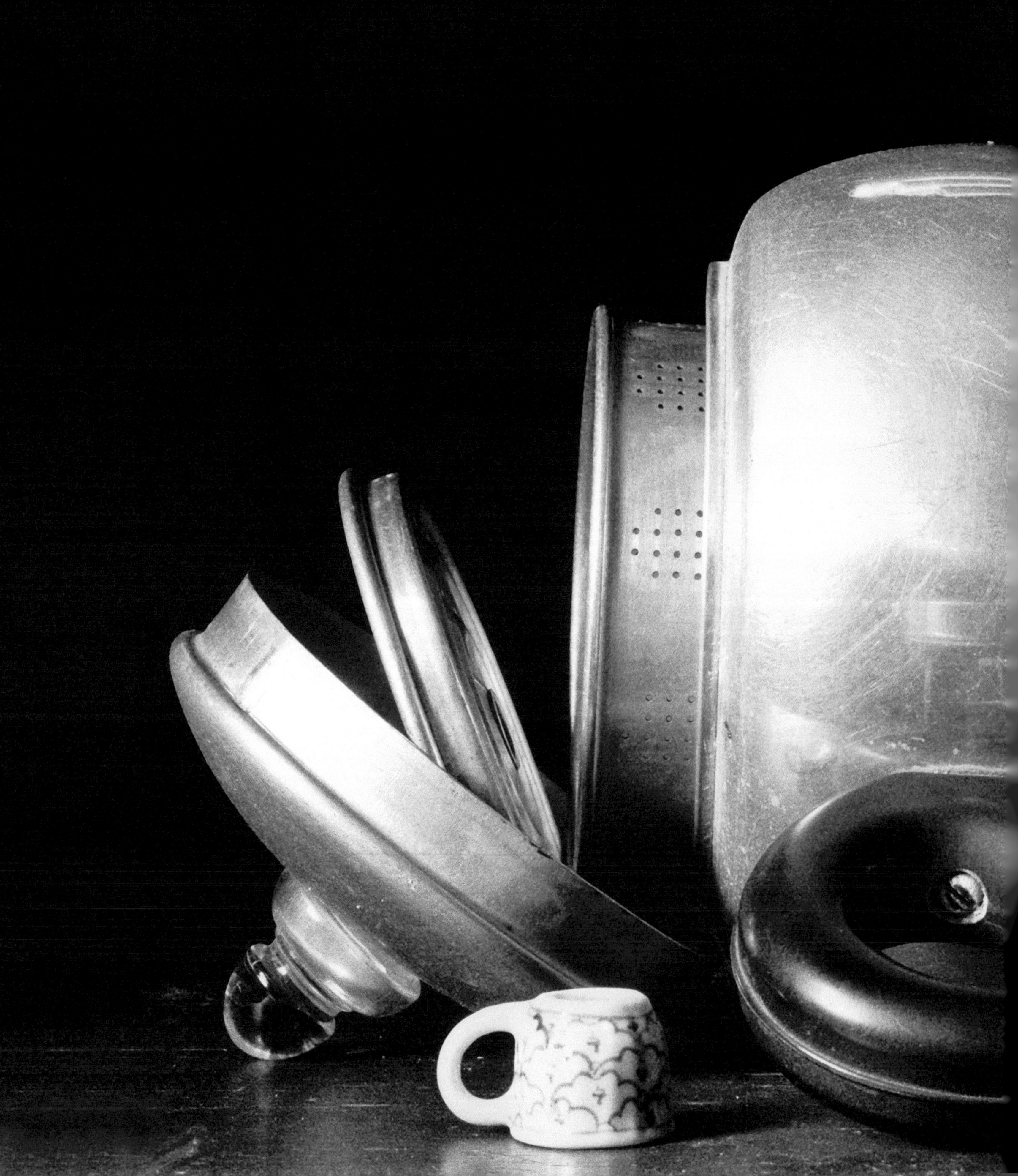

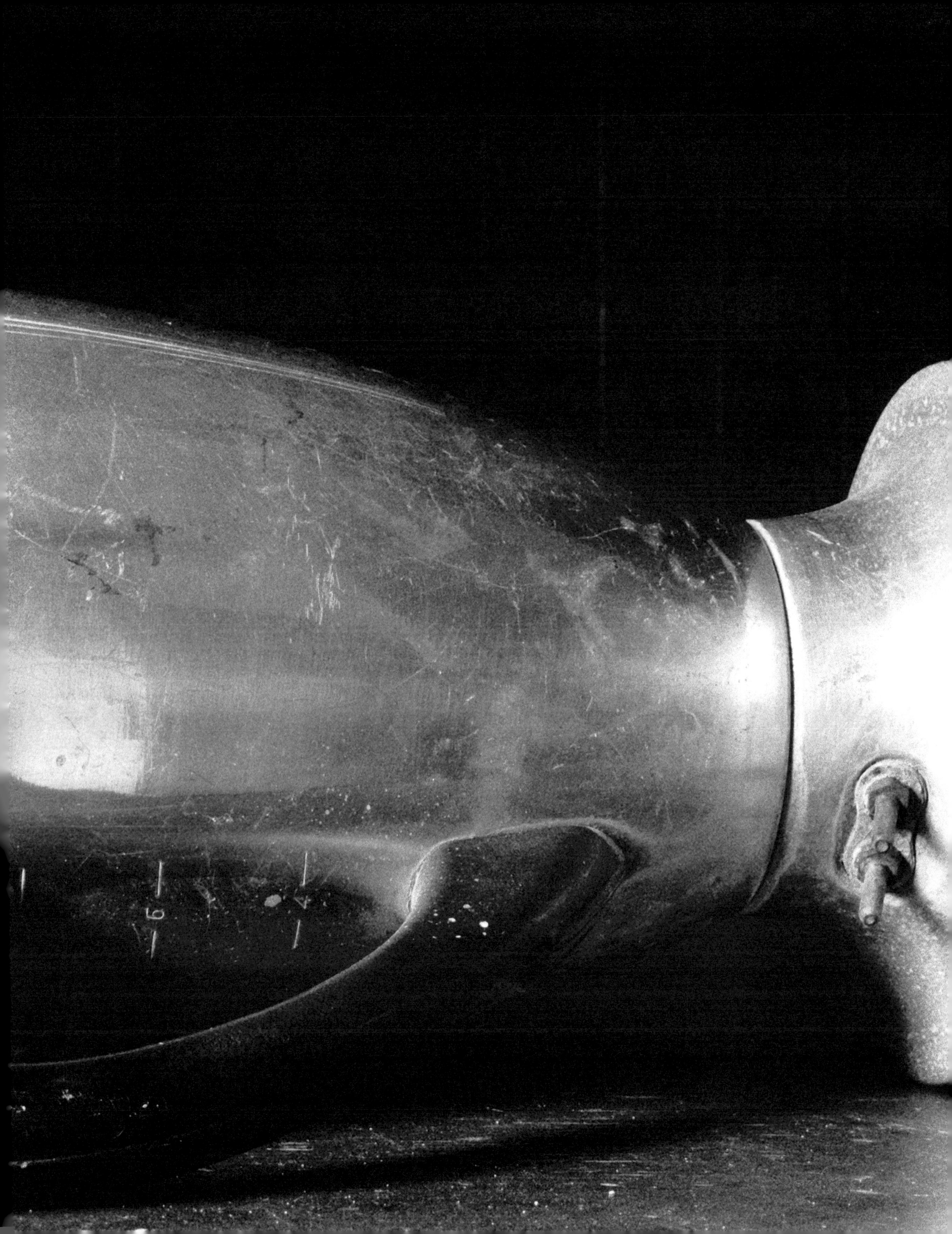

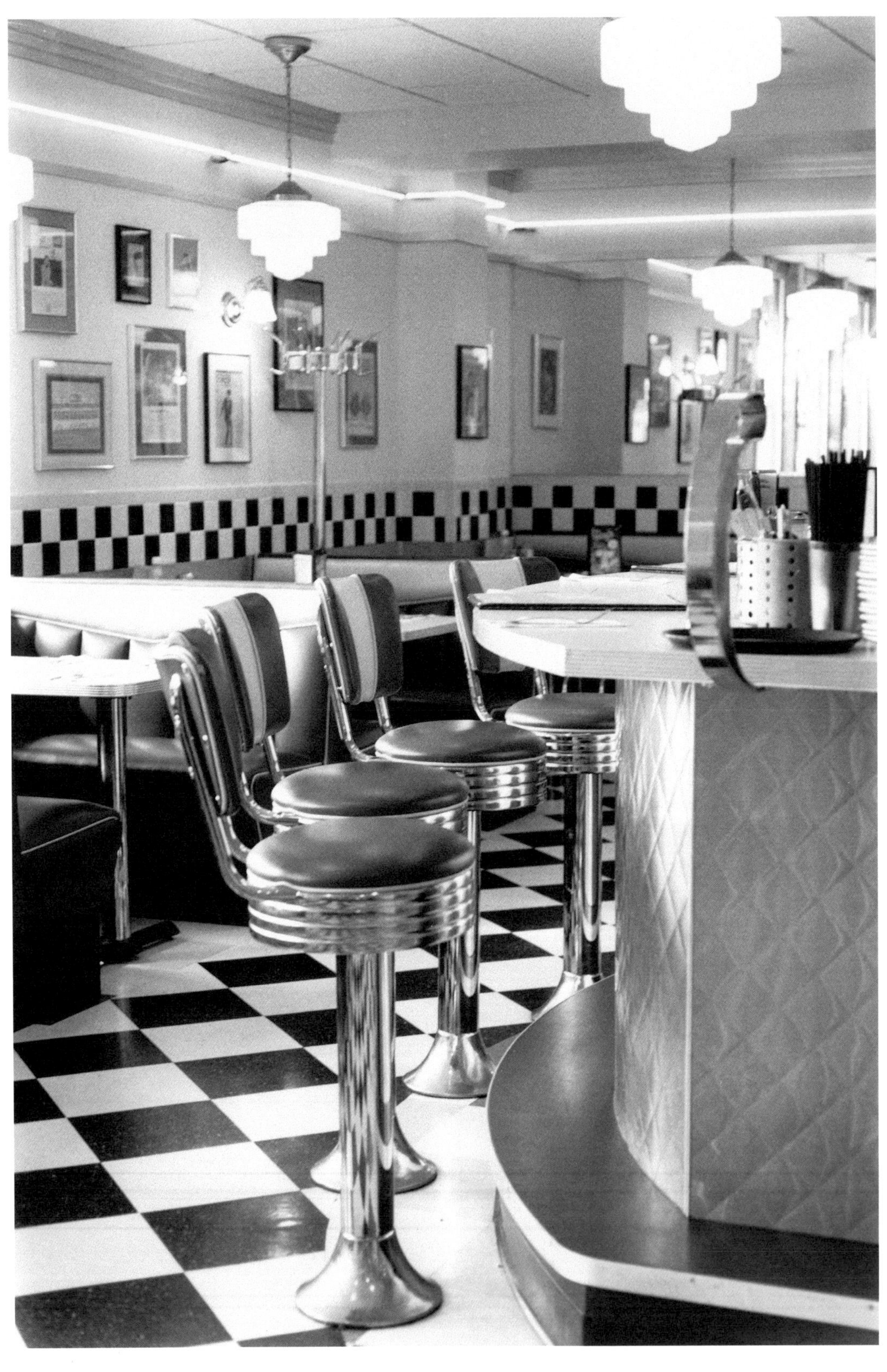

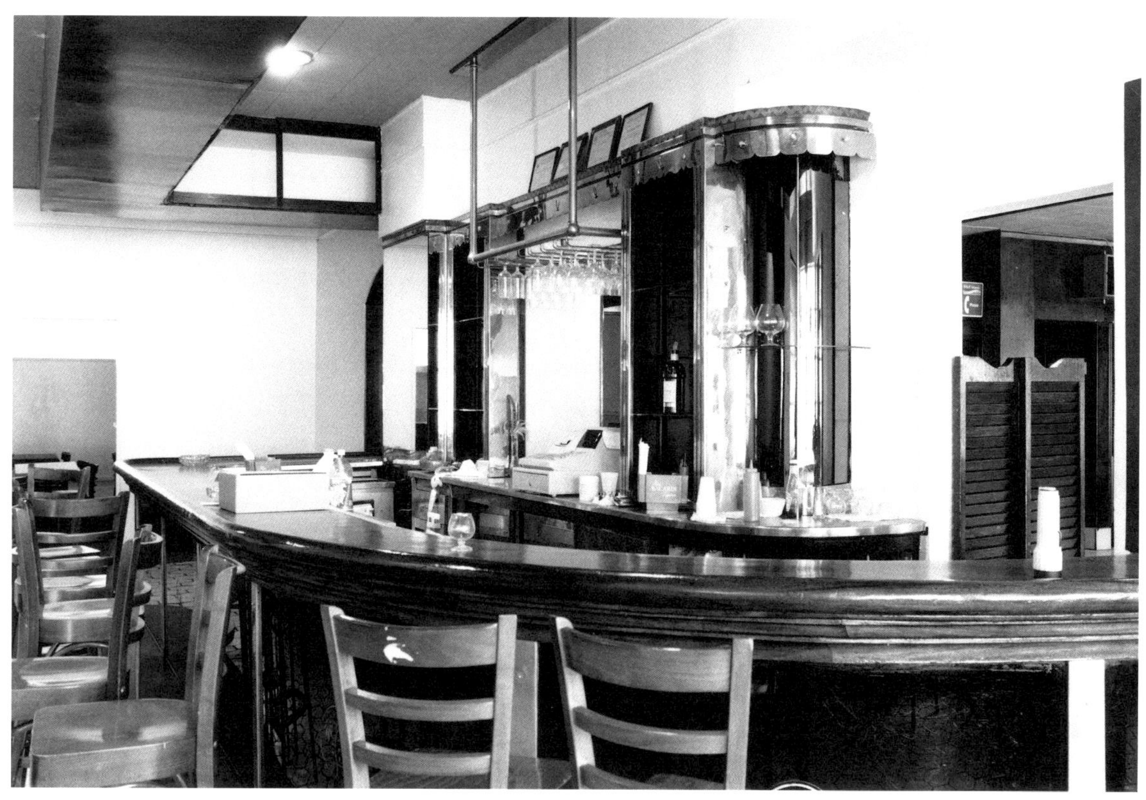

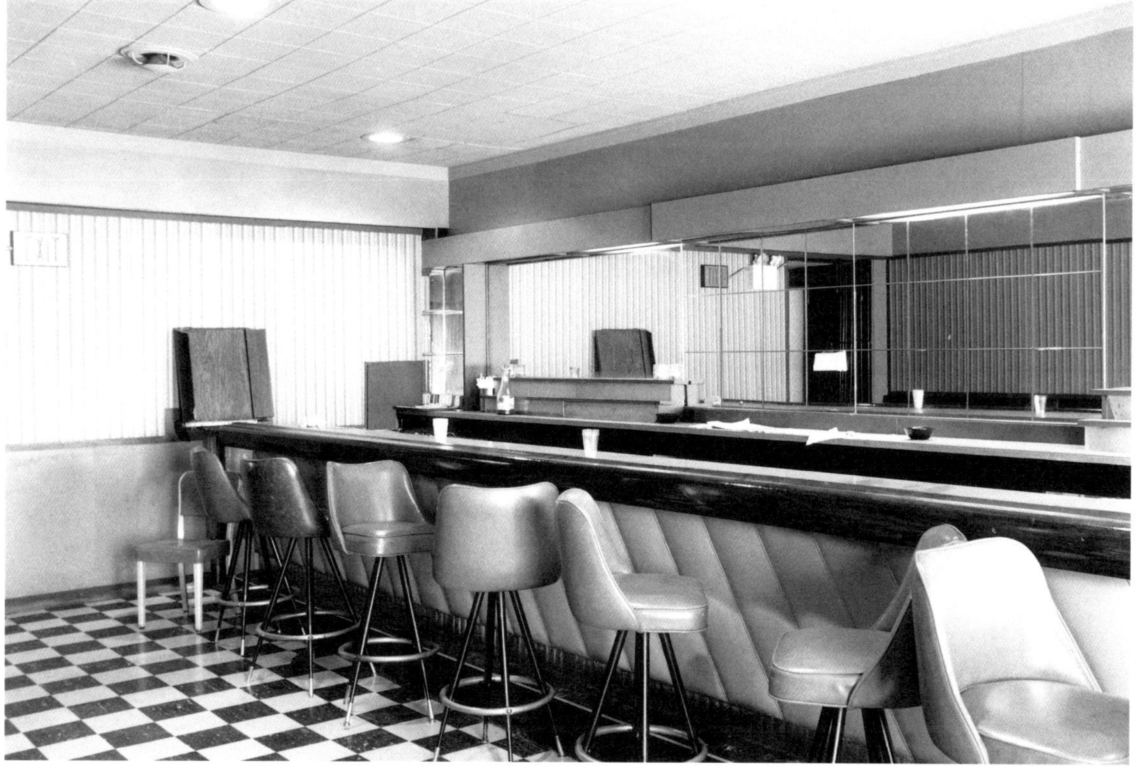

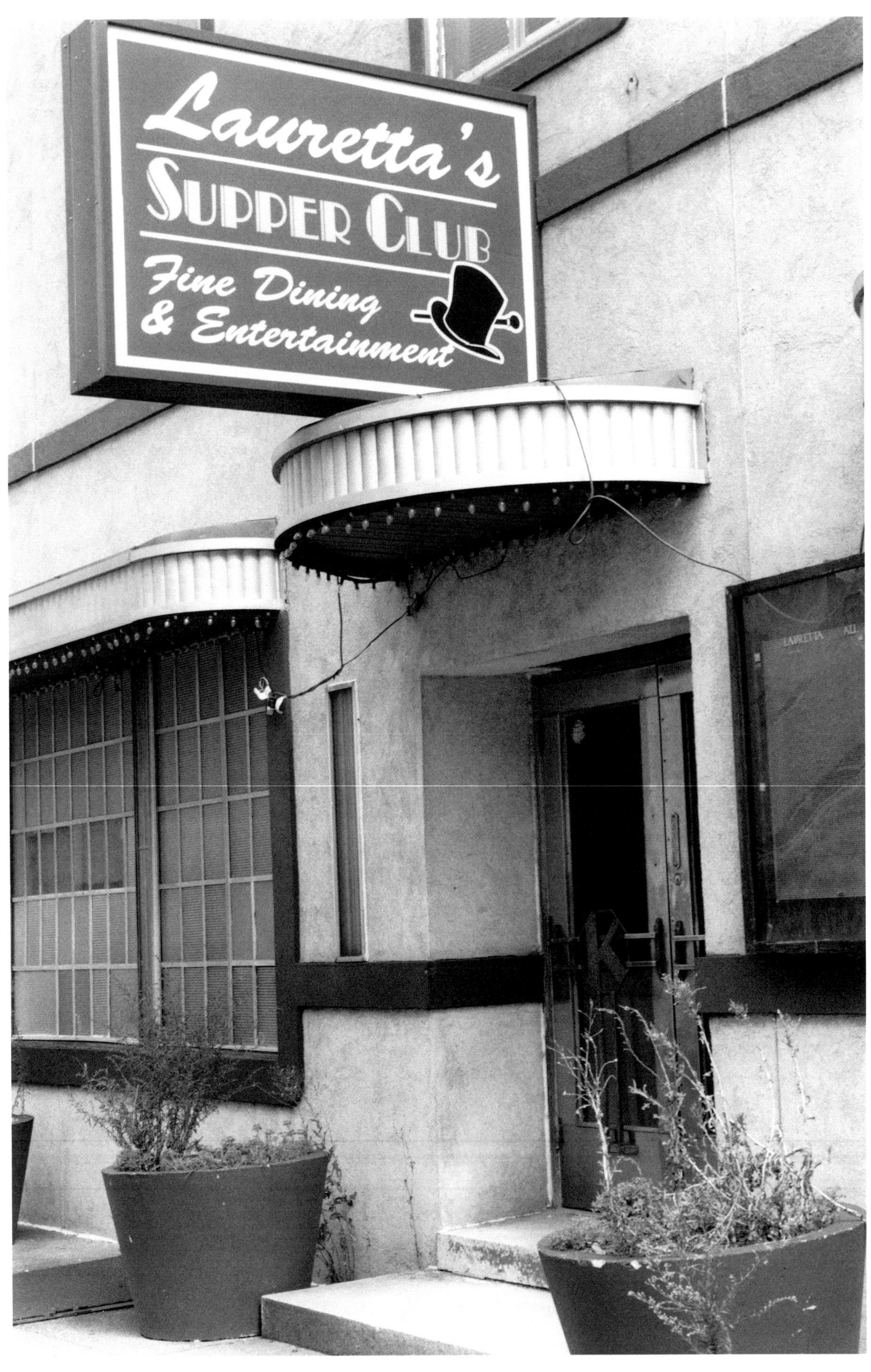

Lauretta's
Supper Club
Fine Dining
& Entertainment

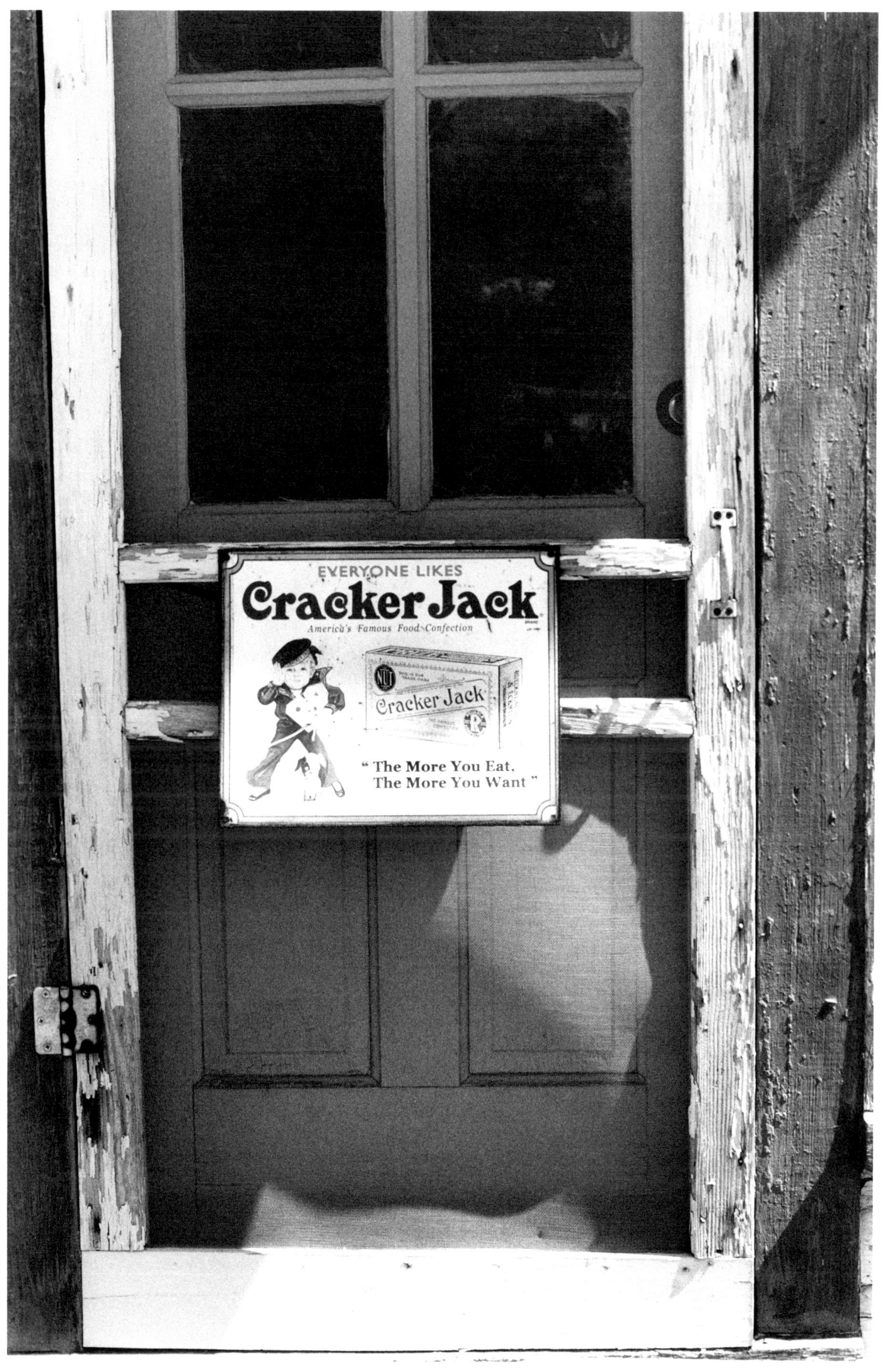
EVERYONE LIKES
Cracker Jack
America's Famous Food Confection
Cracker Jack
" The More You Eat,
The More You Want "

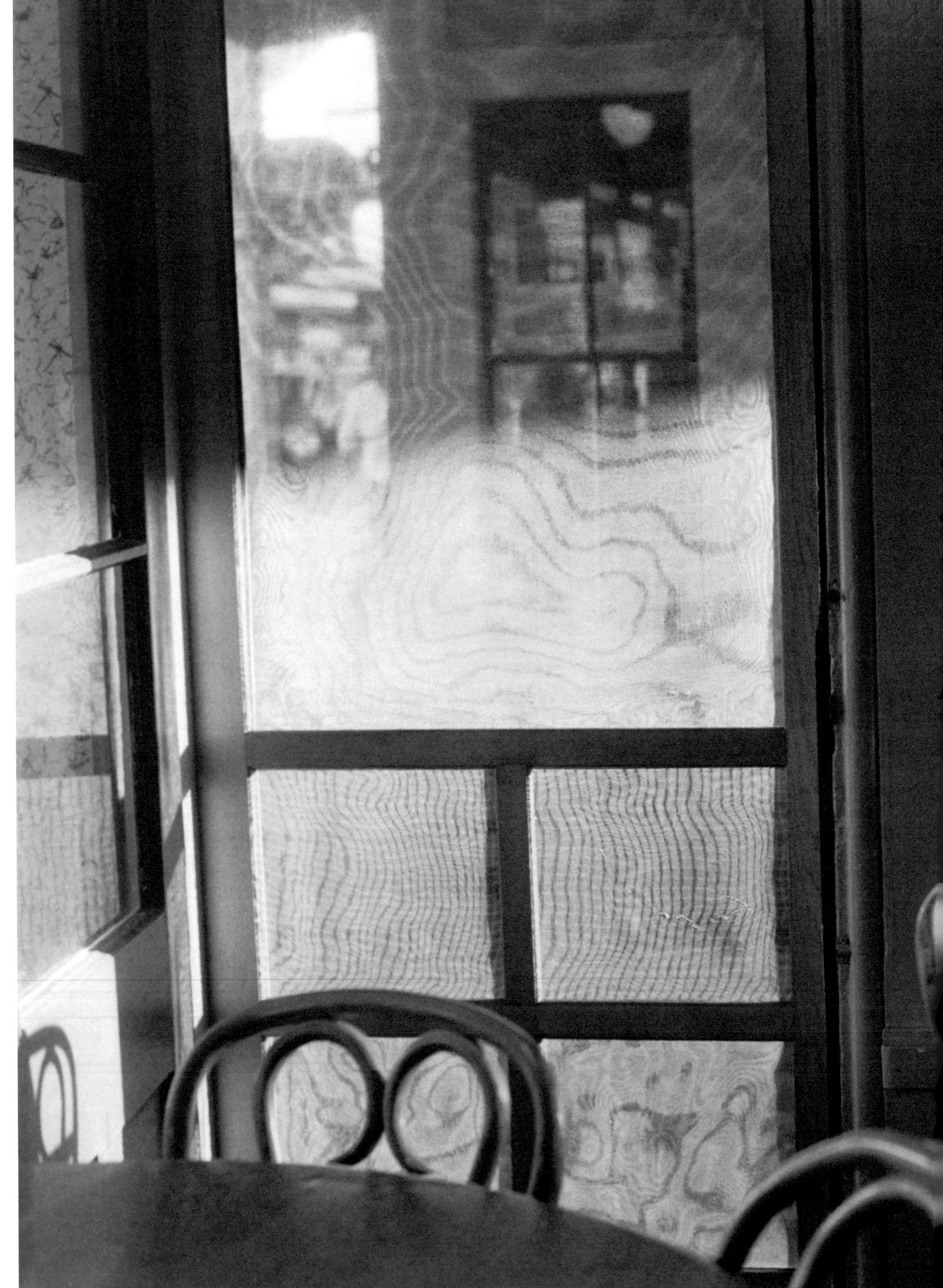

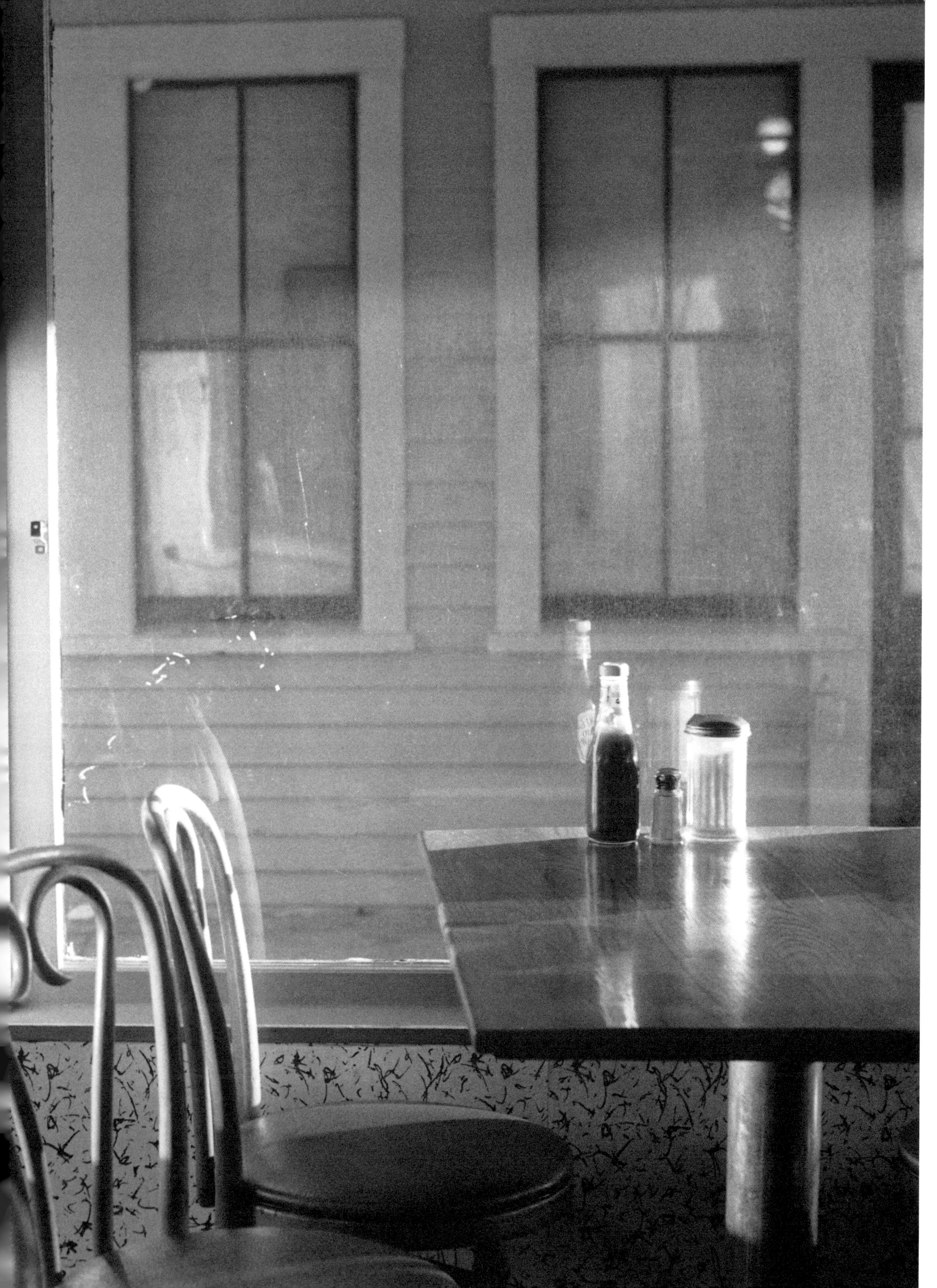

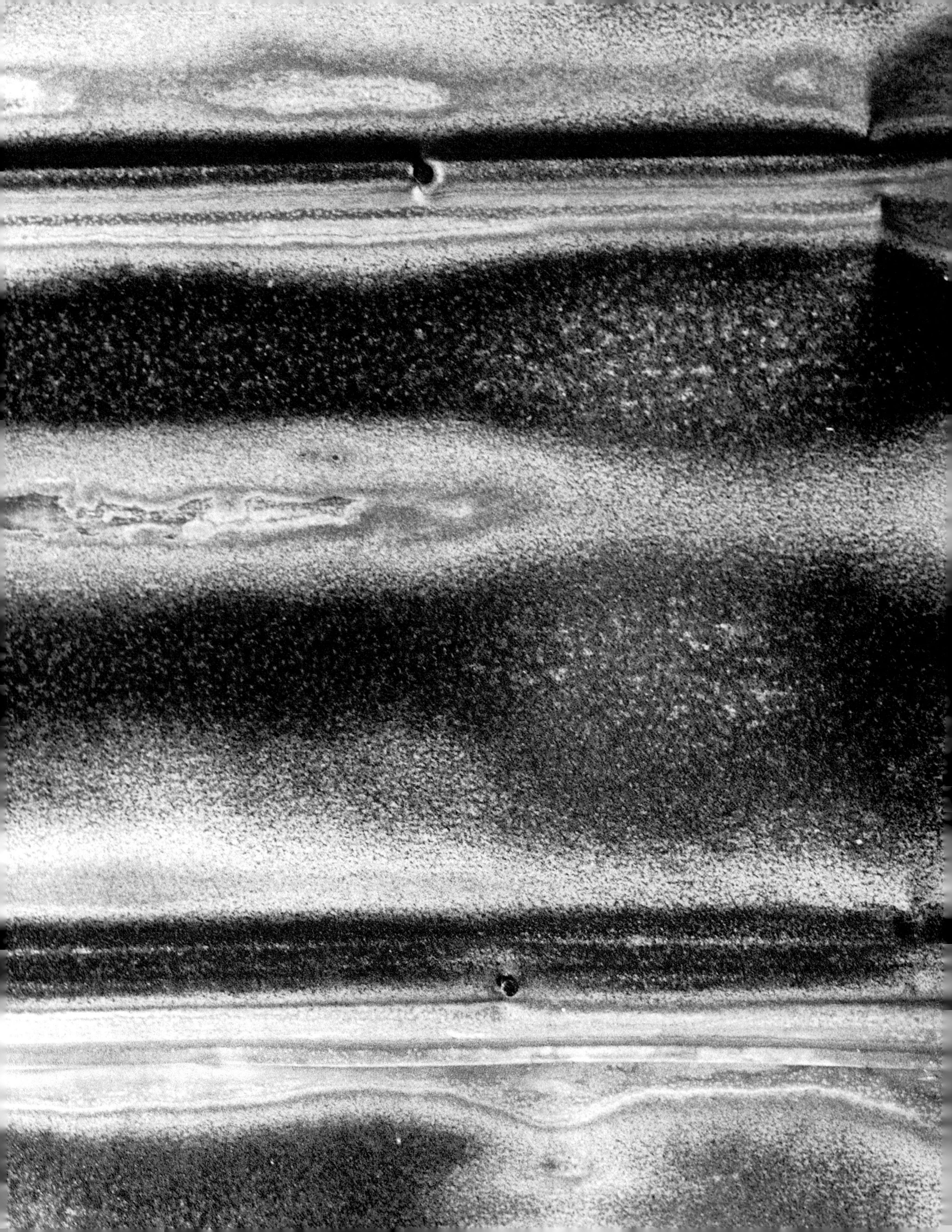

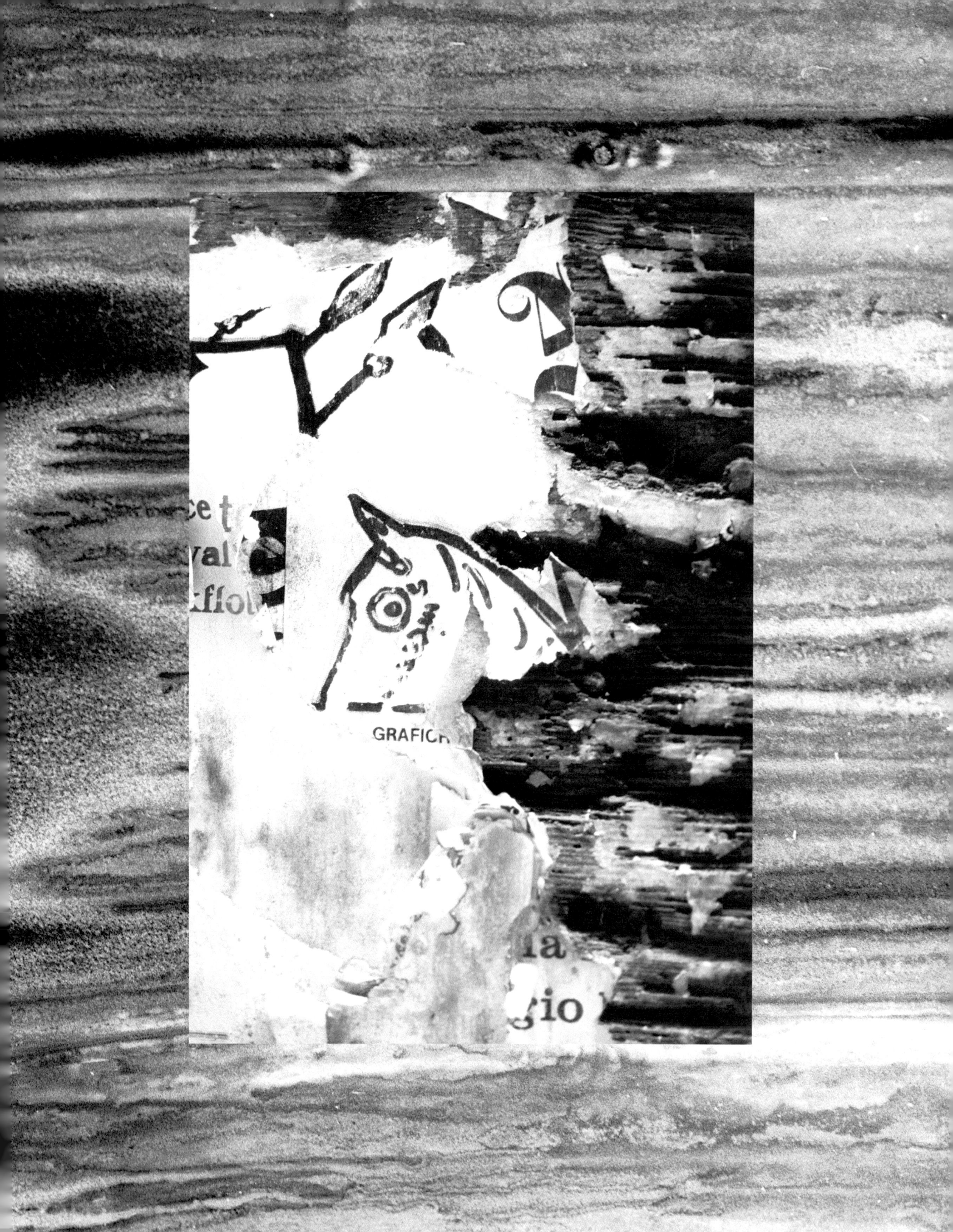
GRAFICH

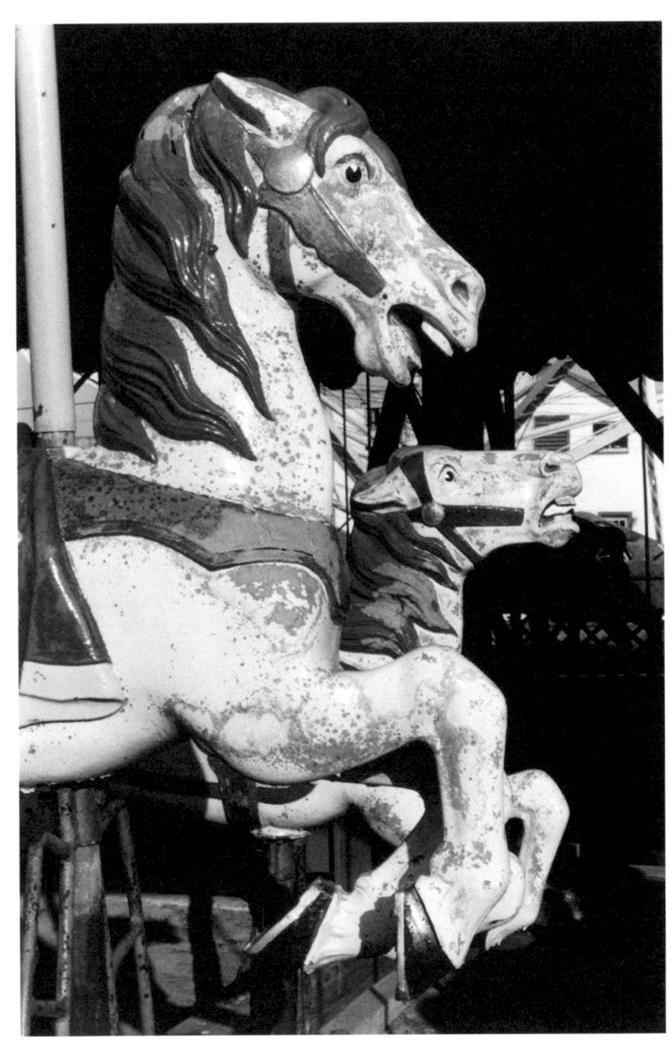

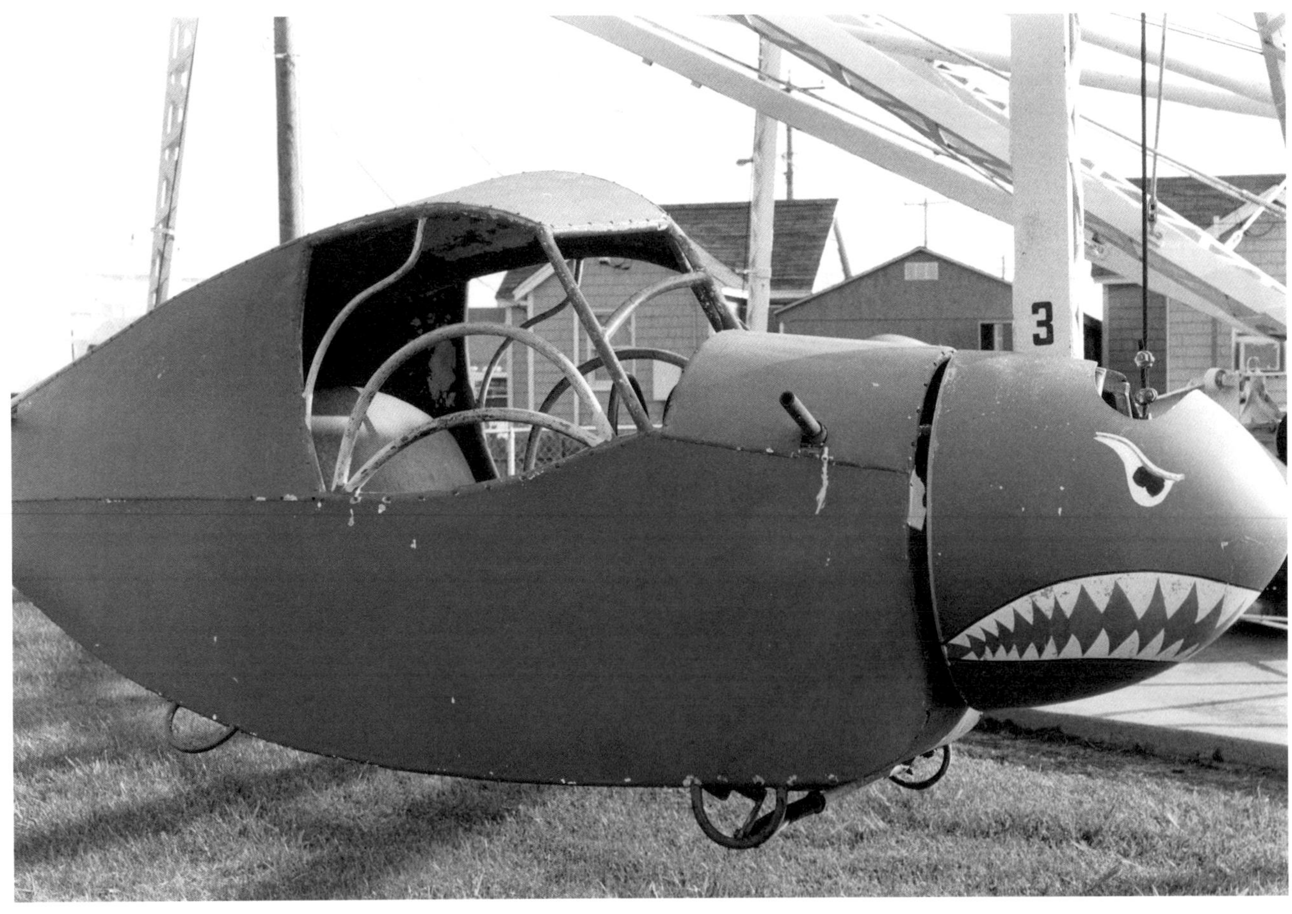

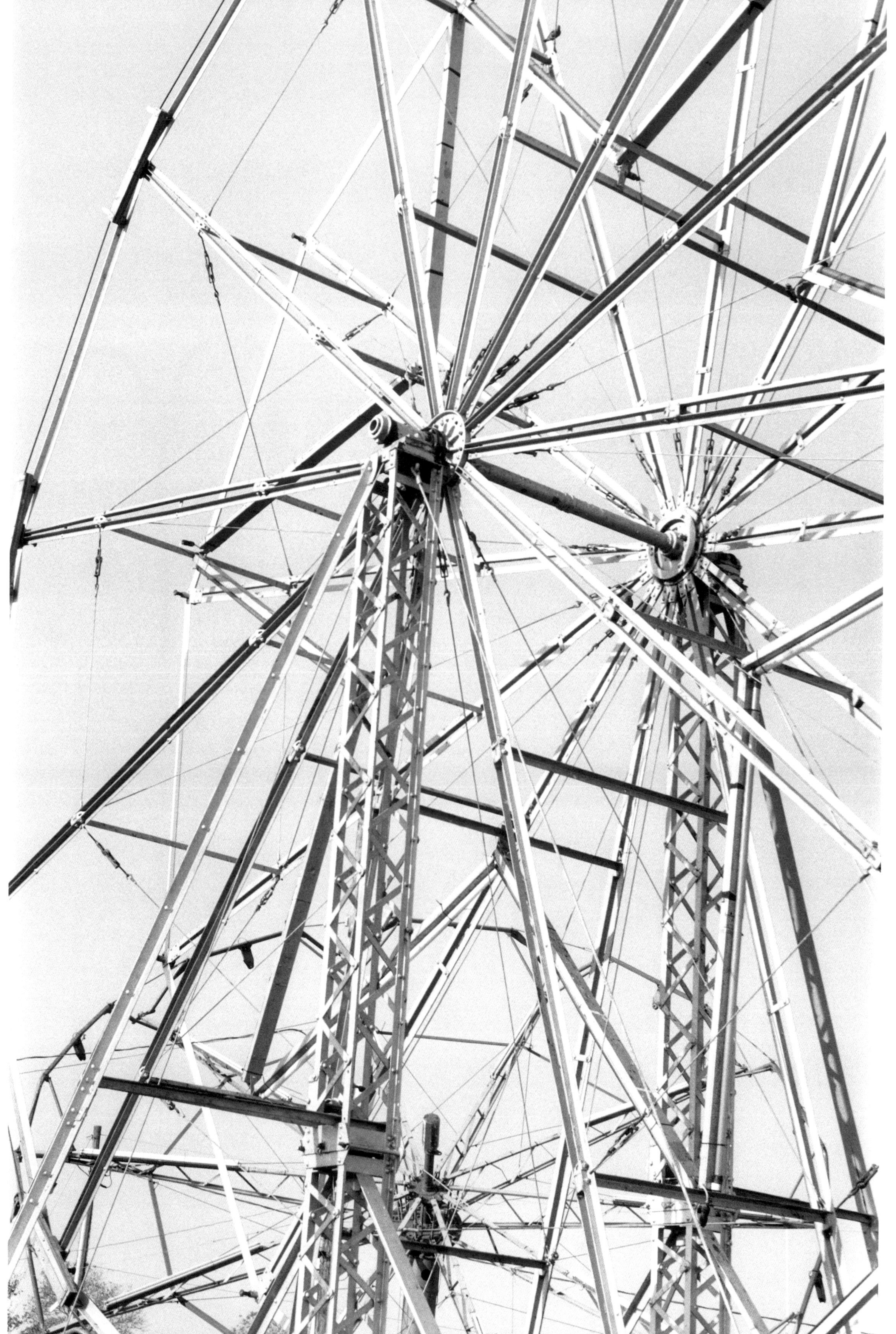

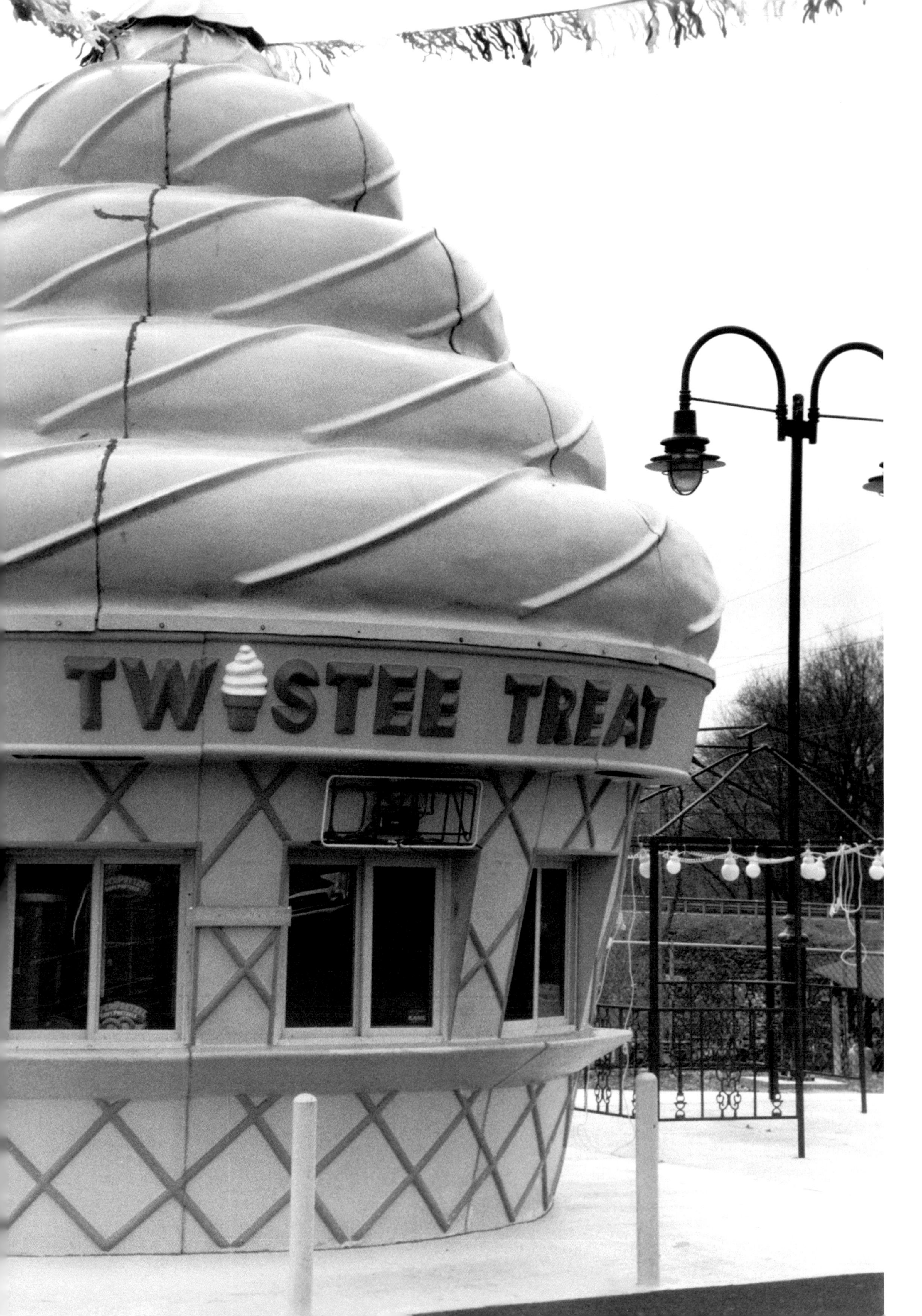

TWISTEE TREAT

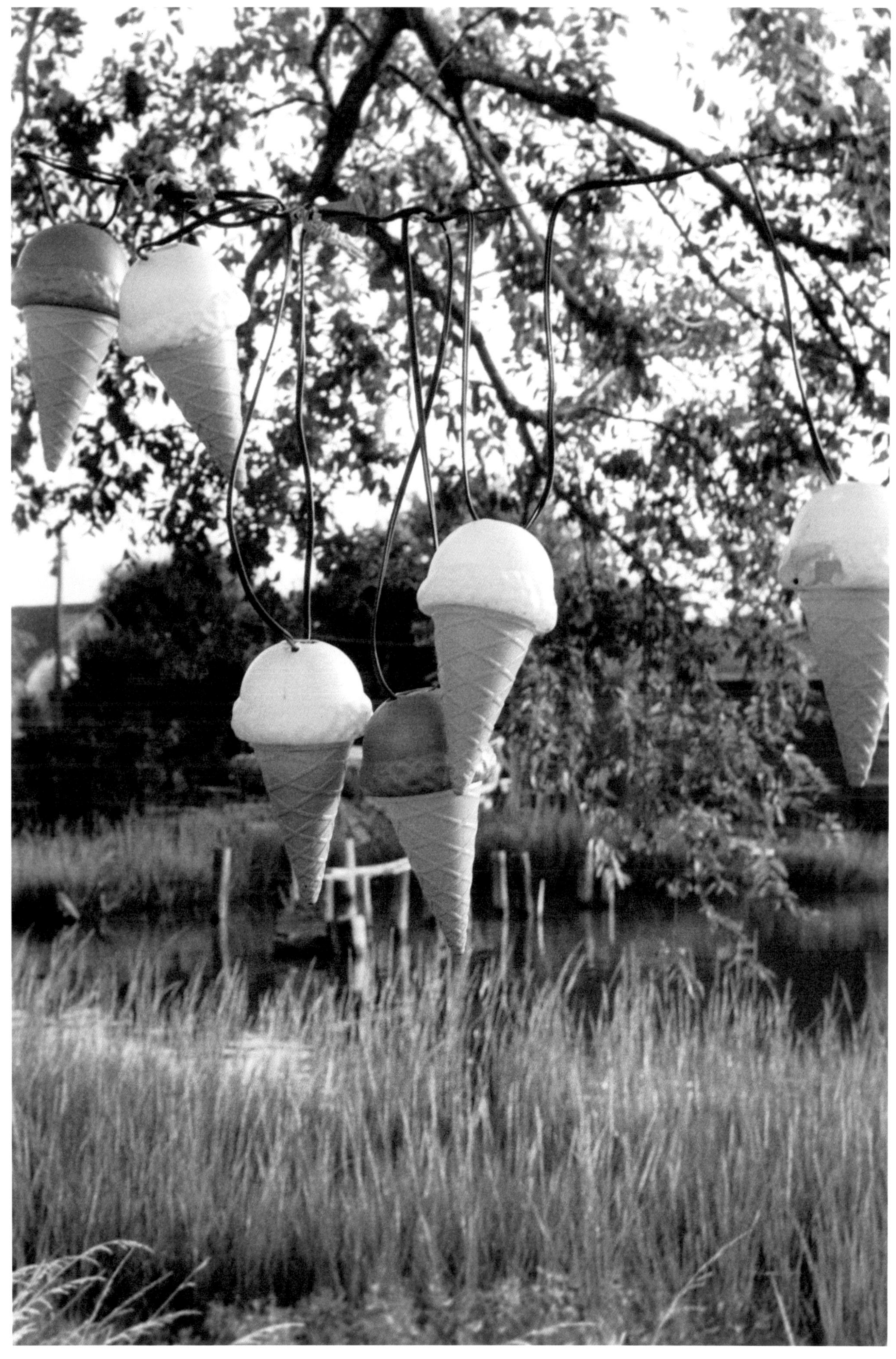

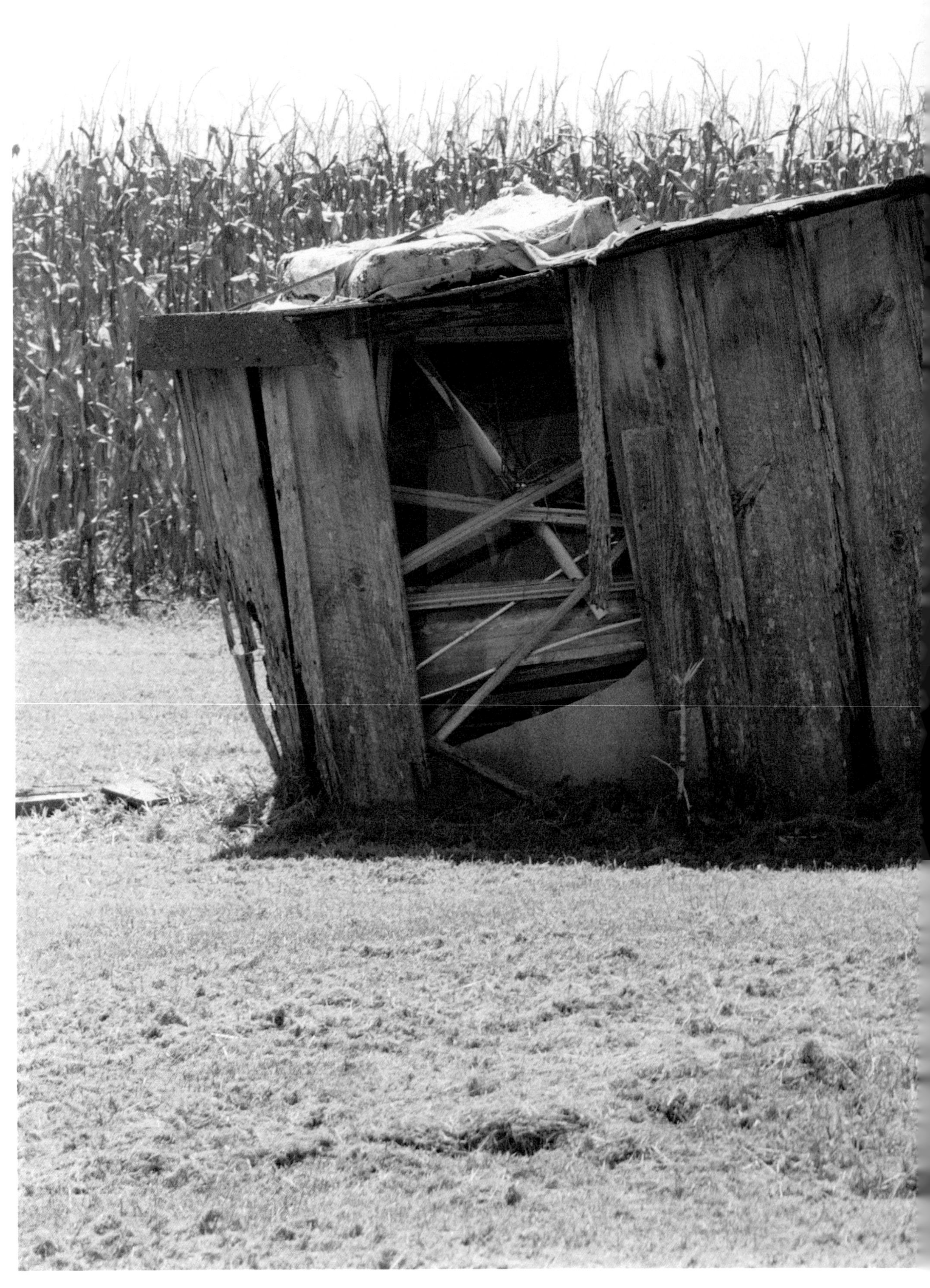

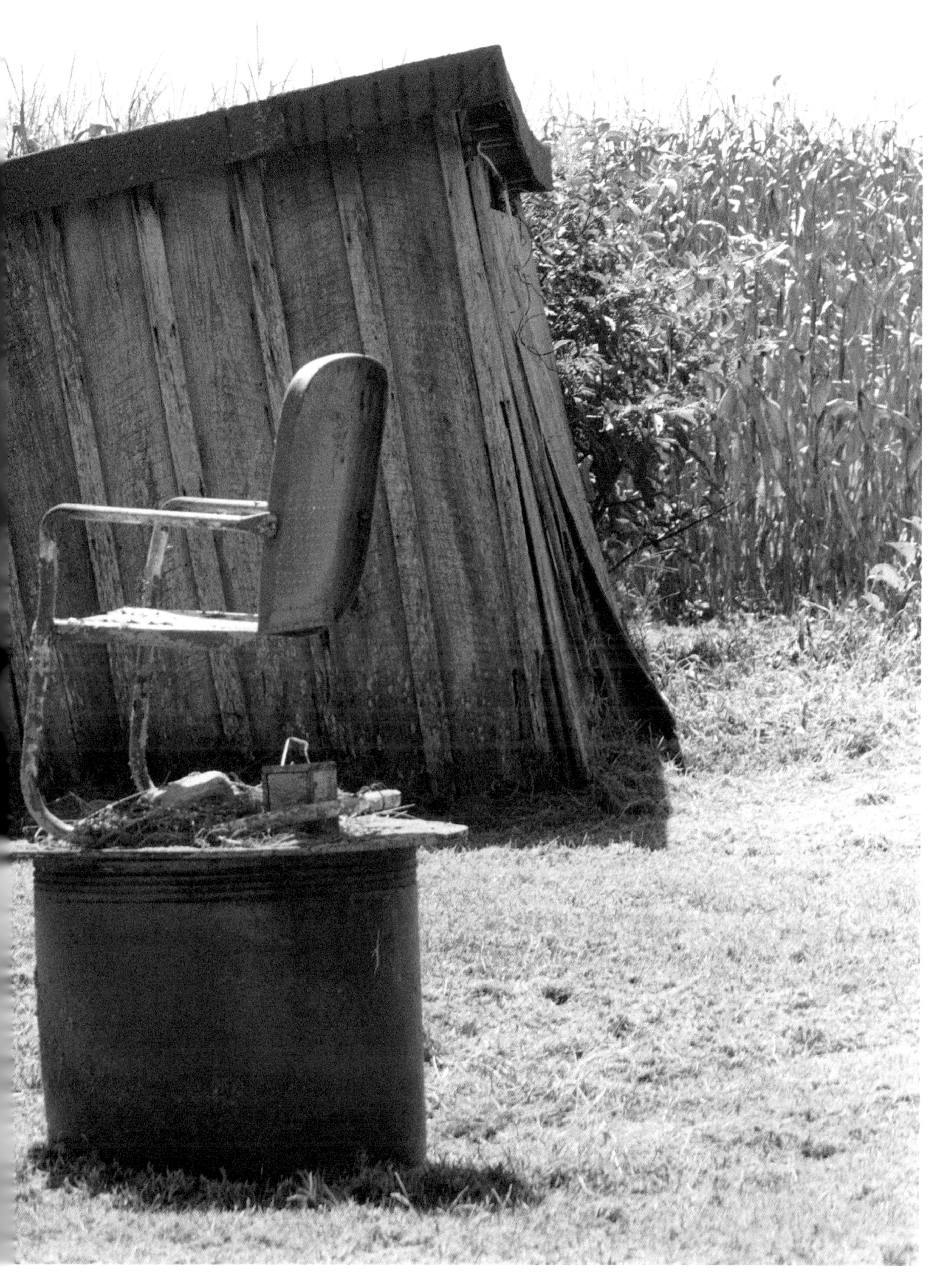

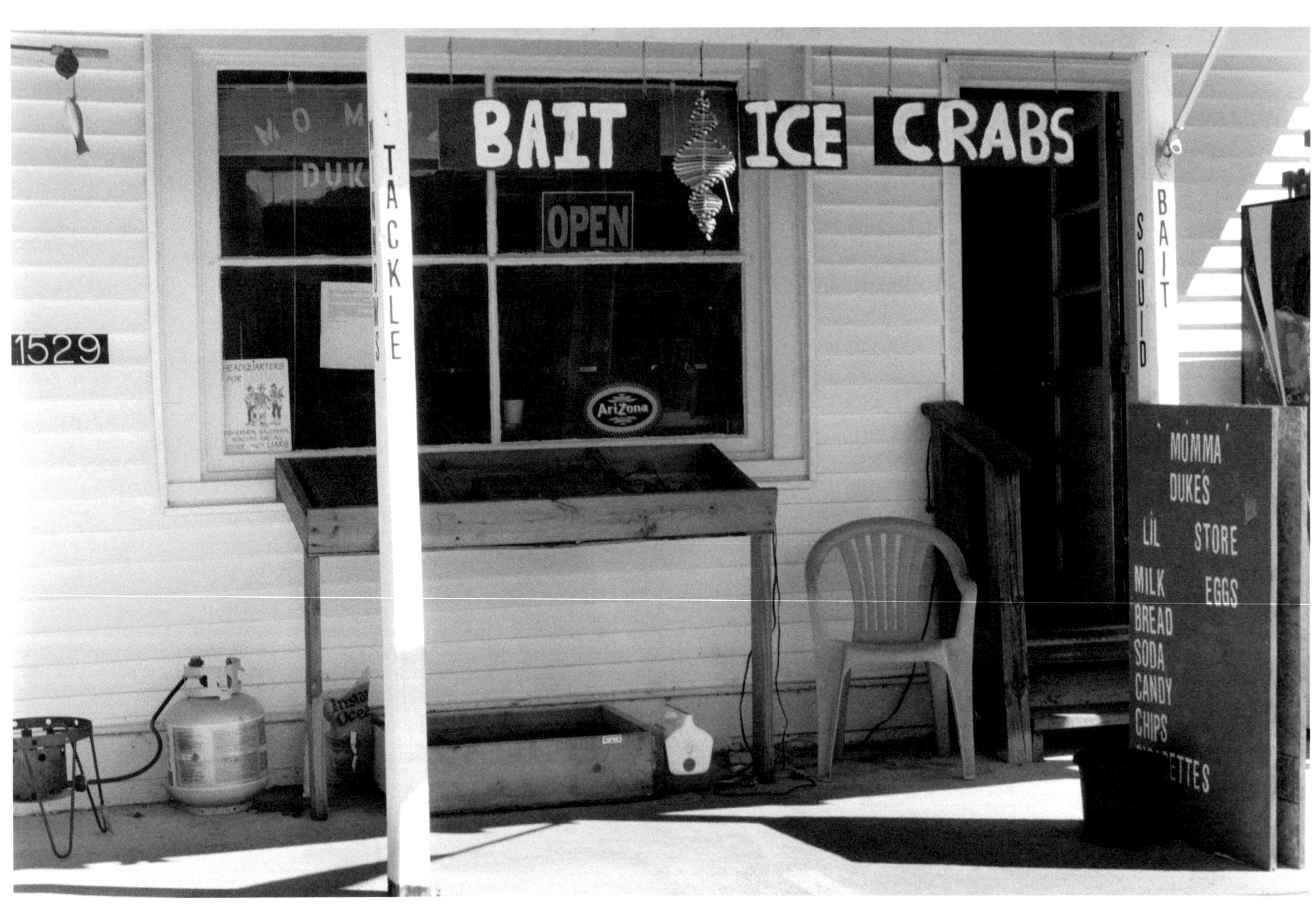
BAIT ICE CRABS
OPEN
TACKLE
SQUID BAIT
1529
AriZona
MOMMA
DUKES
LiL STORE
MILK EGGS
BREAD
SODA
CANDY
CHIPS
CIGARETTES

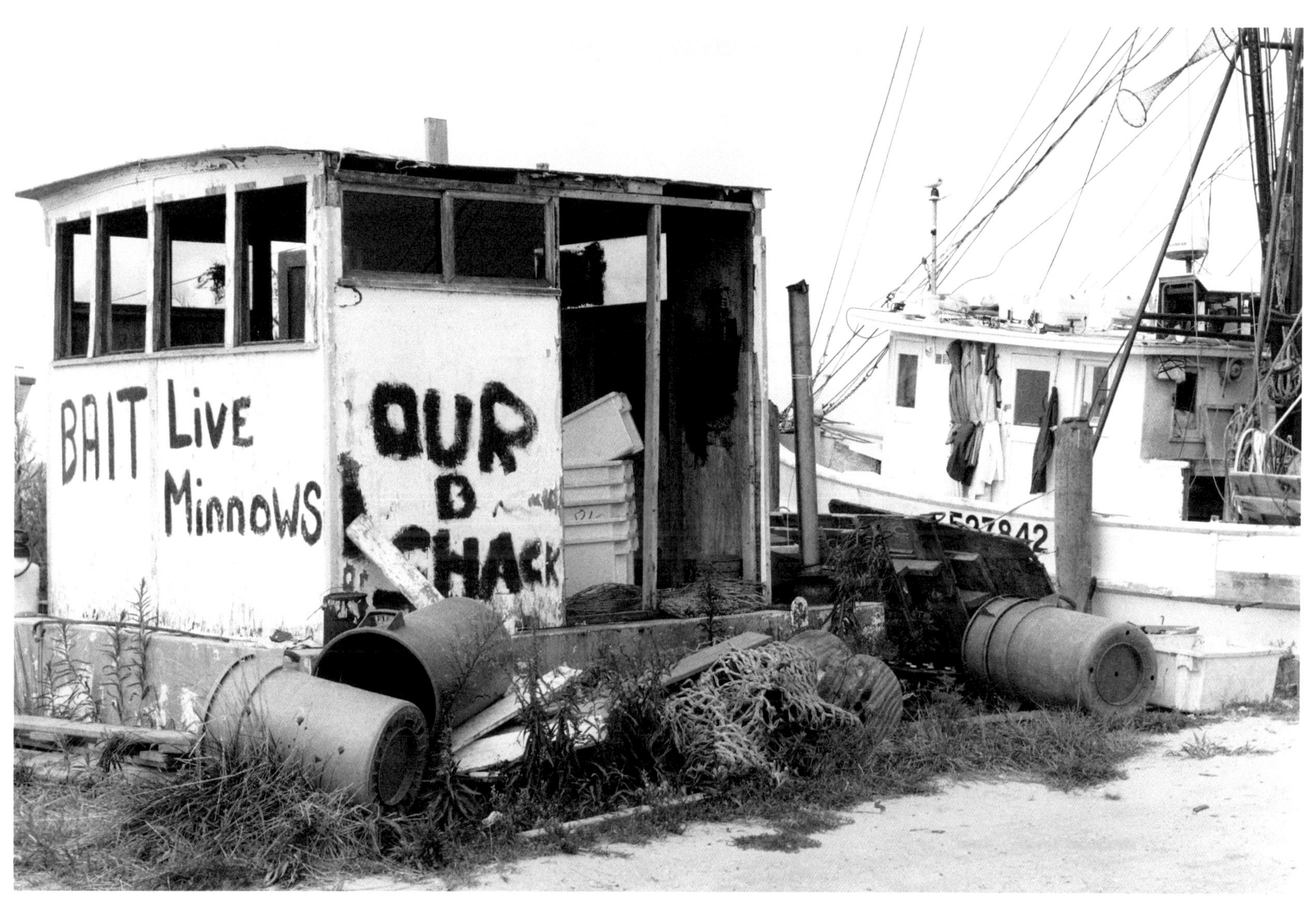

BAIT Live Minnows
OUR
B
SHACK
3527842

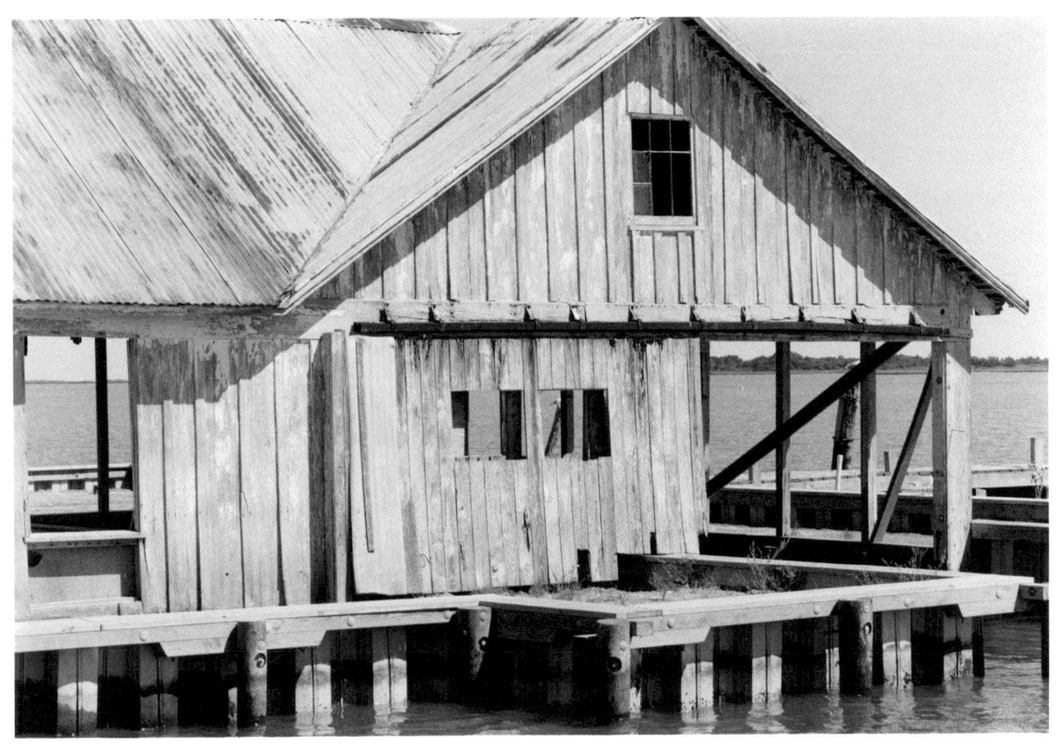

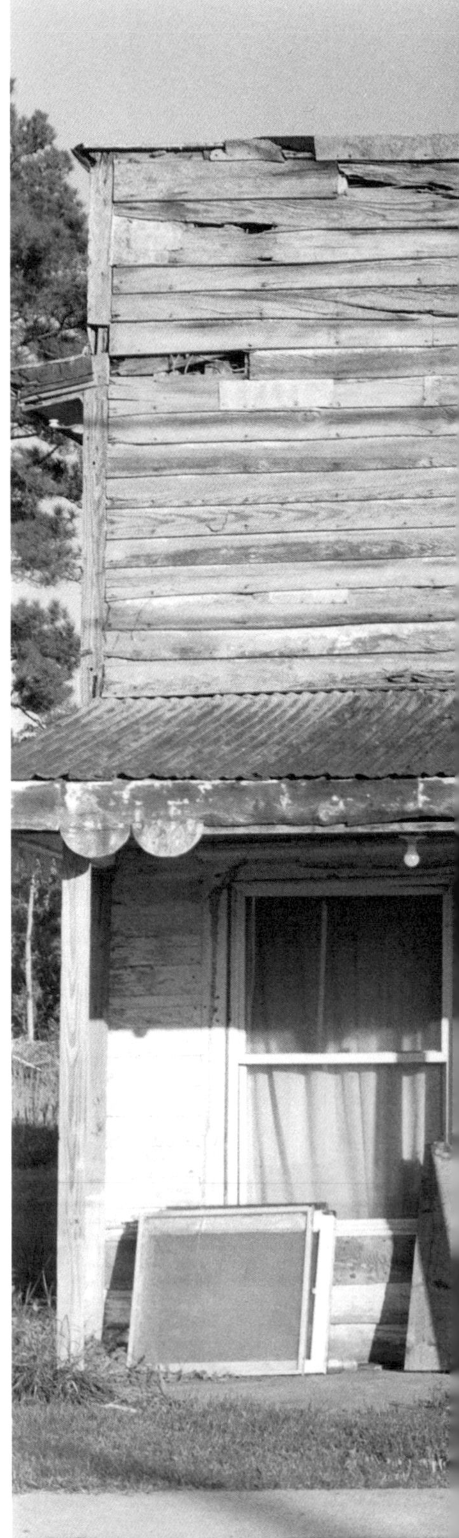

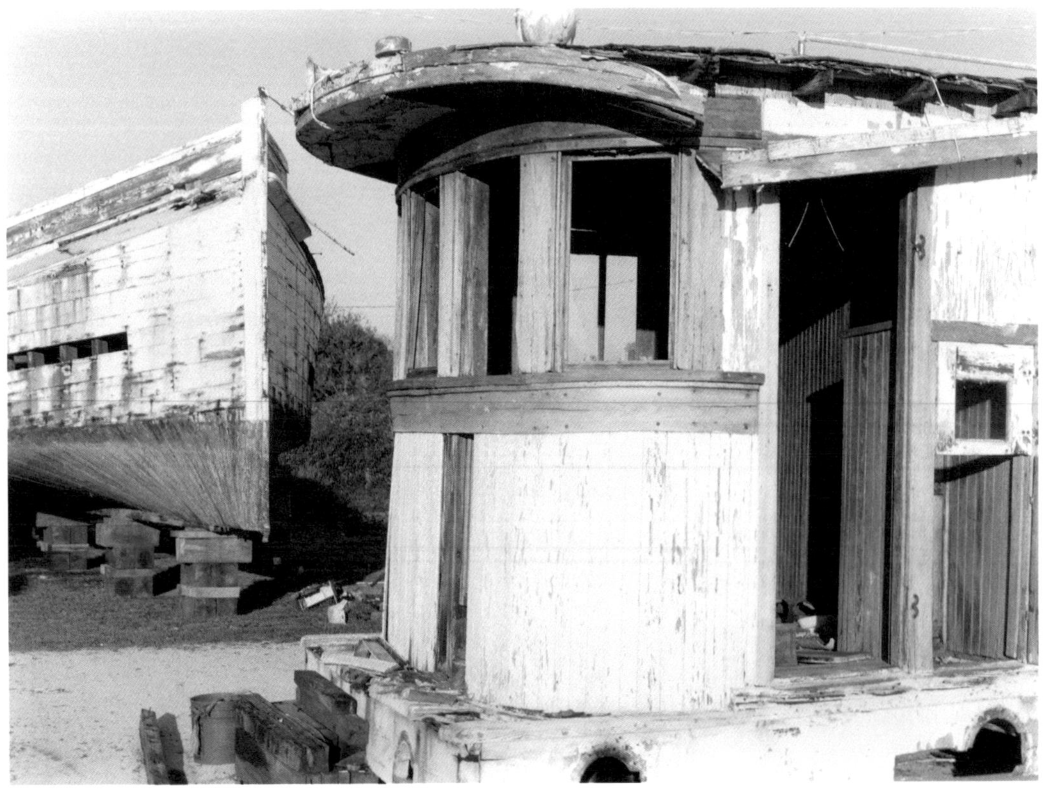

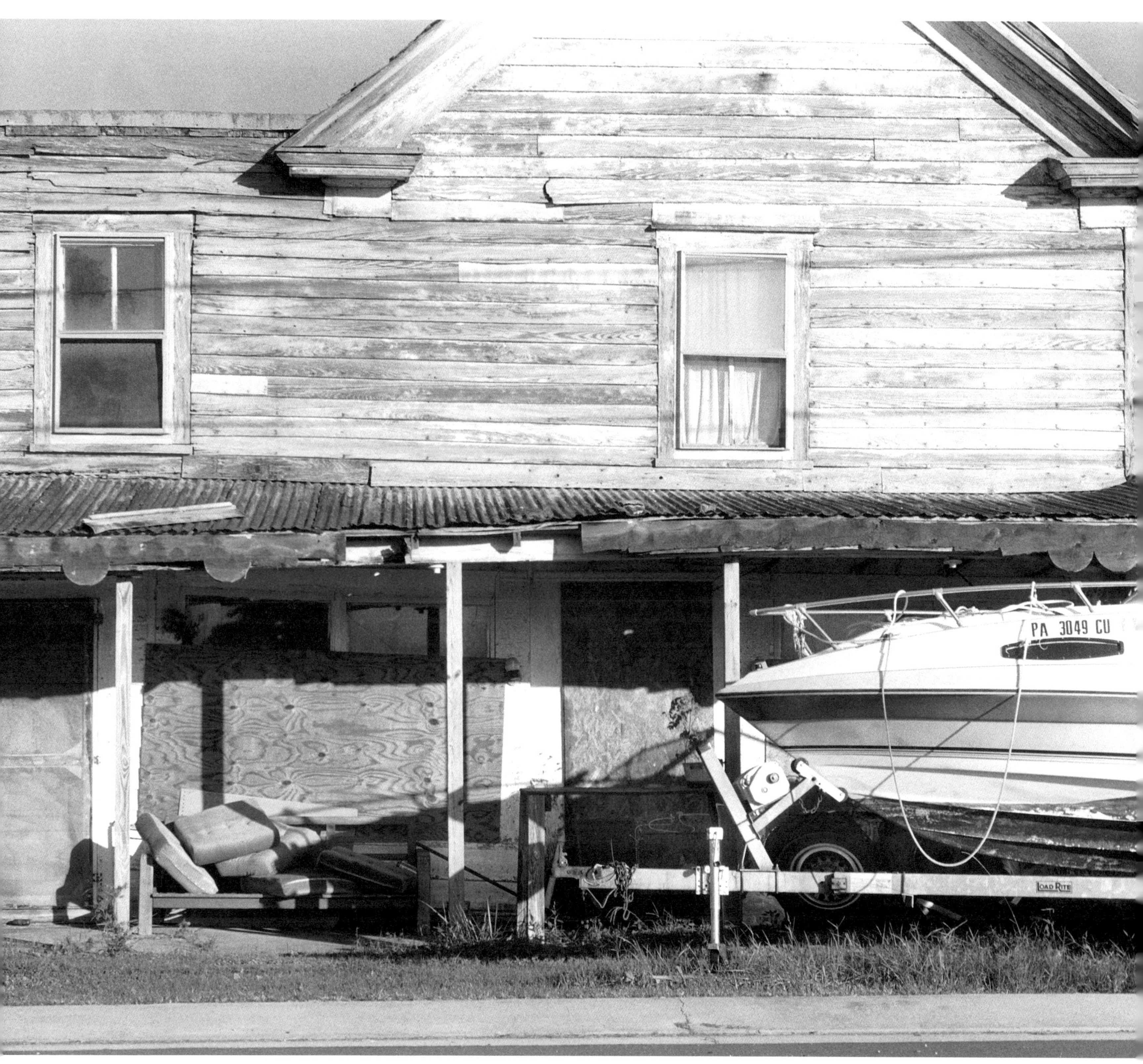
PA 3049 CU
LOAD RITE

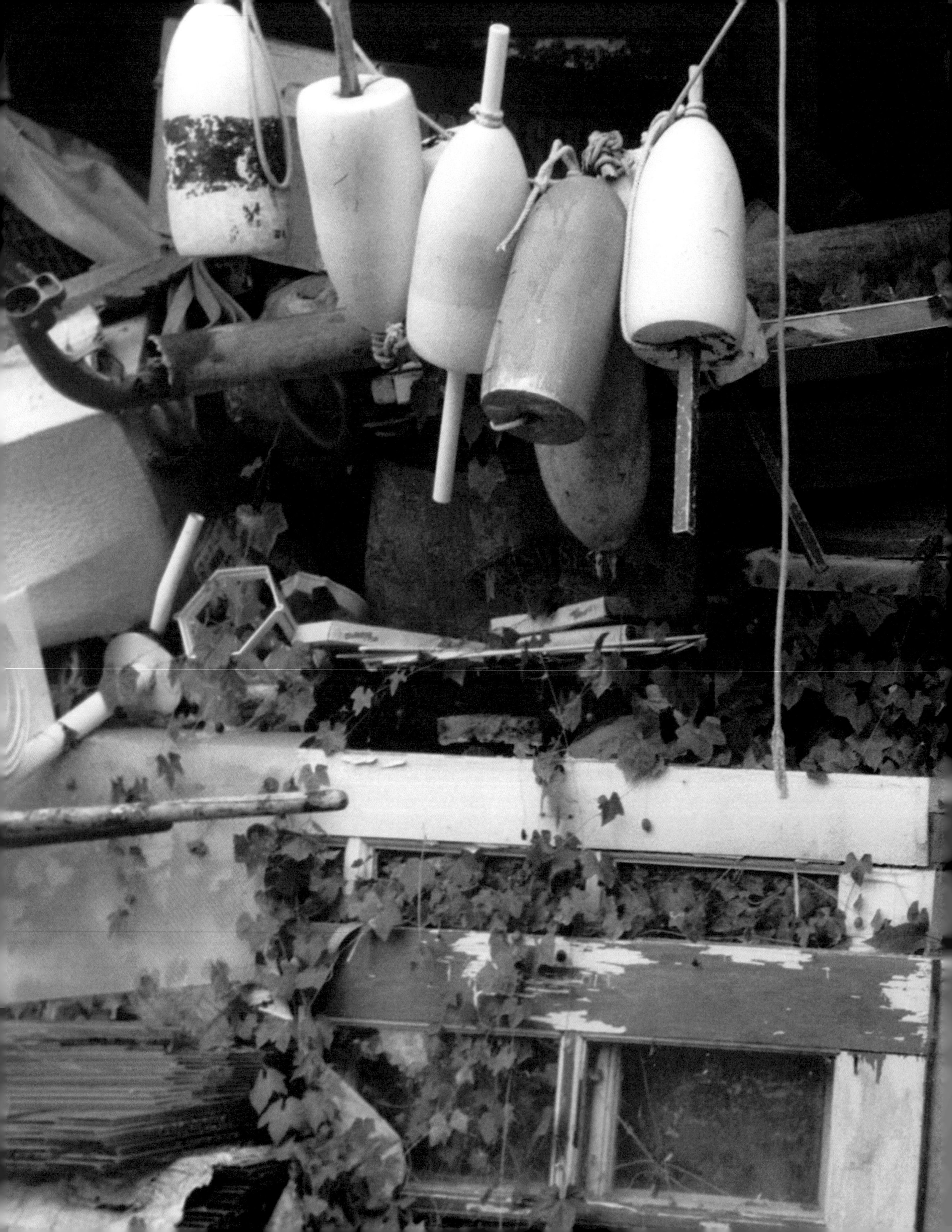

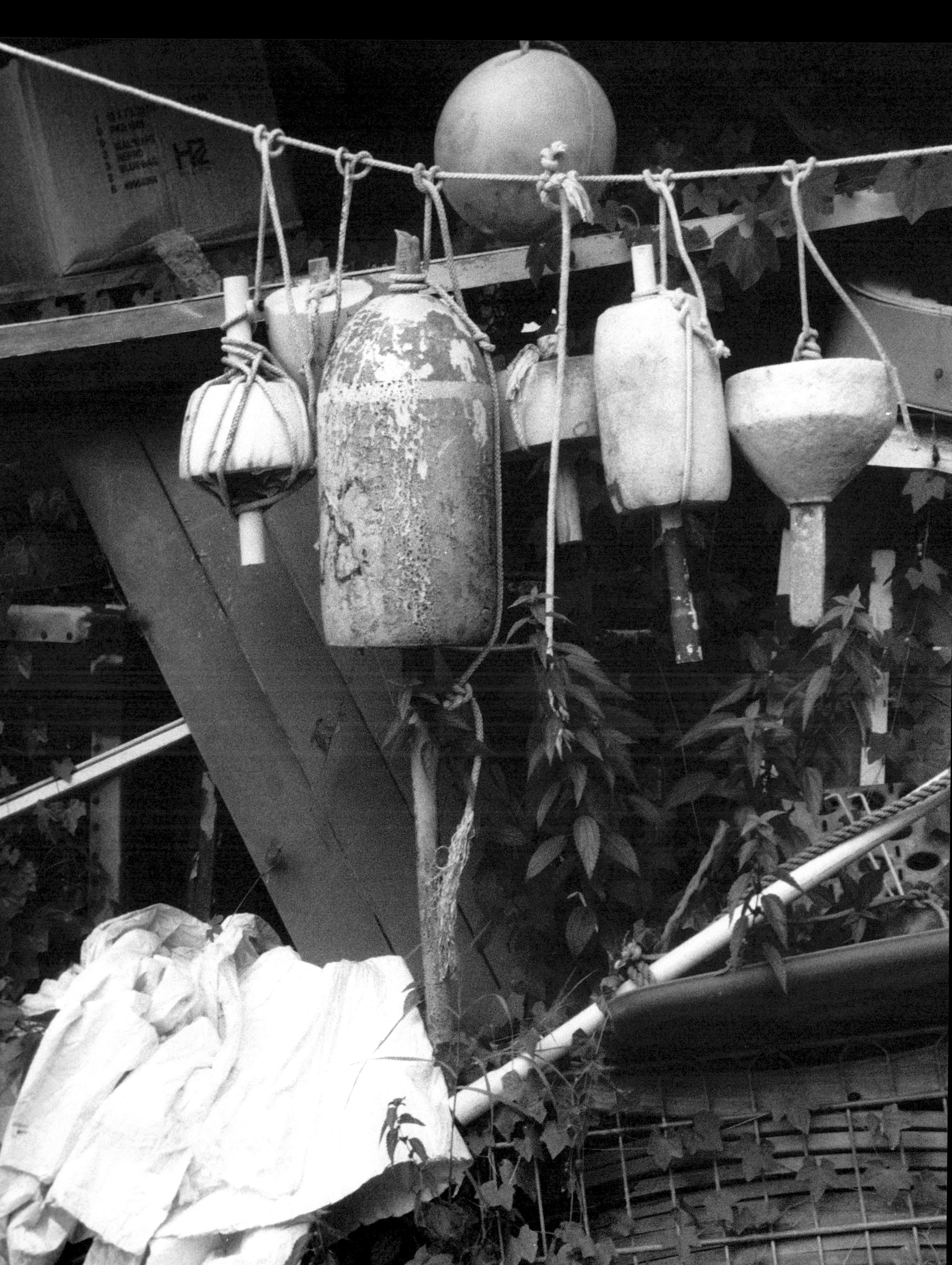

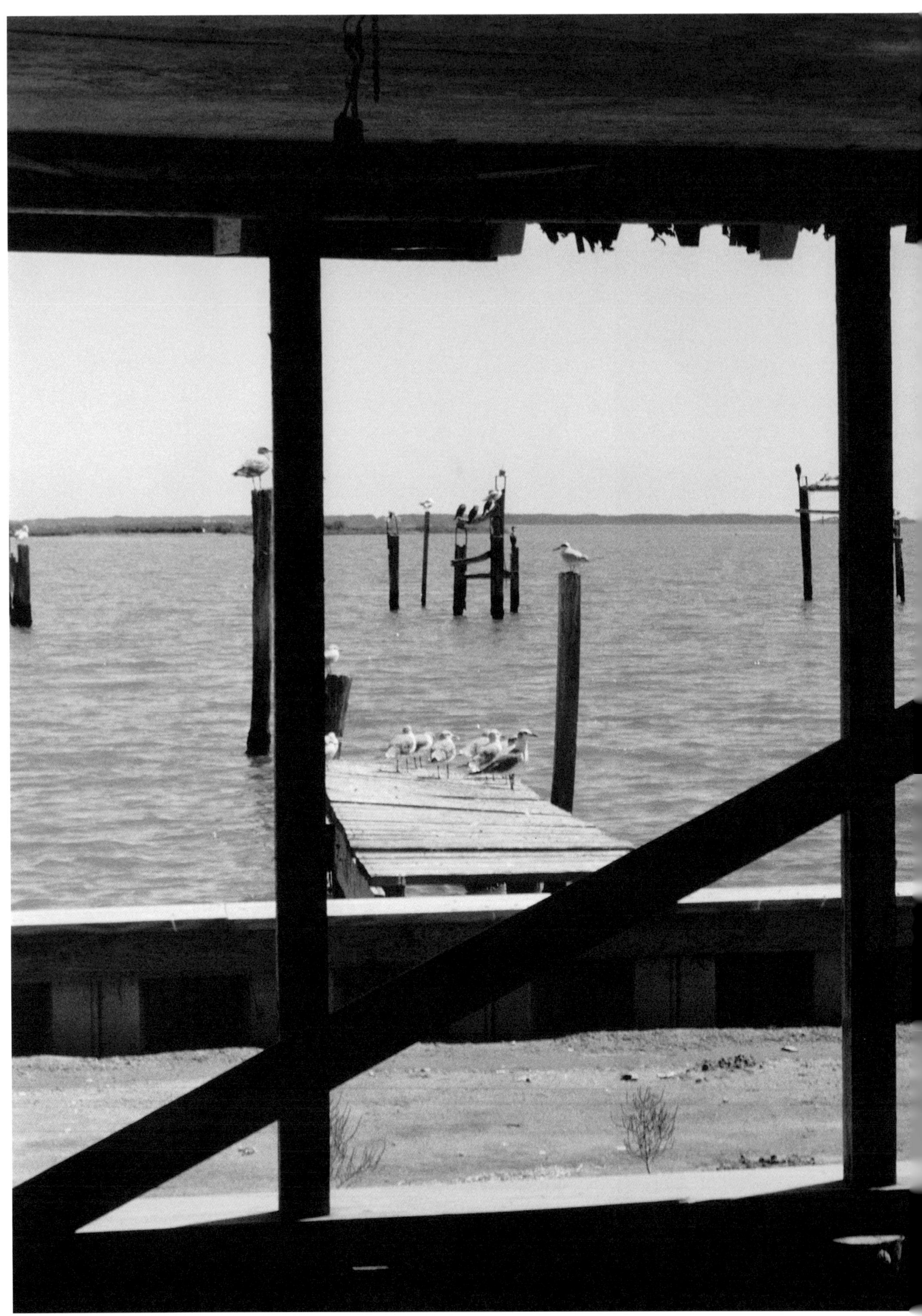

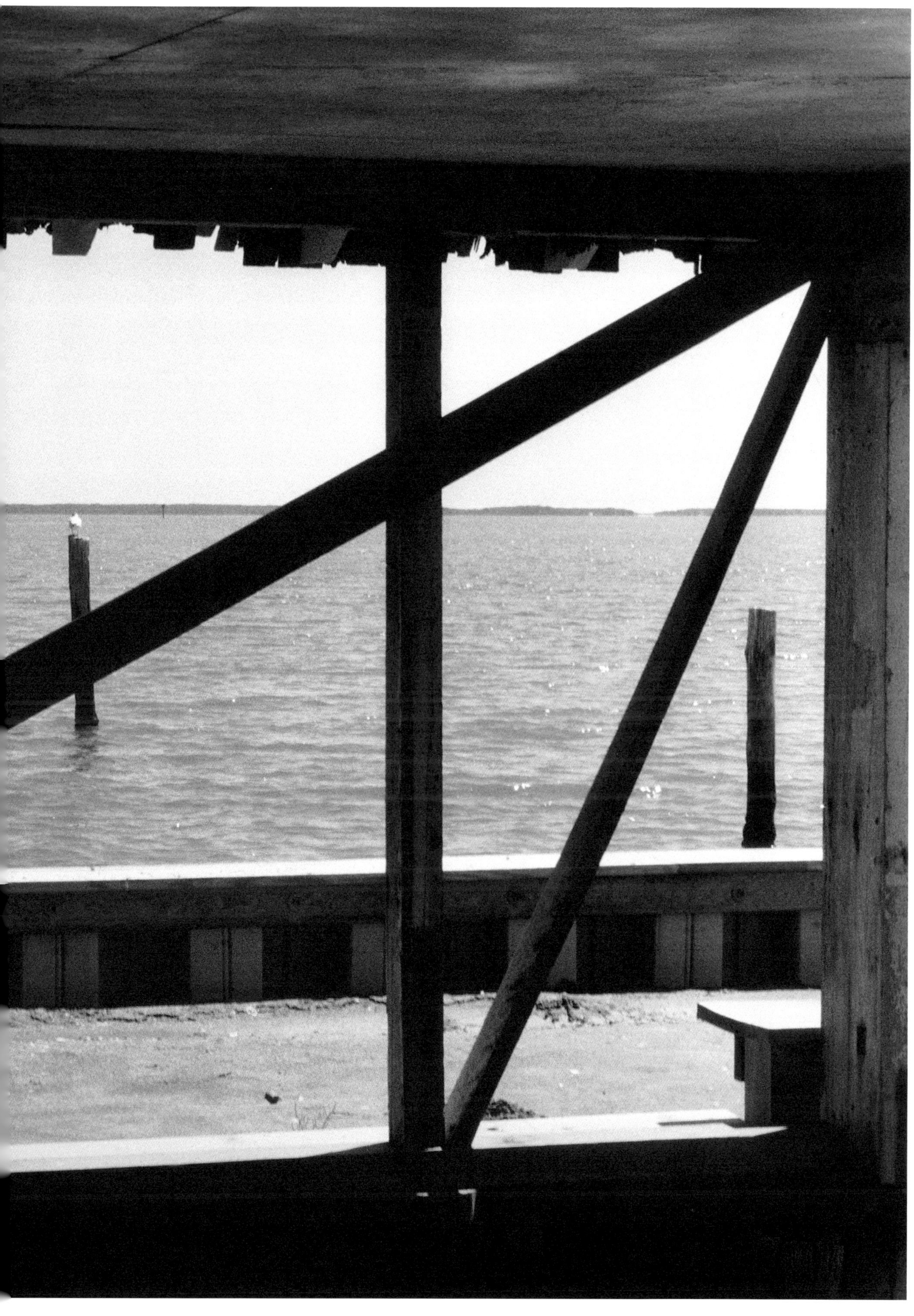

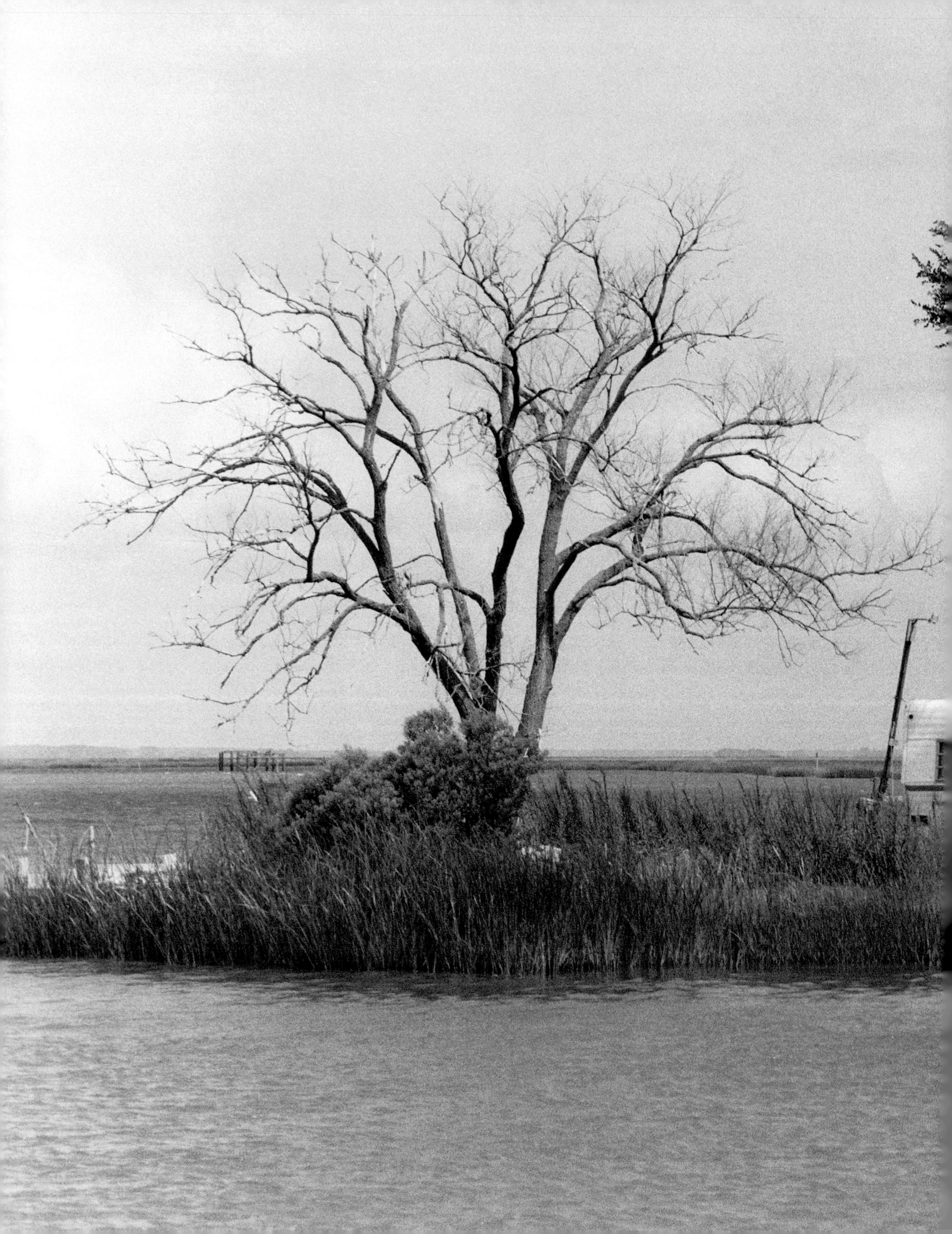

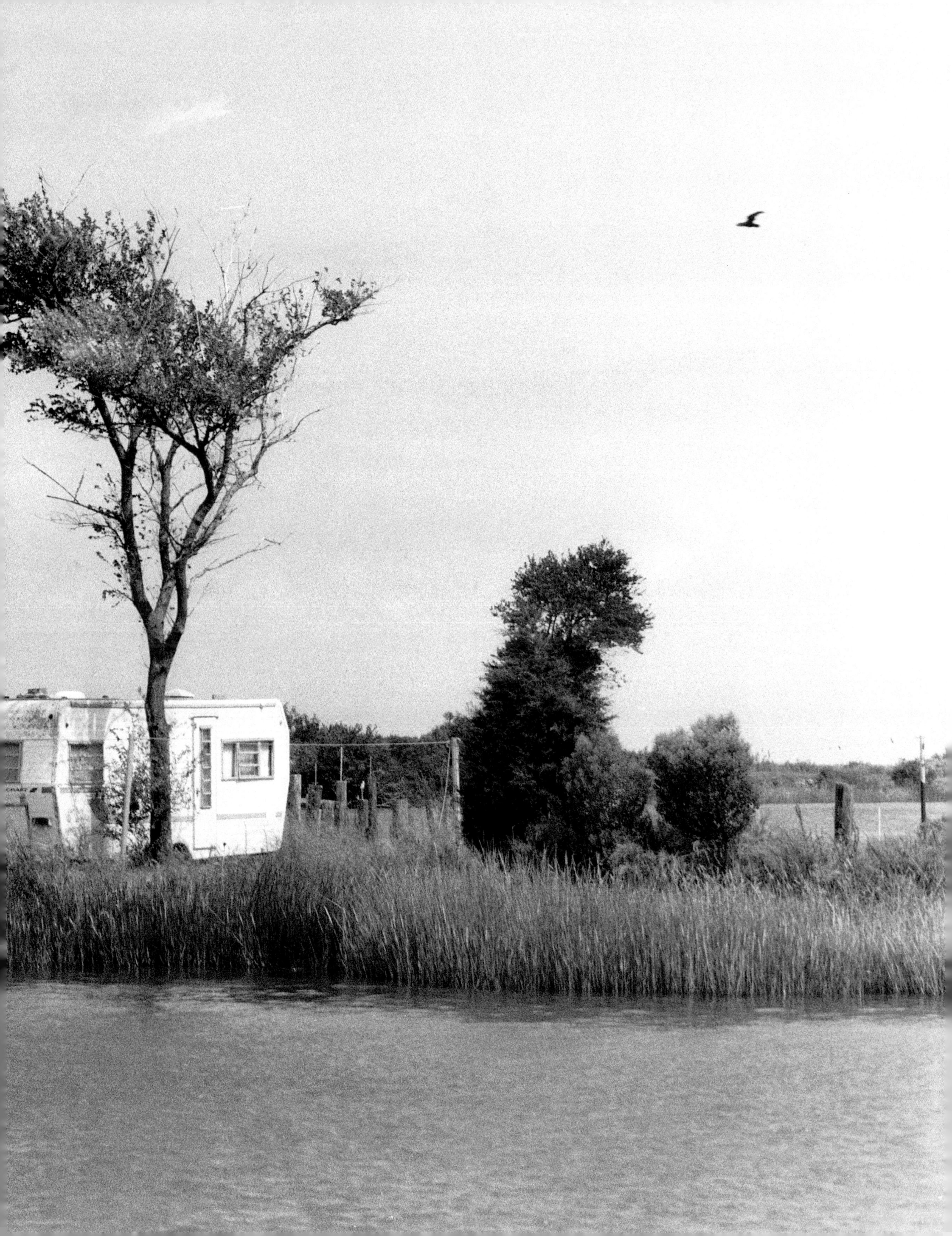

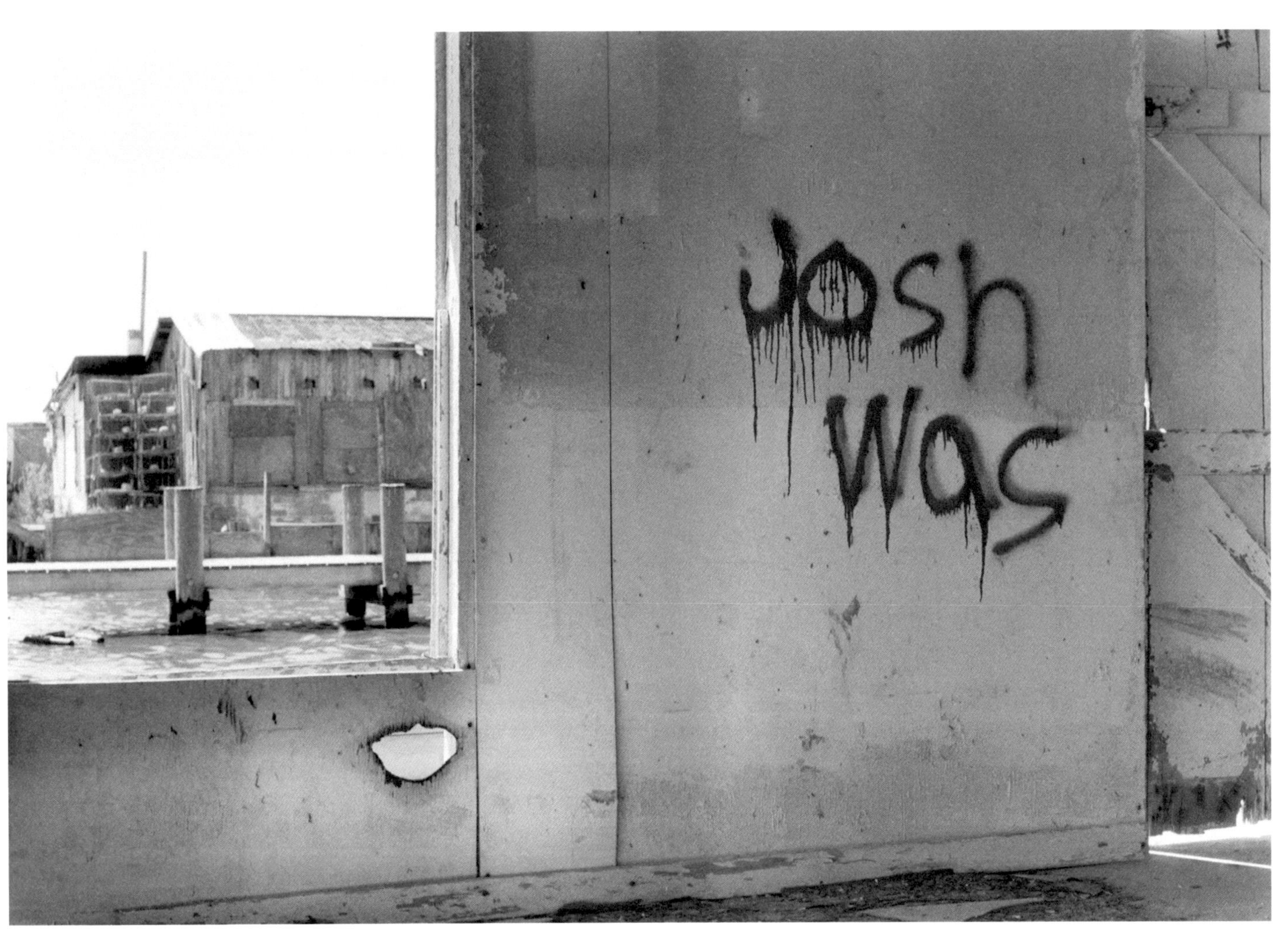
Josh
was

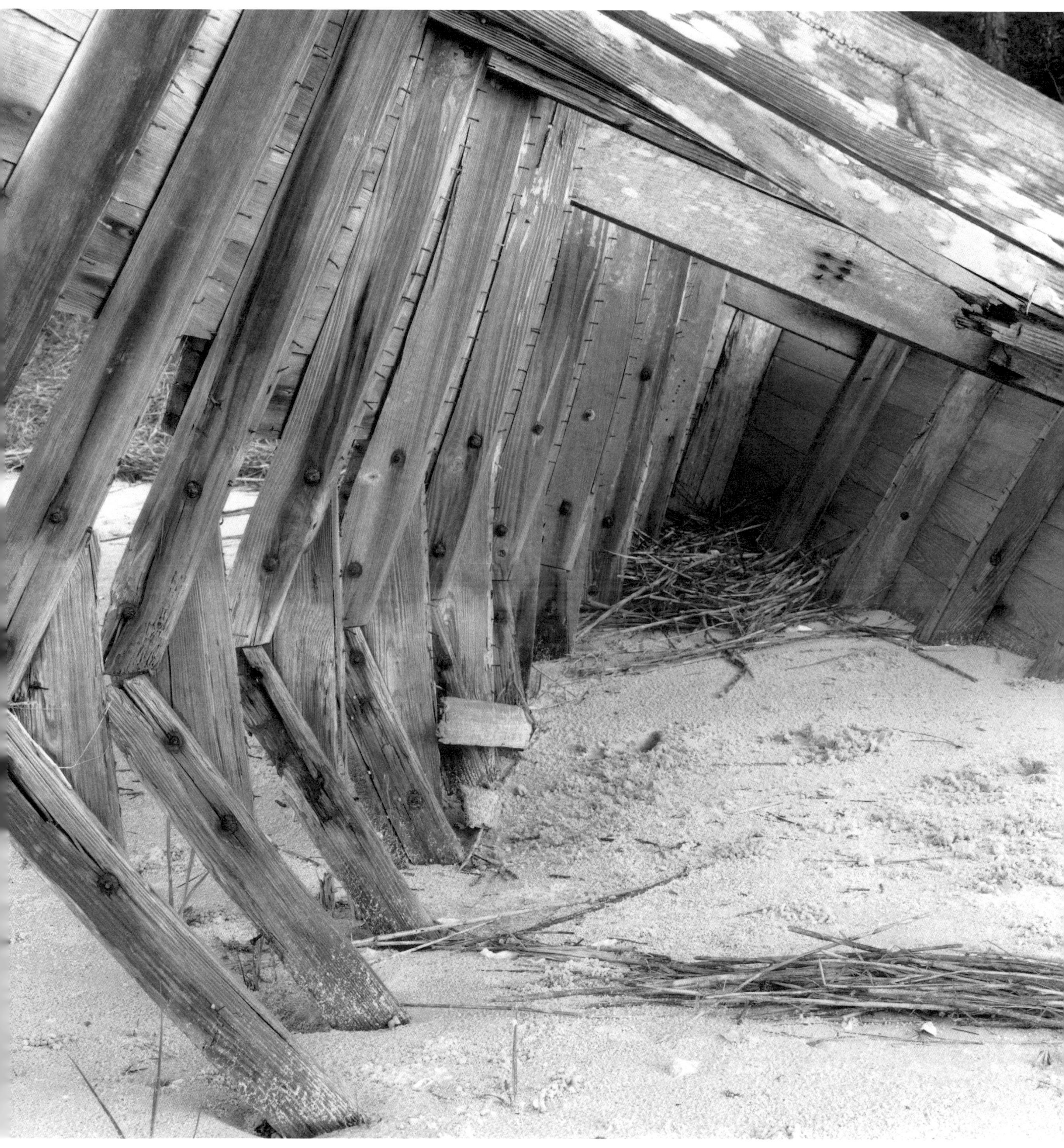

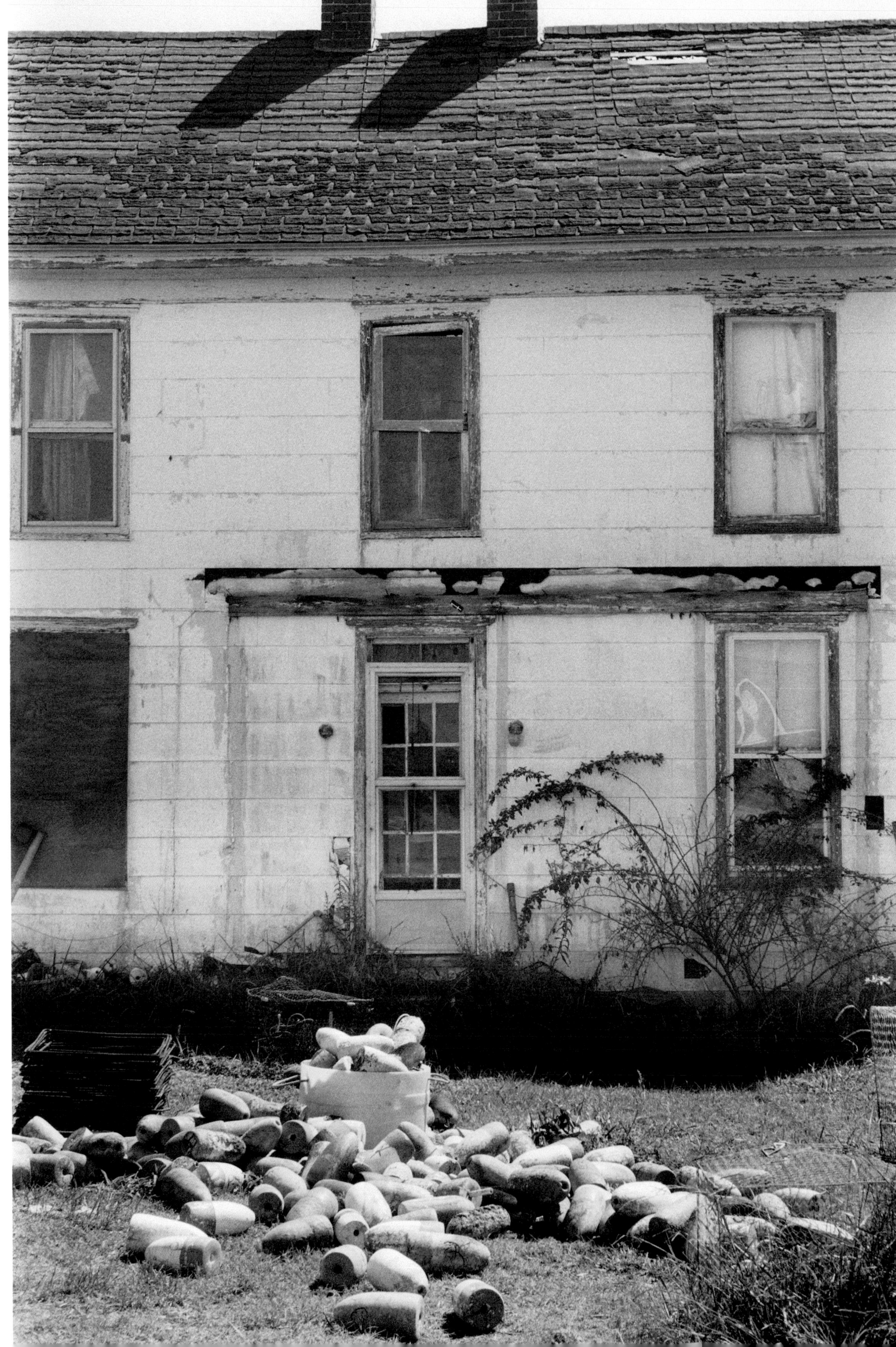

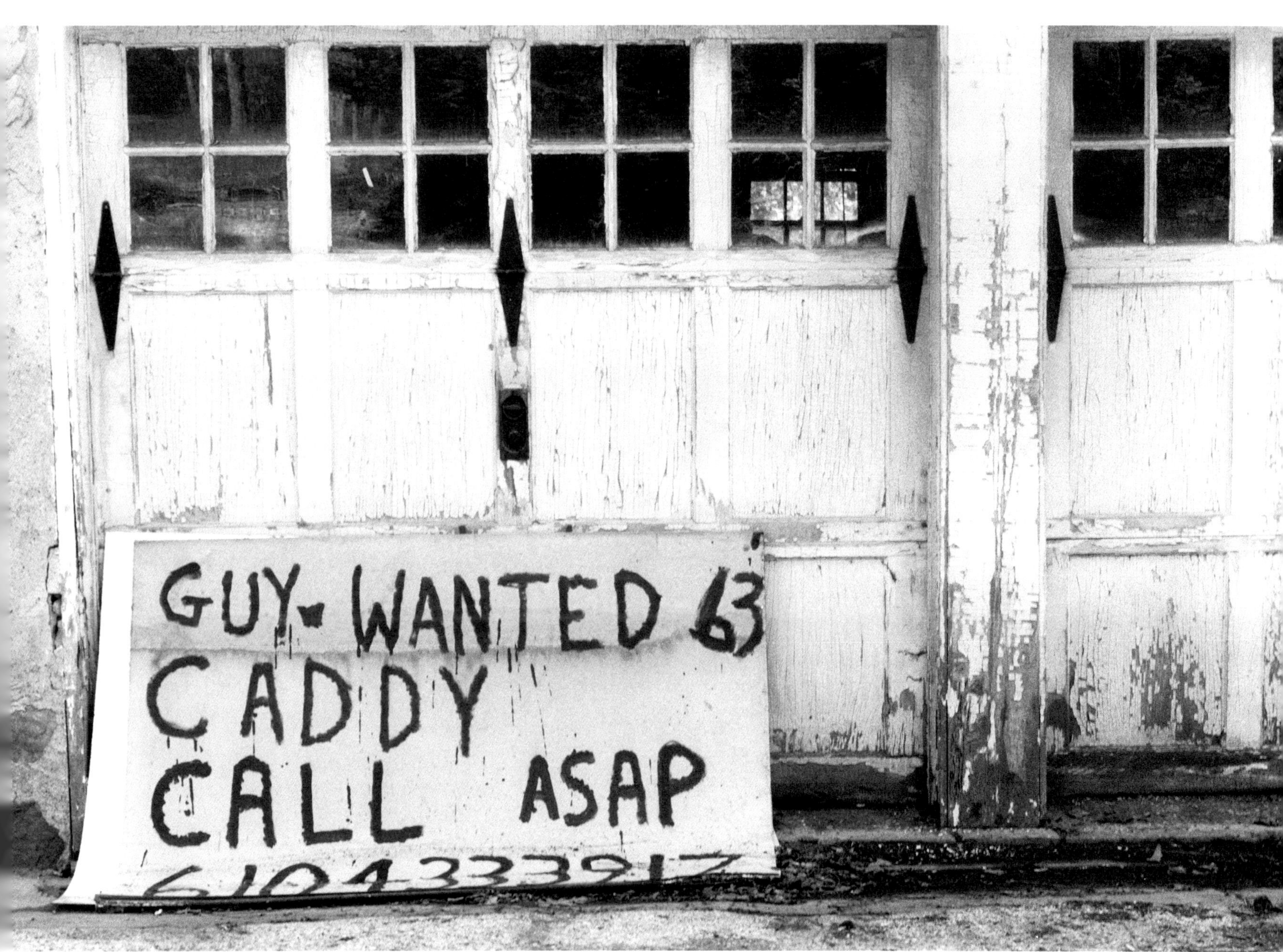
GUY - WANTED 63
CADDY
CALL ASAP
6104333917

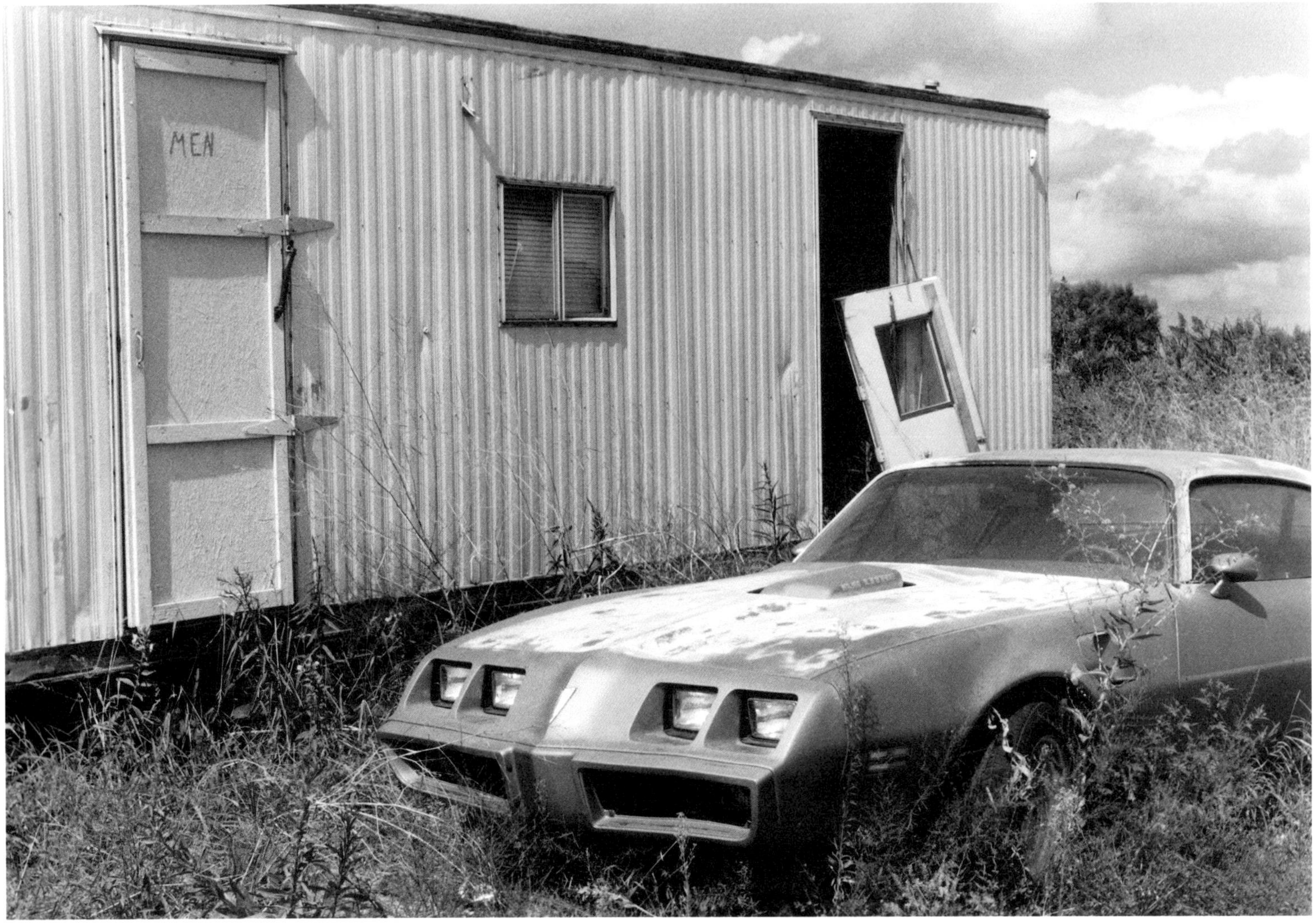

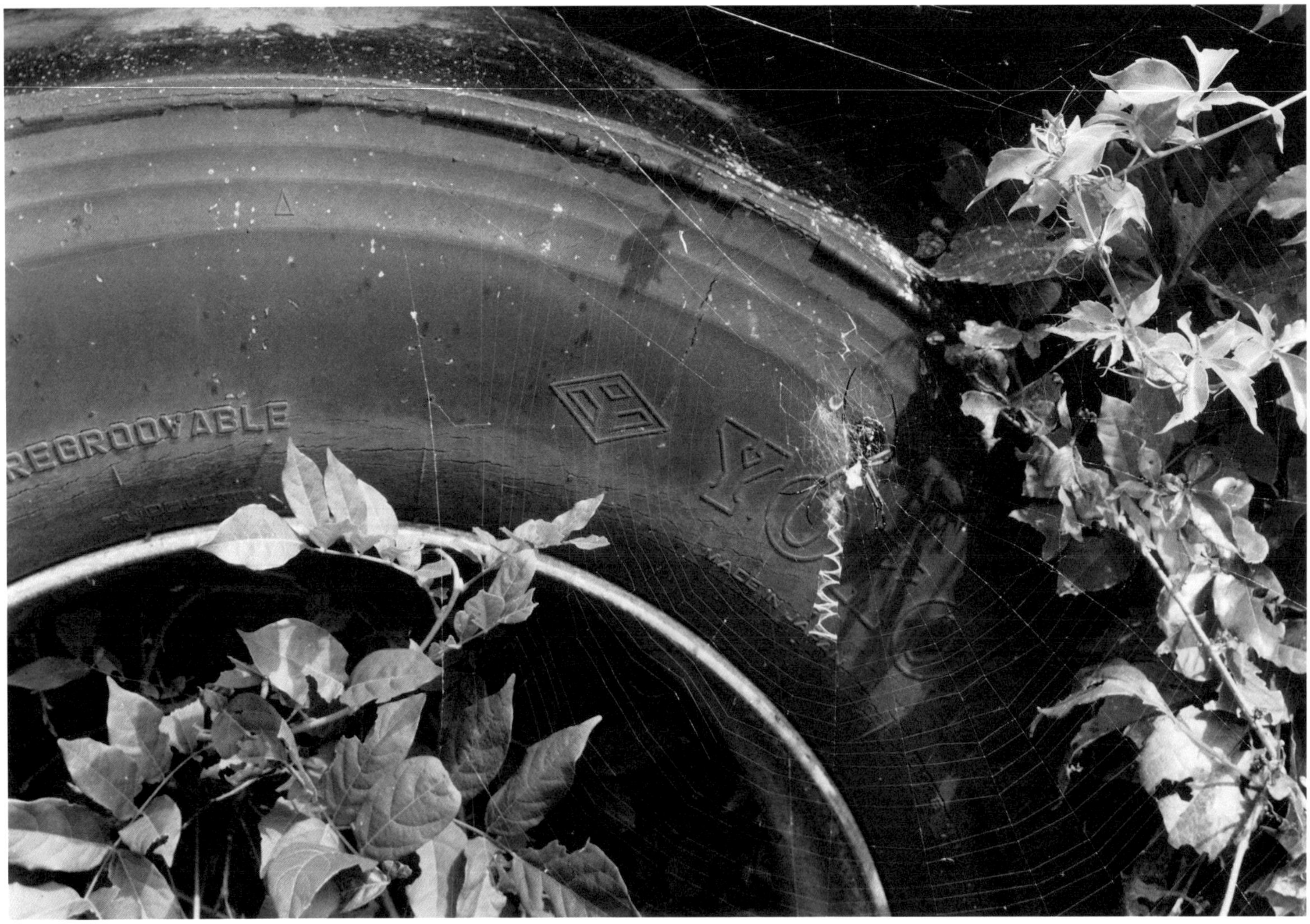

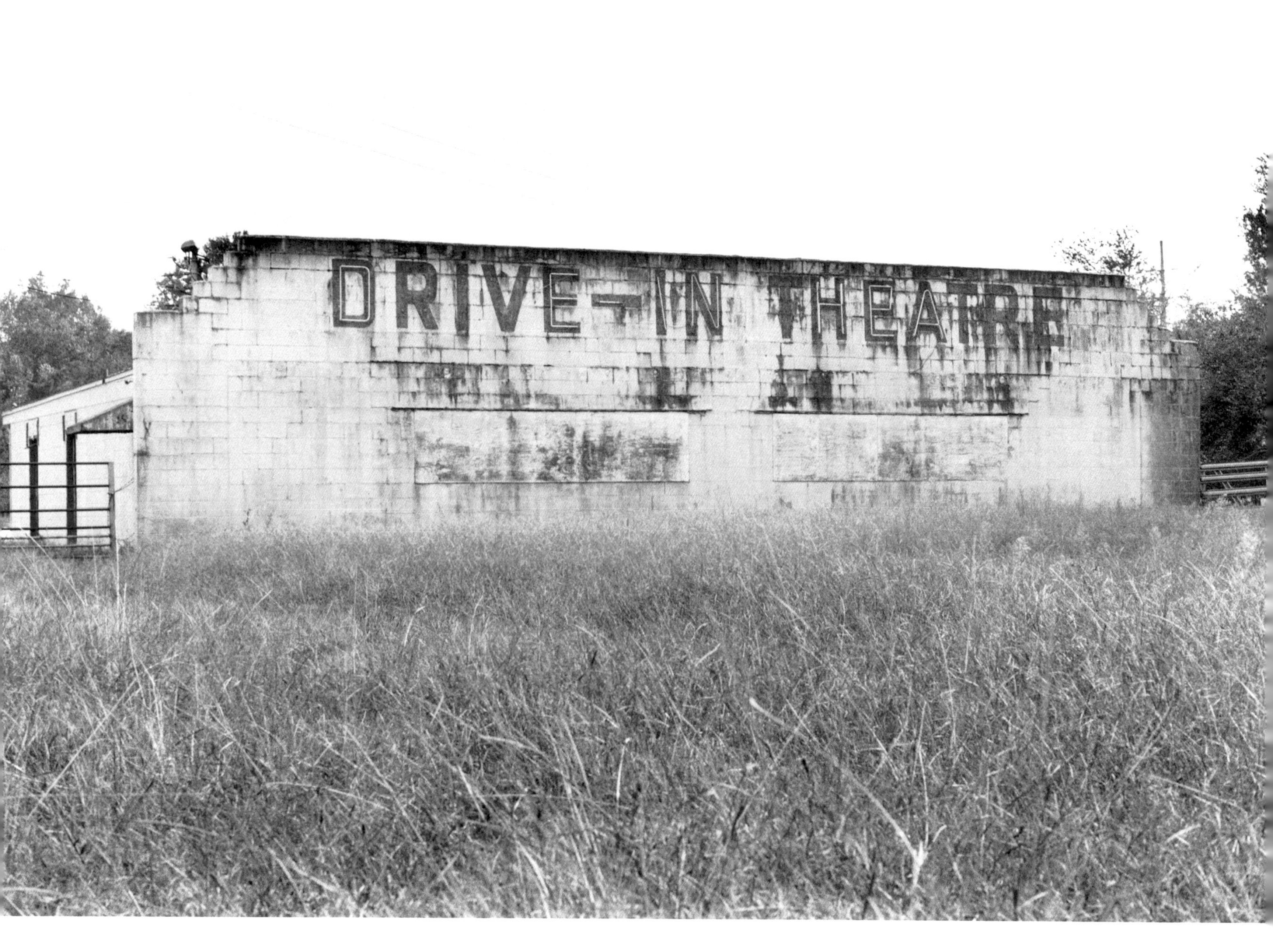

DRIVE-IN THEATRE

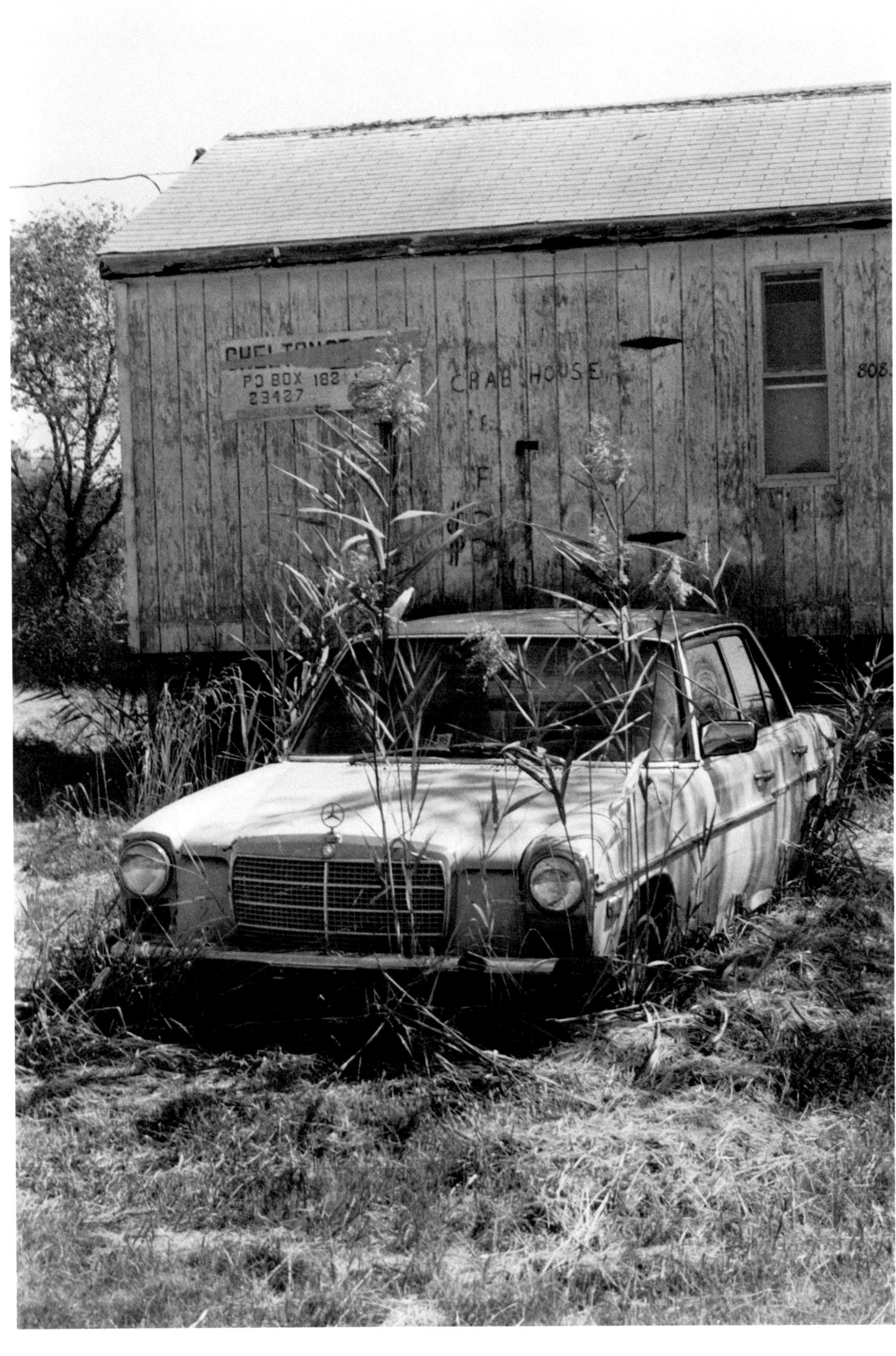

CHELTONST
PO BOX 188
23427
CRAB HOUSE
808

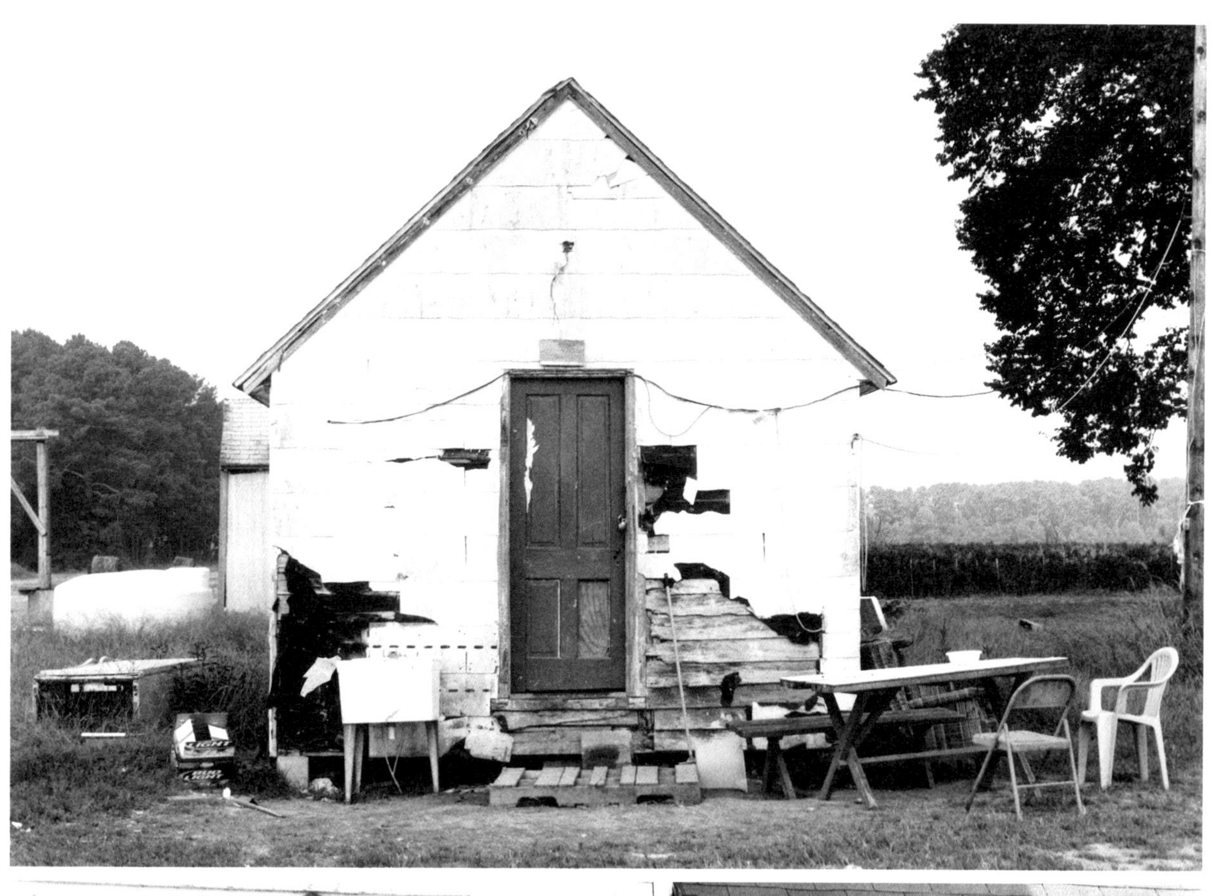

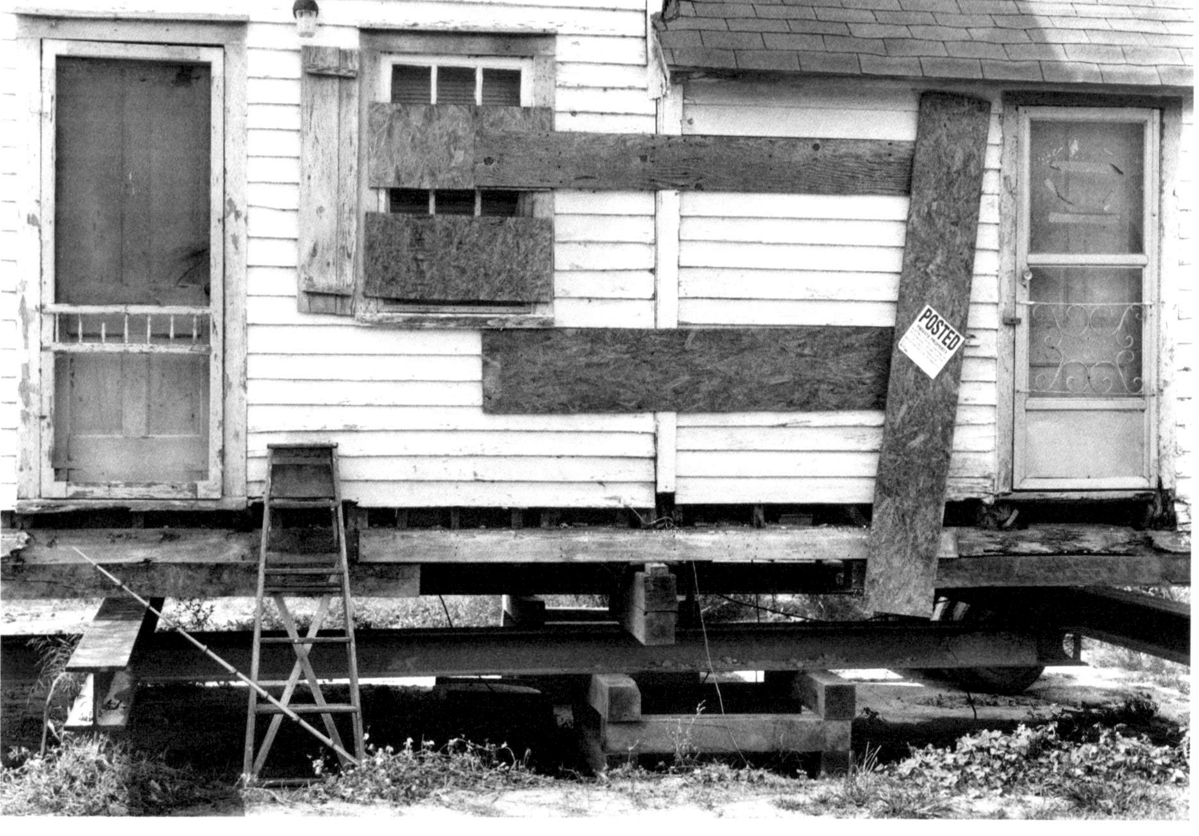

POSTED

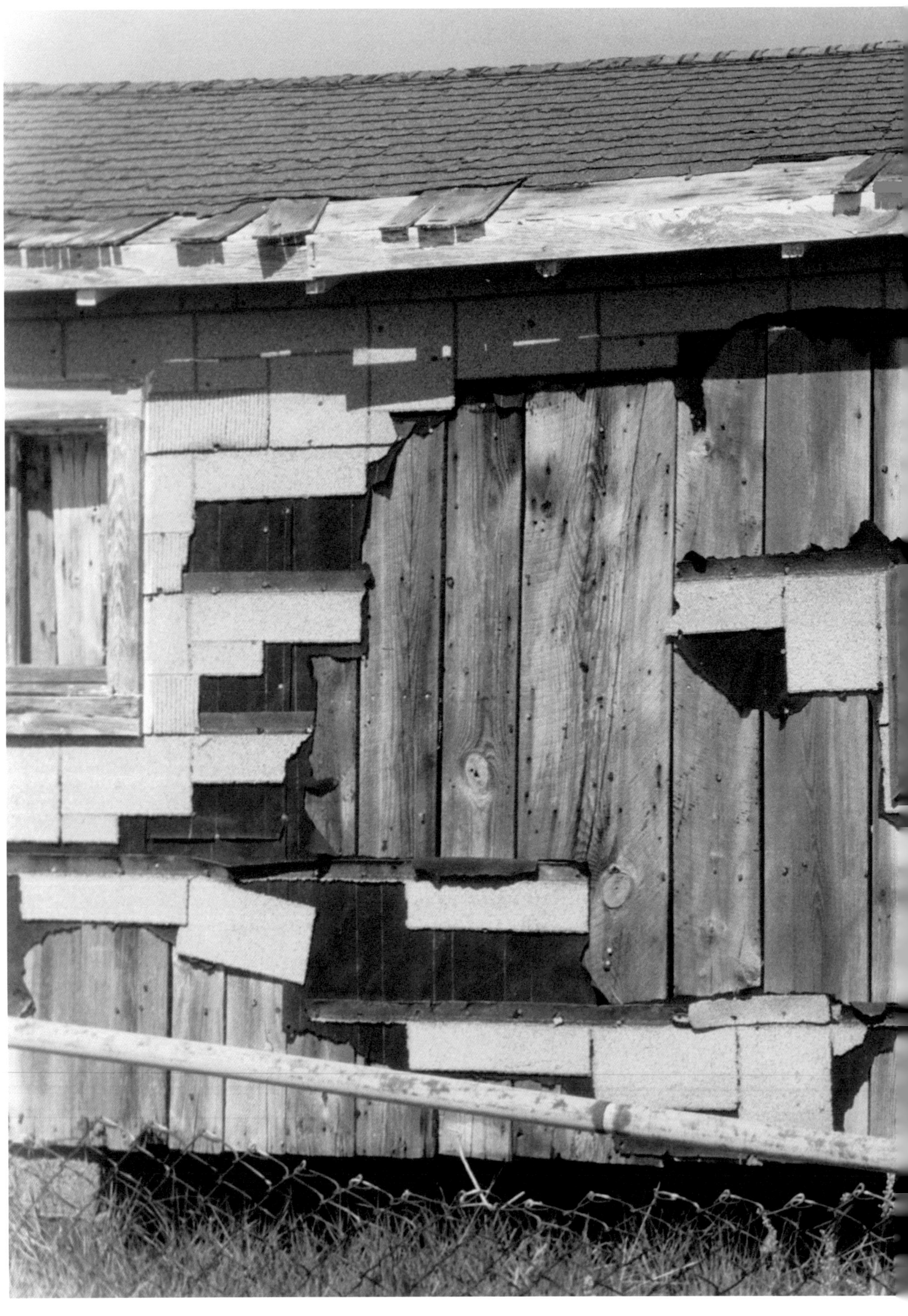

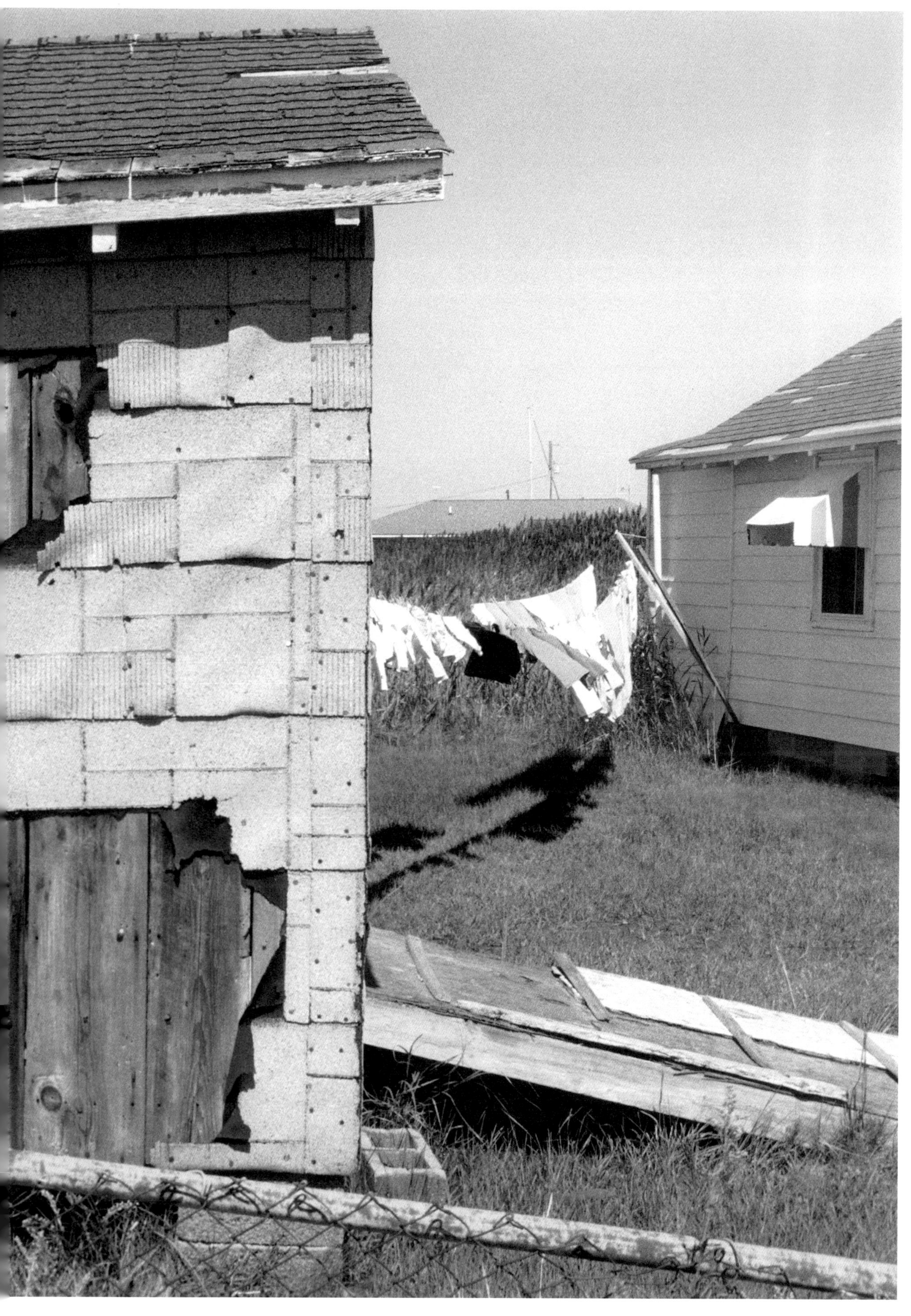

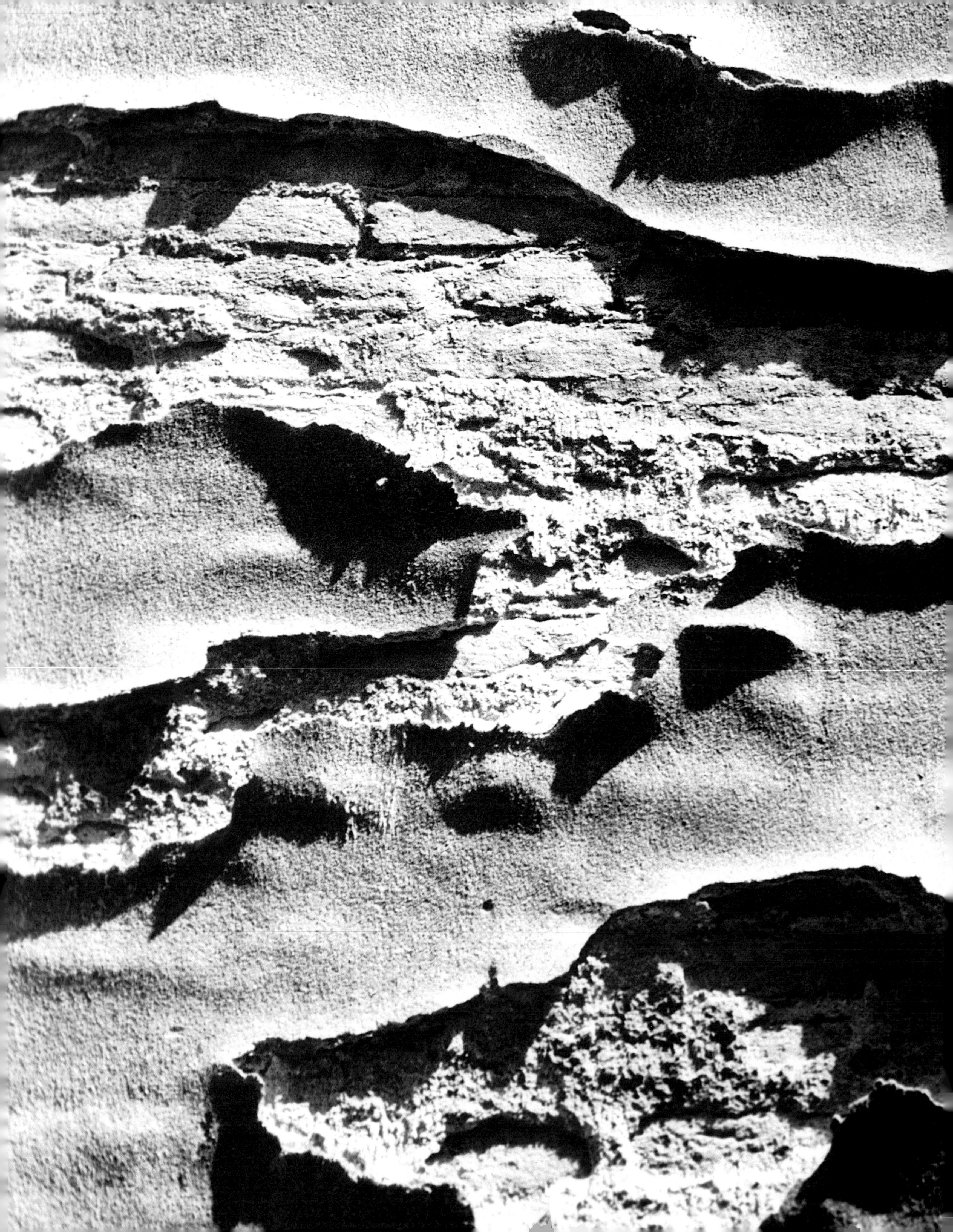

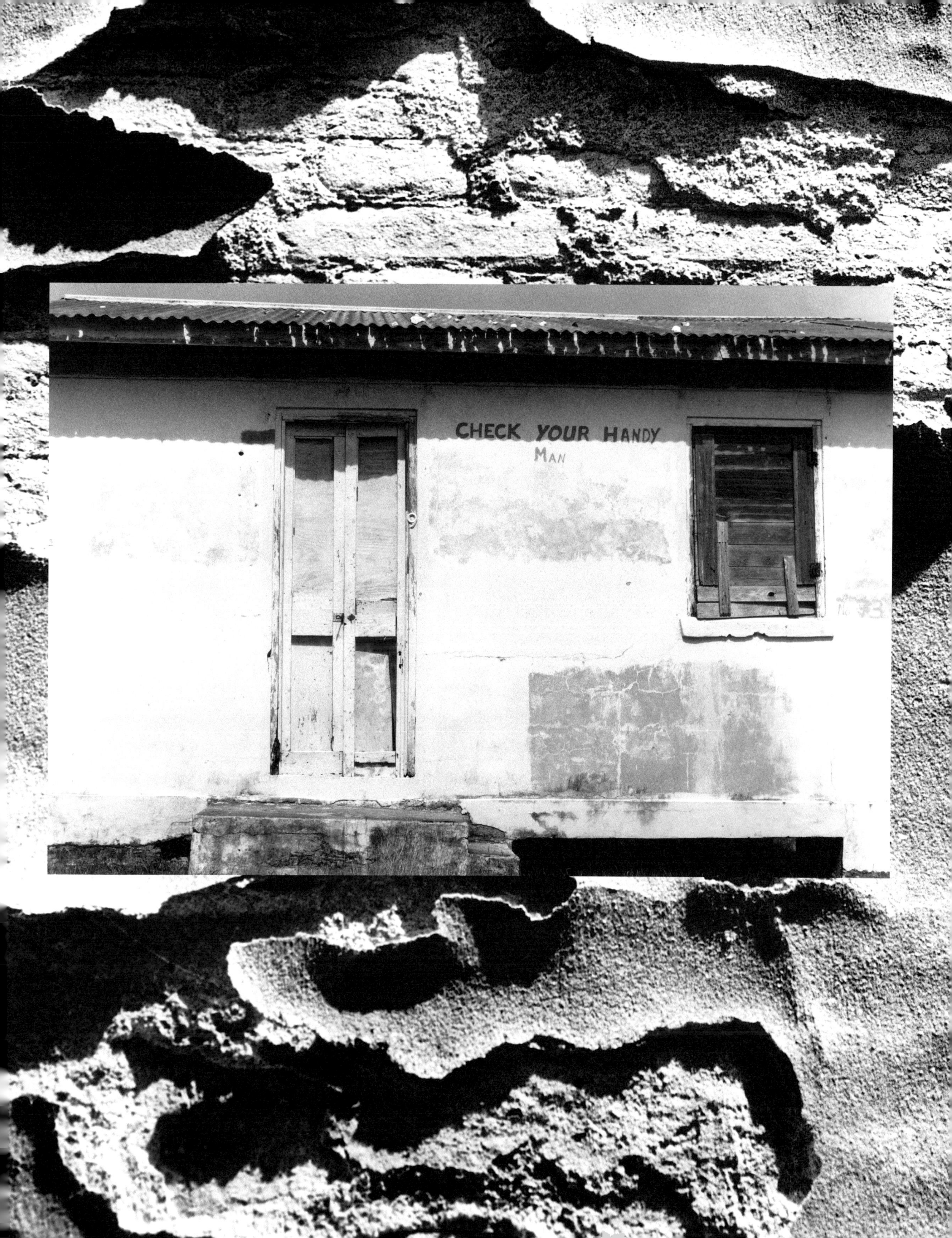

CHECK YOUR HANDY
MAN

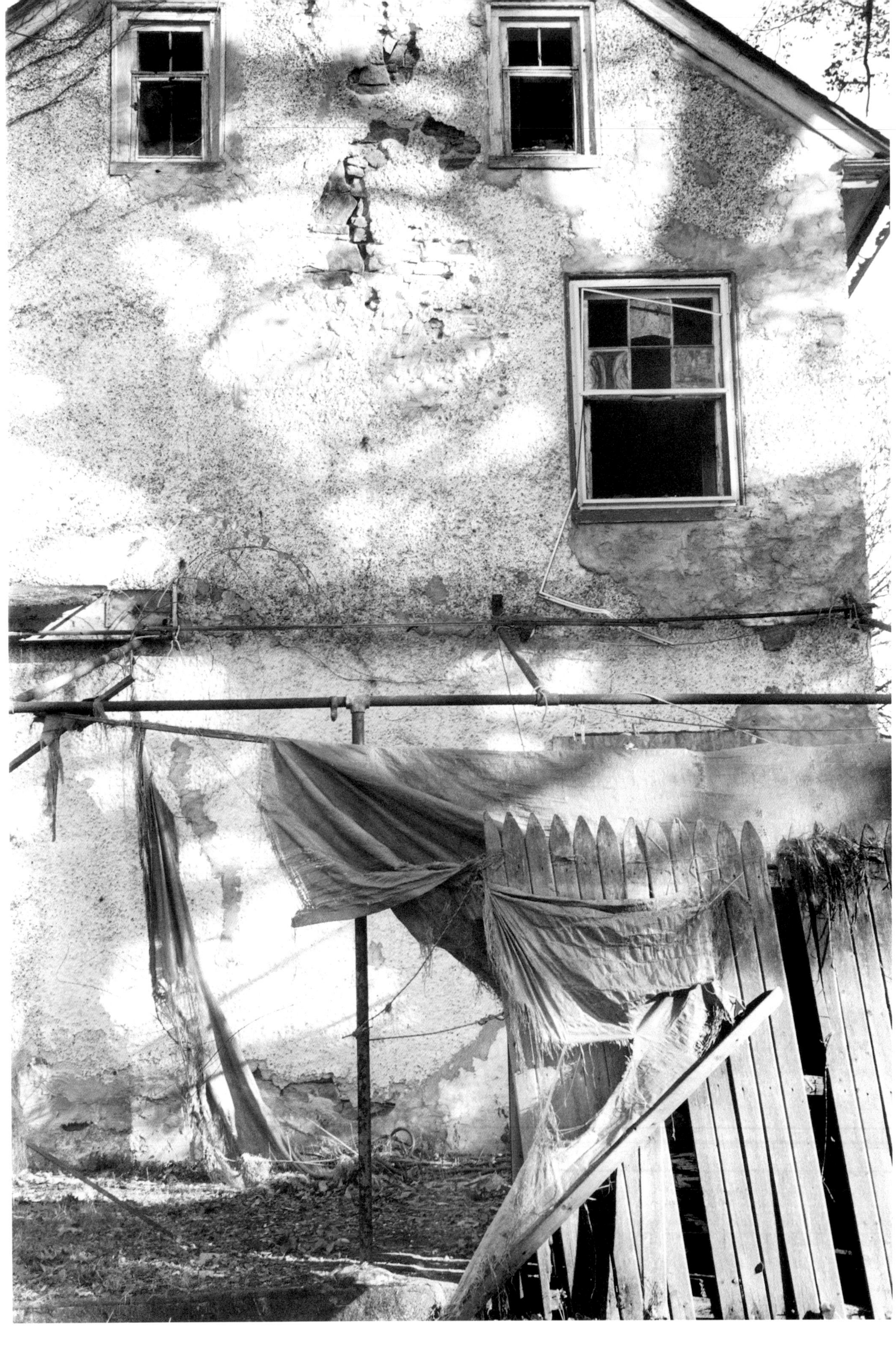

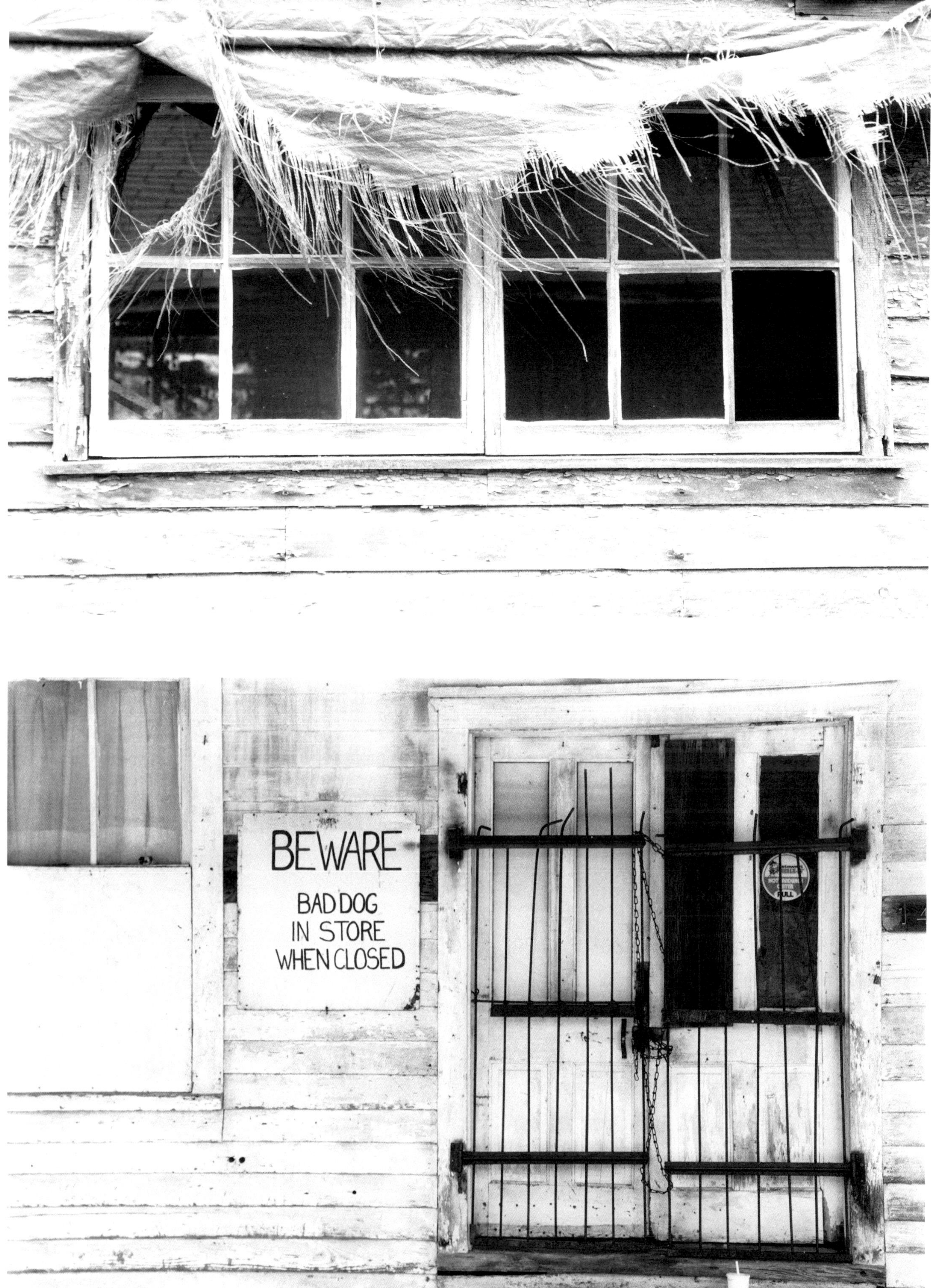
BEWARE
BAD DOG
IN STORE
WHEN CLOSED

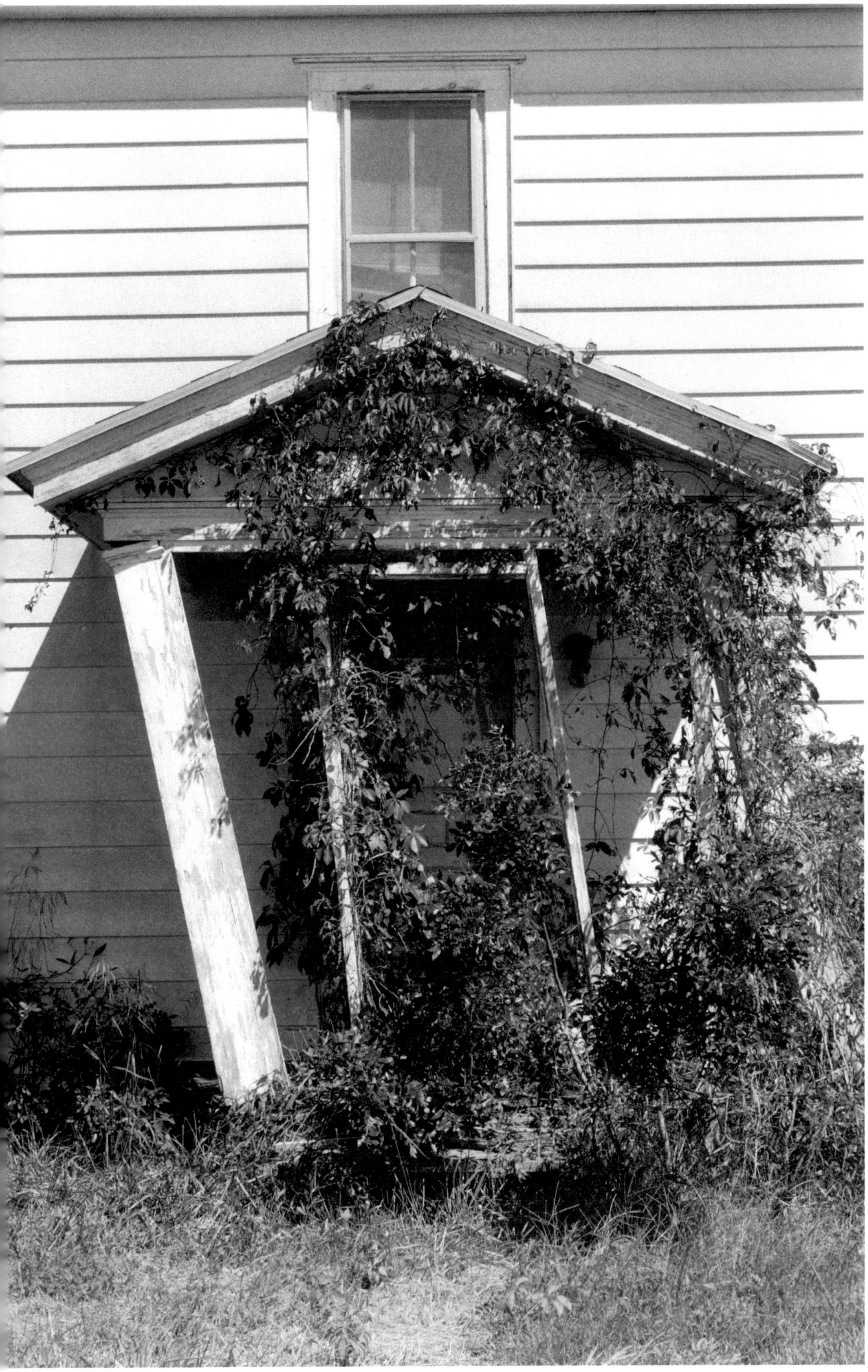

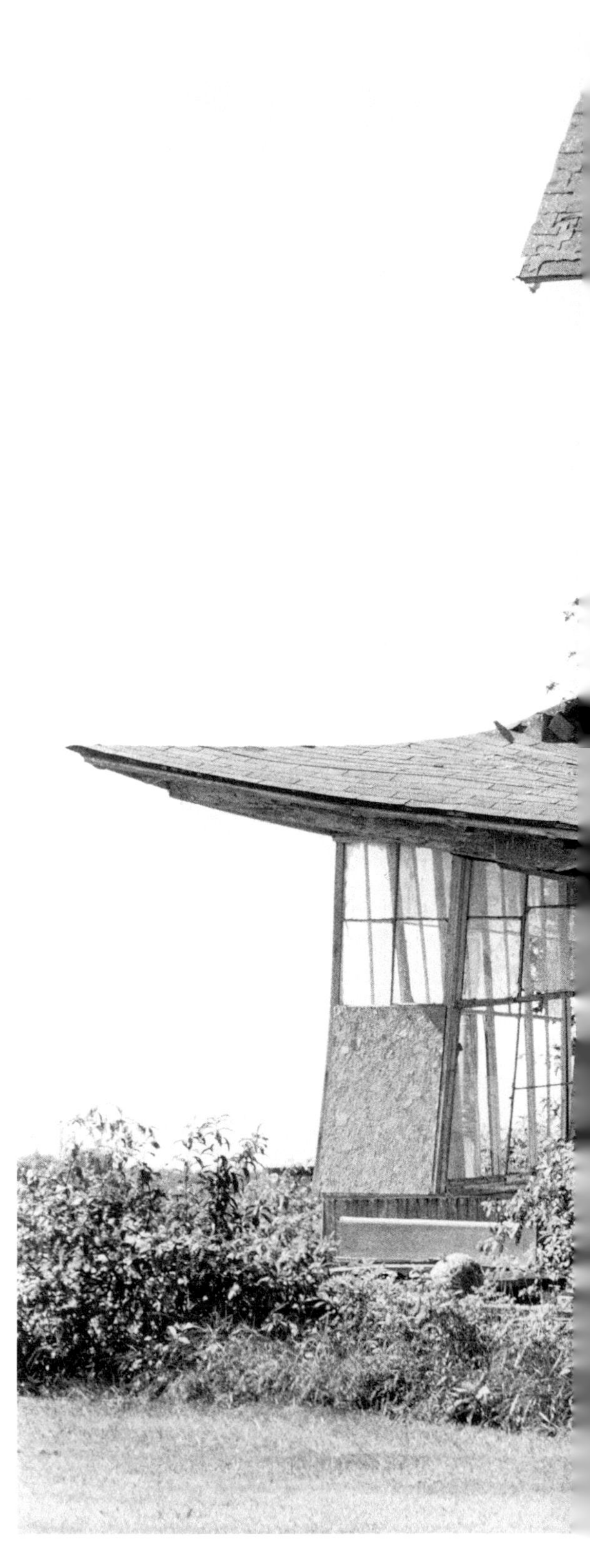

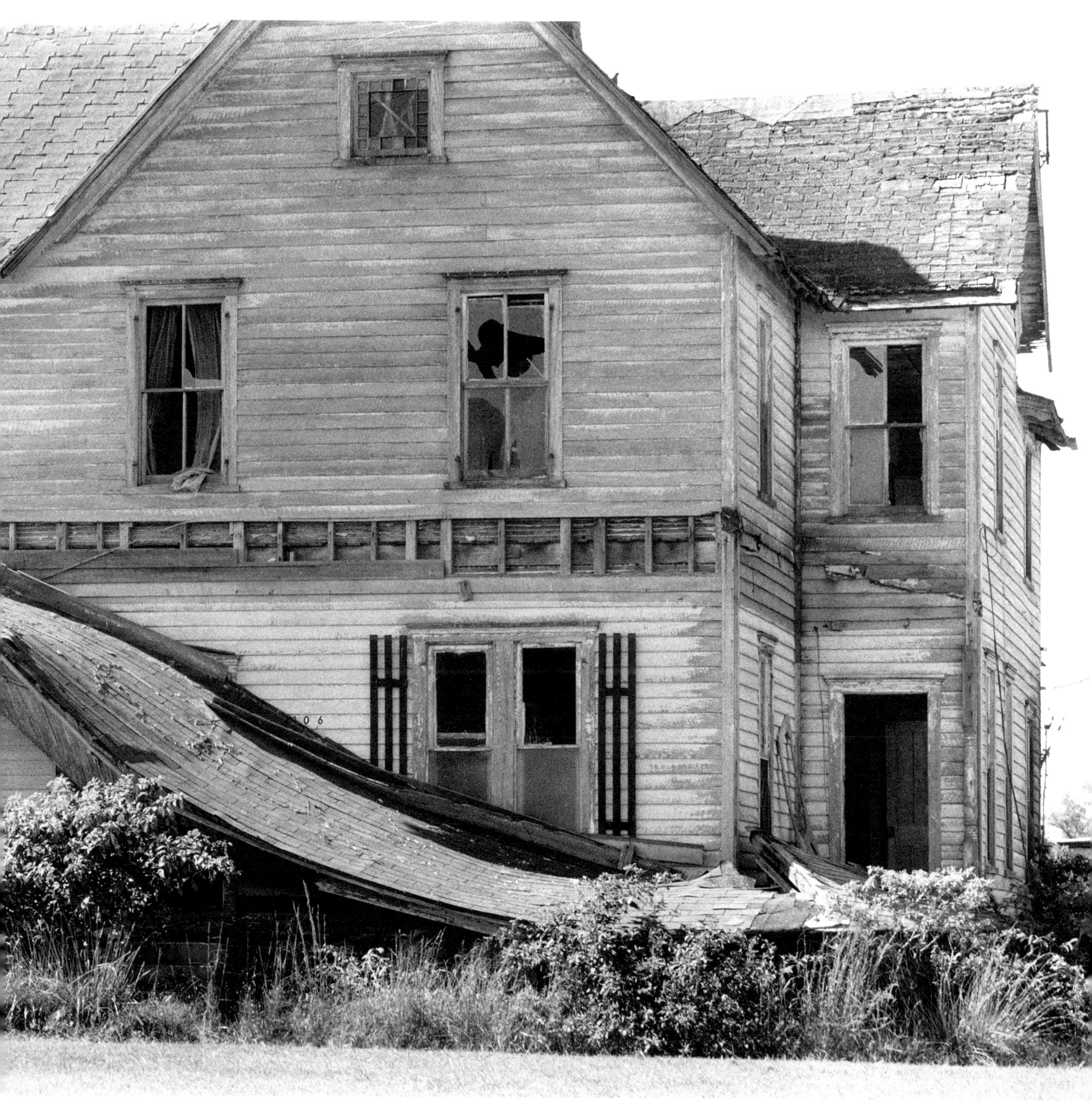

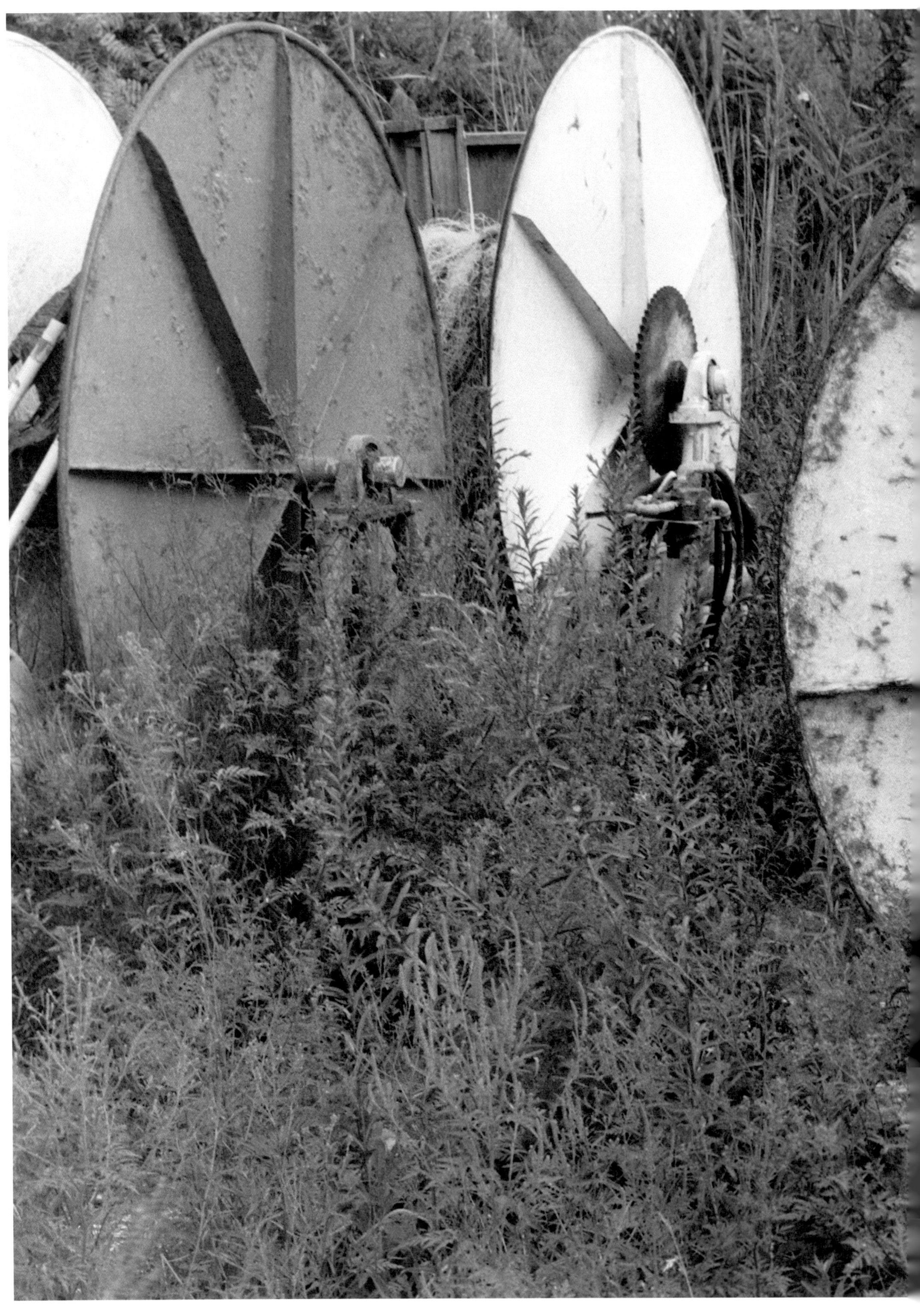

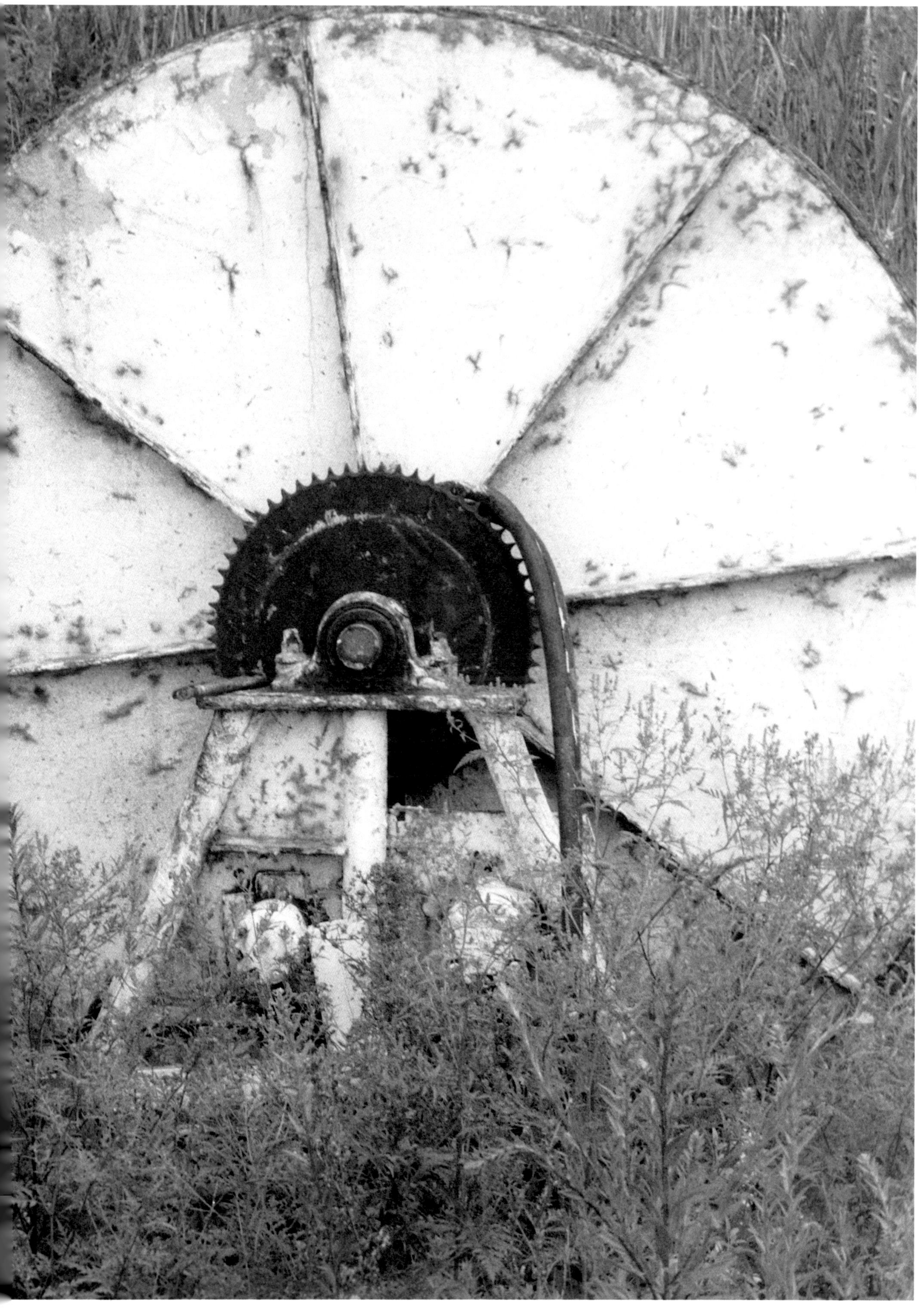

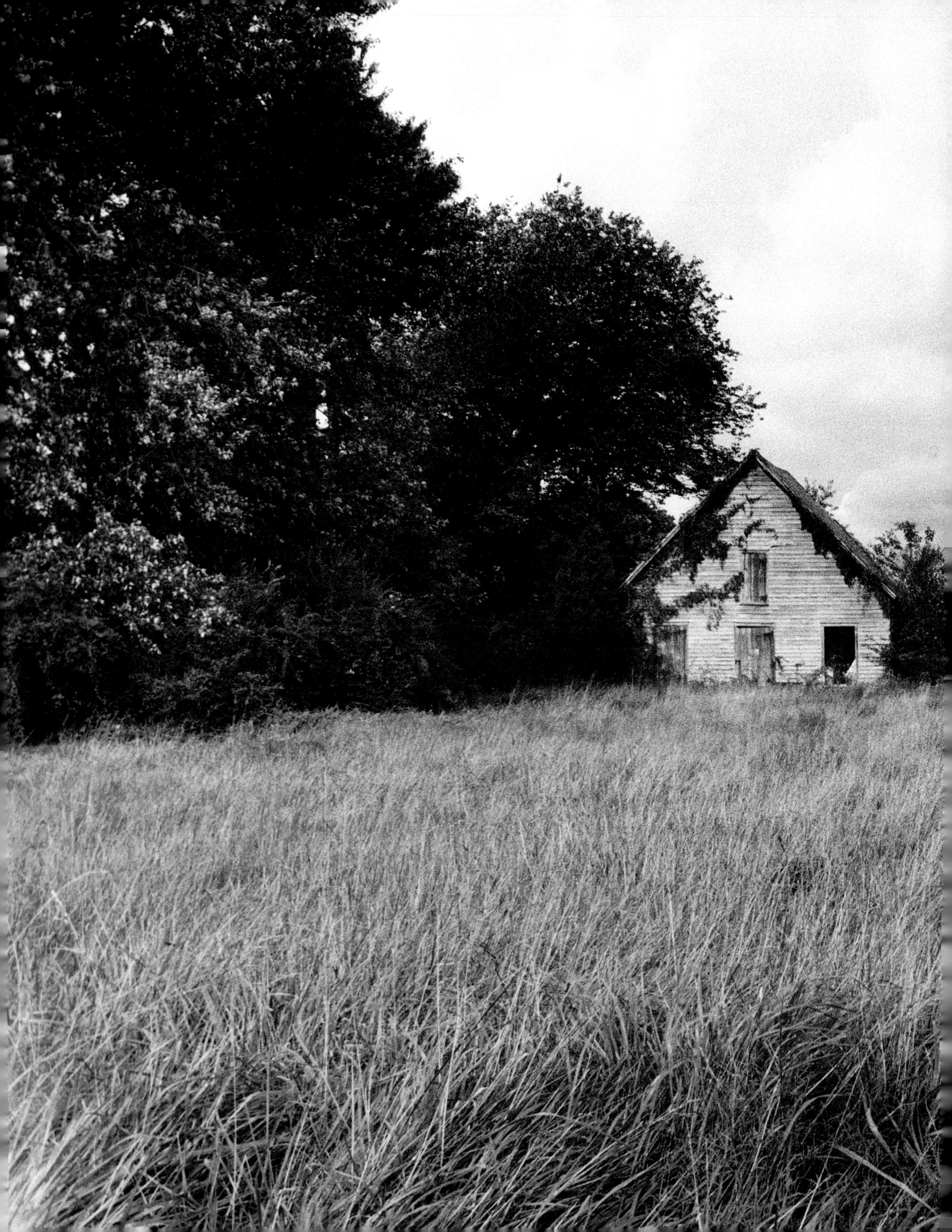

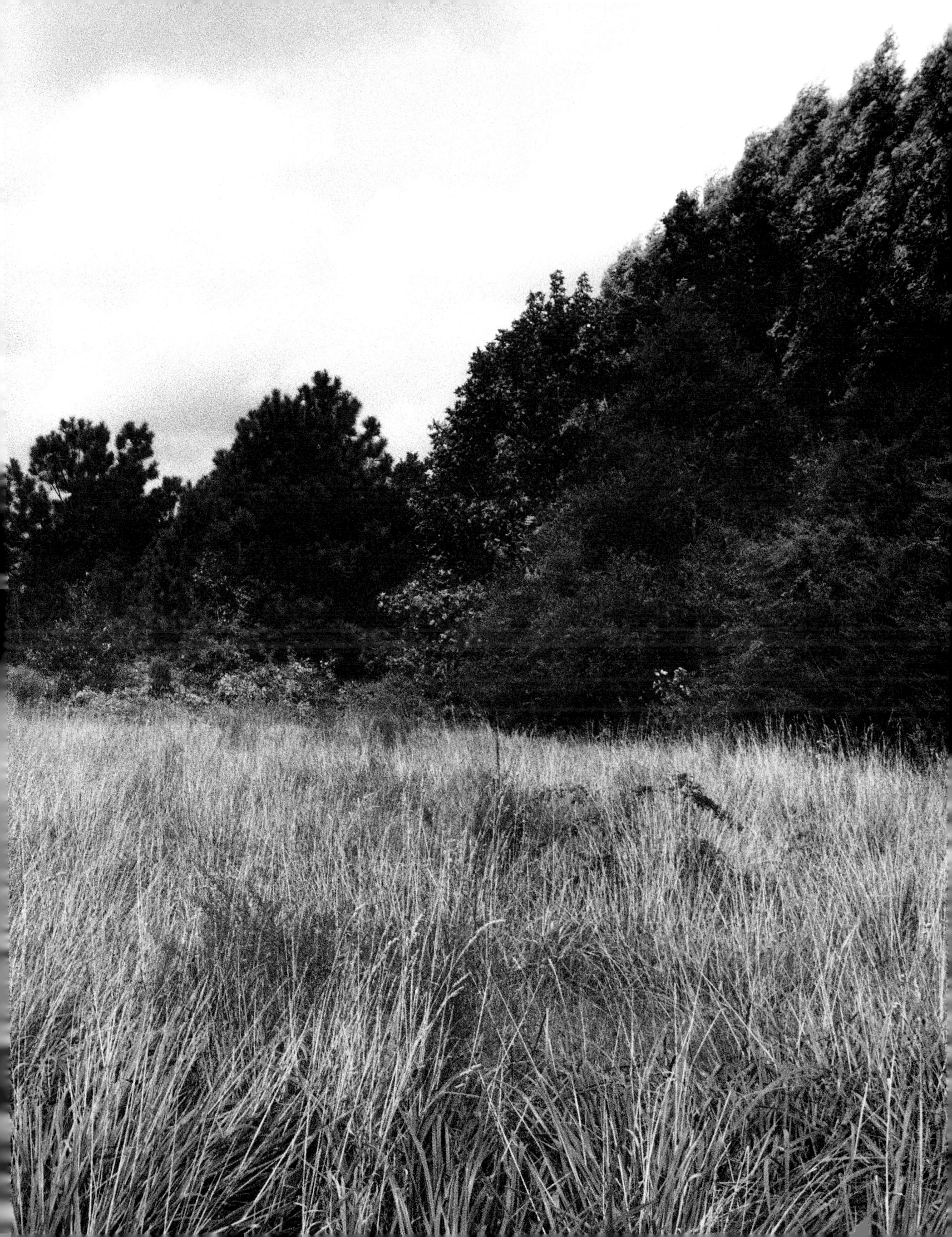

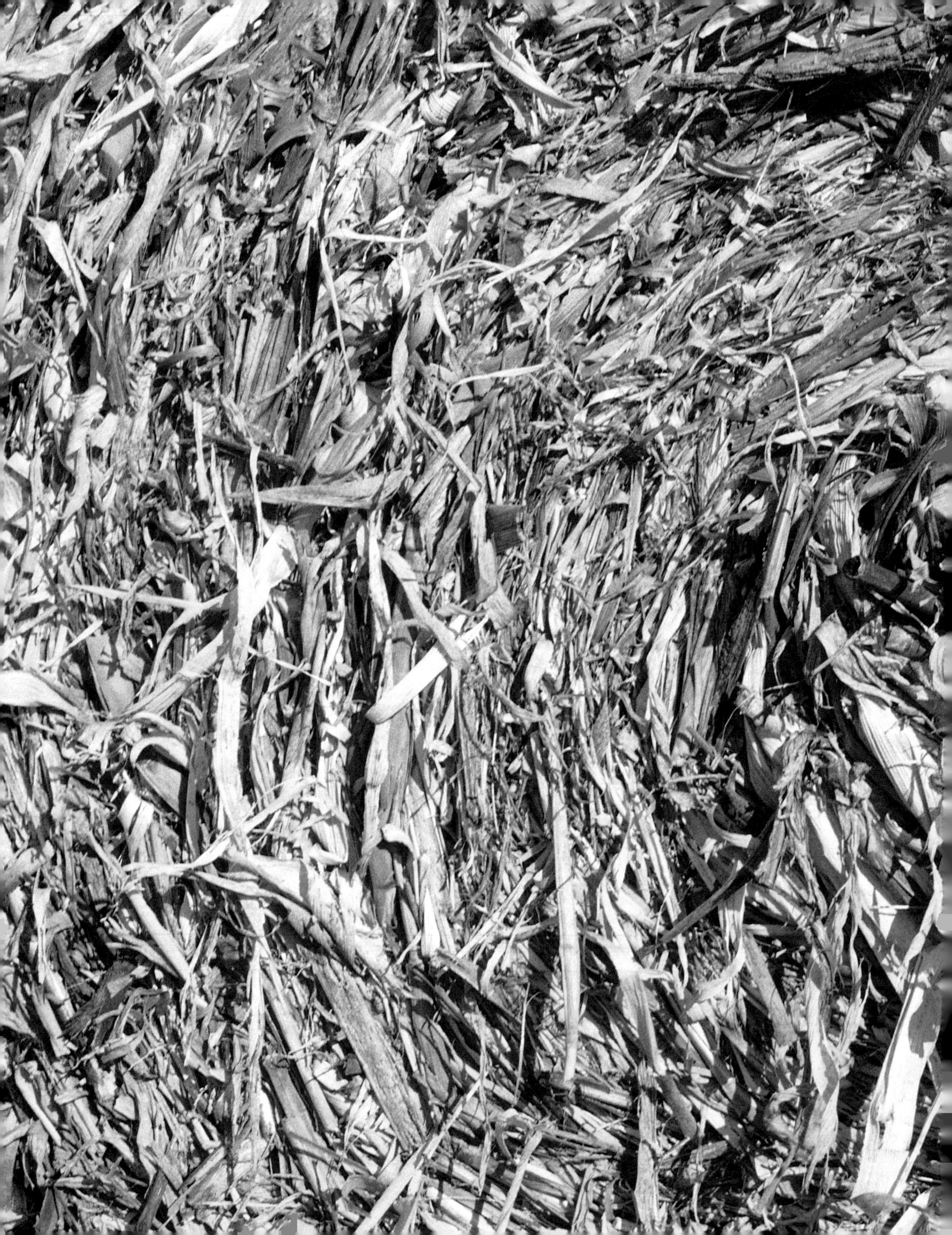

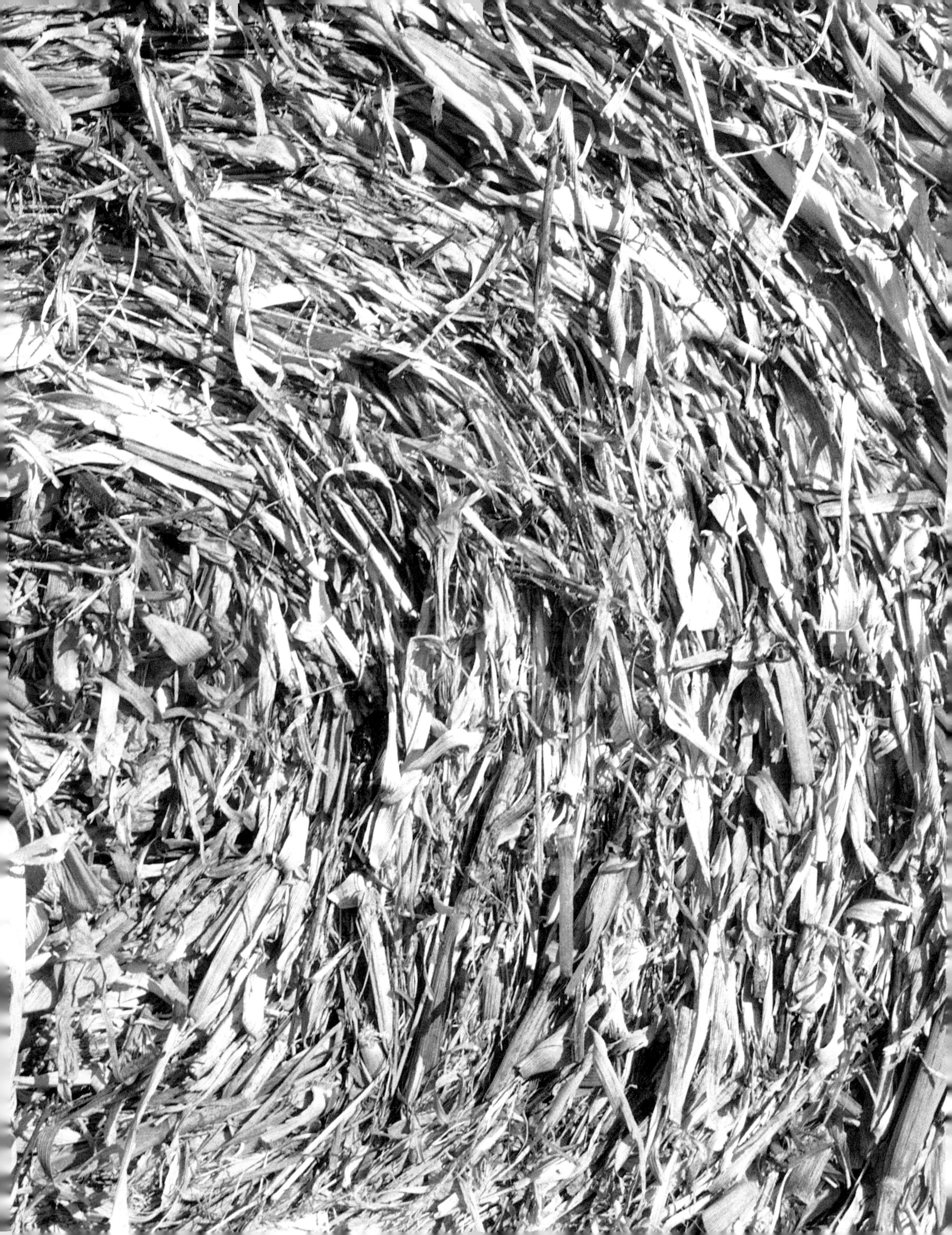

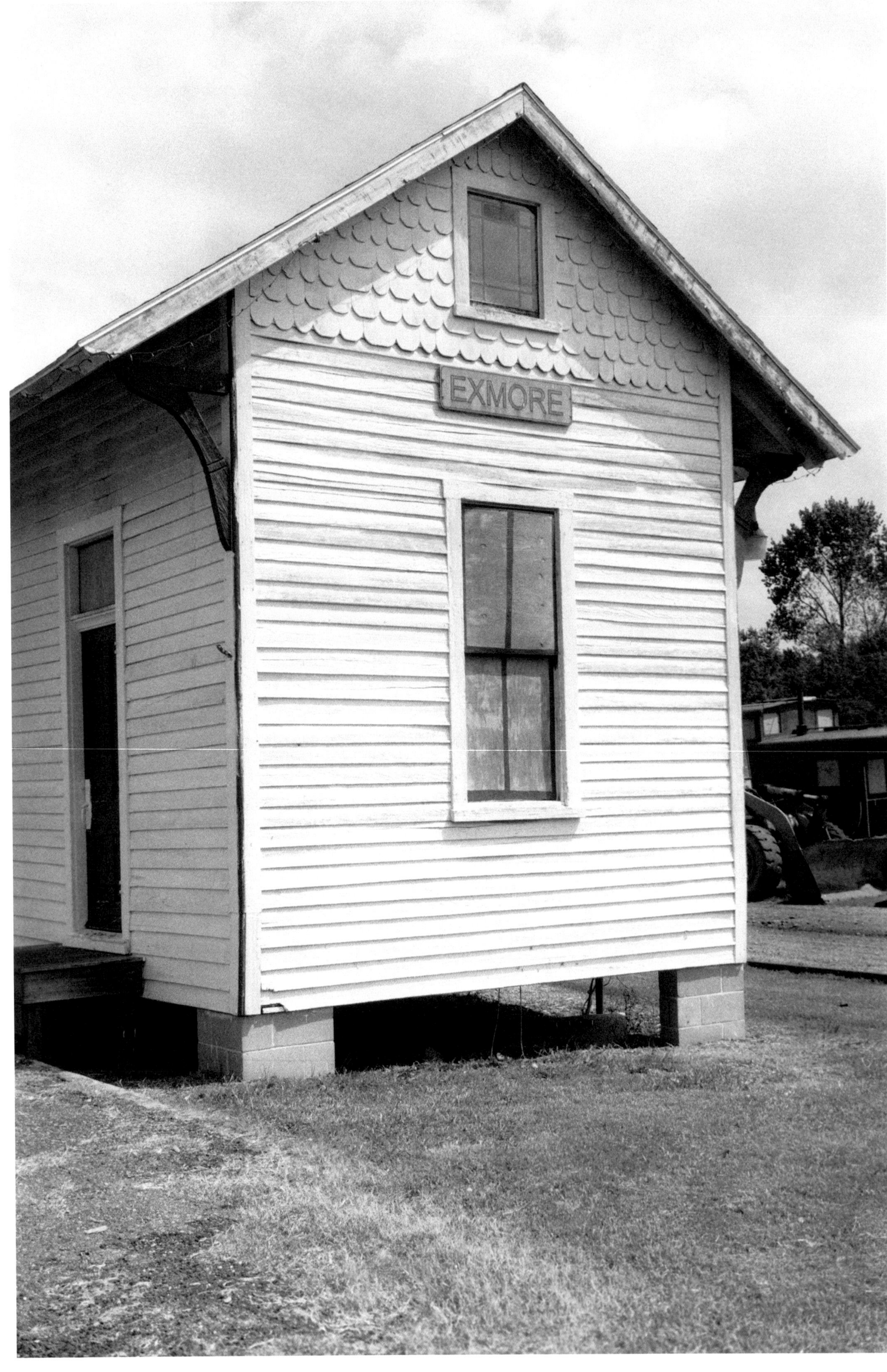

EXMORE

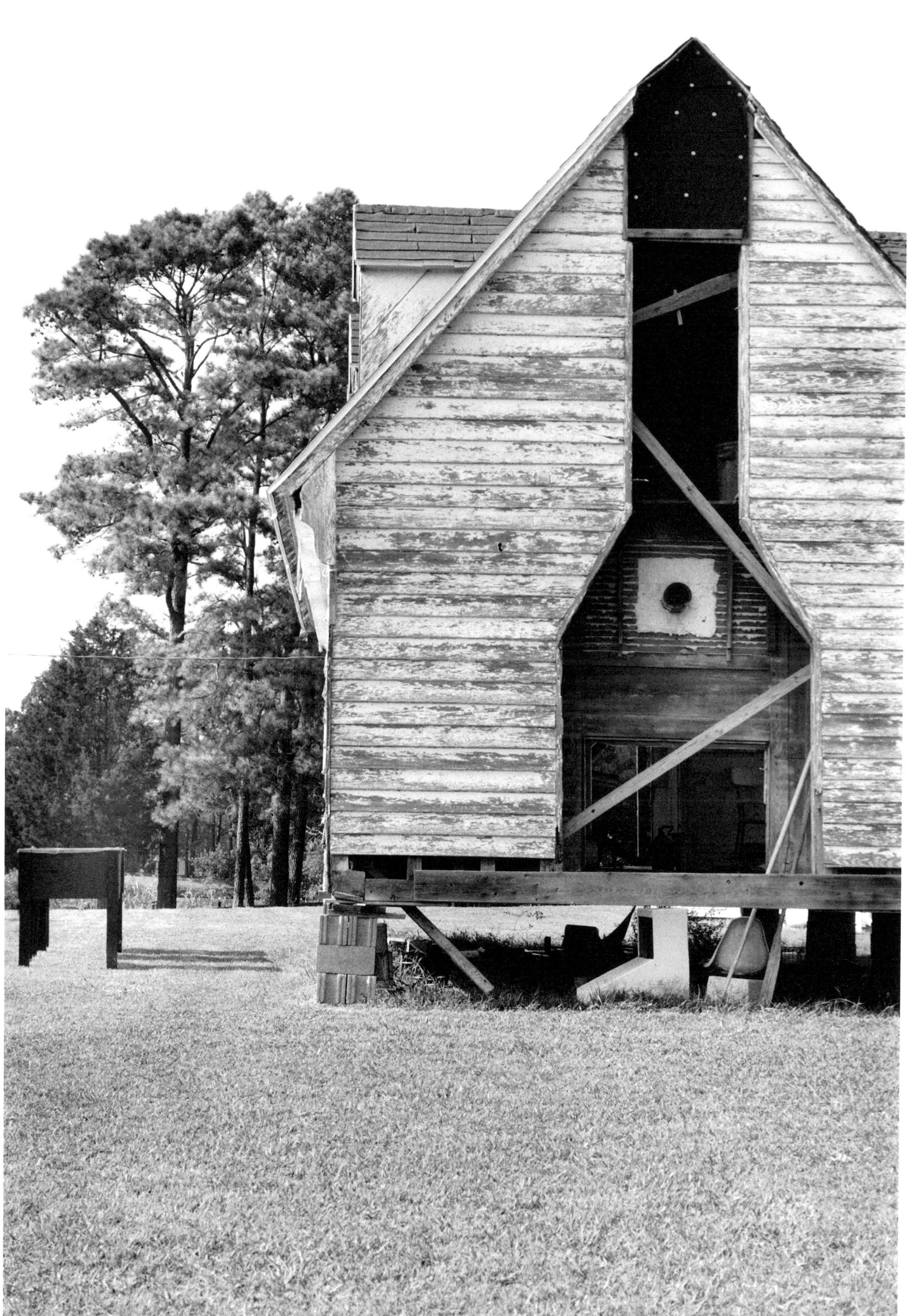

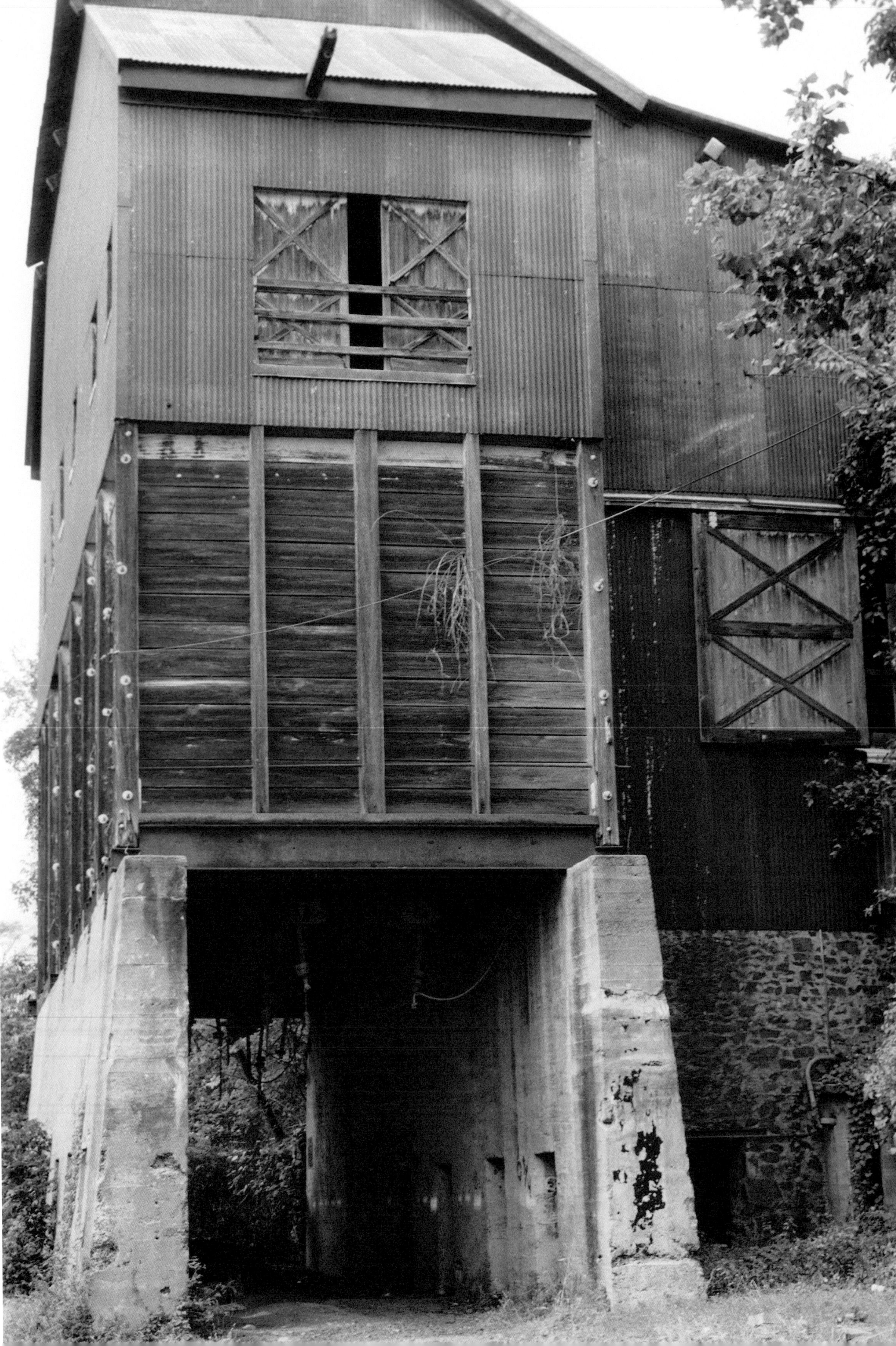

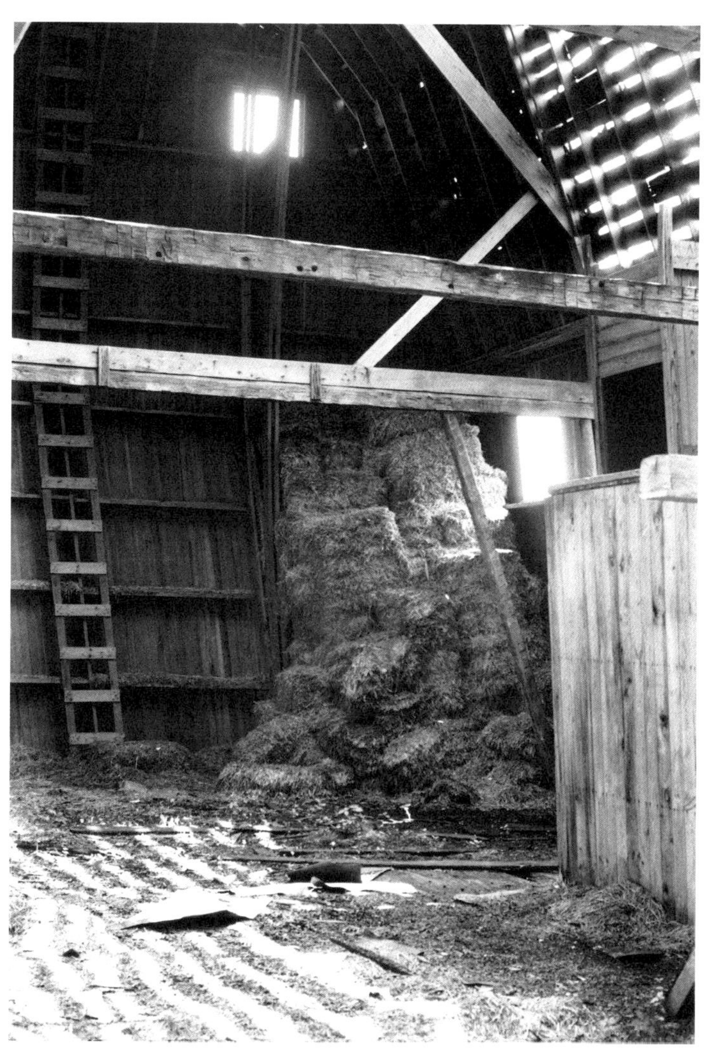 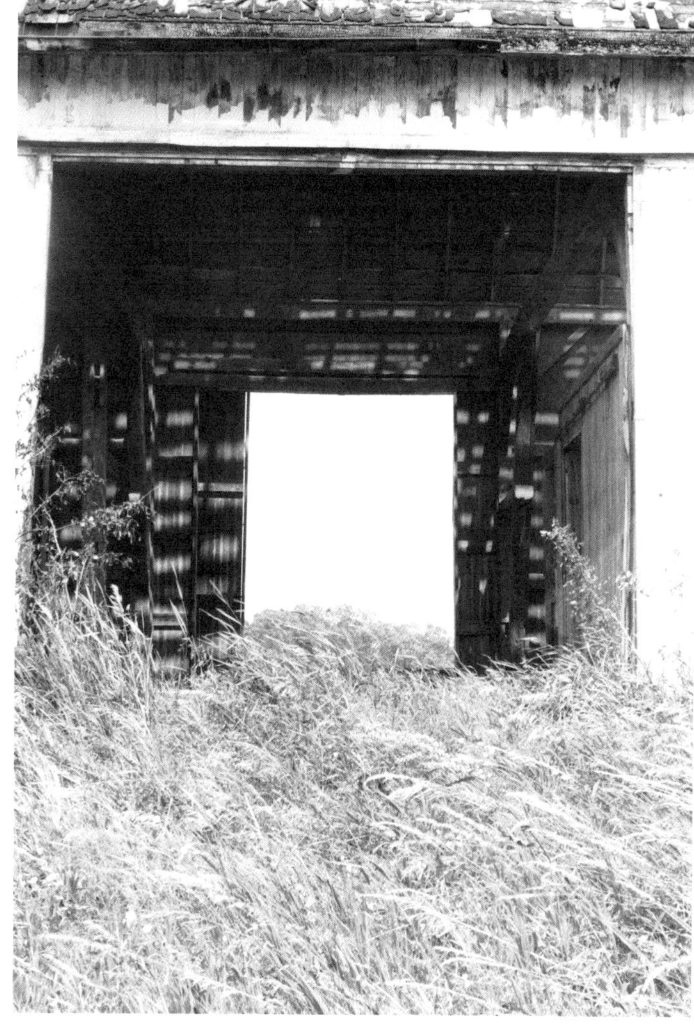

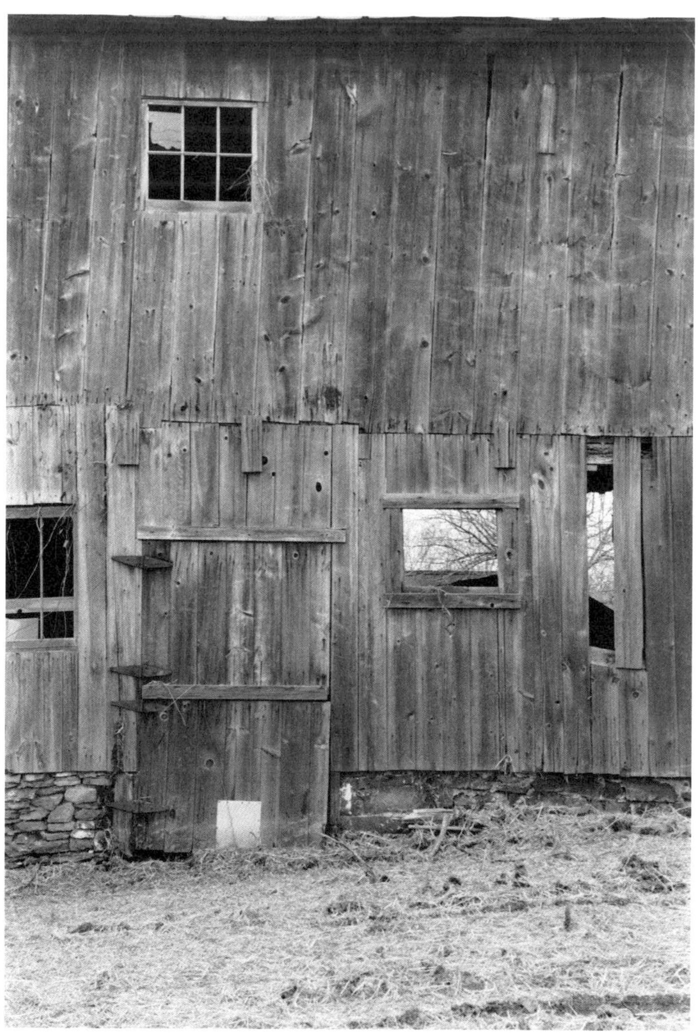 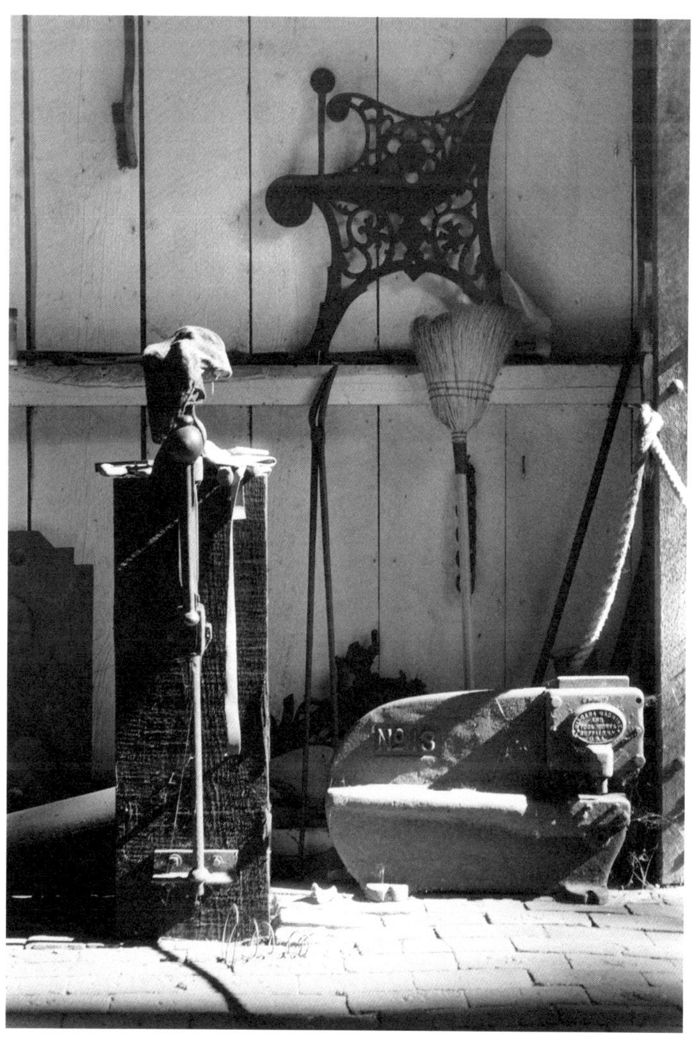

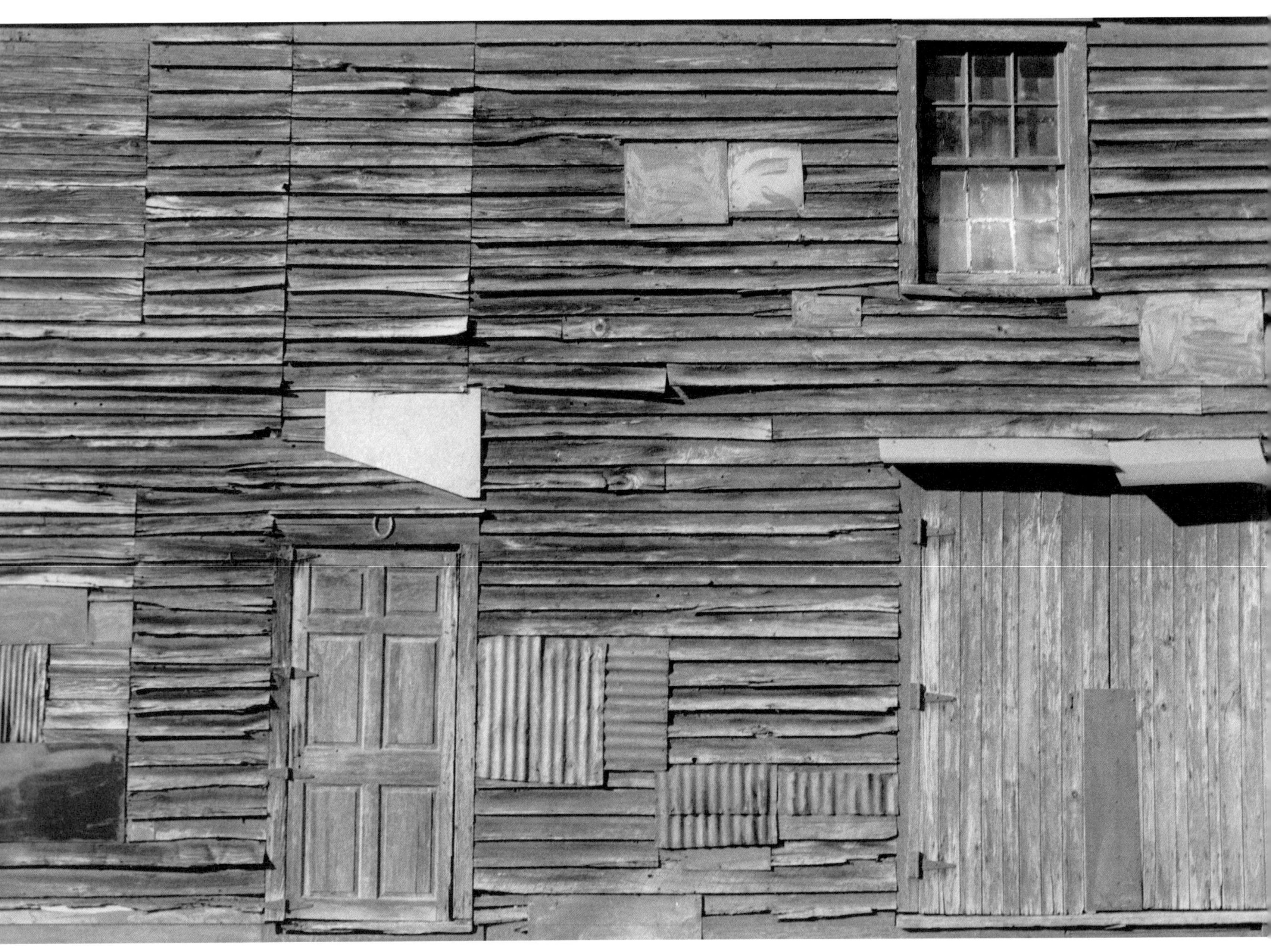

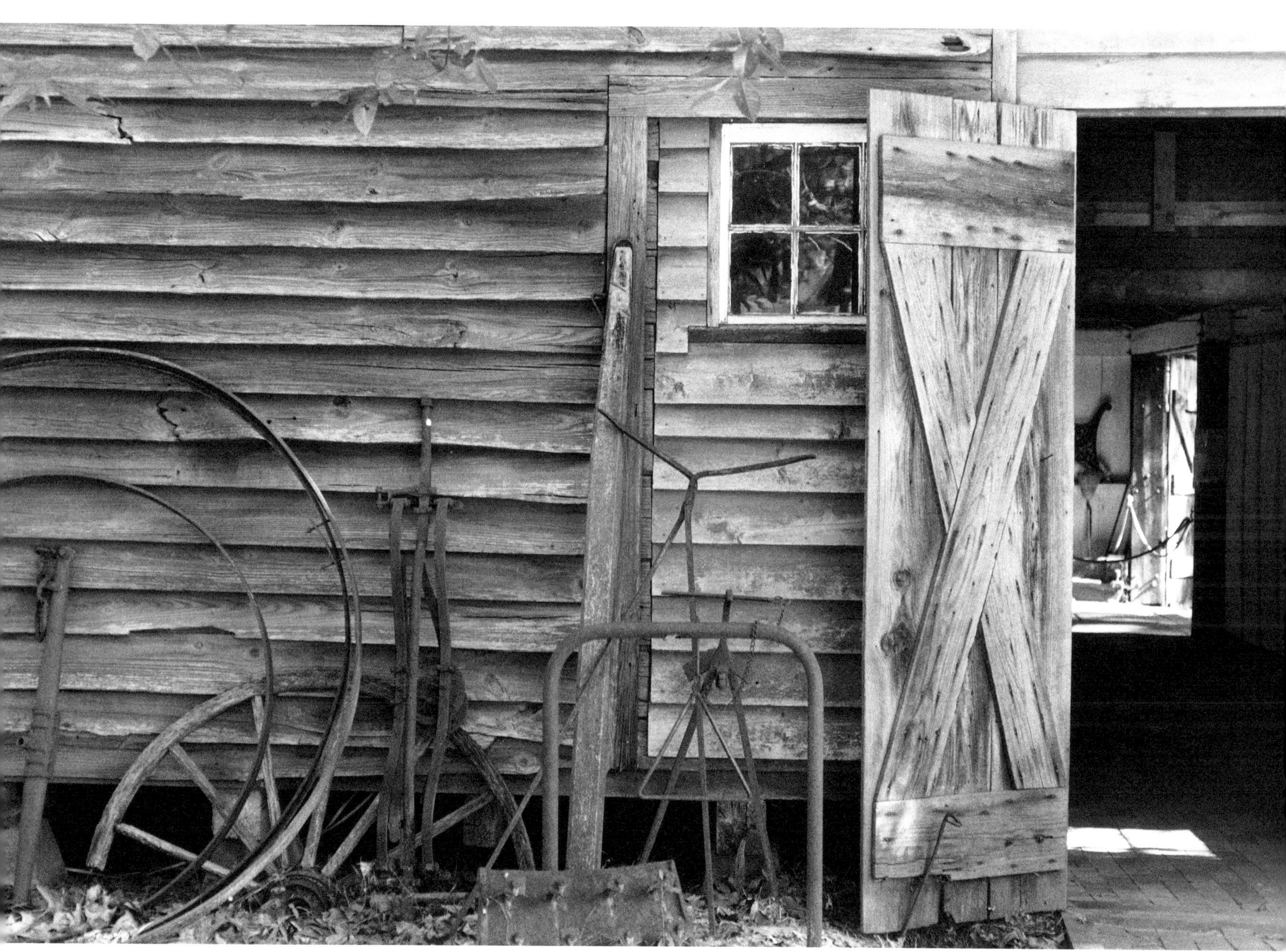

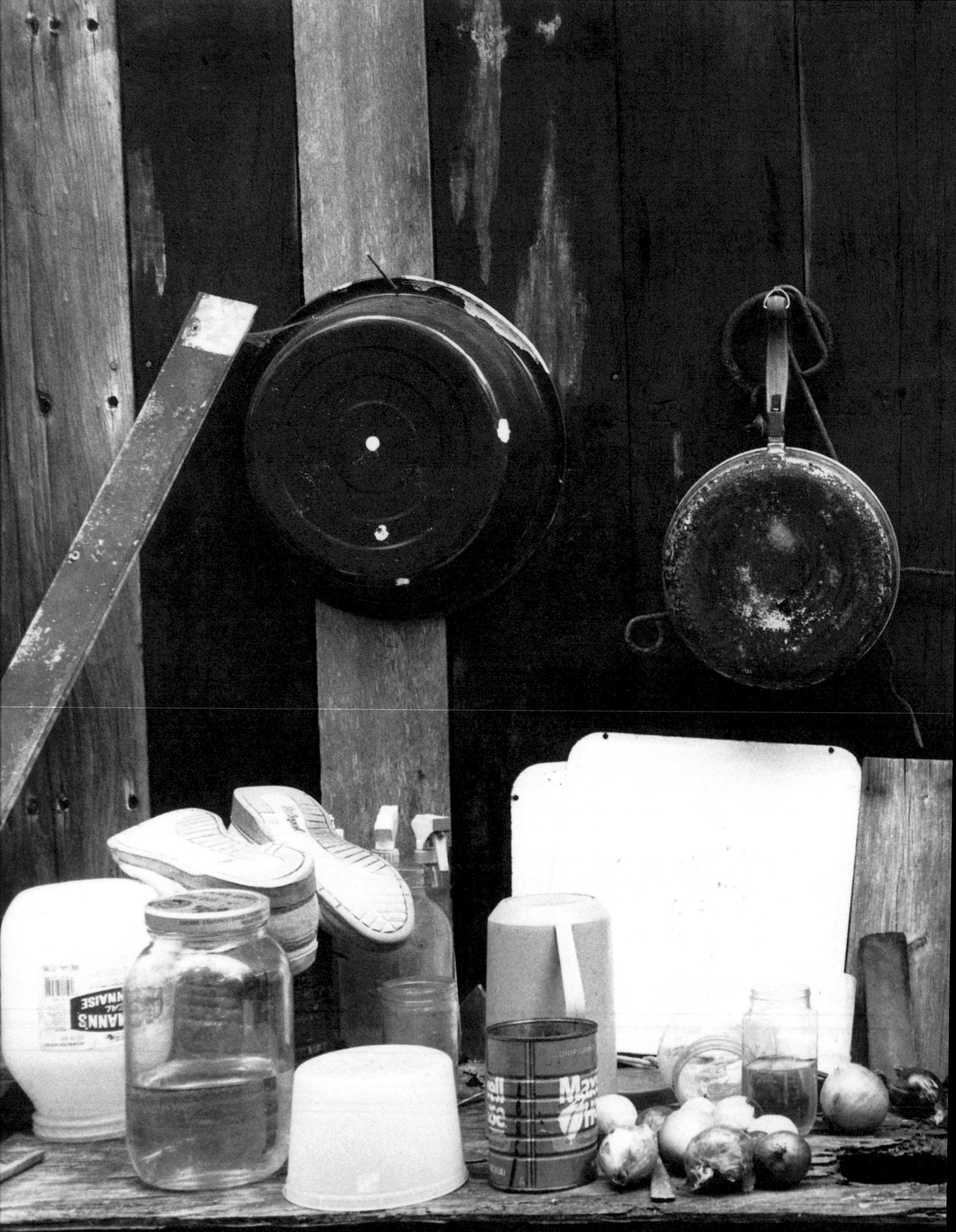

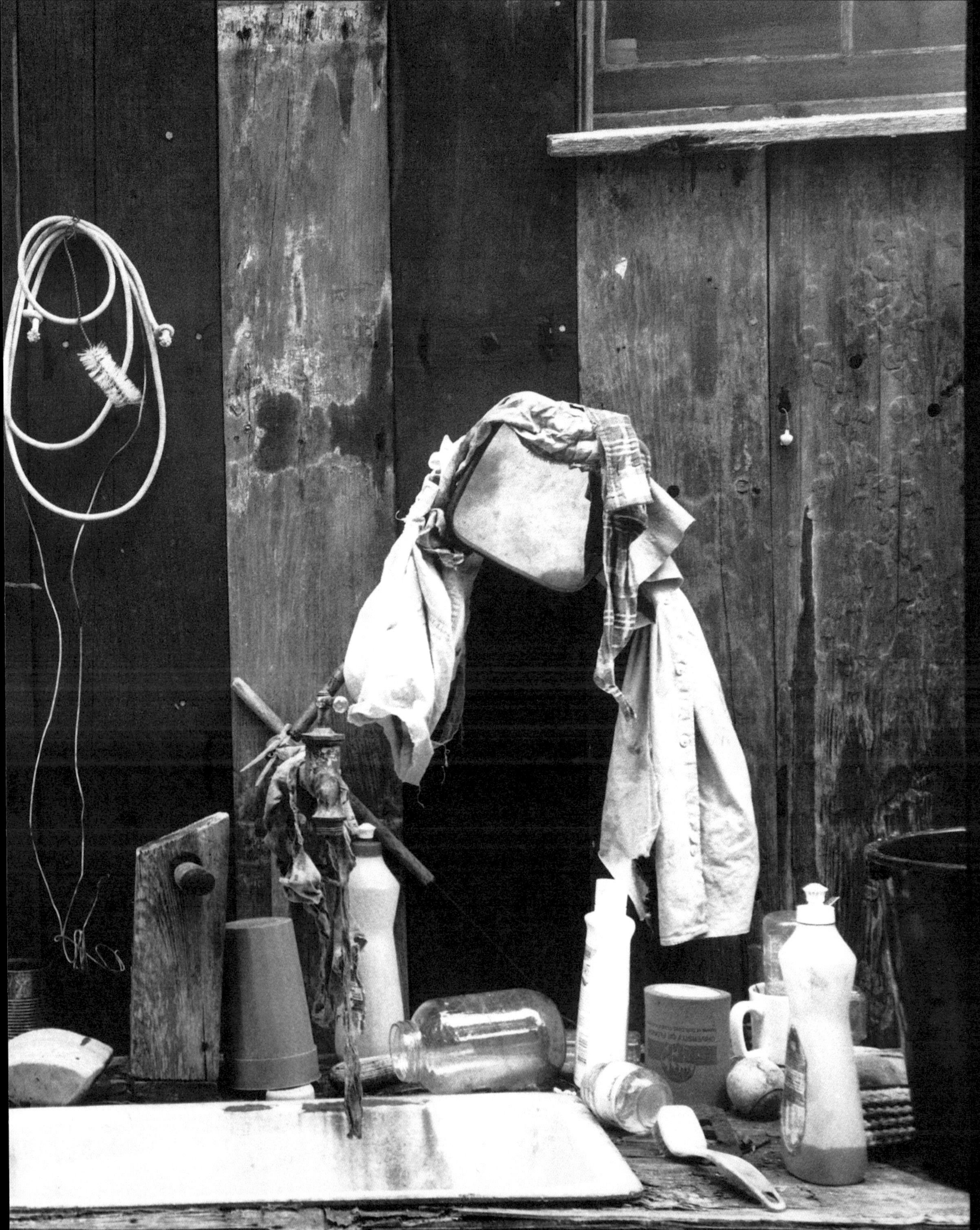

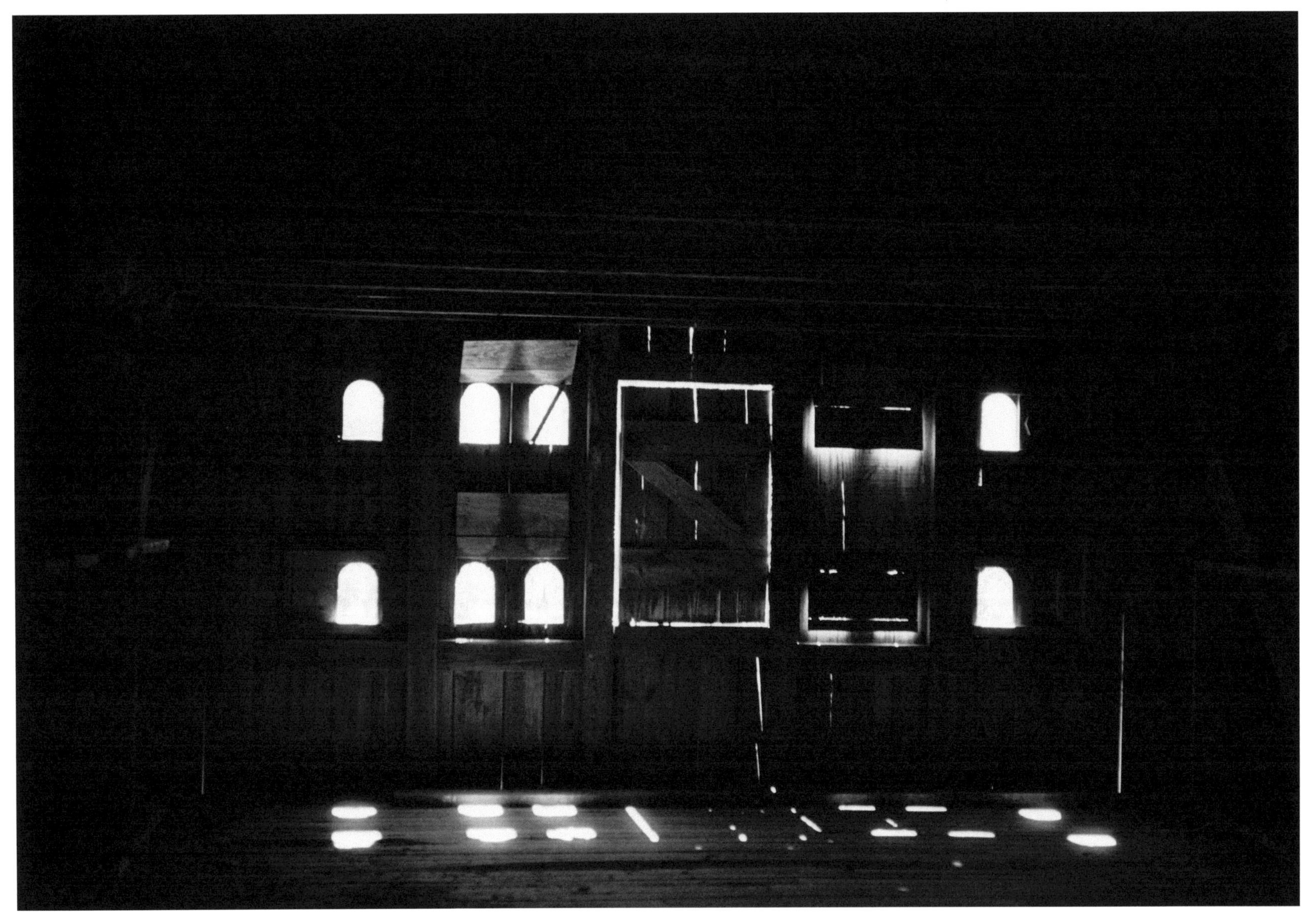

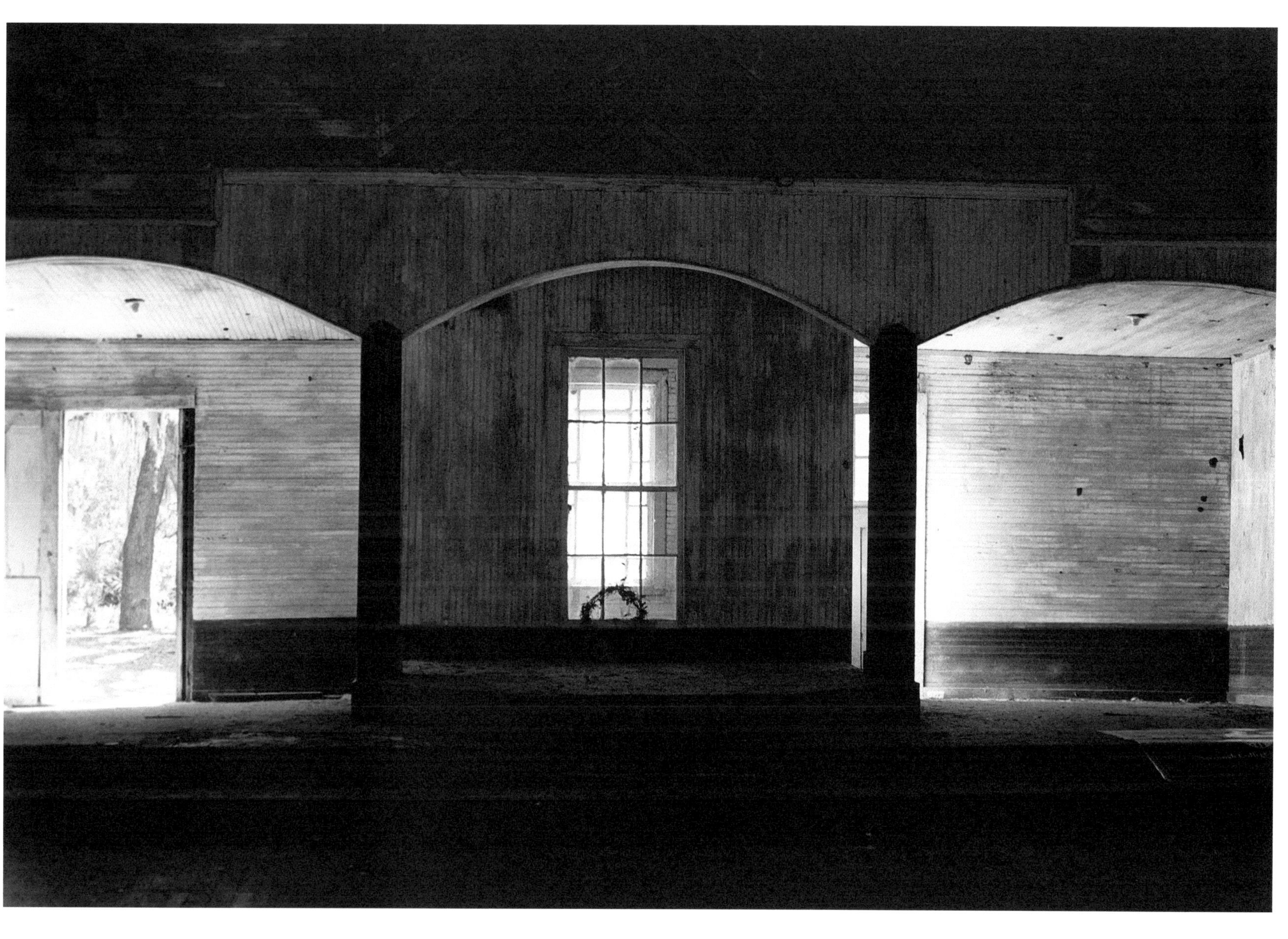

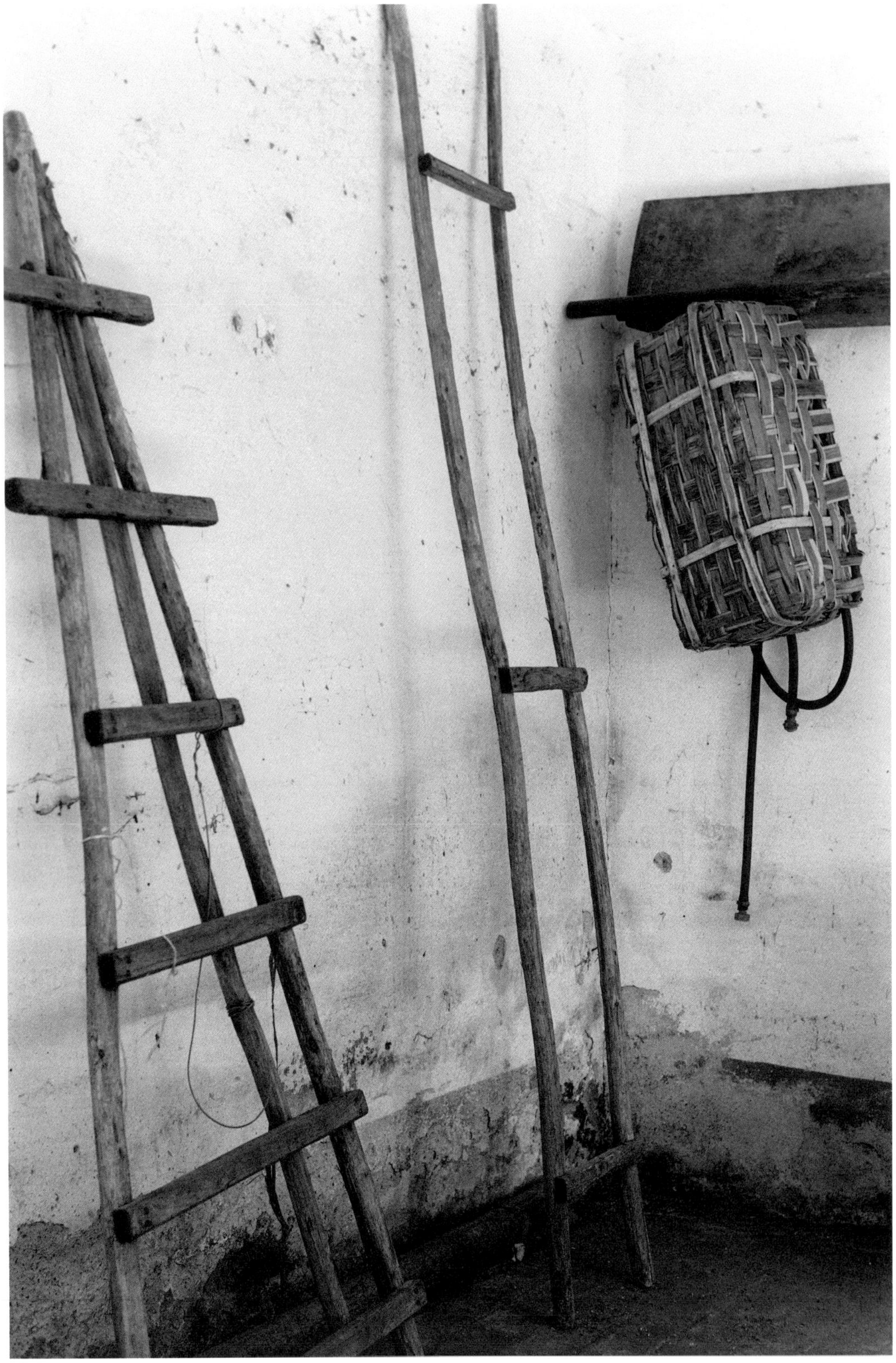

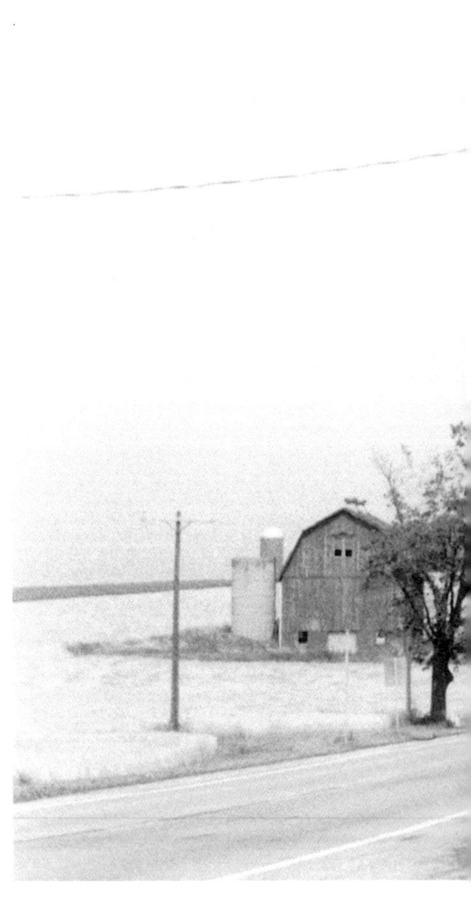

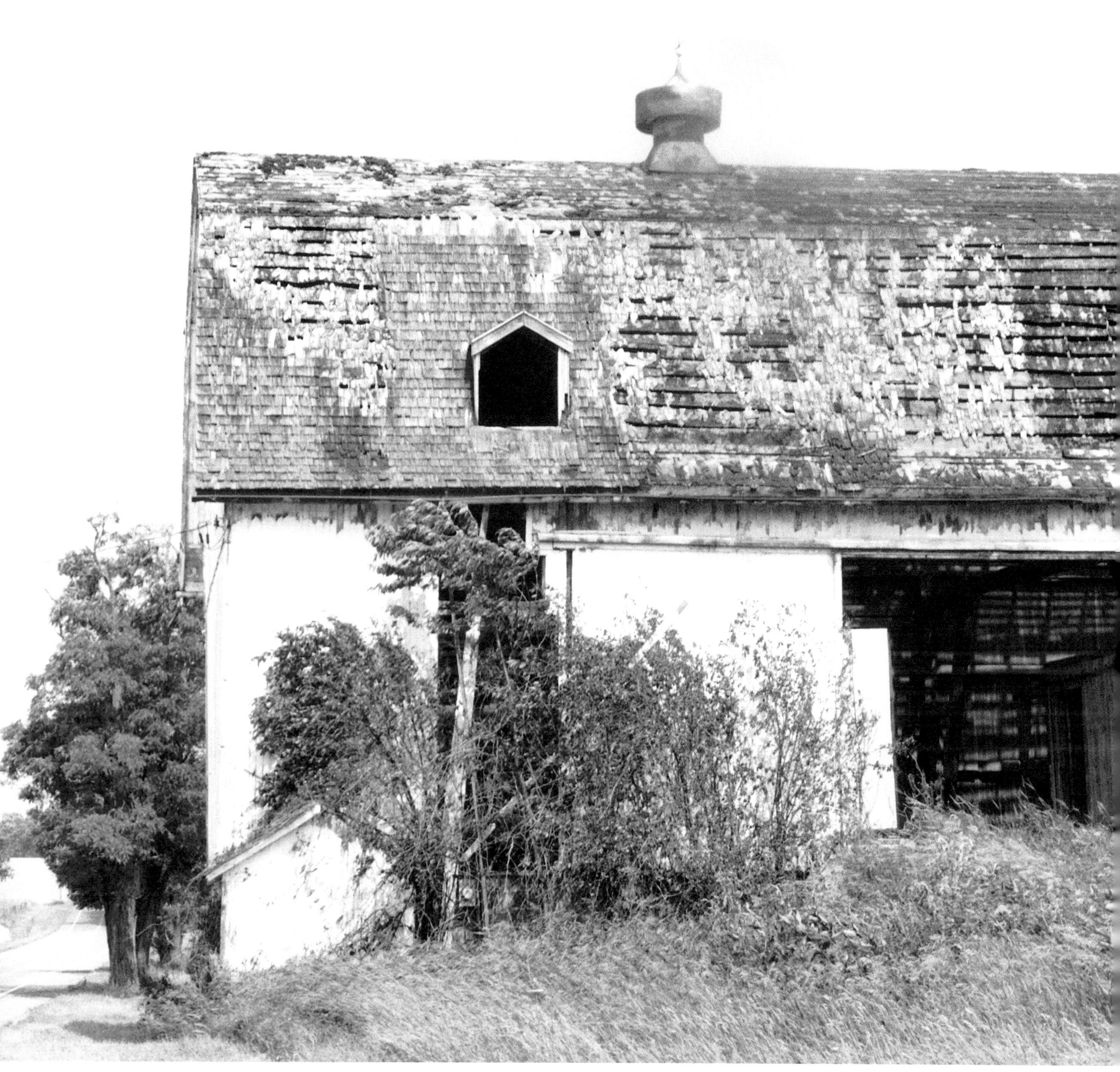

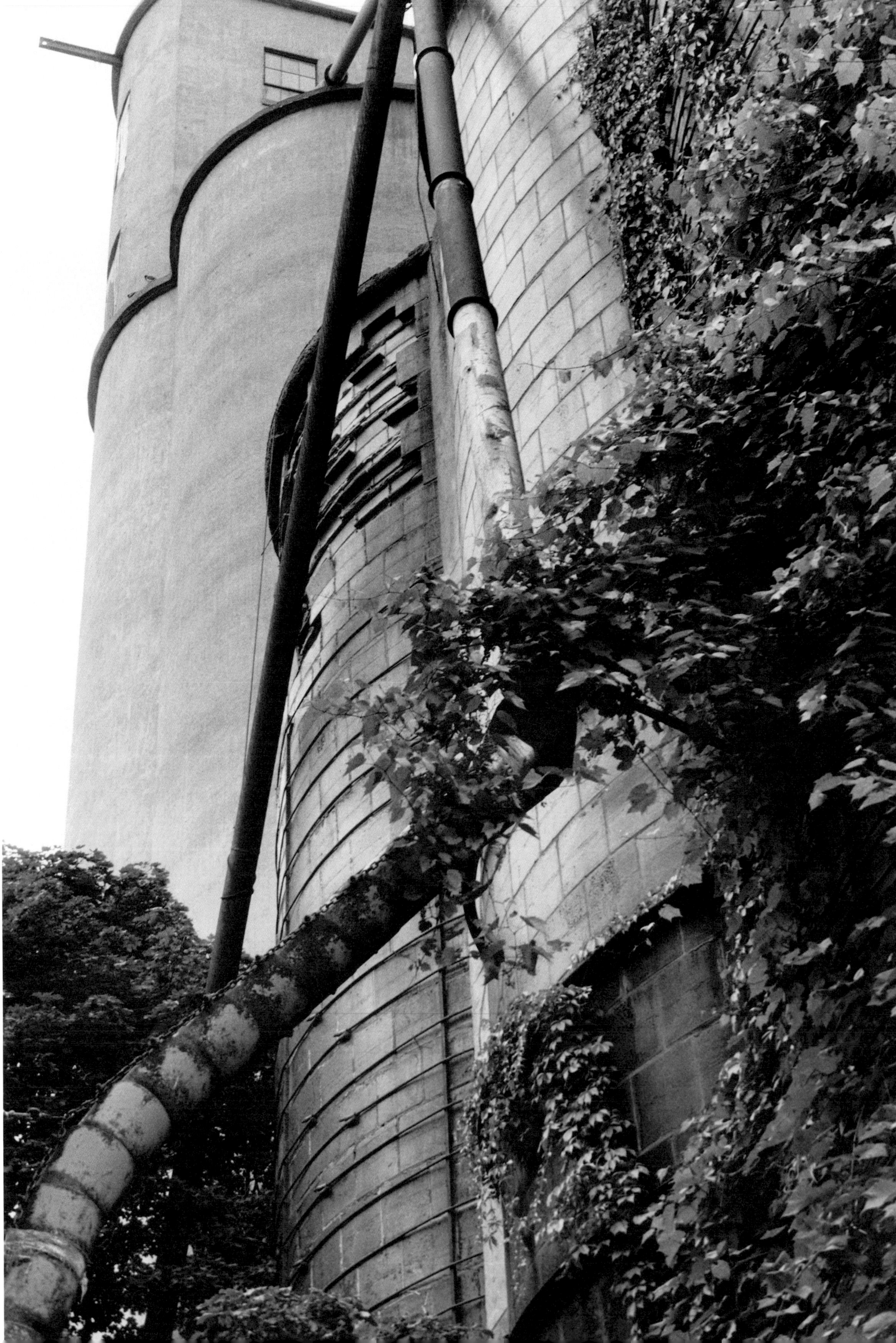

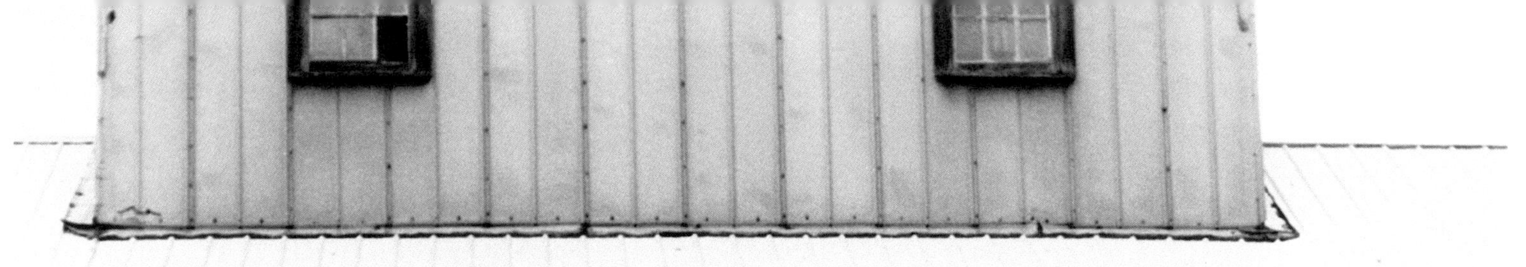

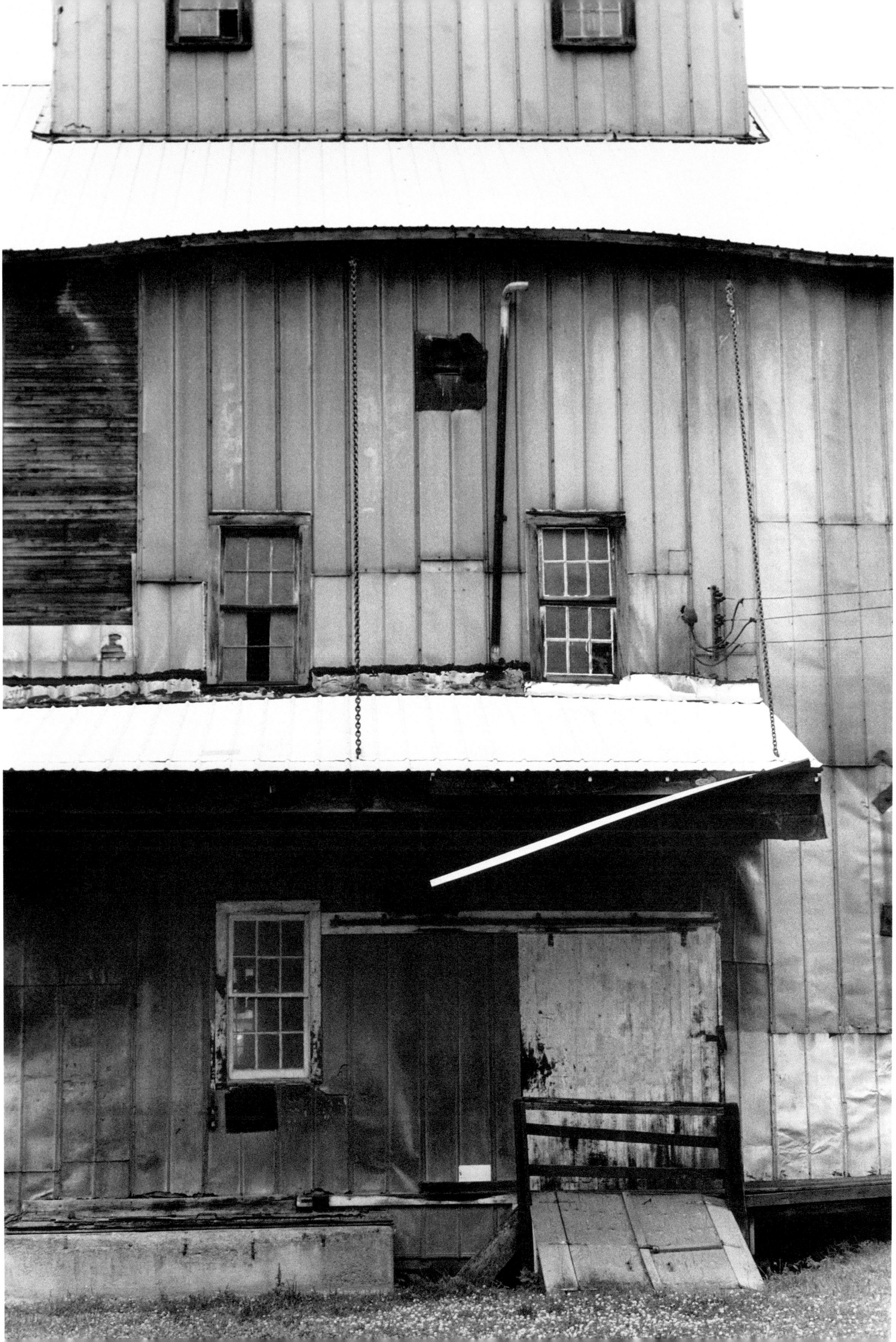

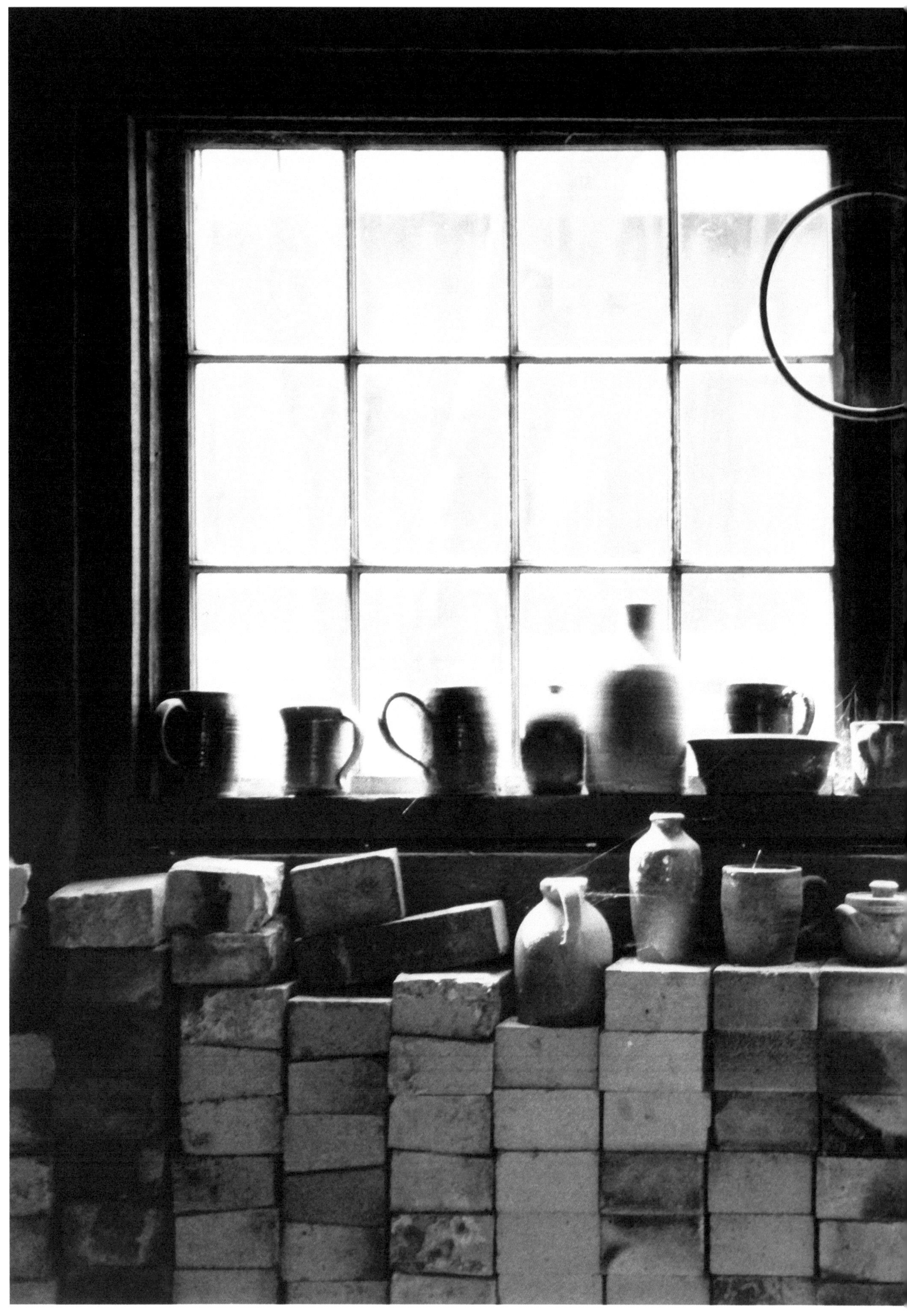

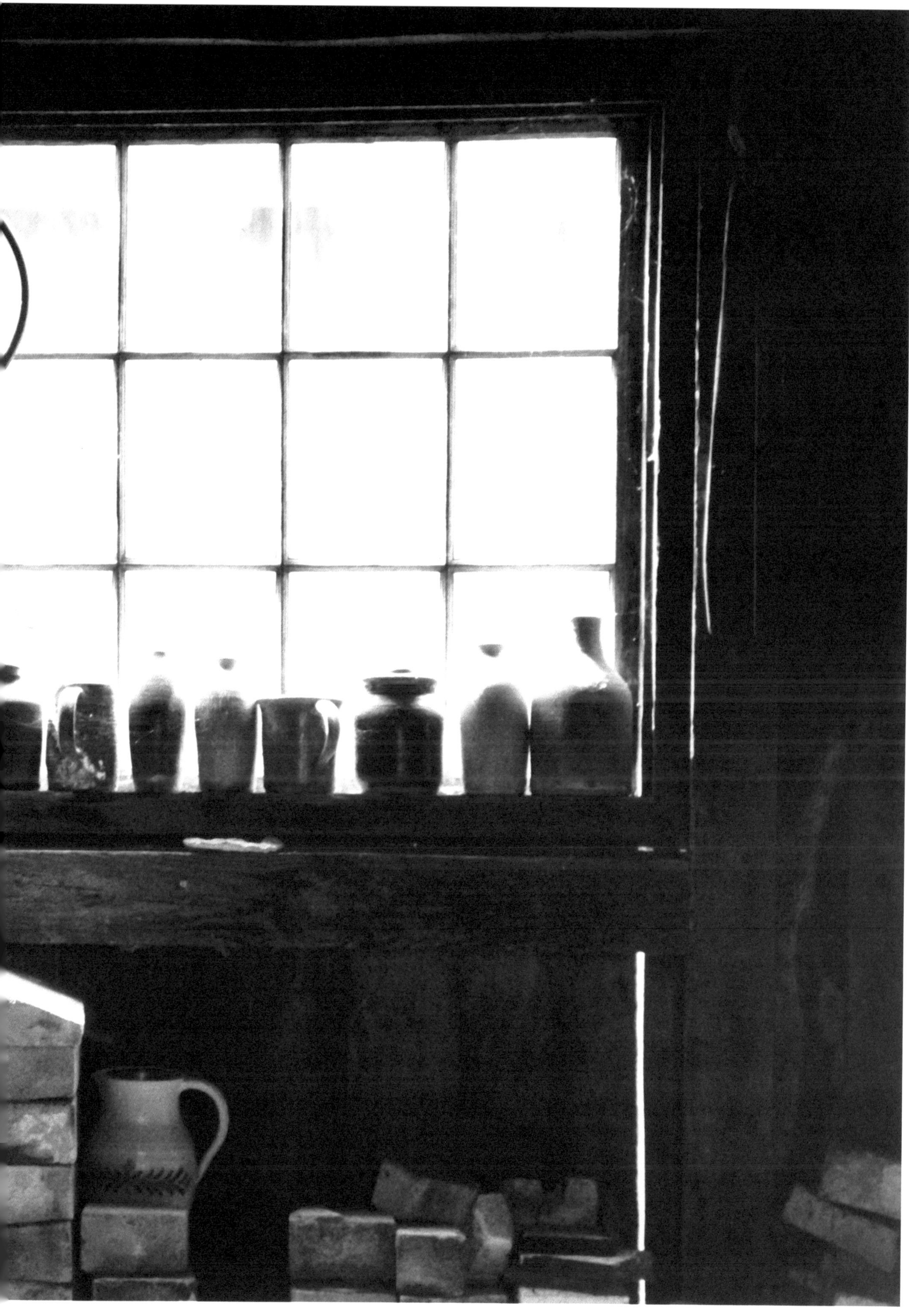

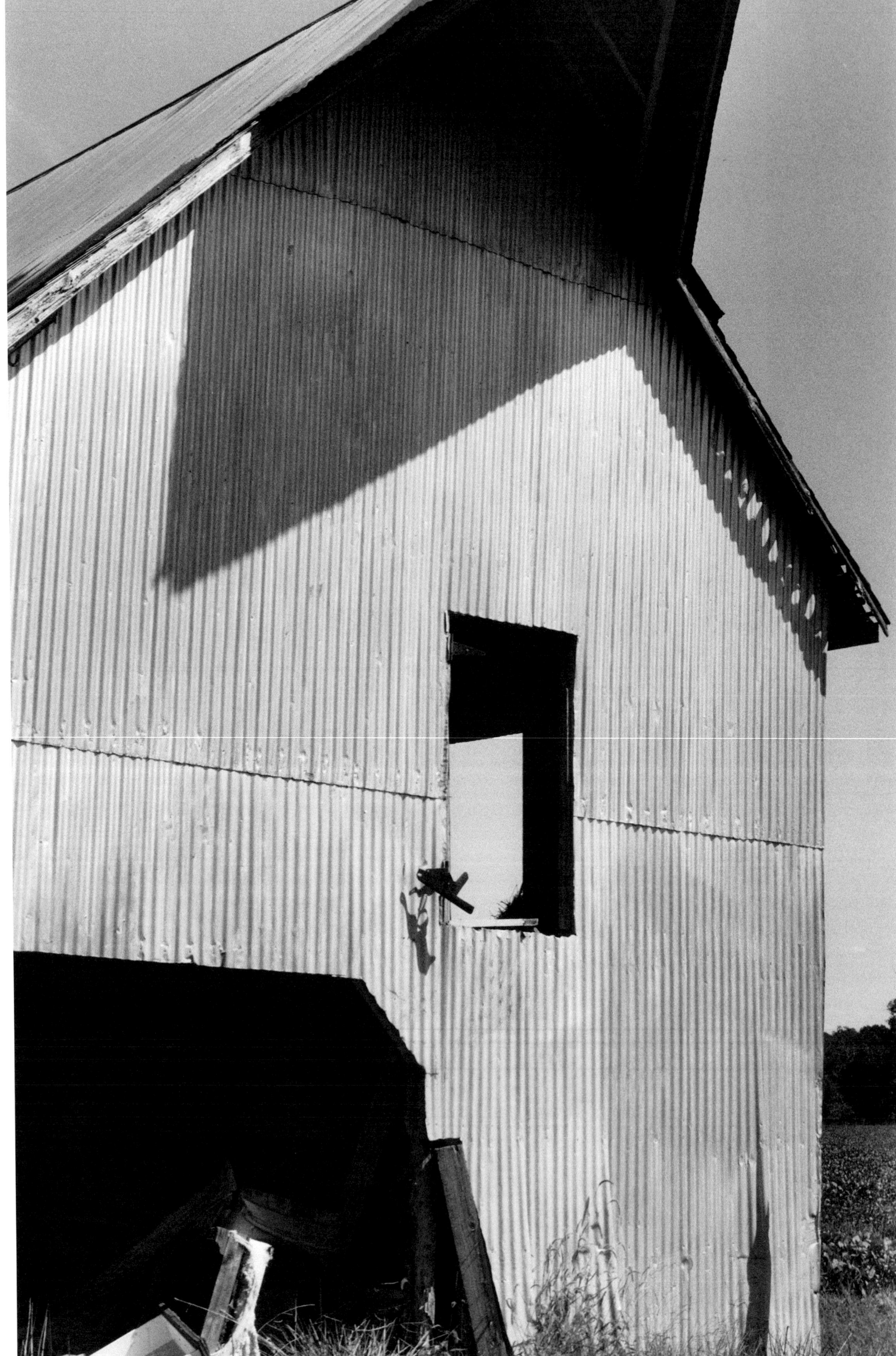

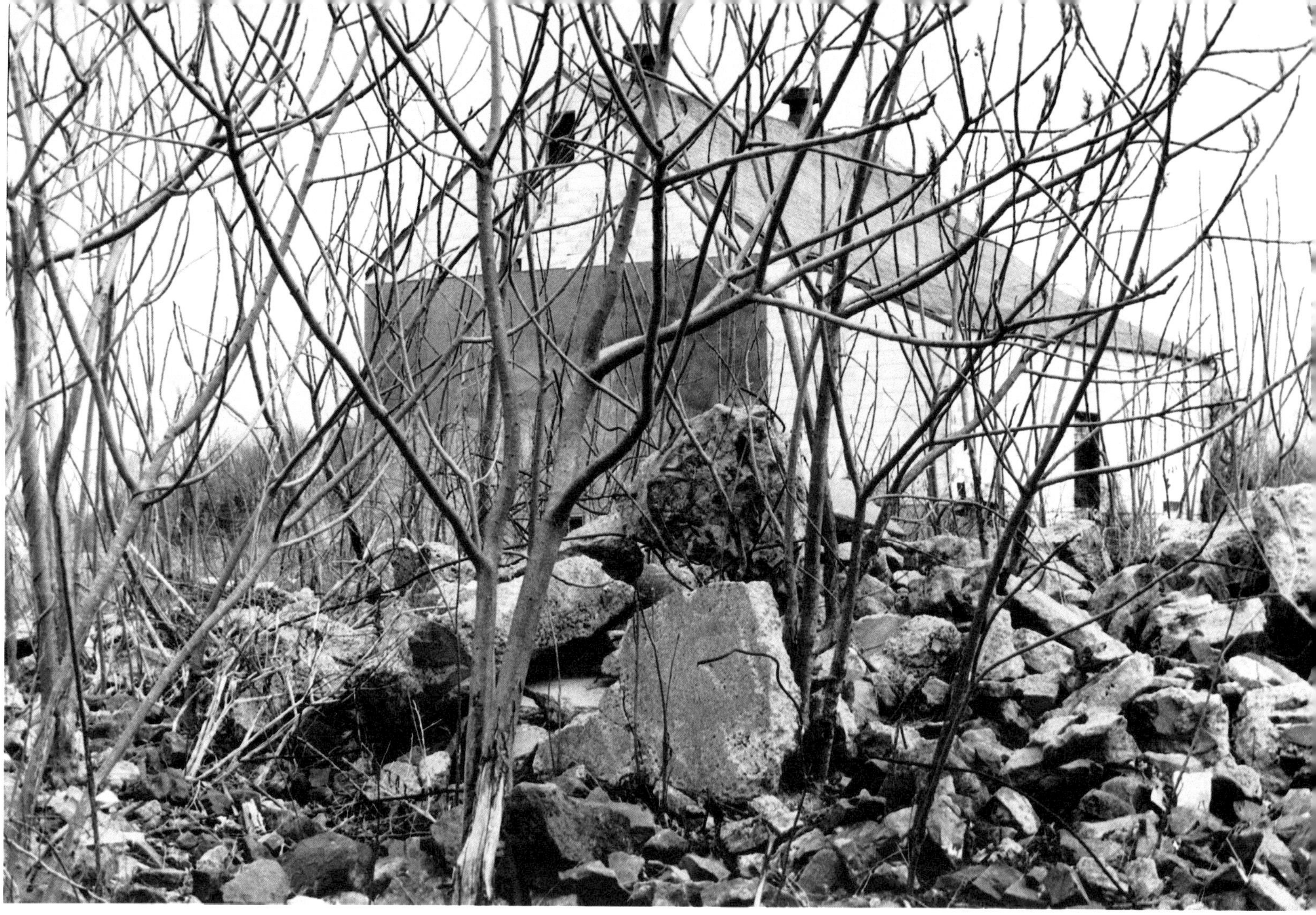

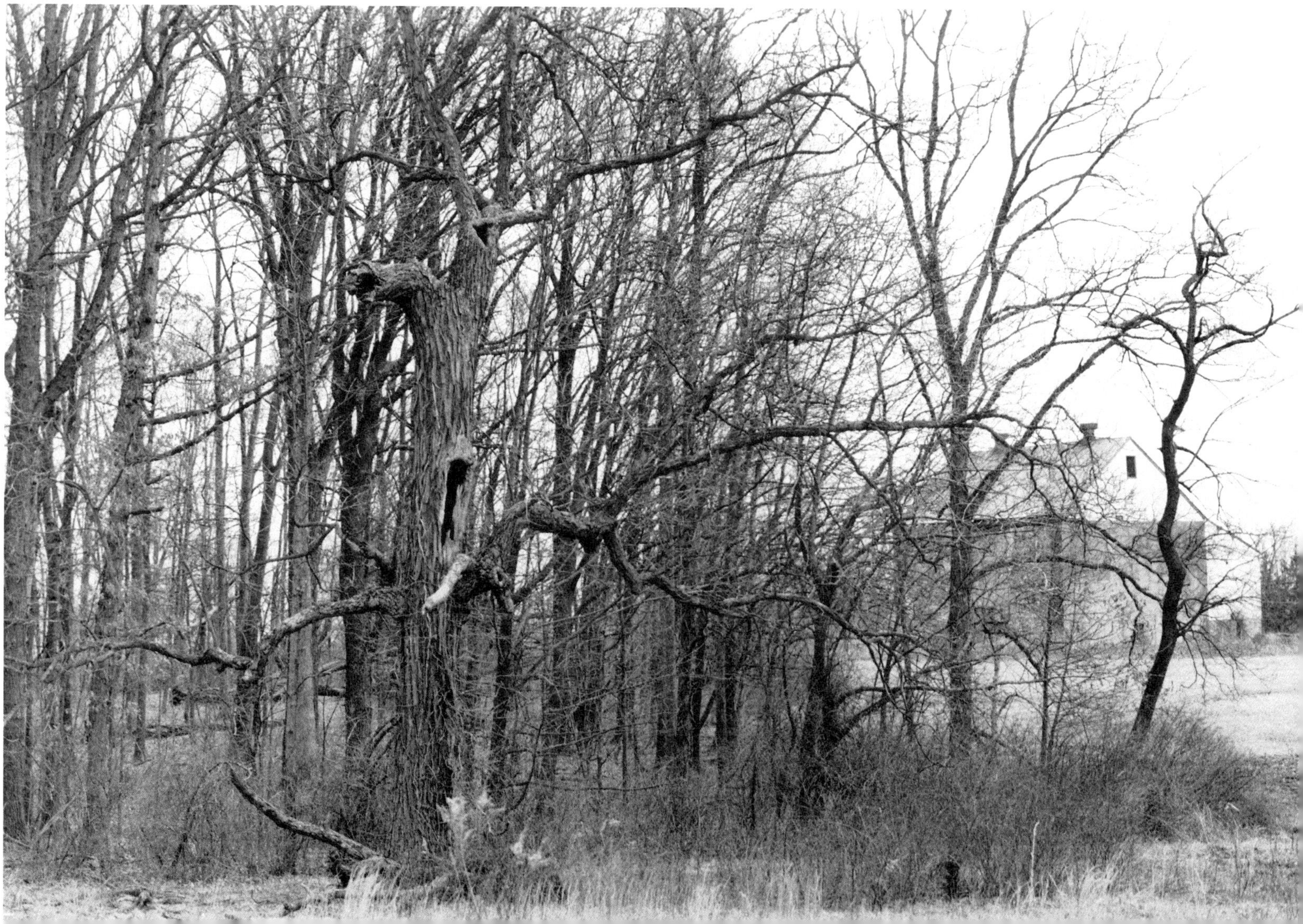

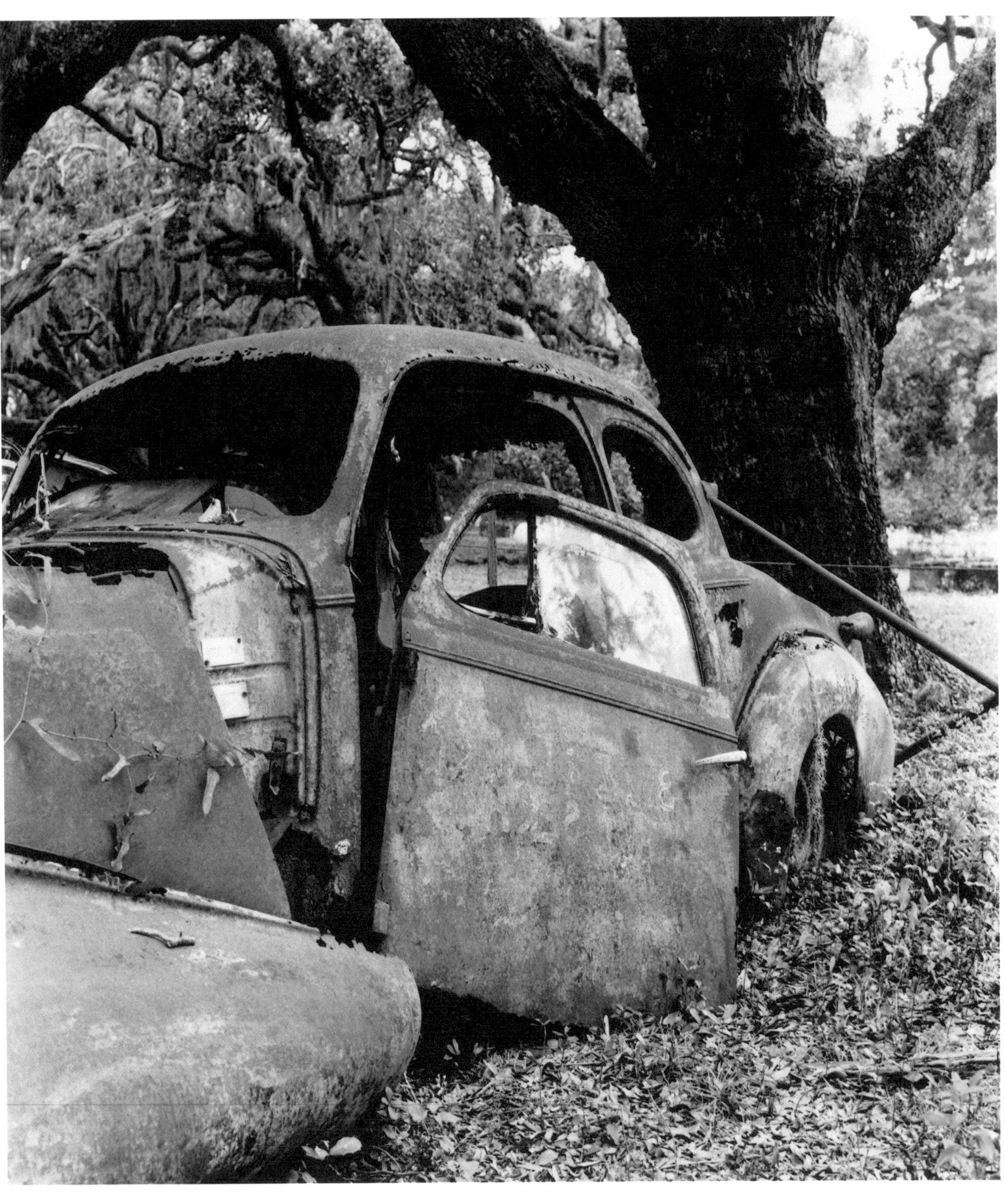

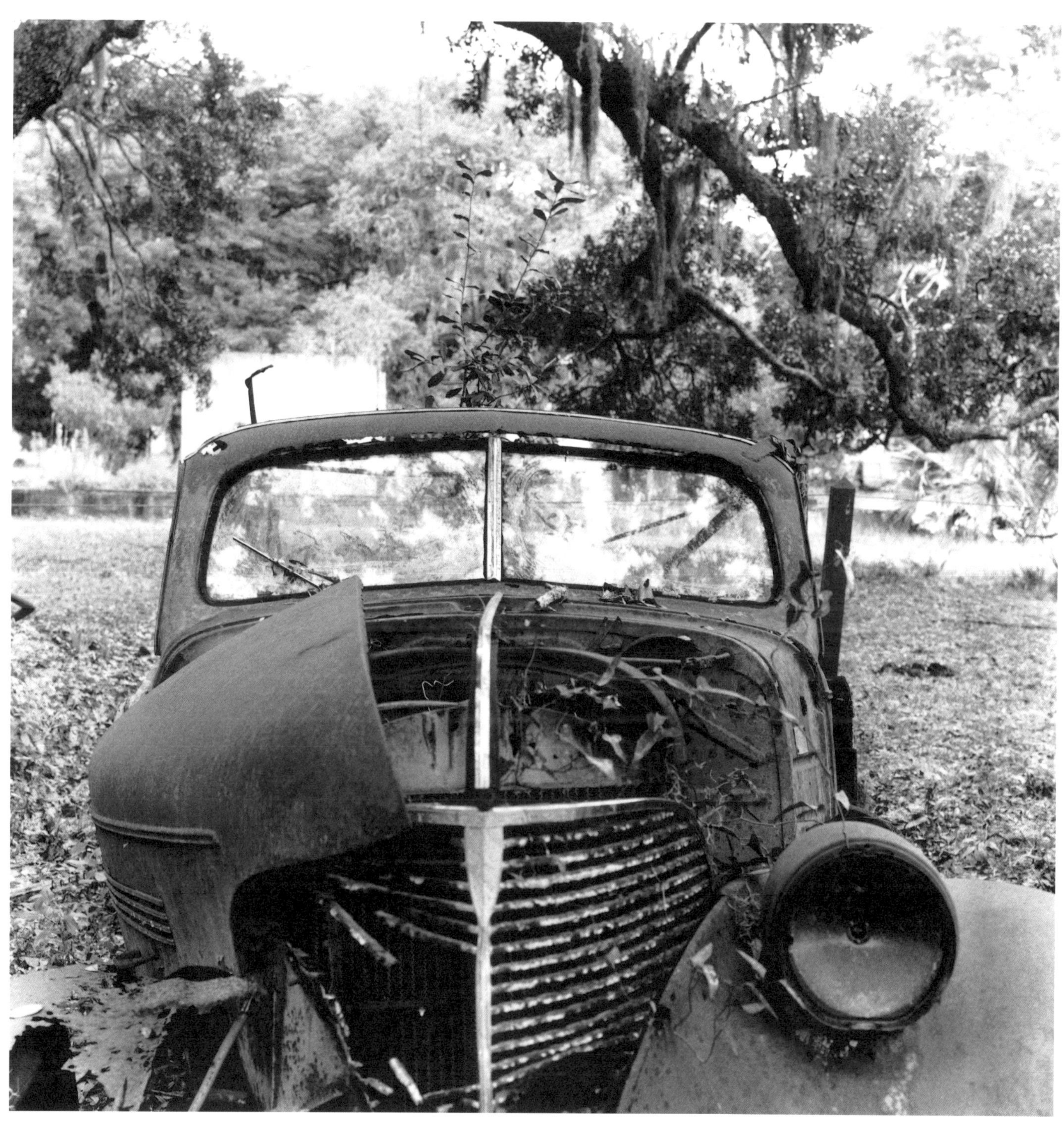

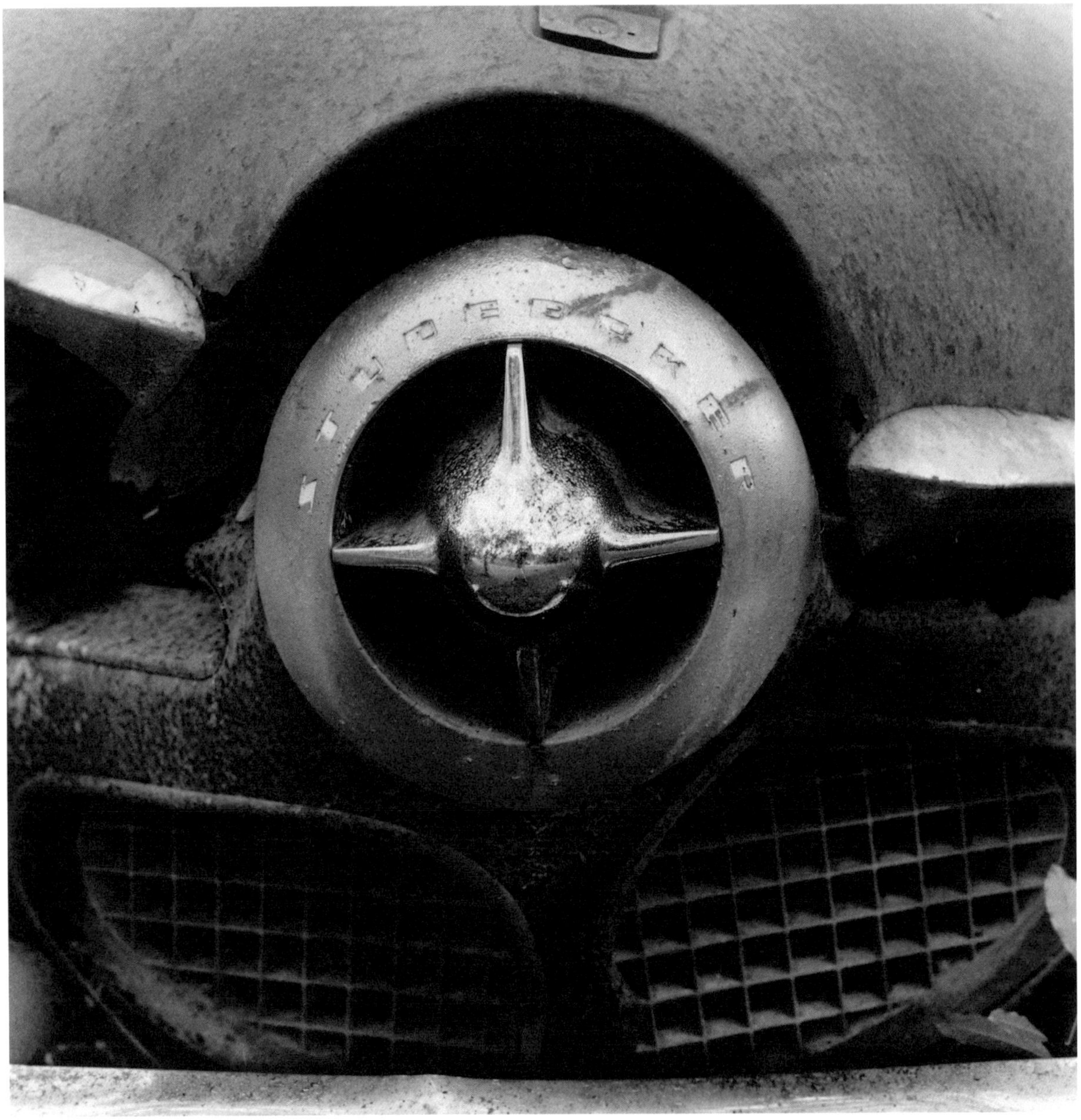

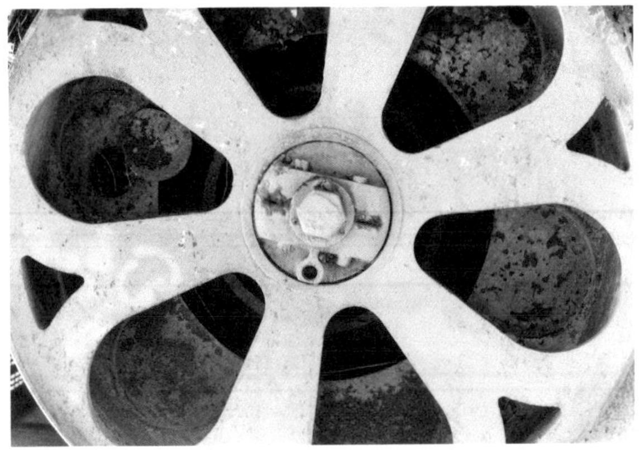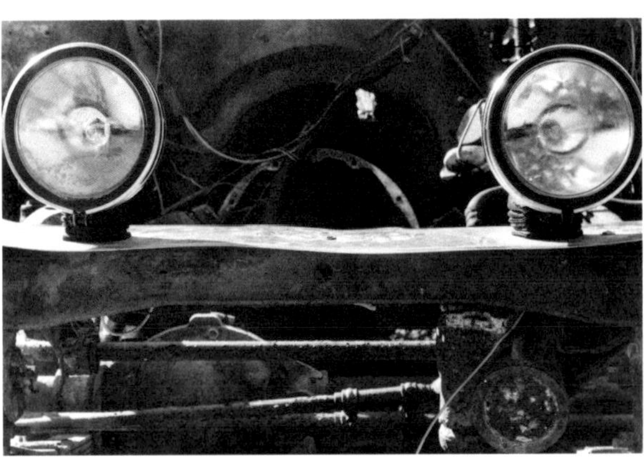

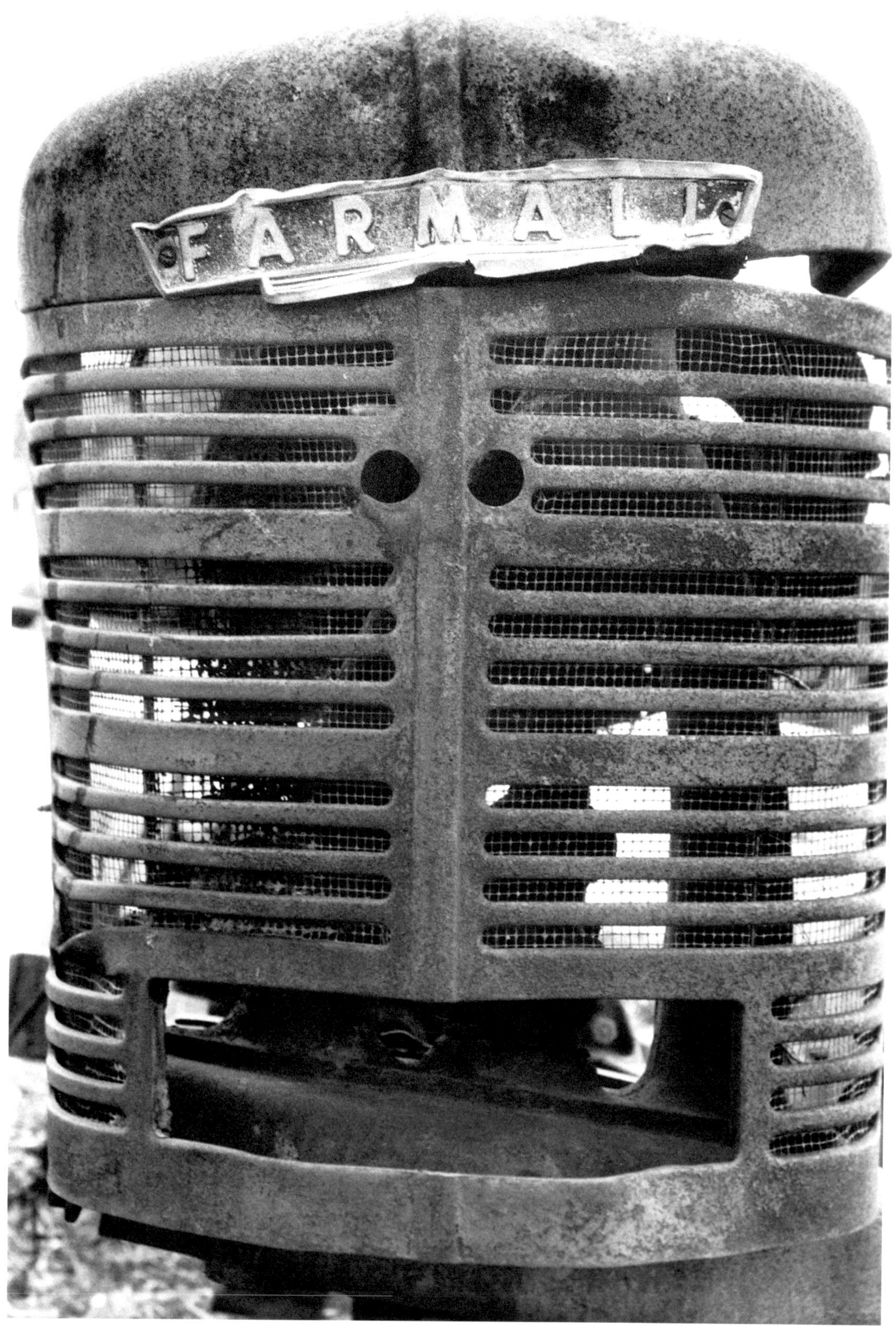
FARMALL

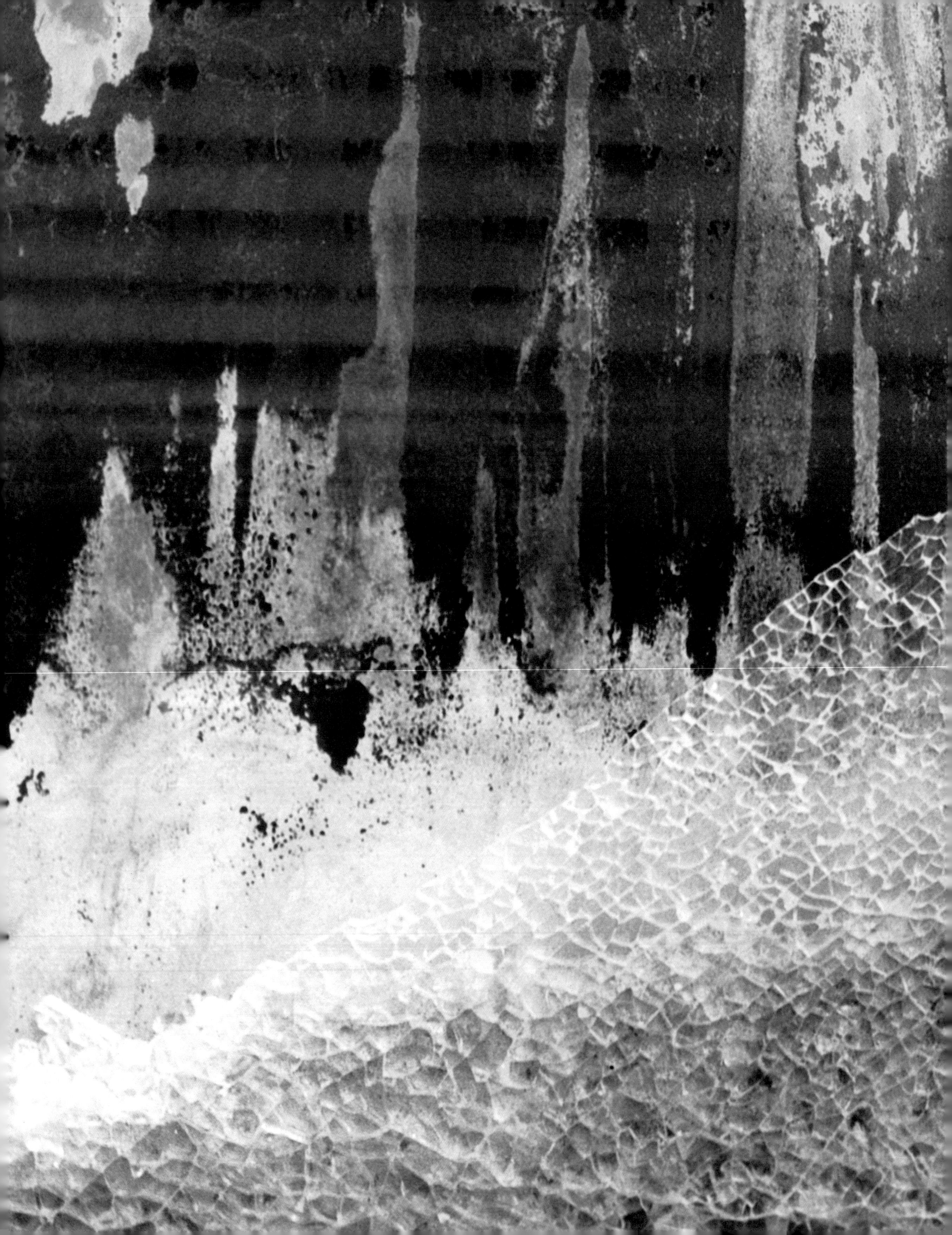

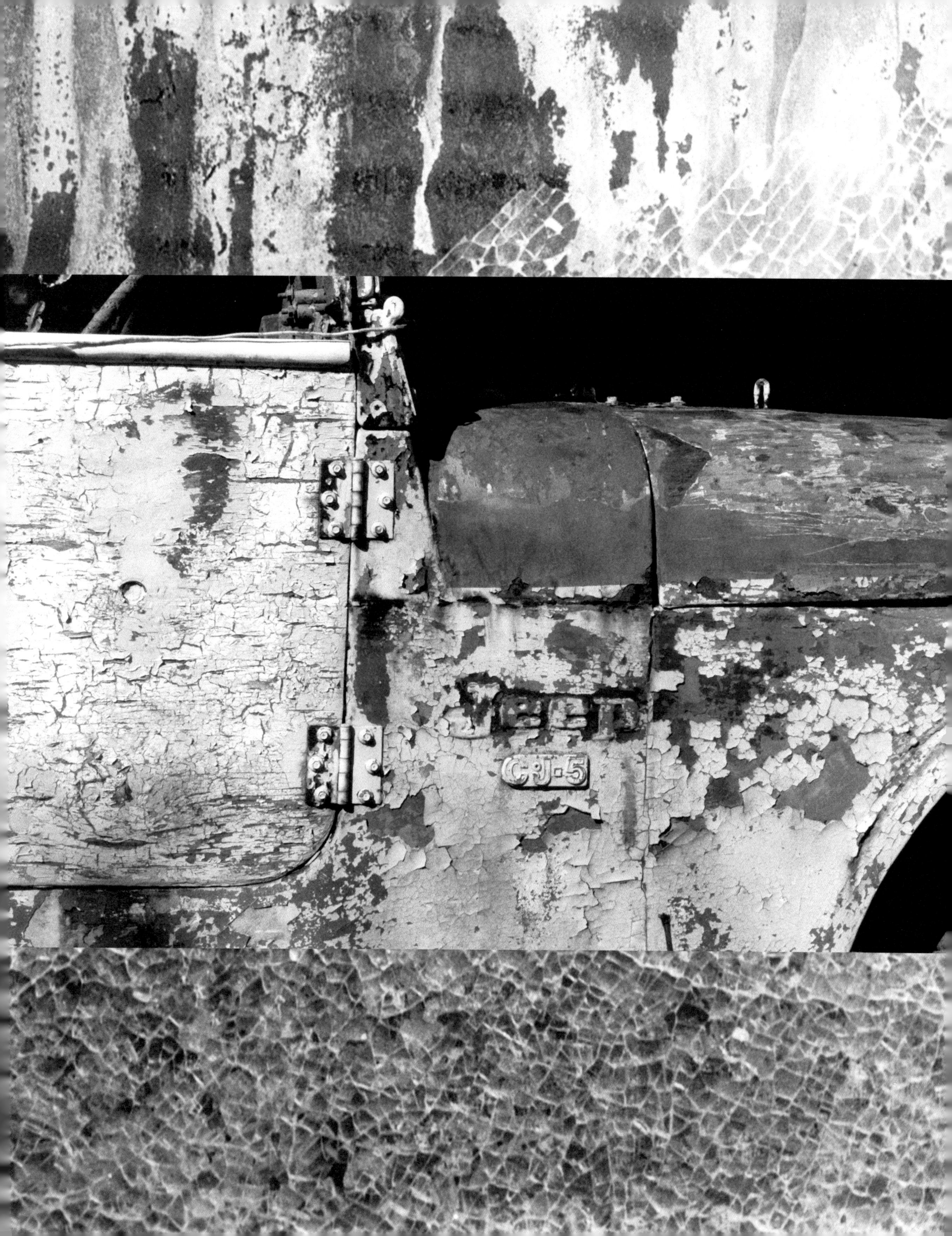
JEEP
CJ-5

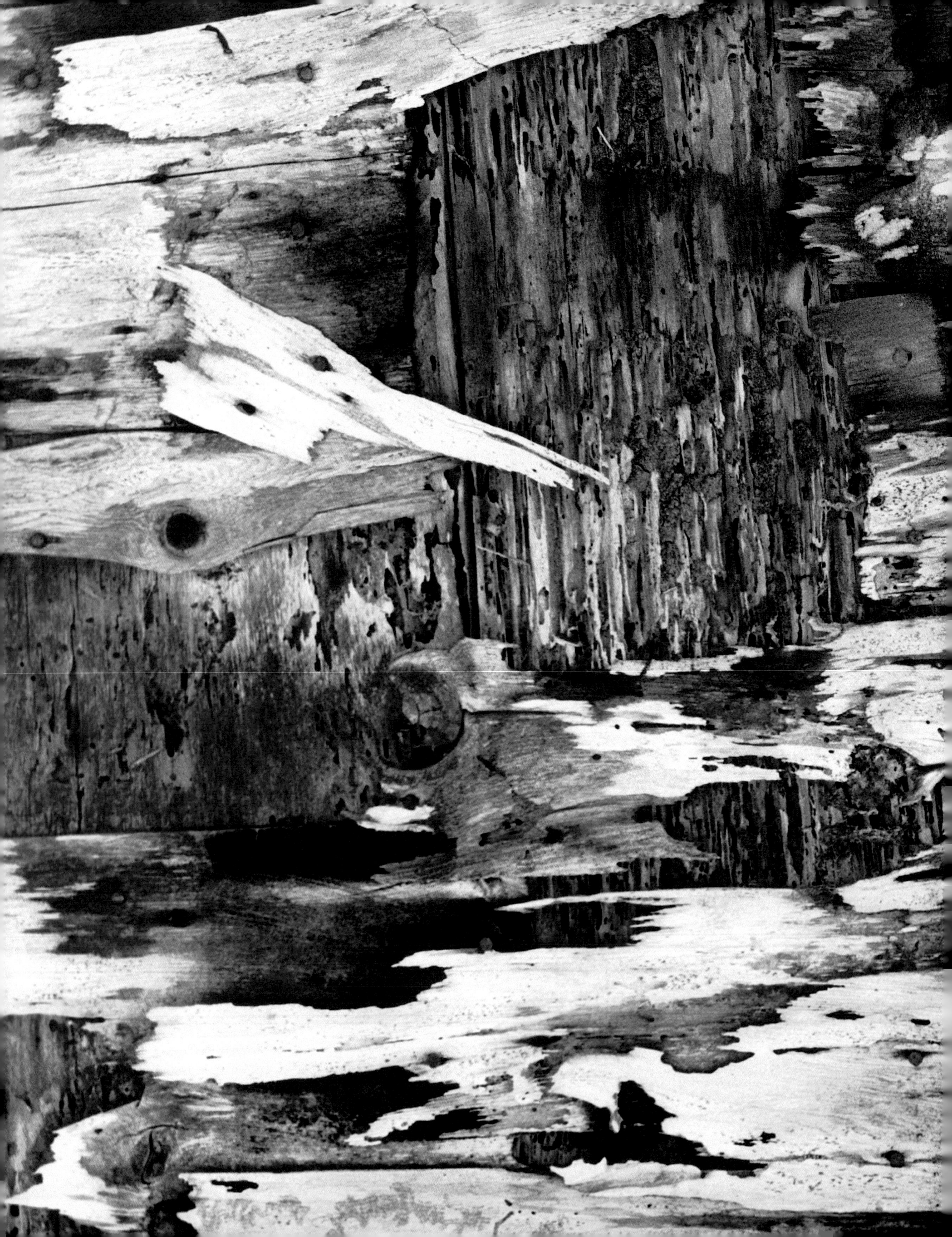

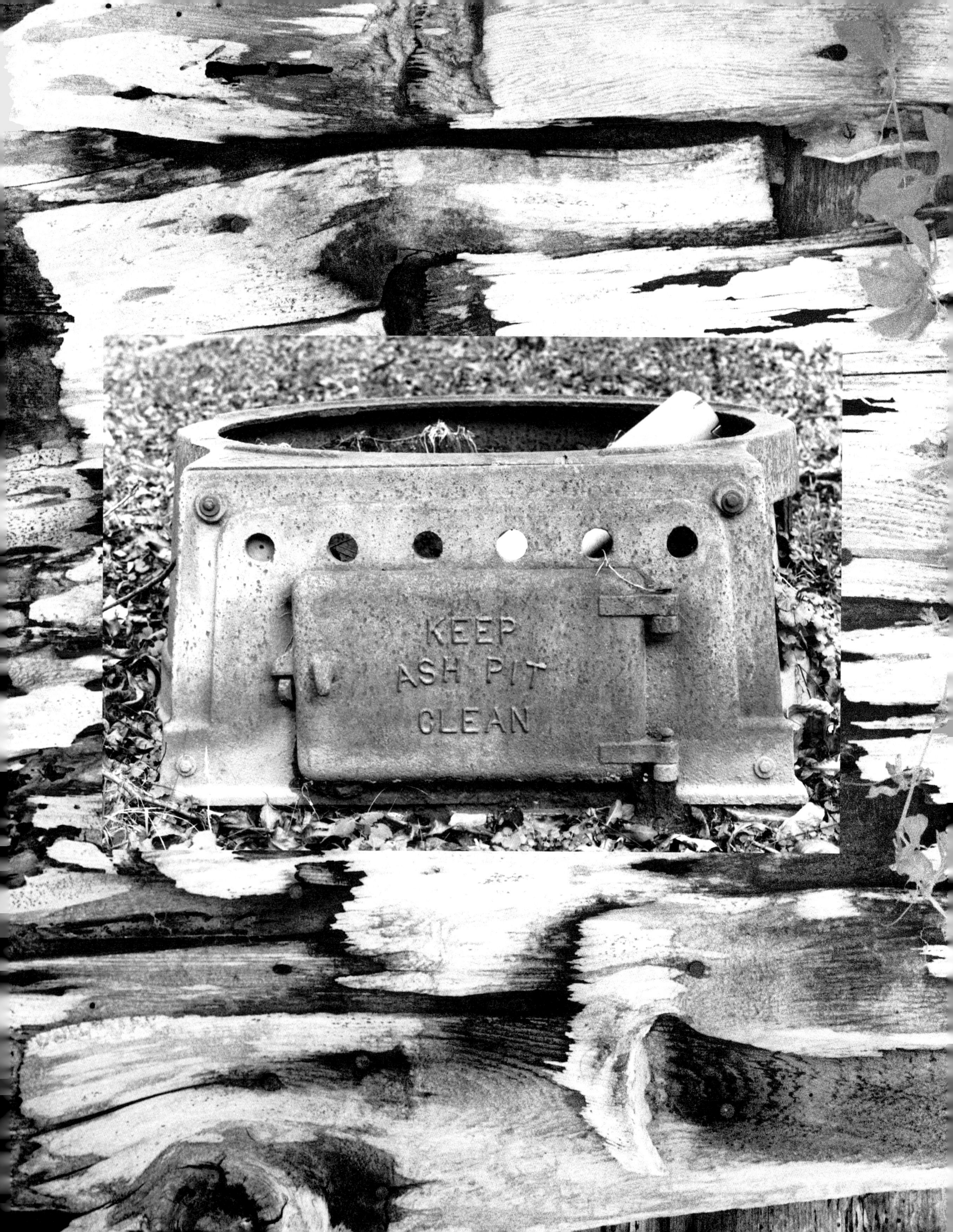
KEEP
ASH PIT
CLEAN

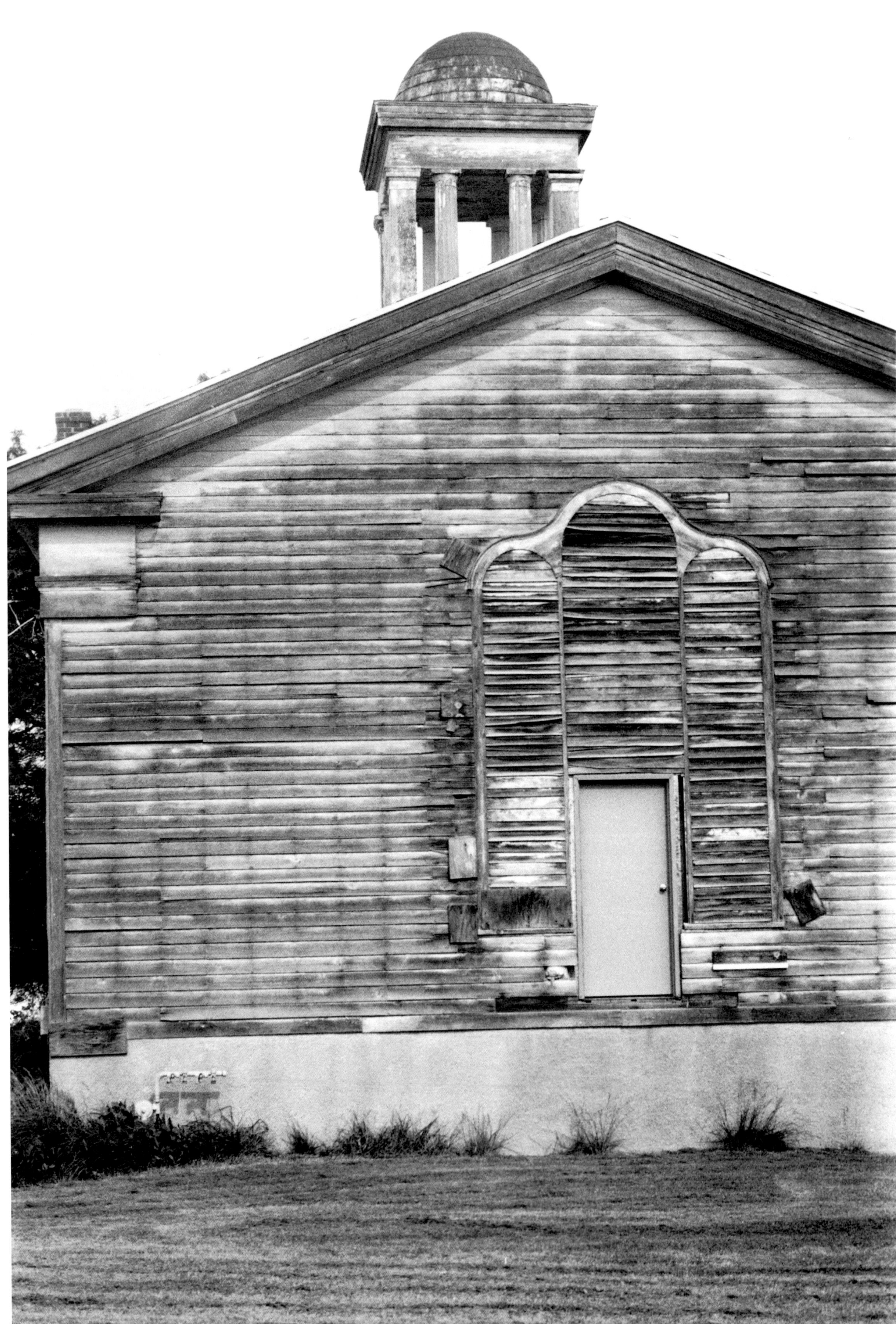

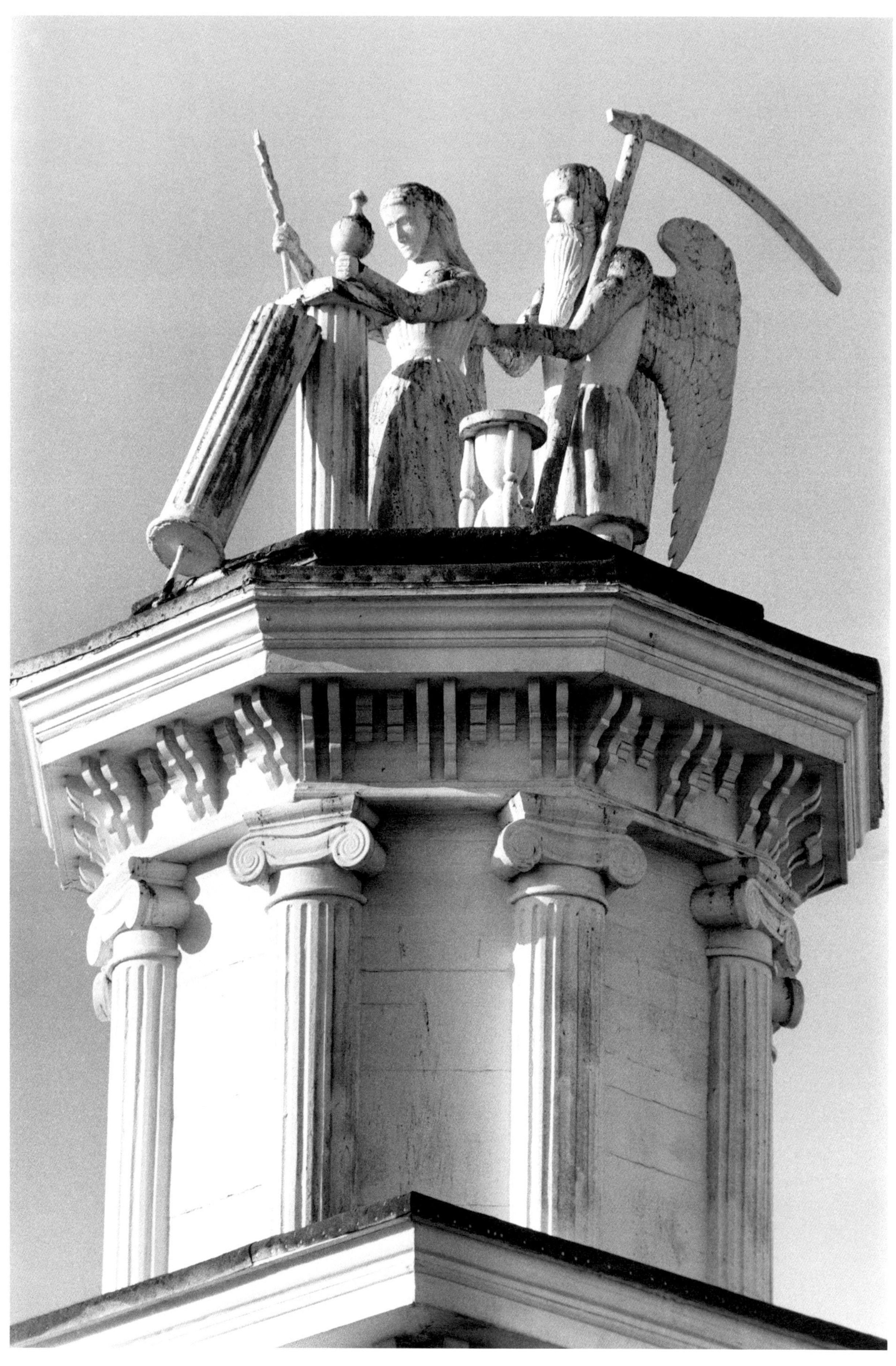

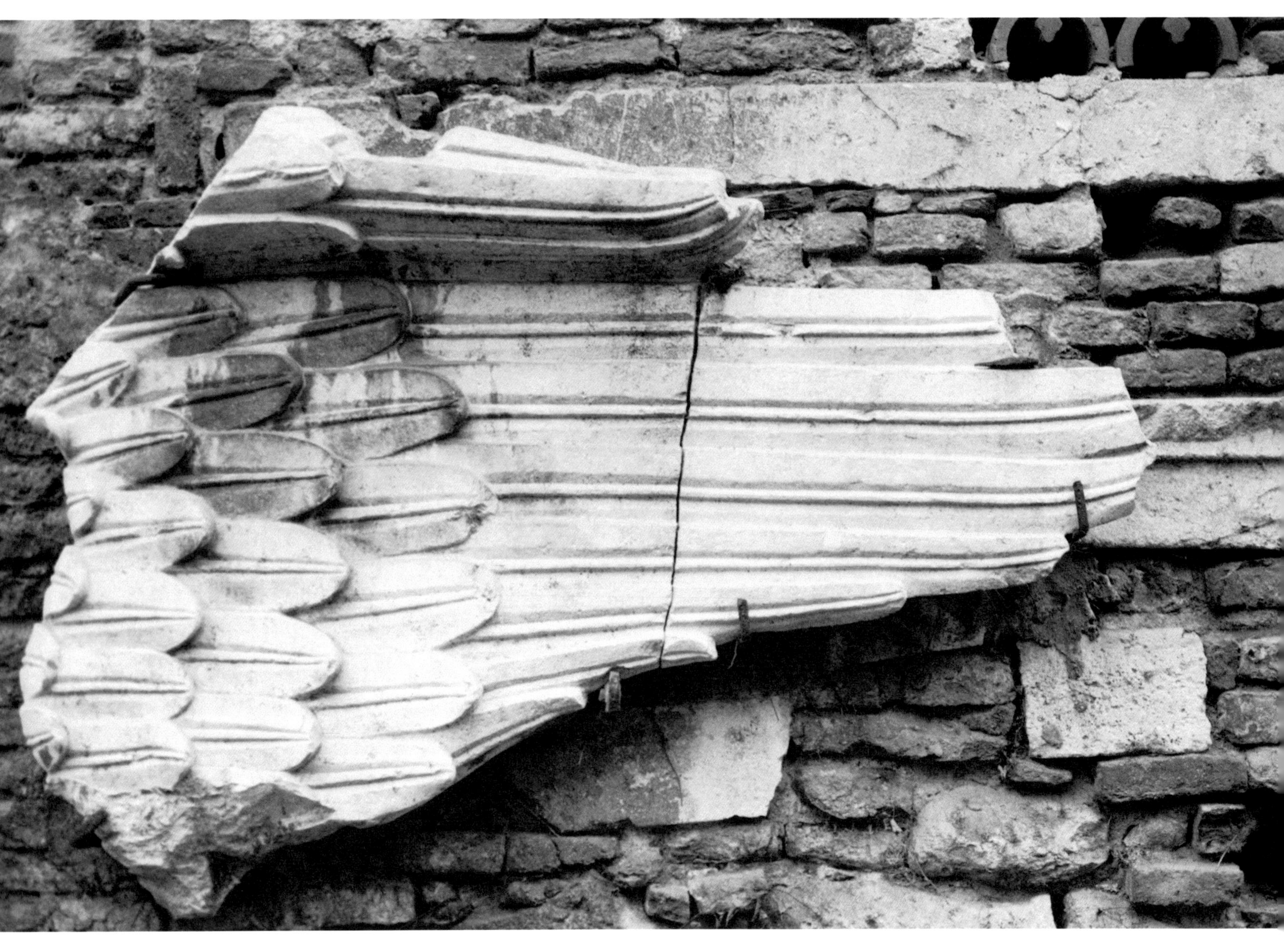

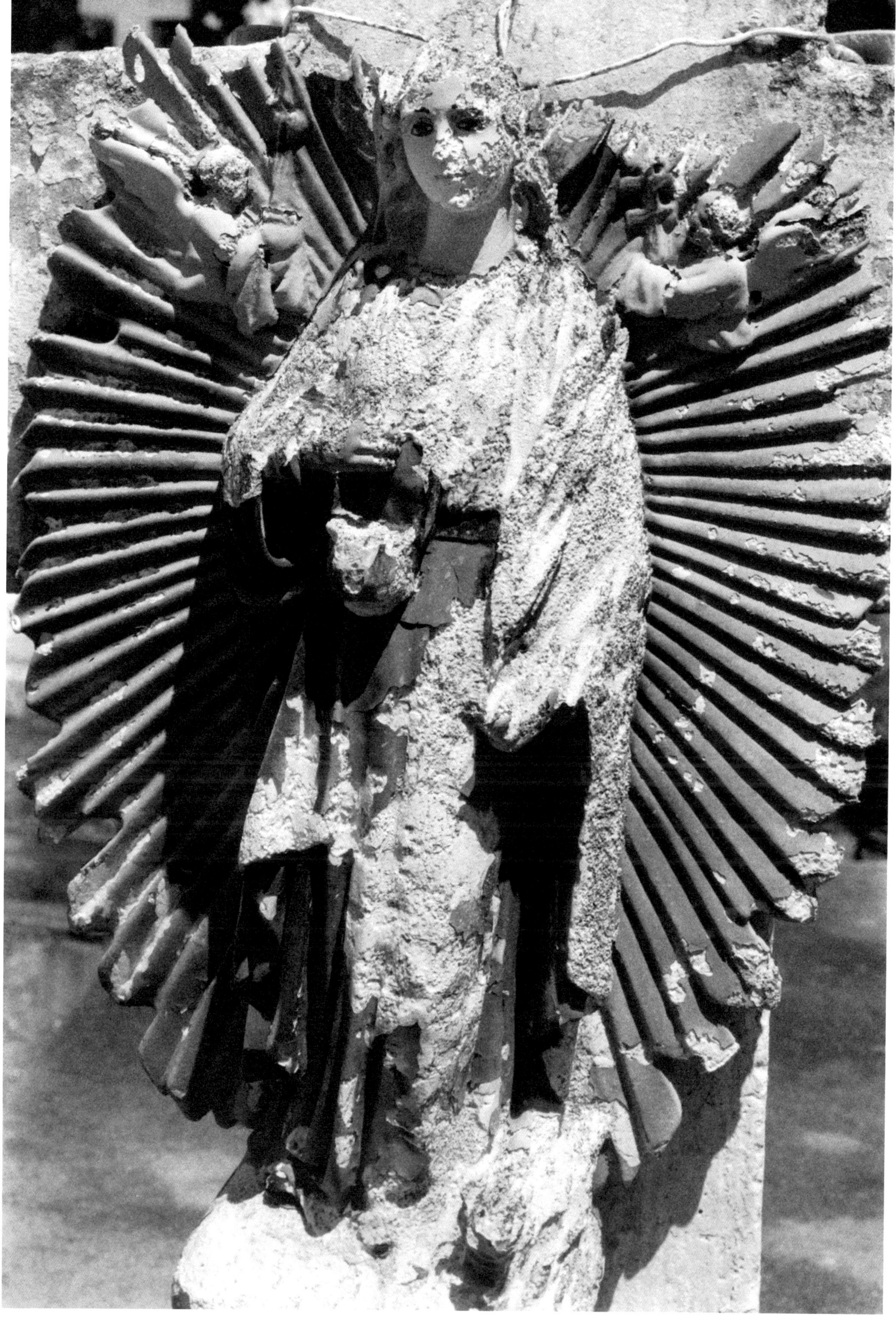

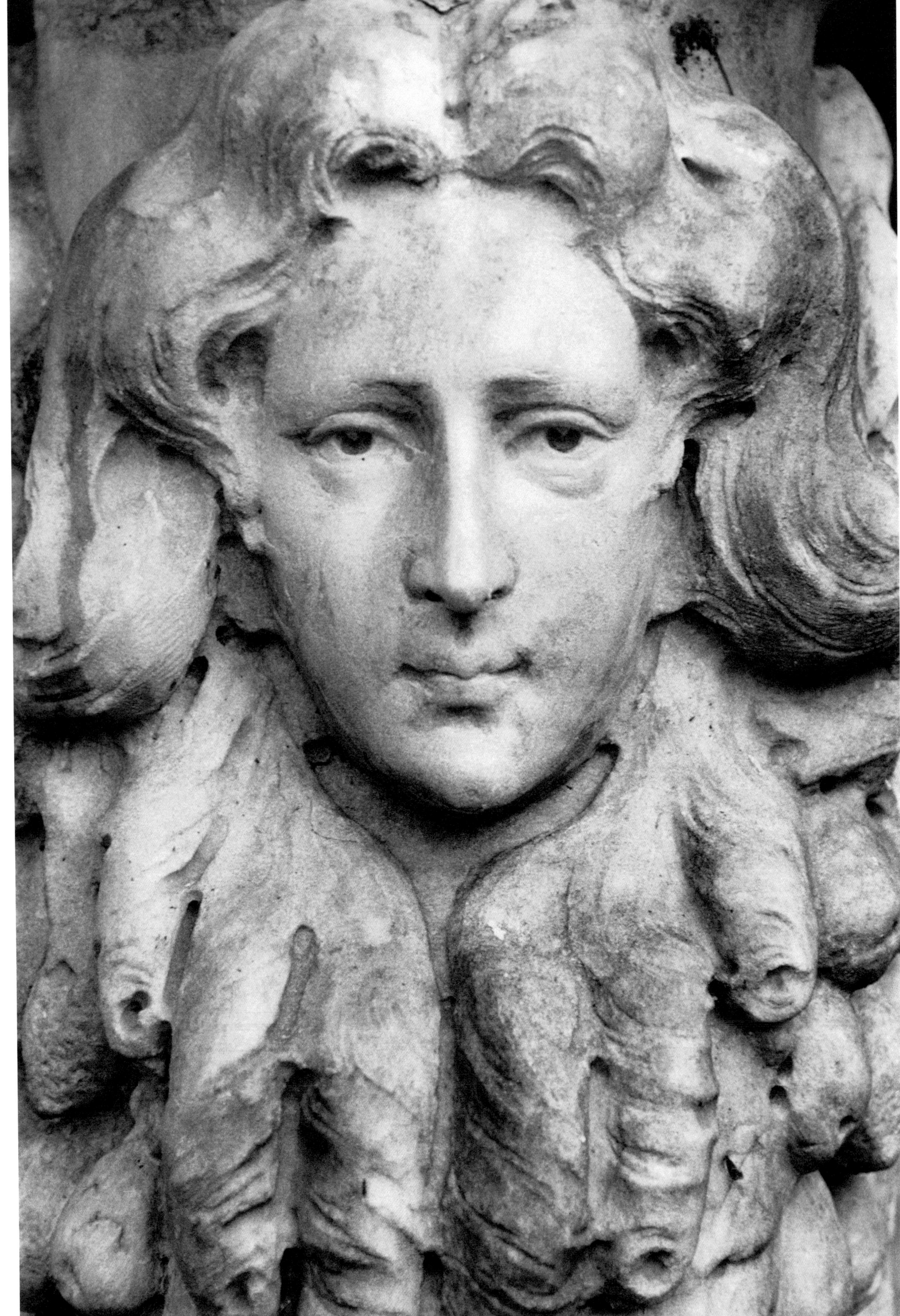

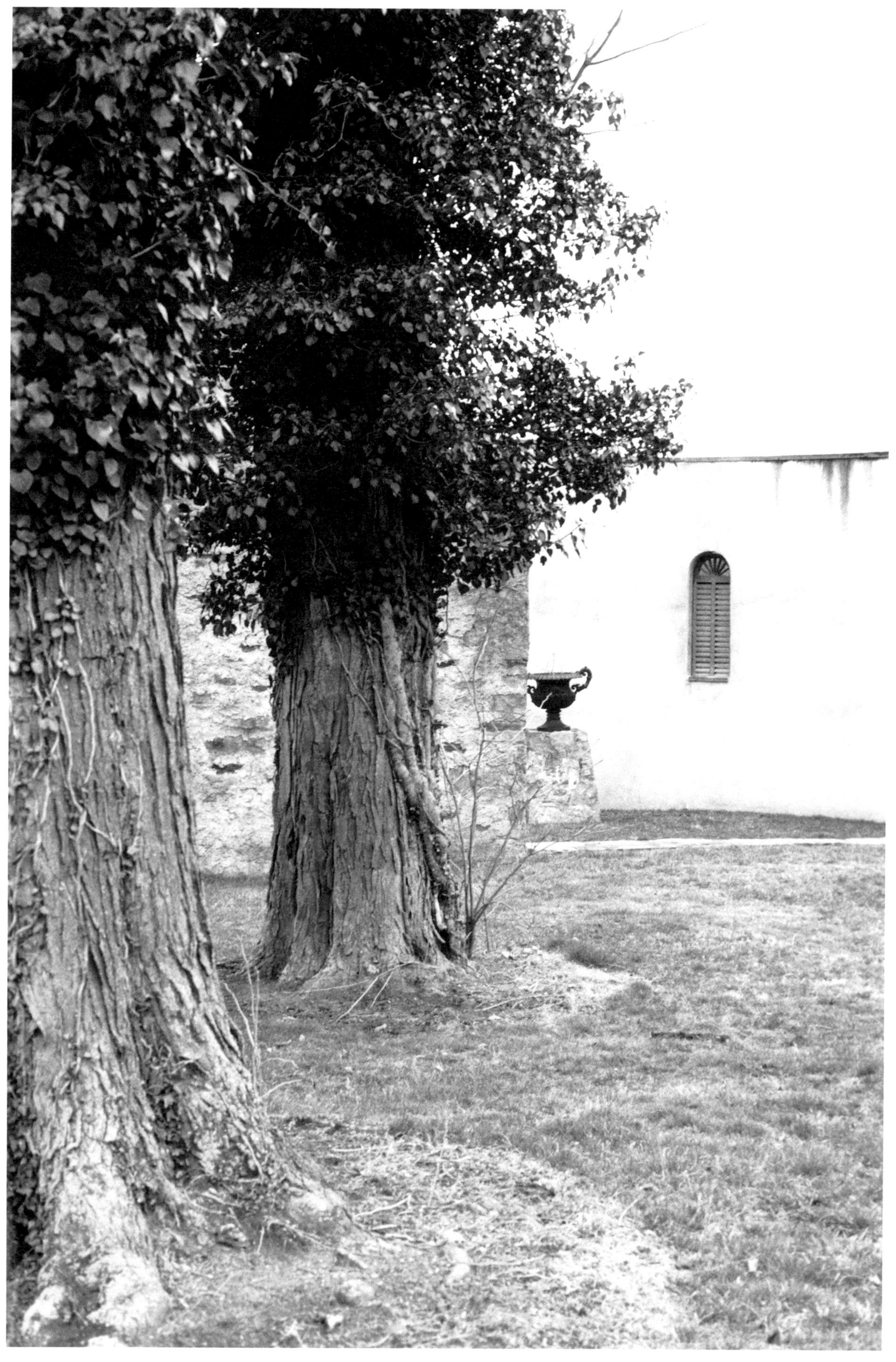

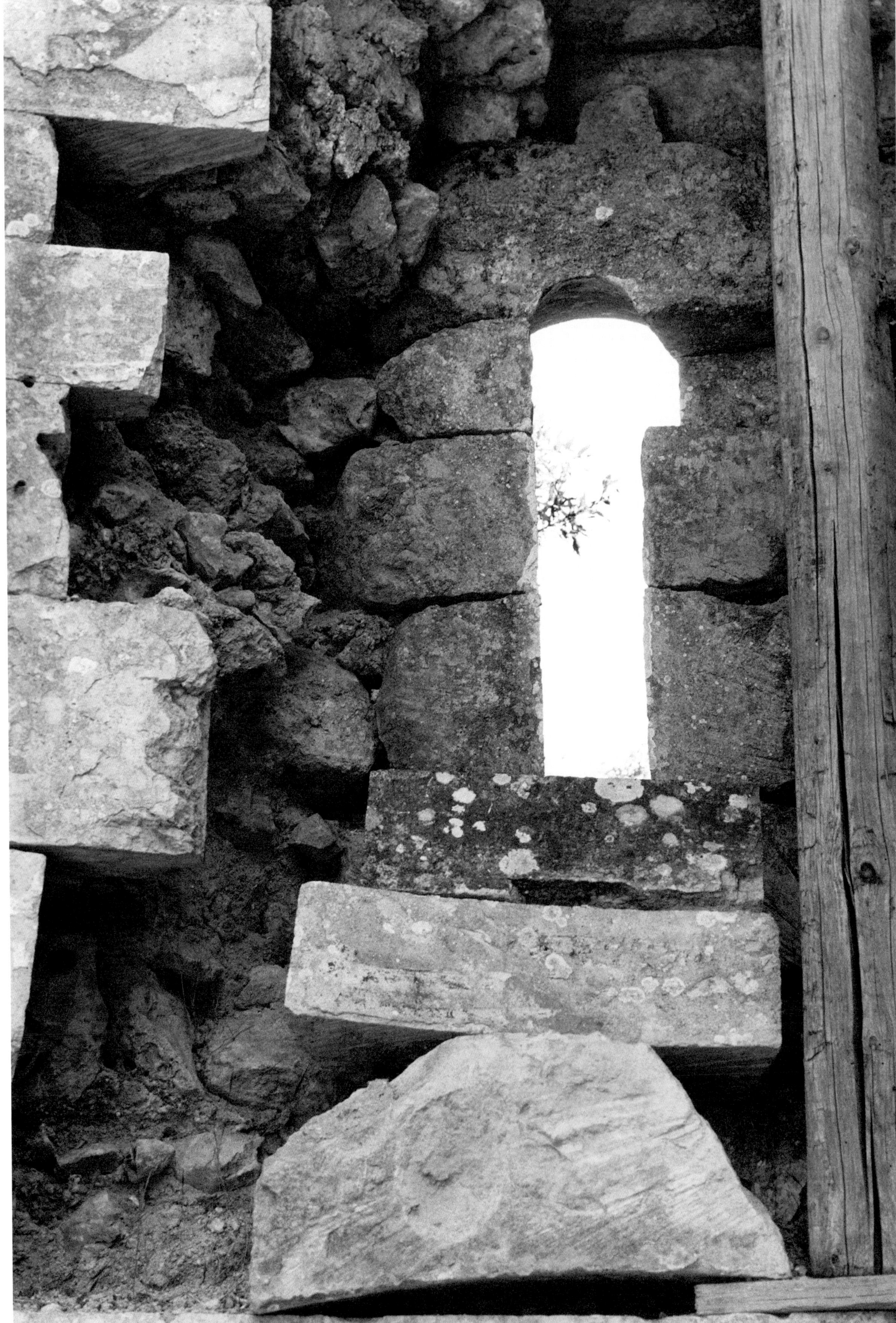

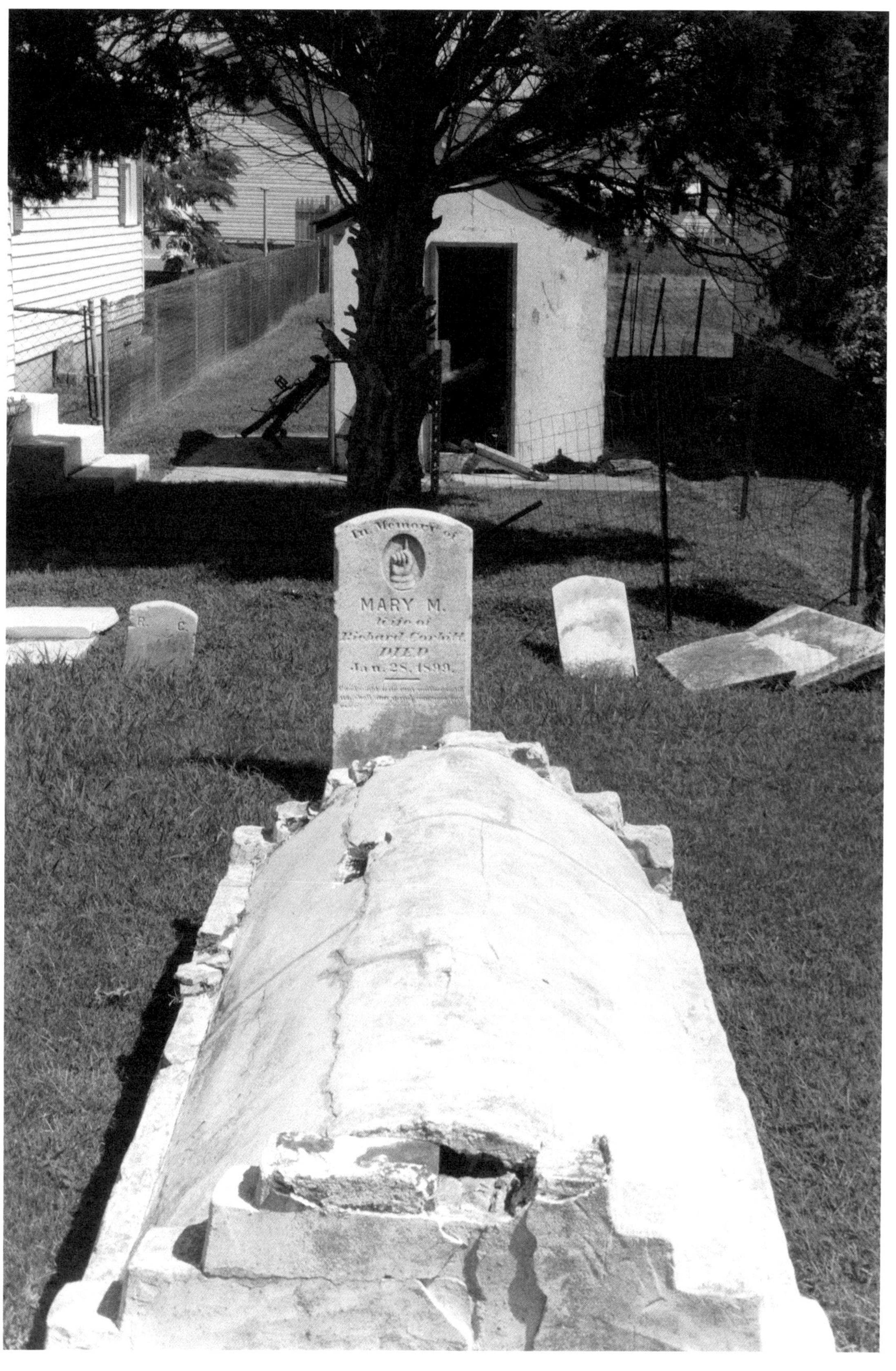
In Memory of
MARY M.
wife of
Richard Corbill
DIED
Jan. 28, 1899

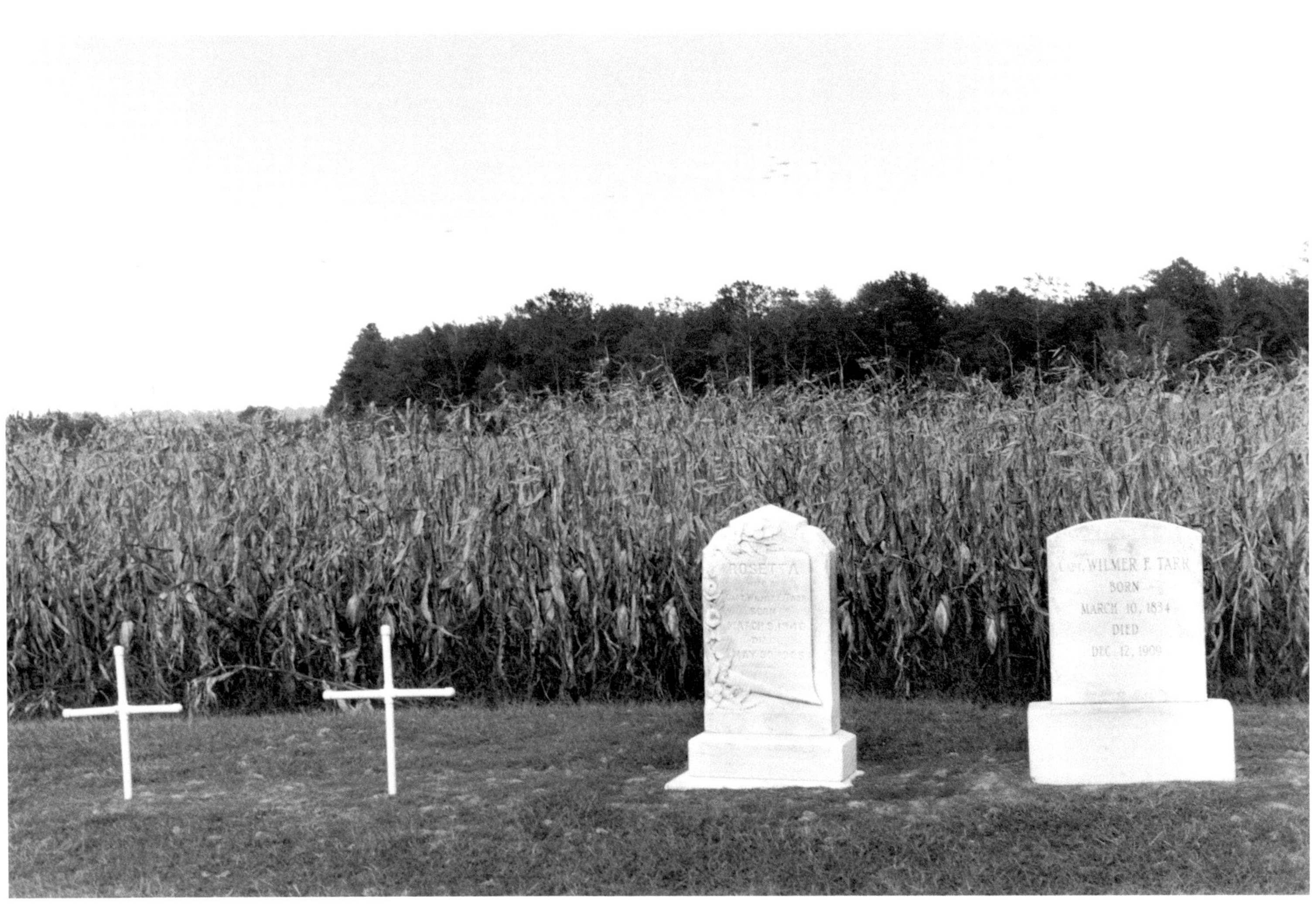

ROSETTA
BORN
DIED
CAPT. WILMER F. TARR
BORN
MARCH 10, 1834
DIED
DEC. 12, 1909

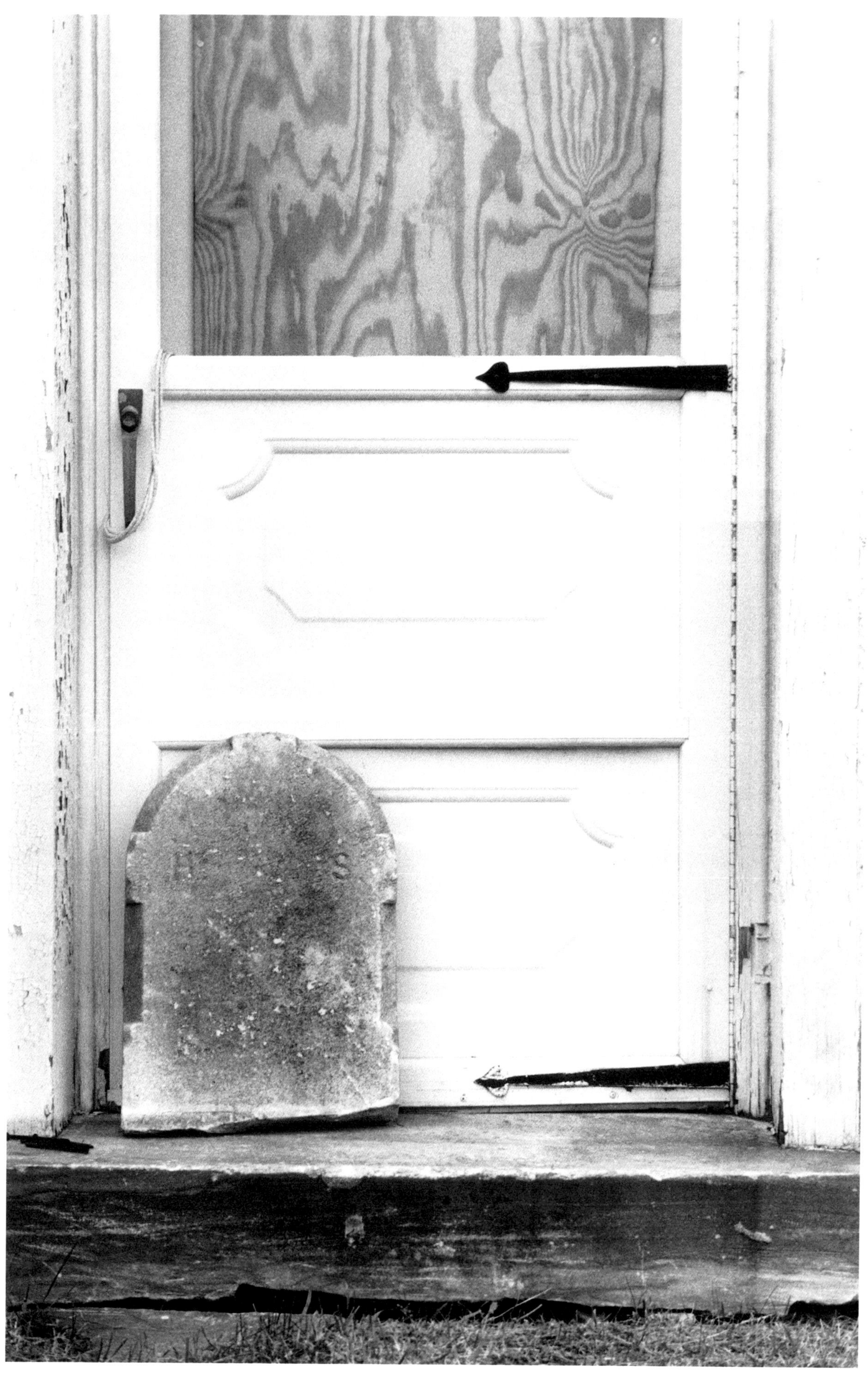

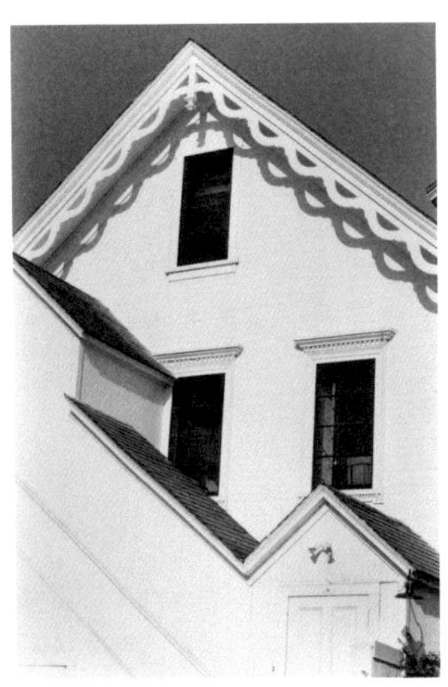

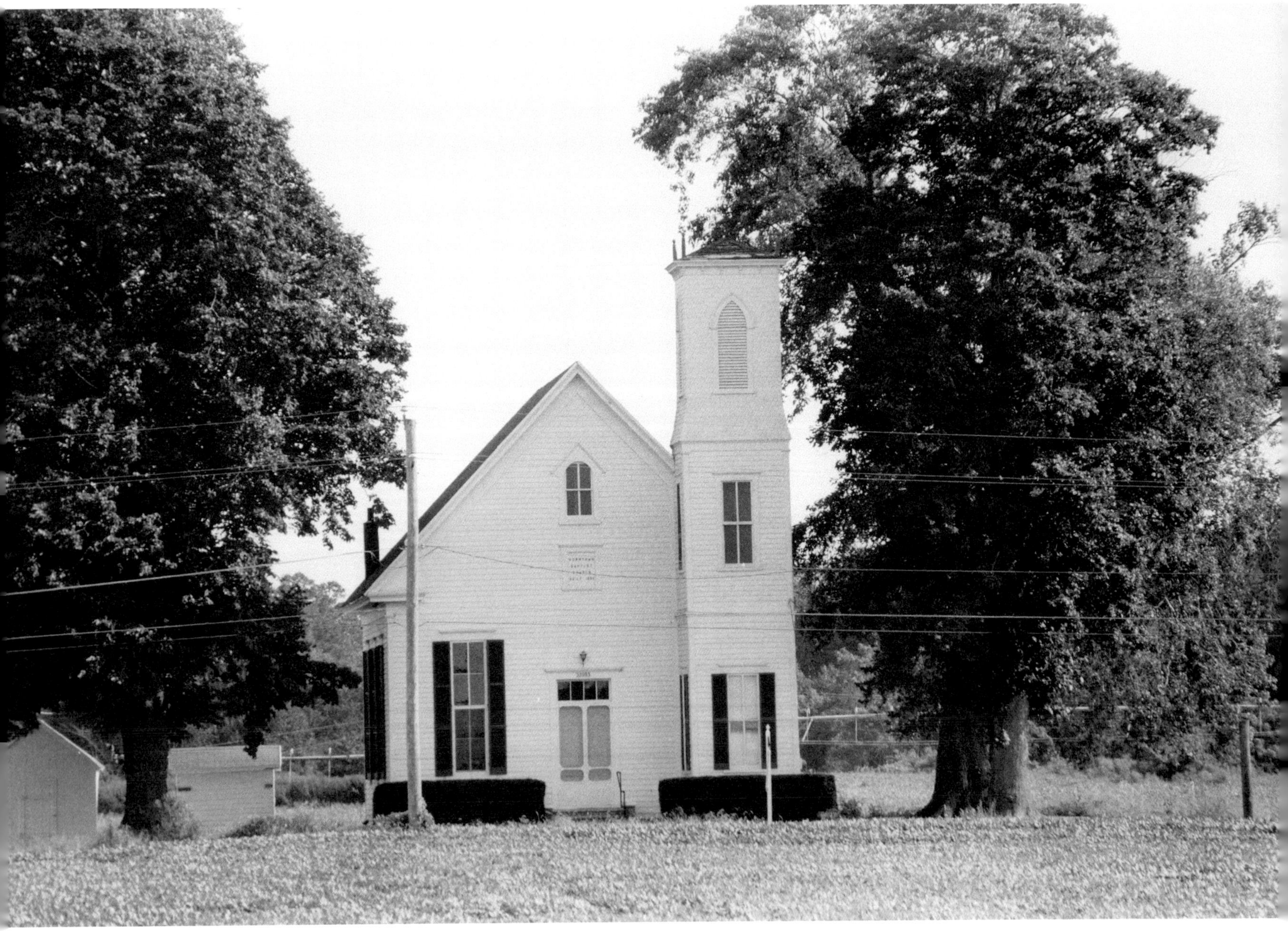

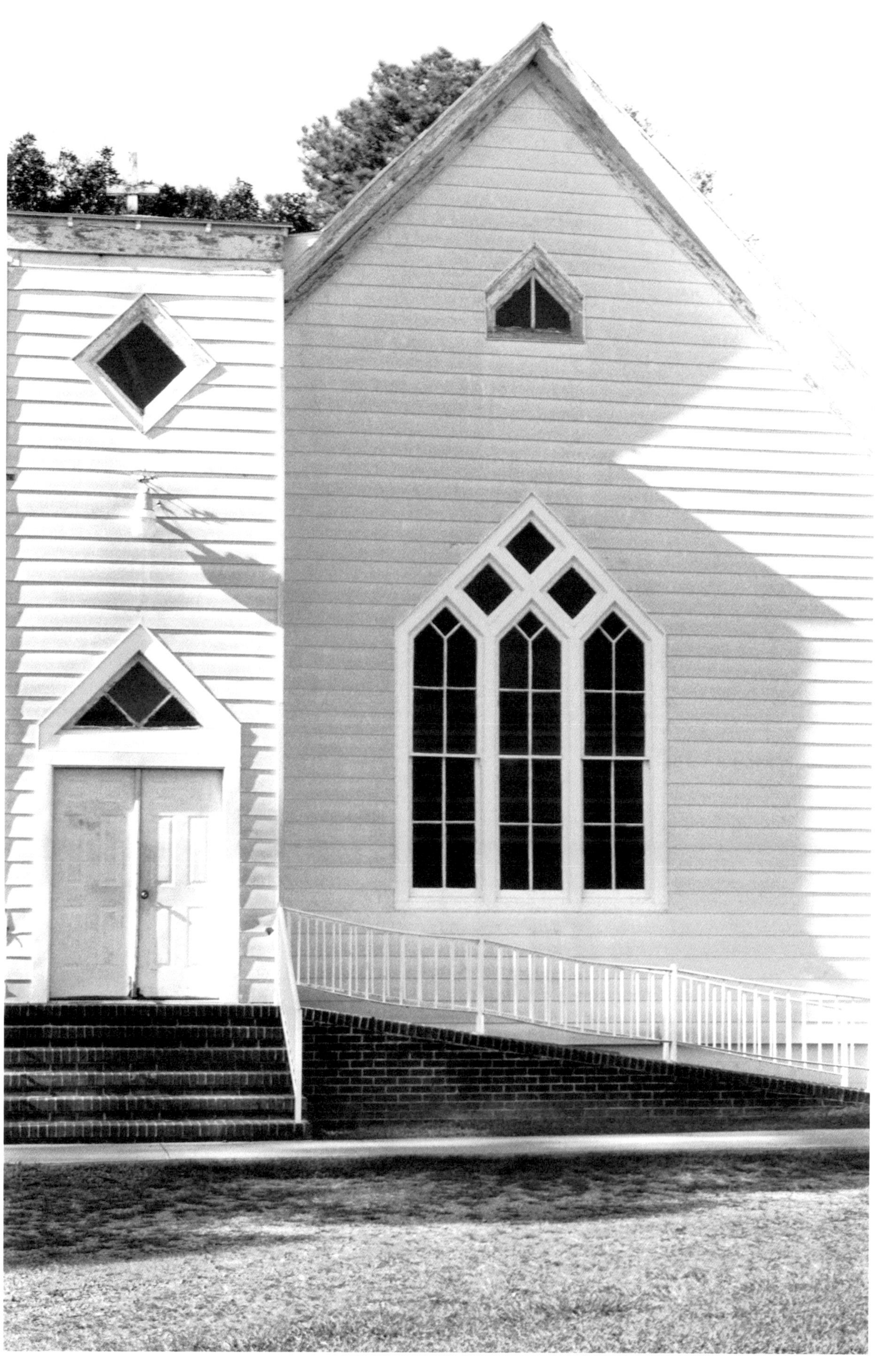

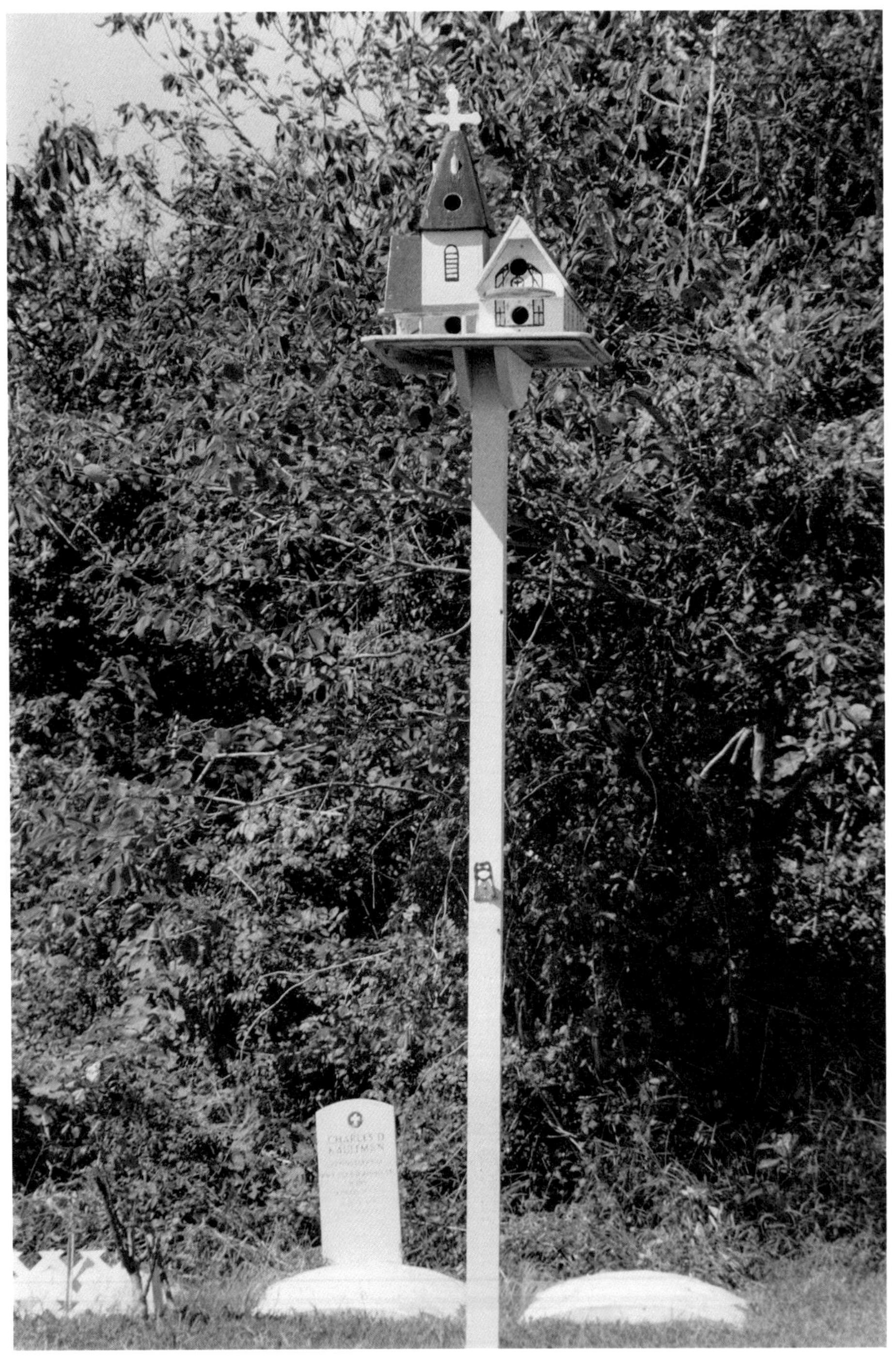

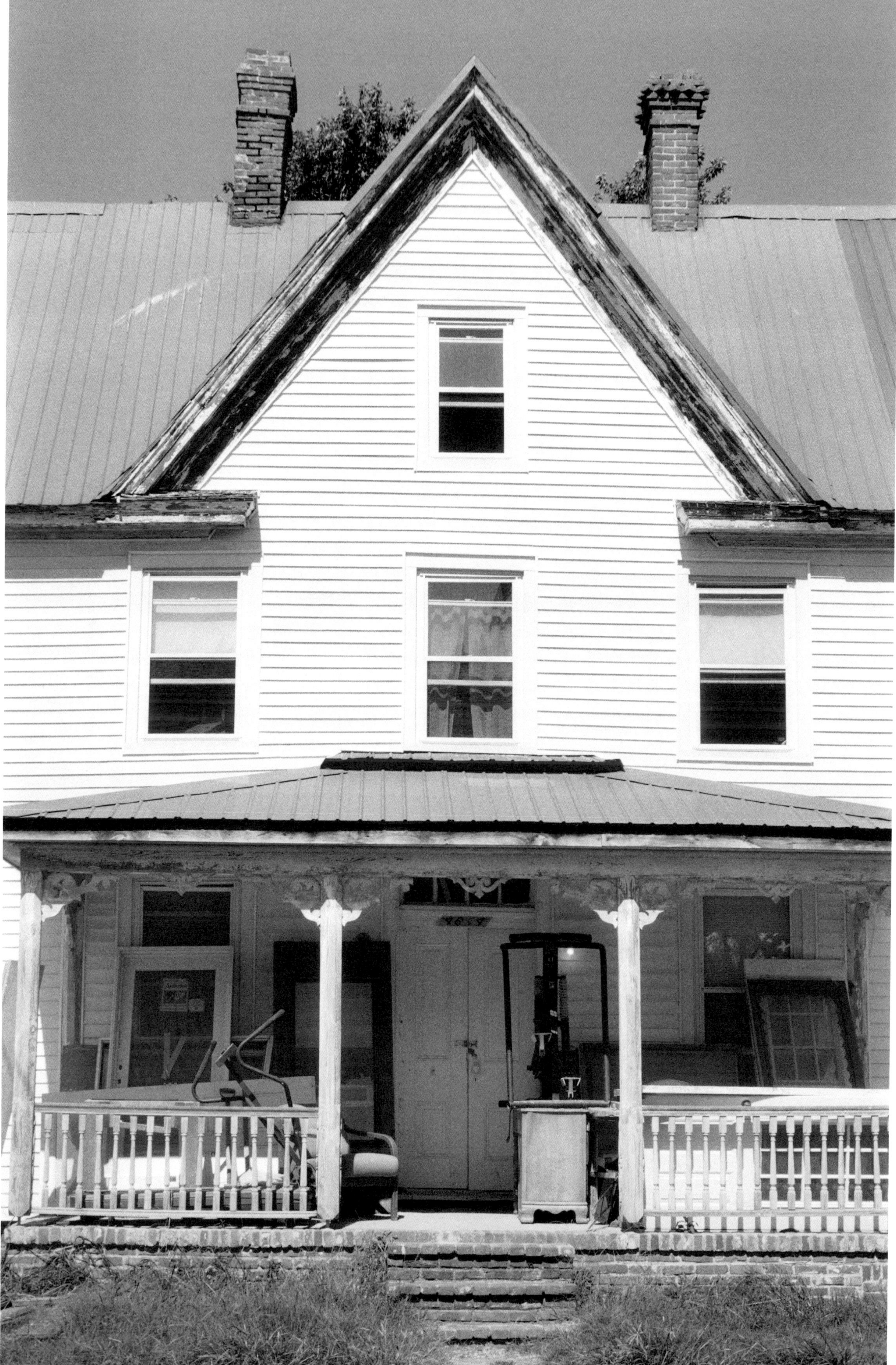

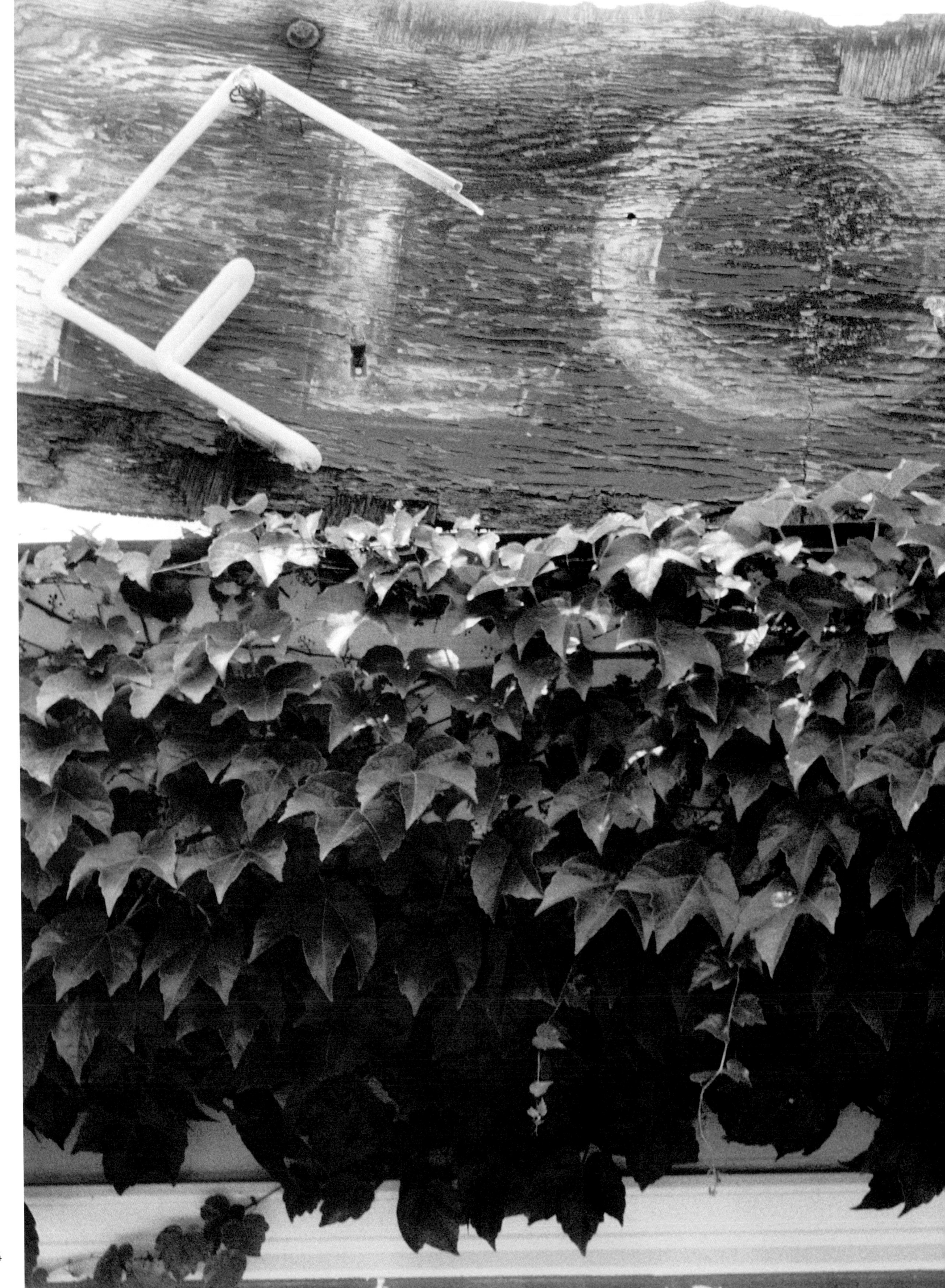

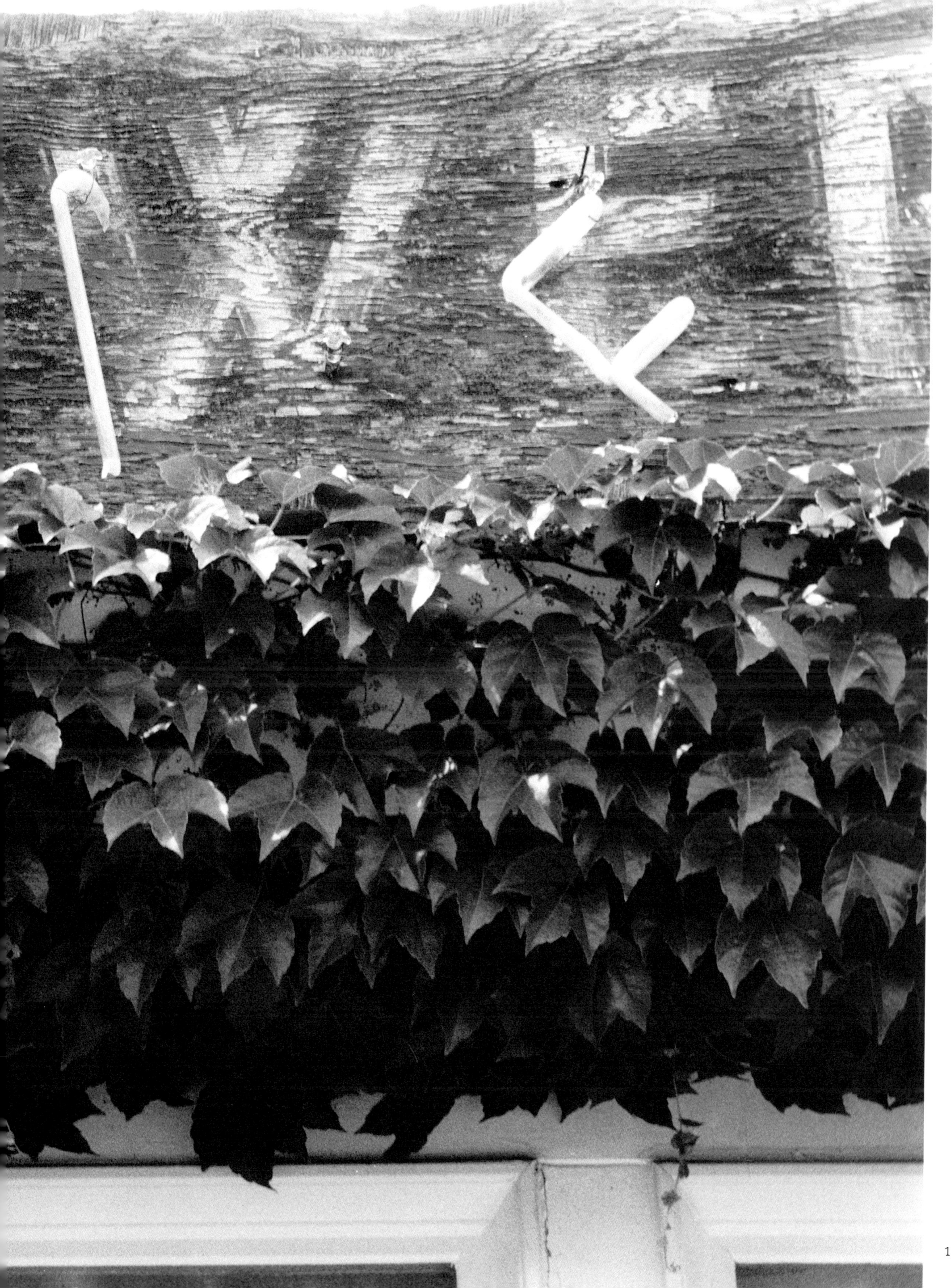

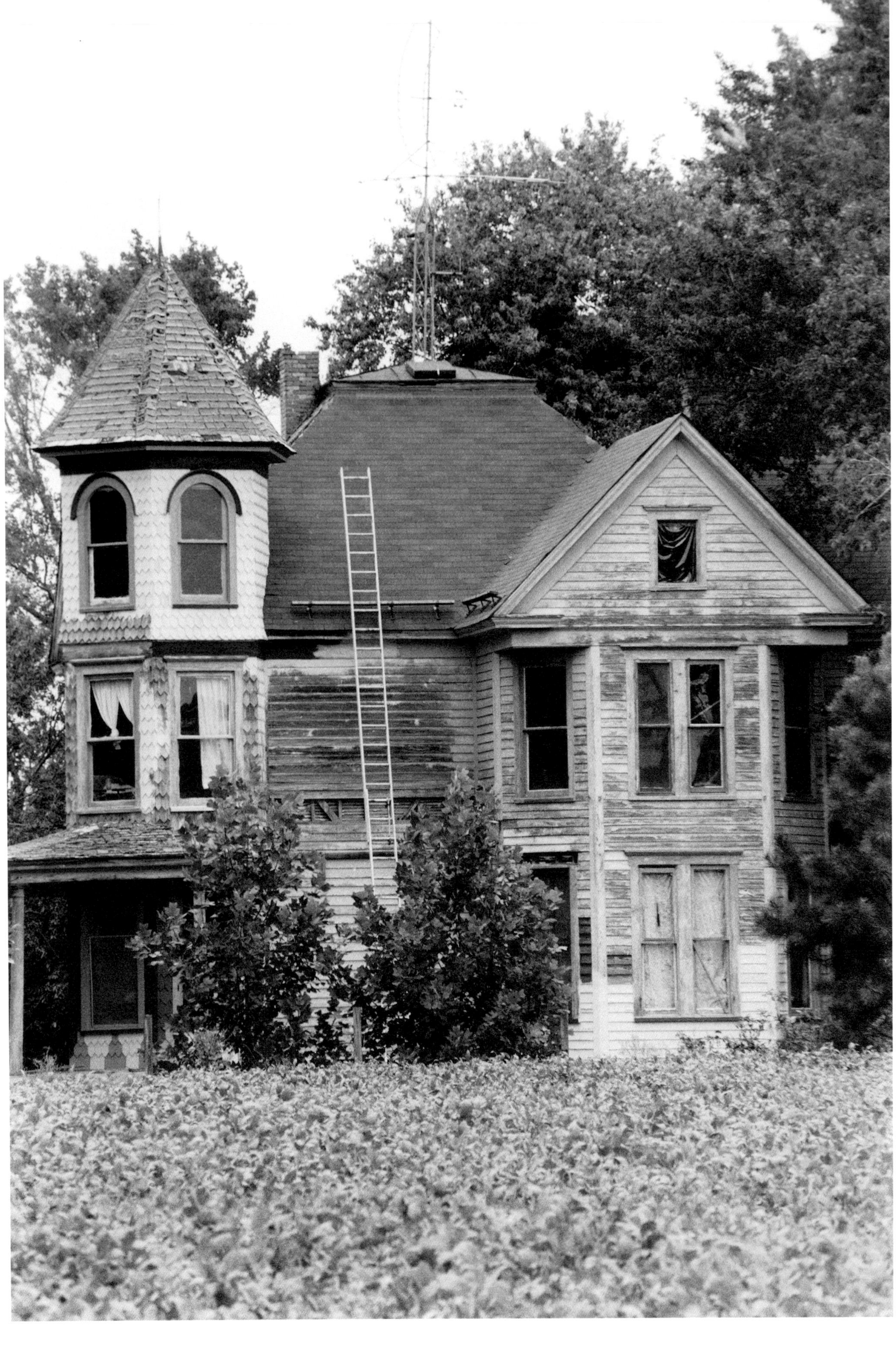

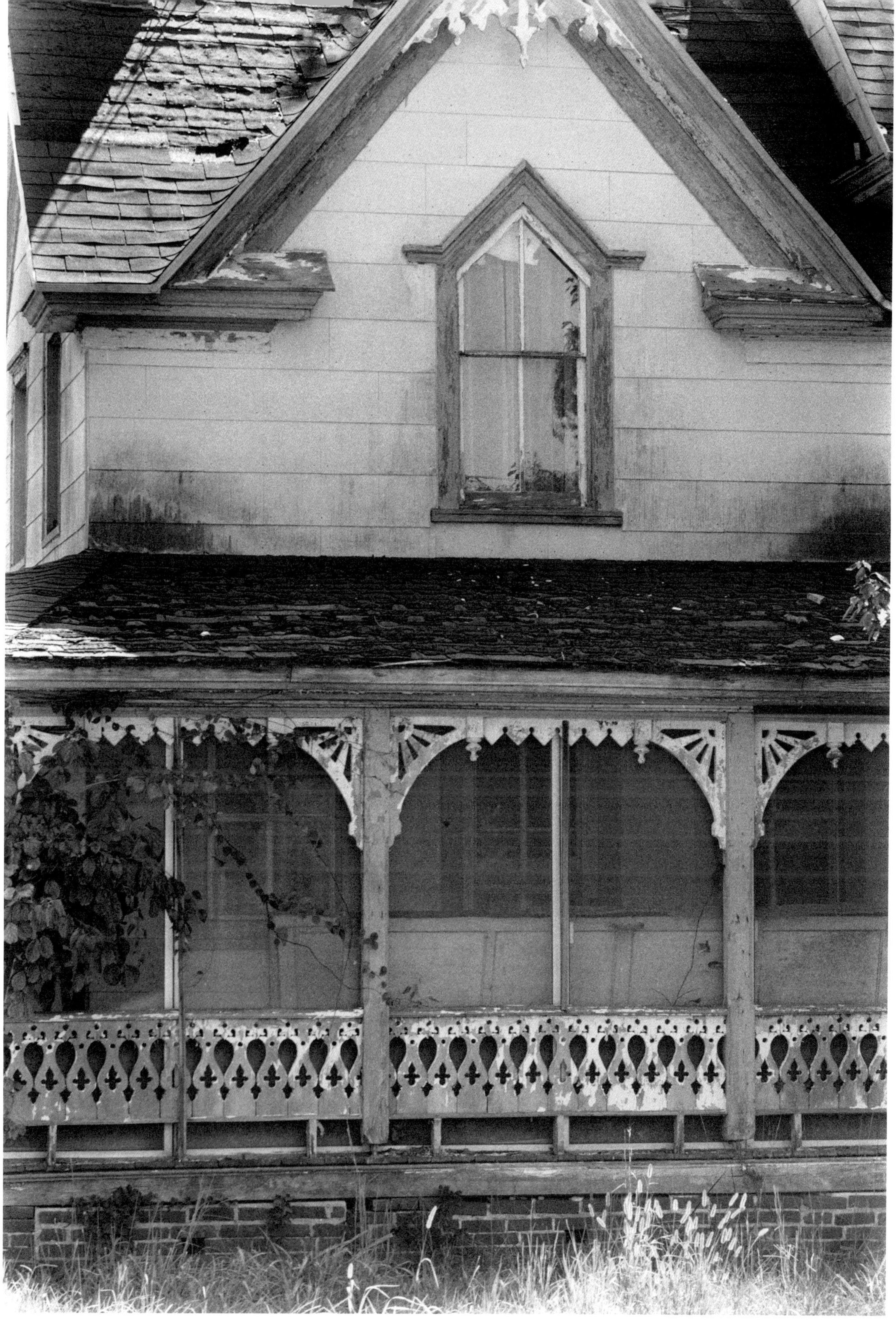

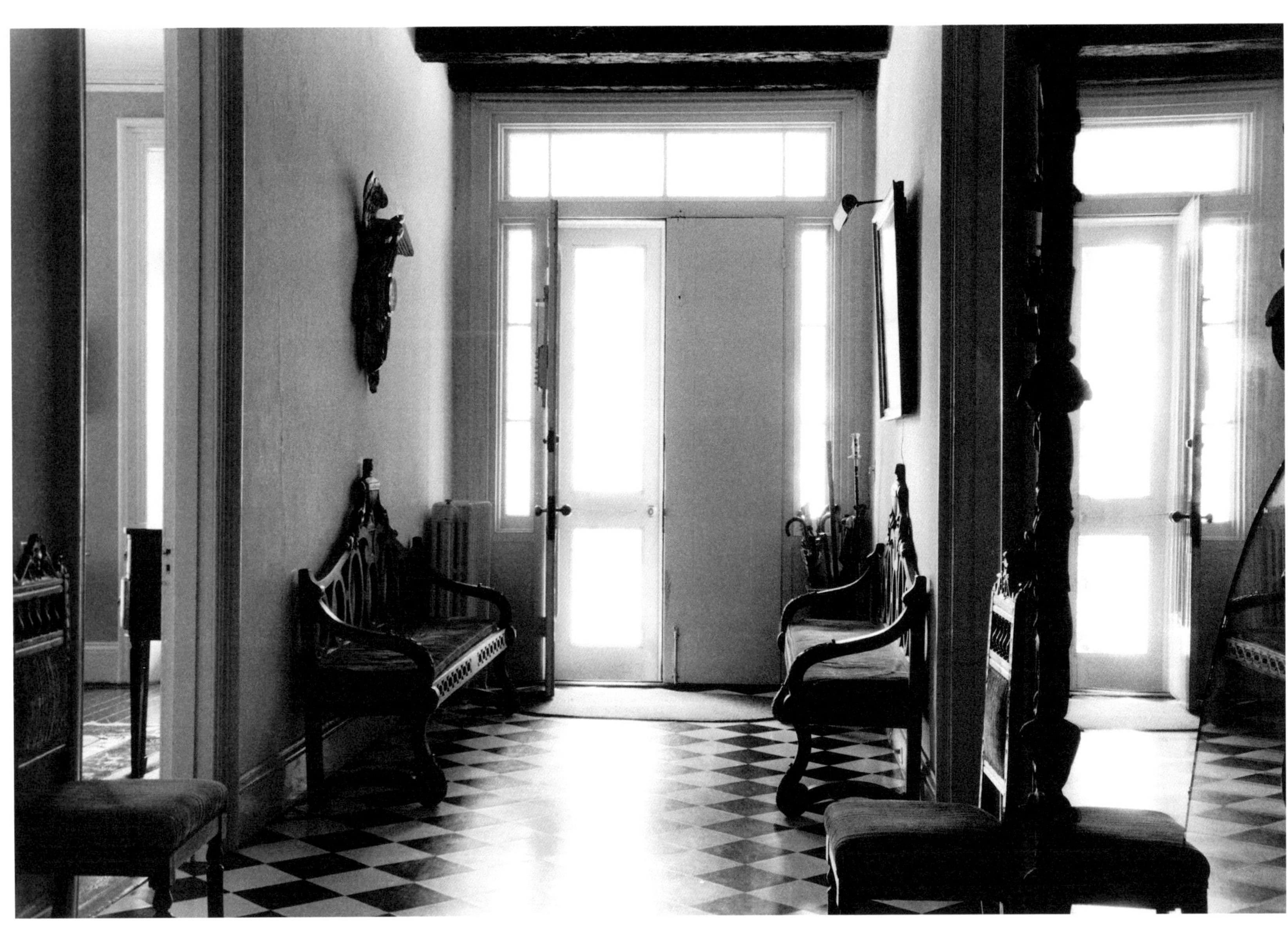

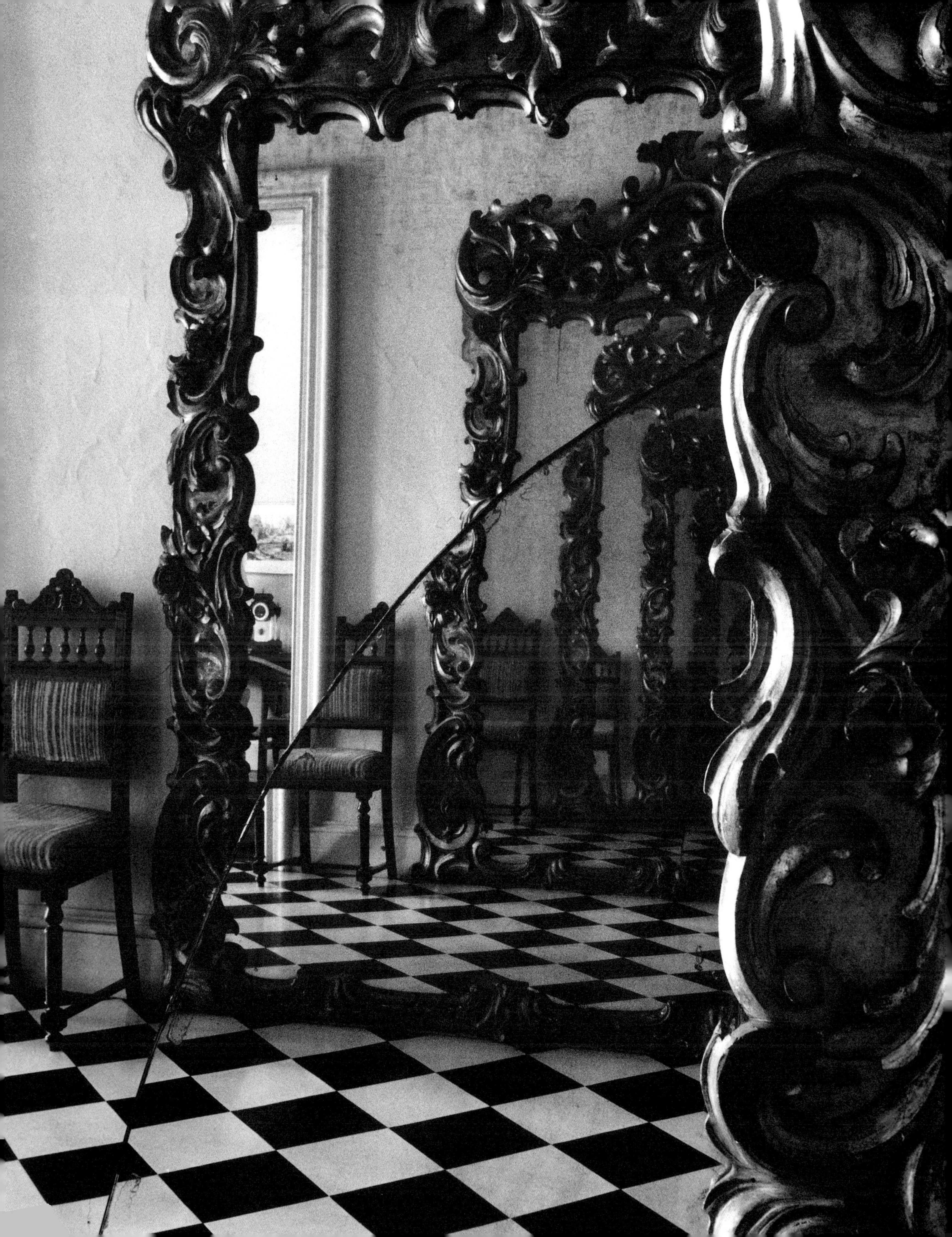

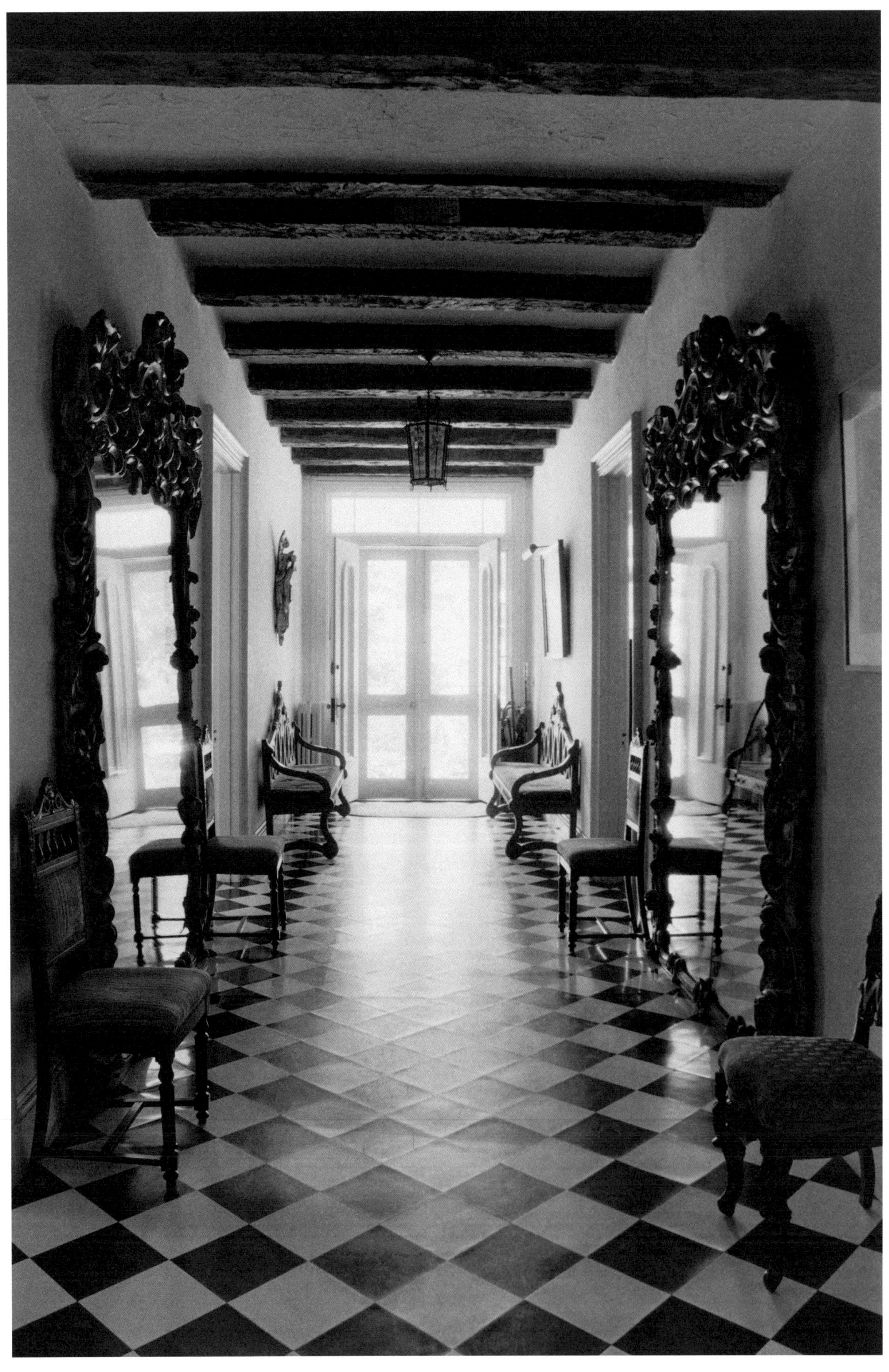

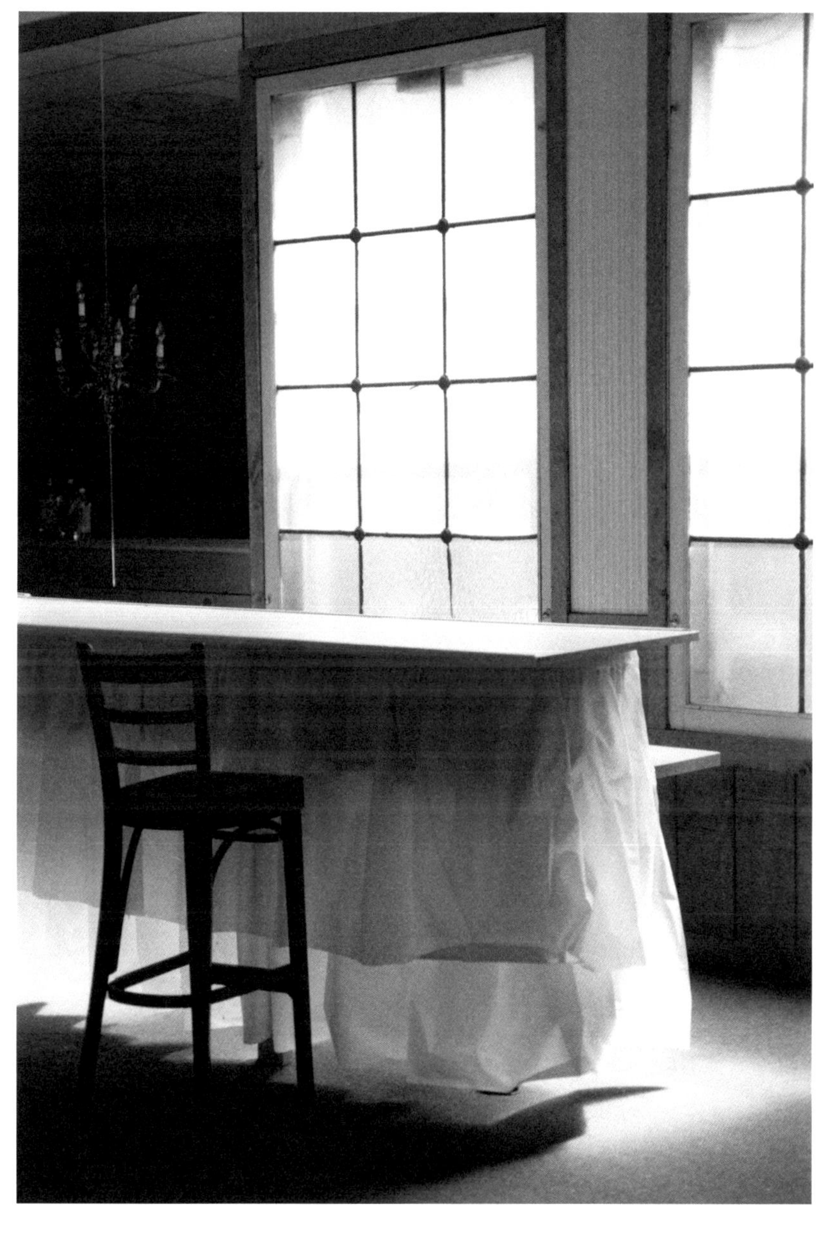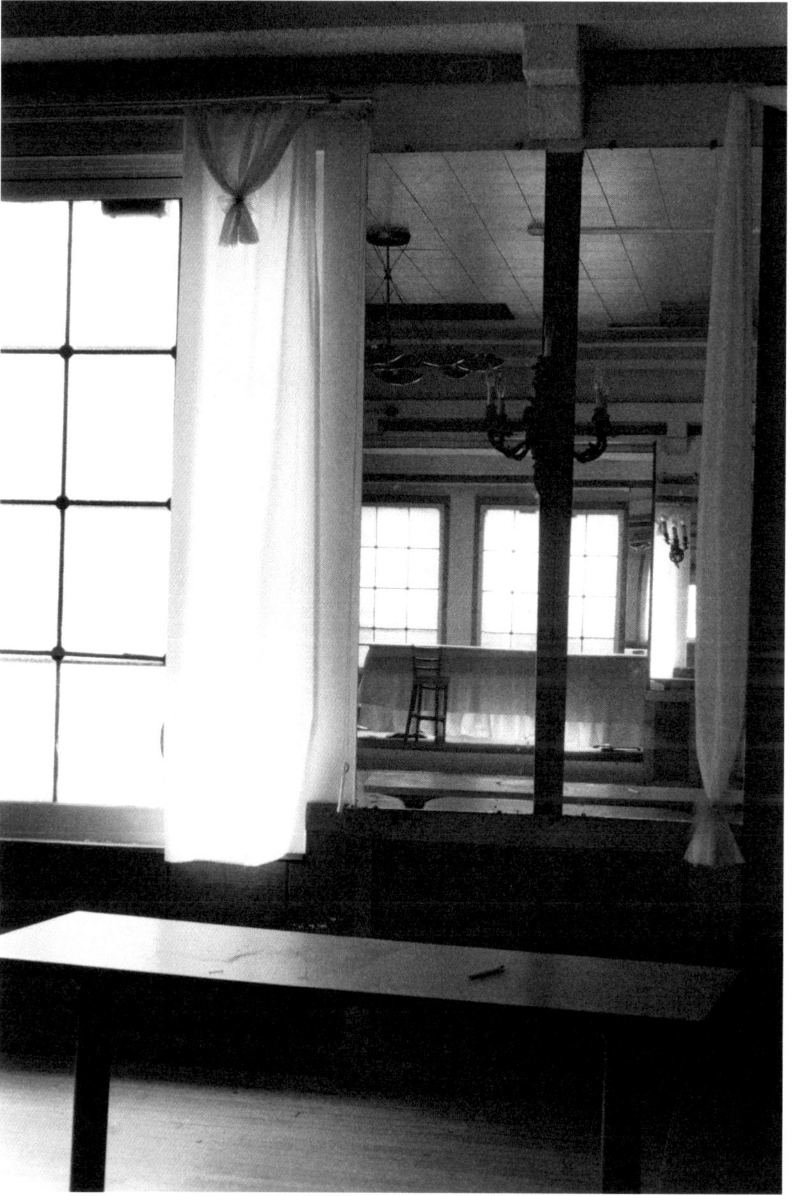

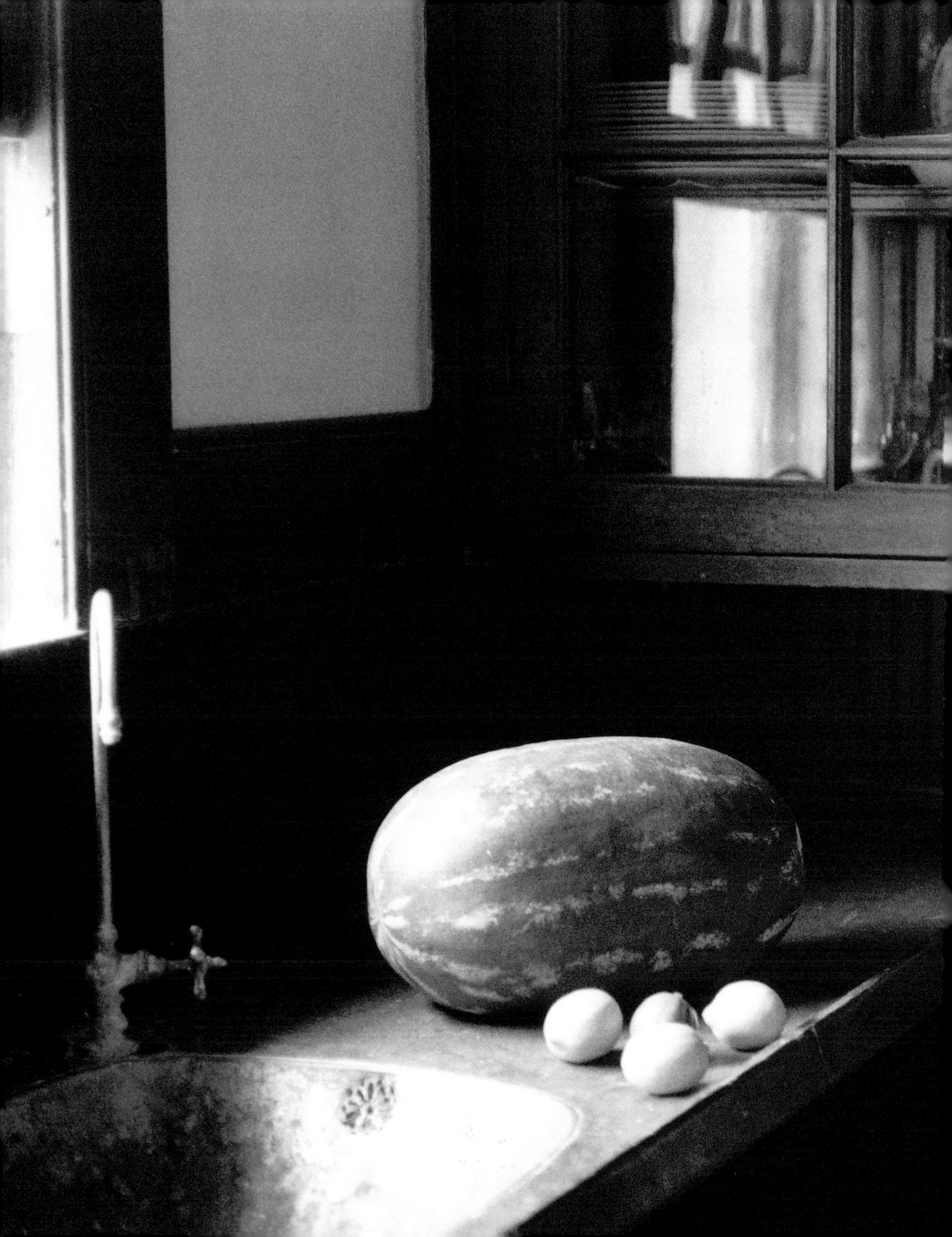

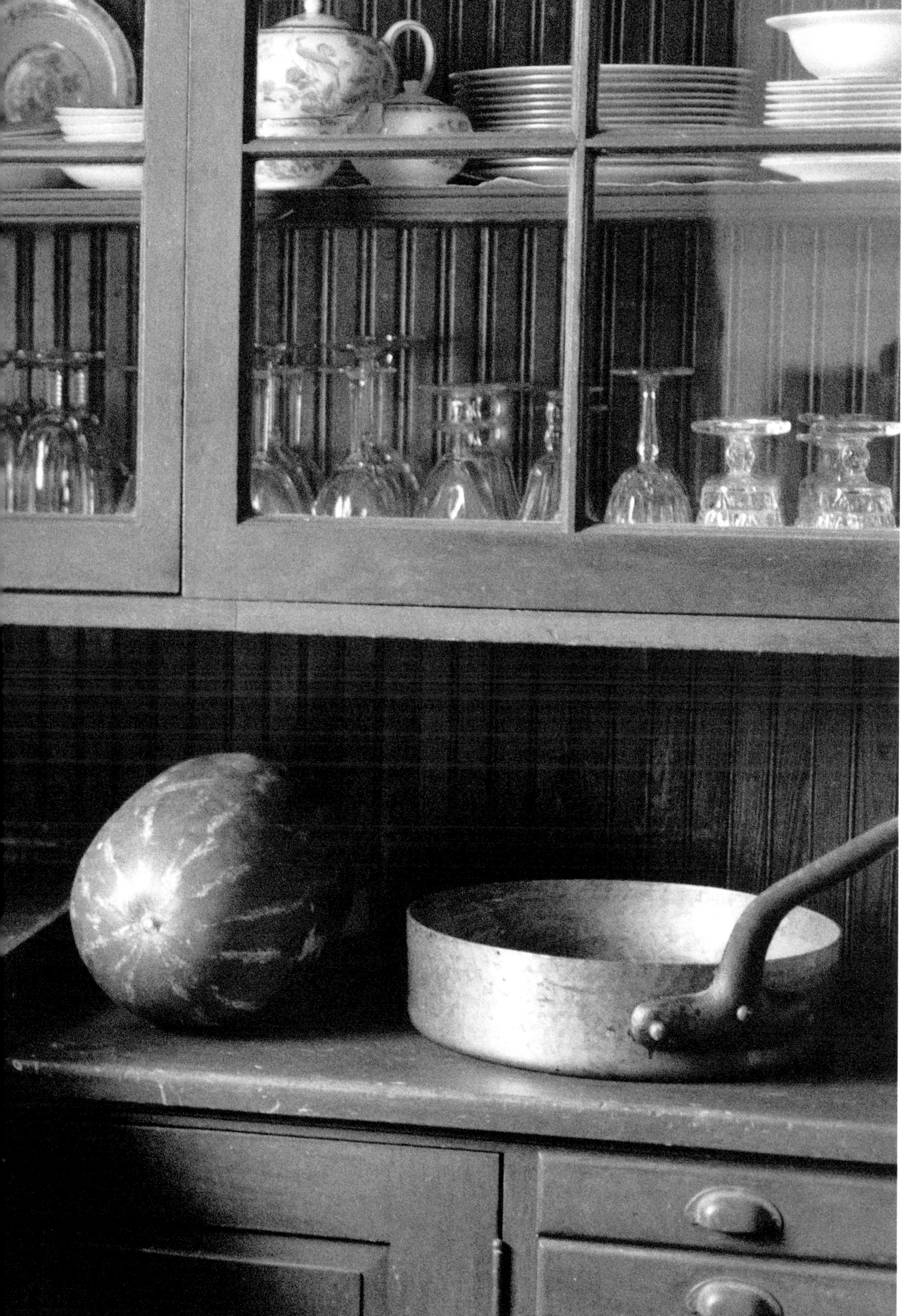

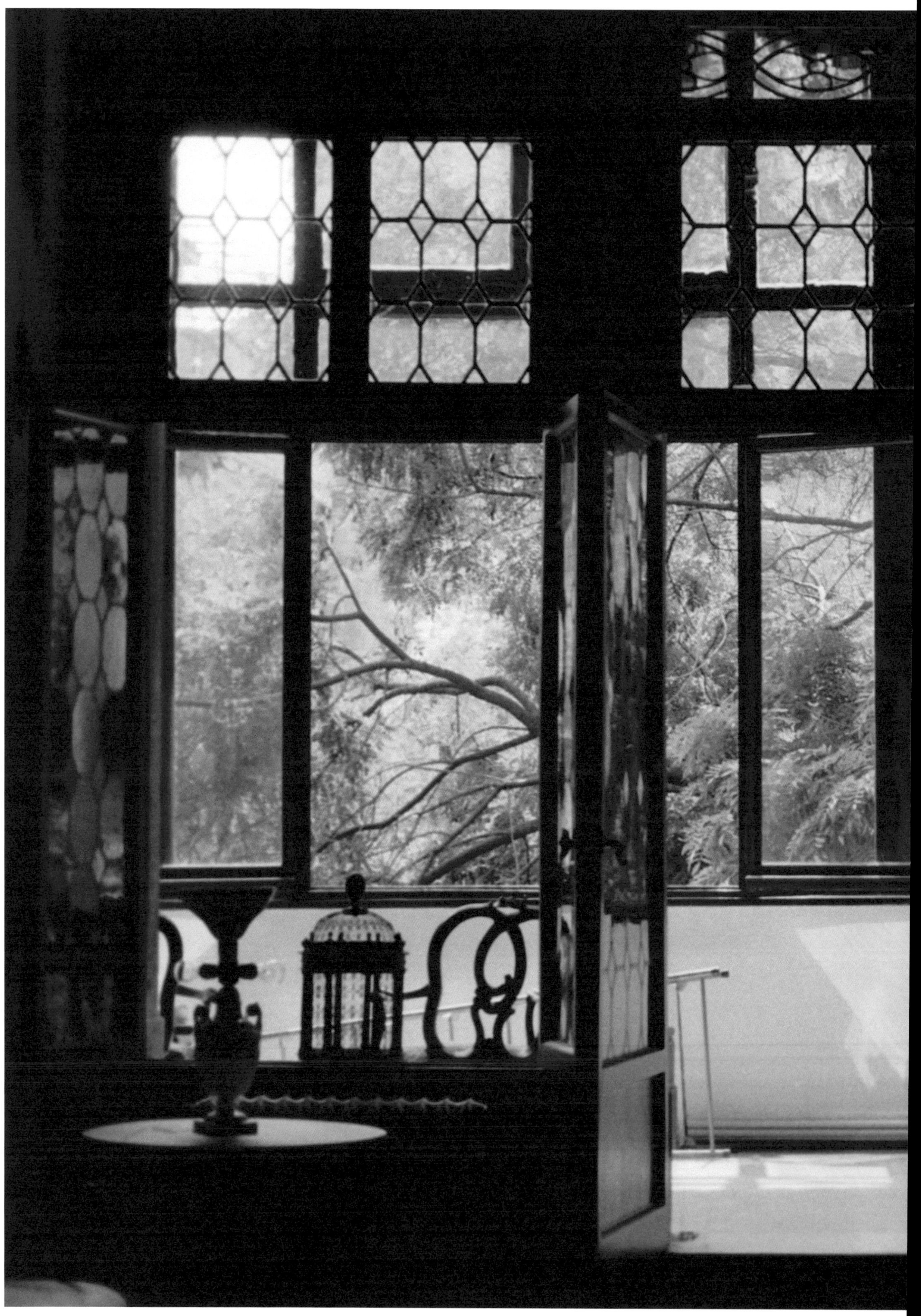

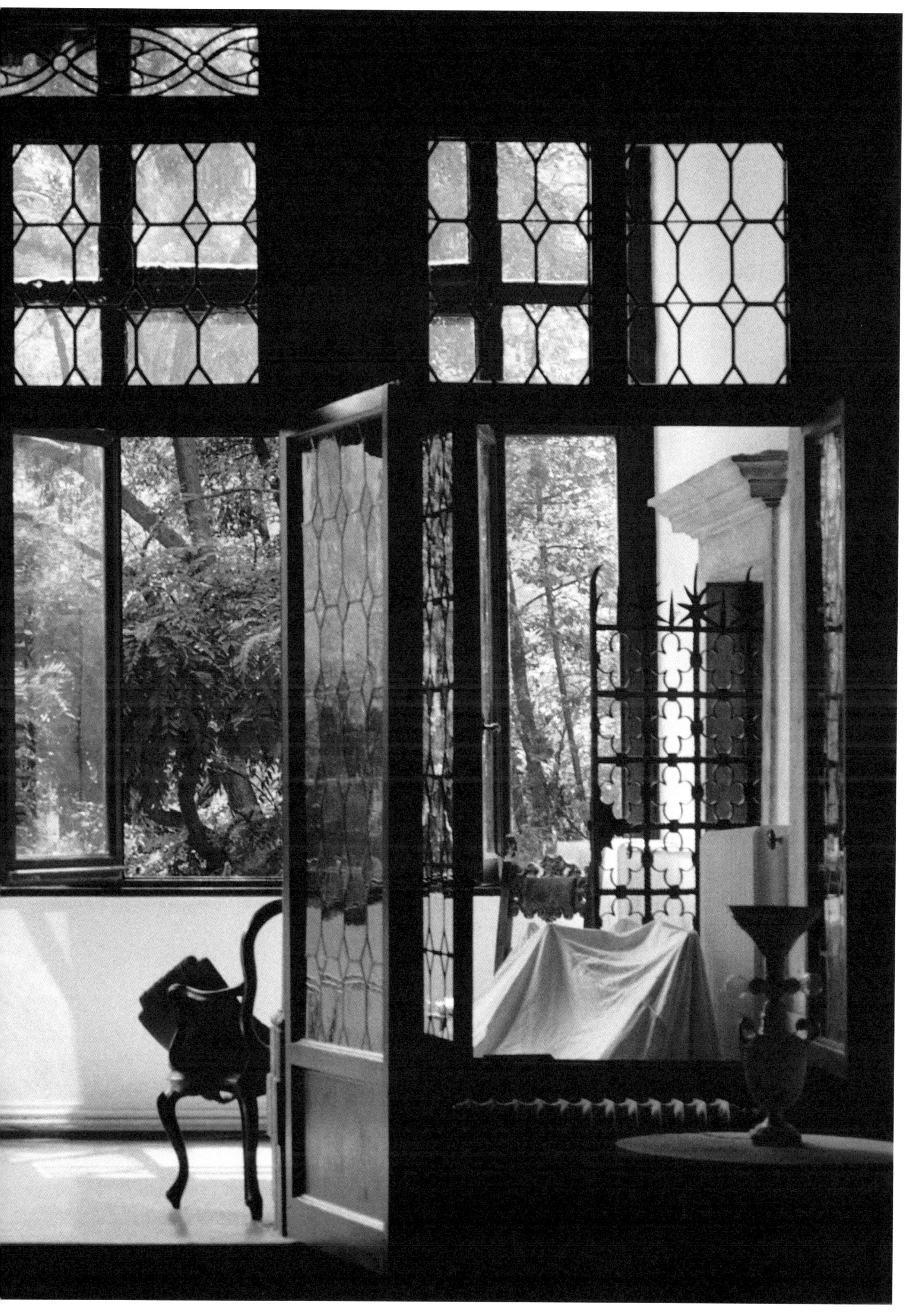

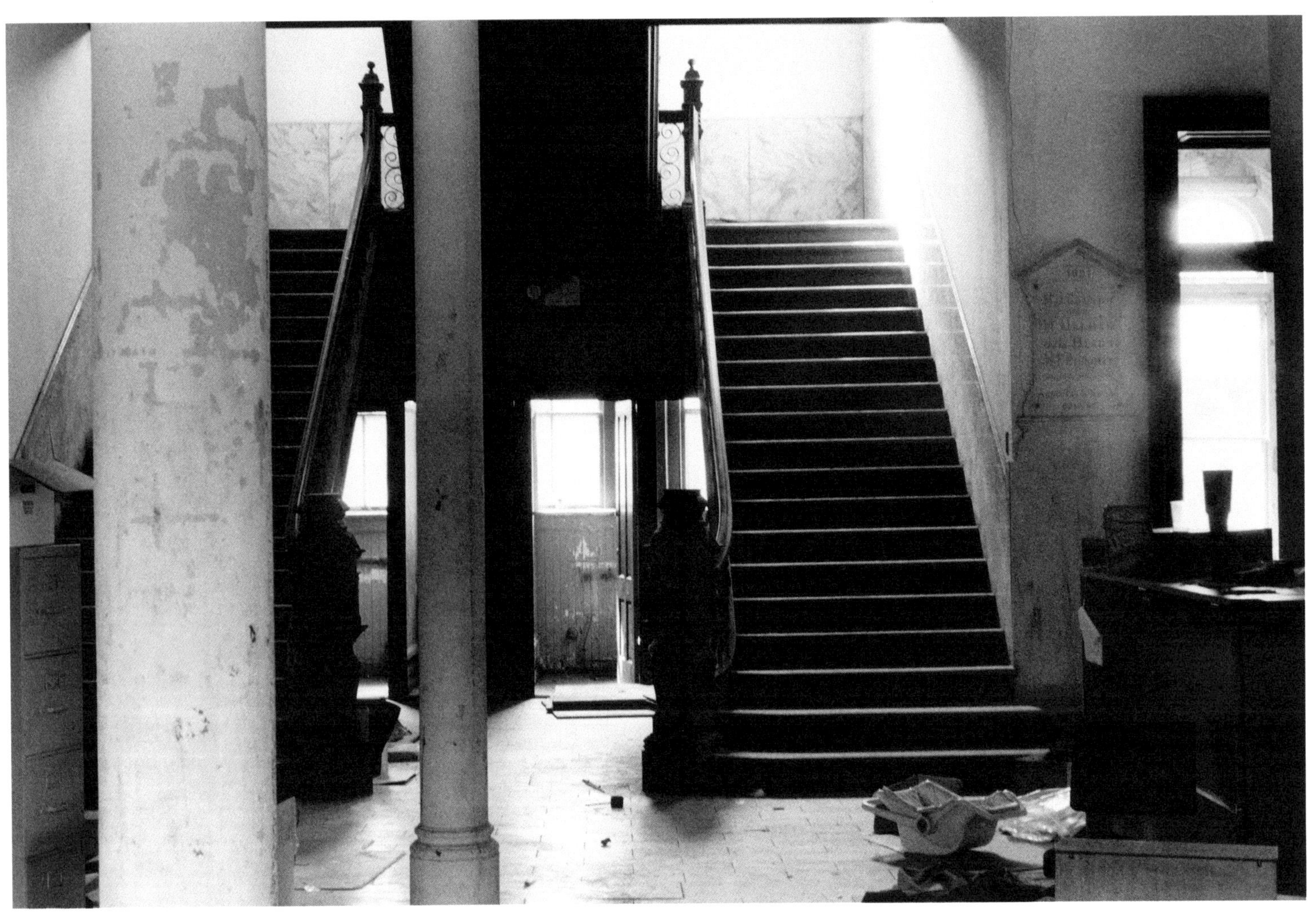

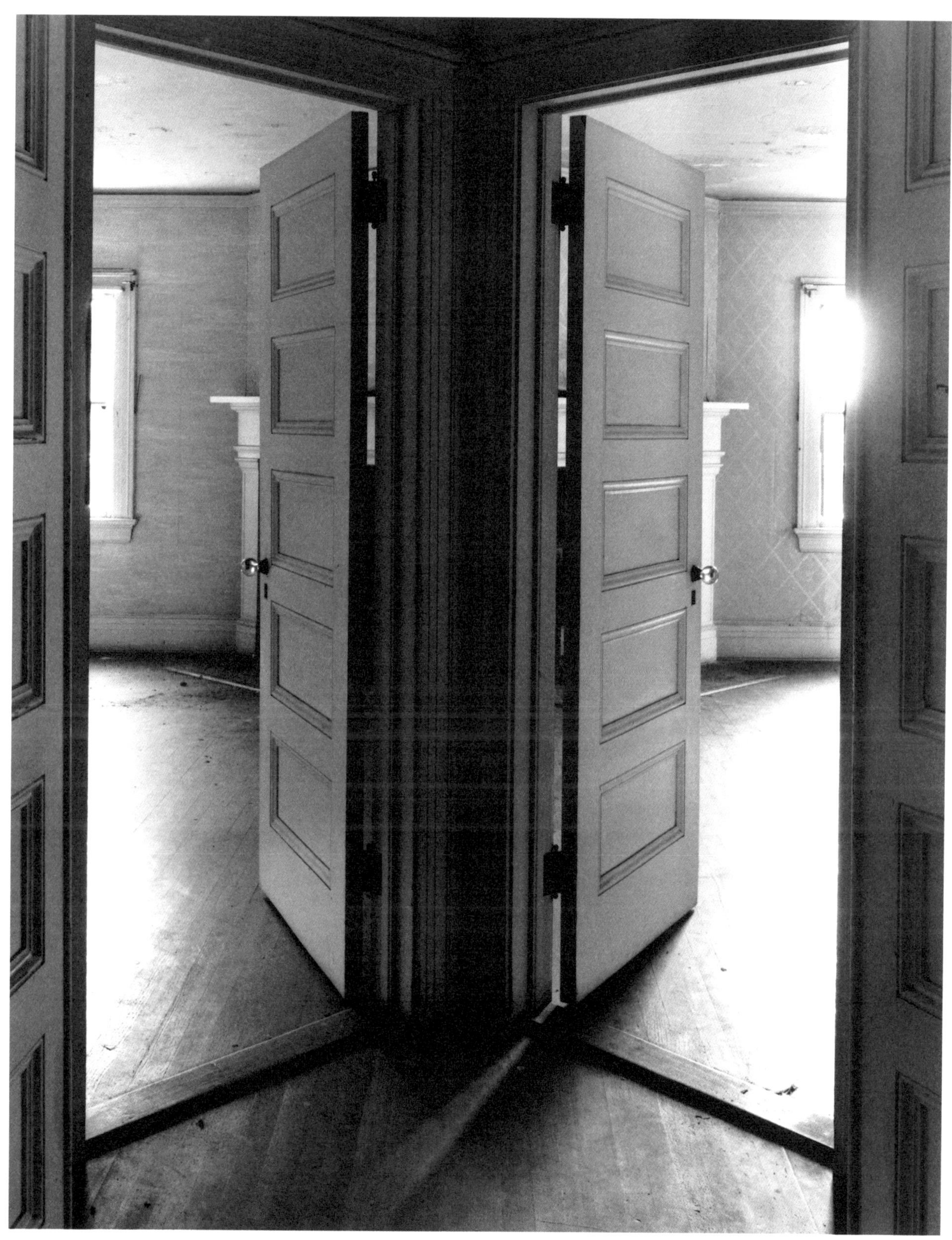

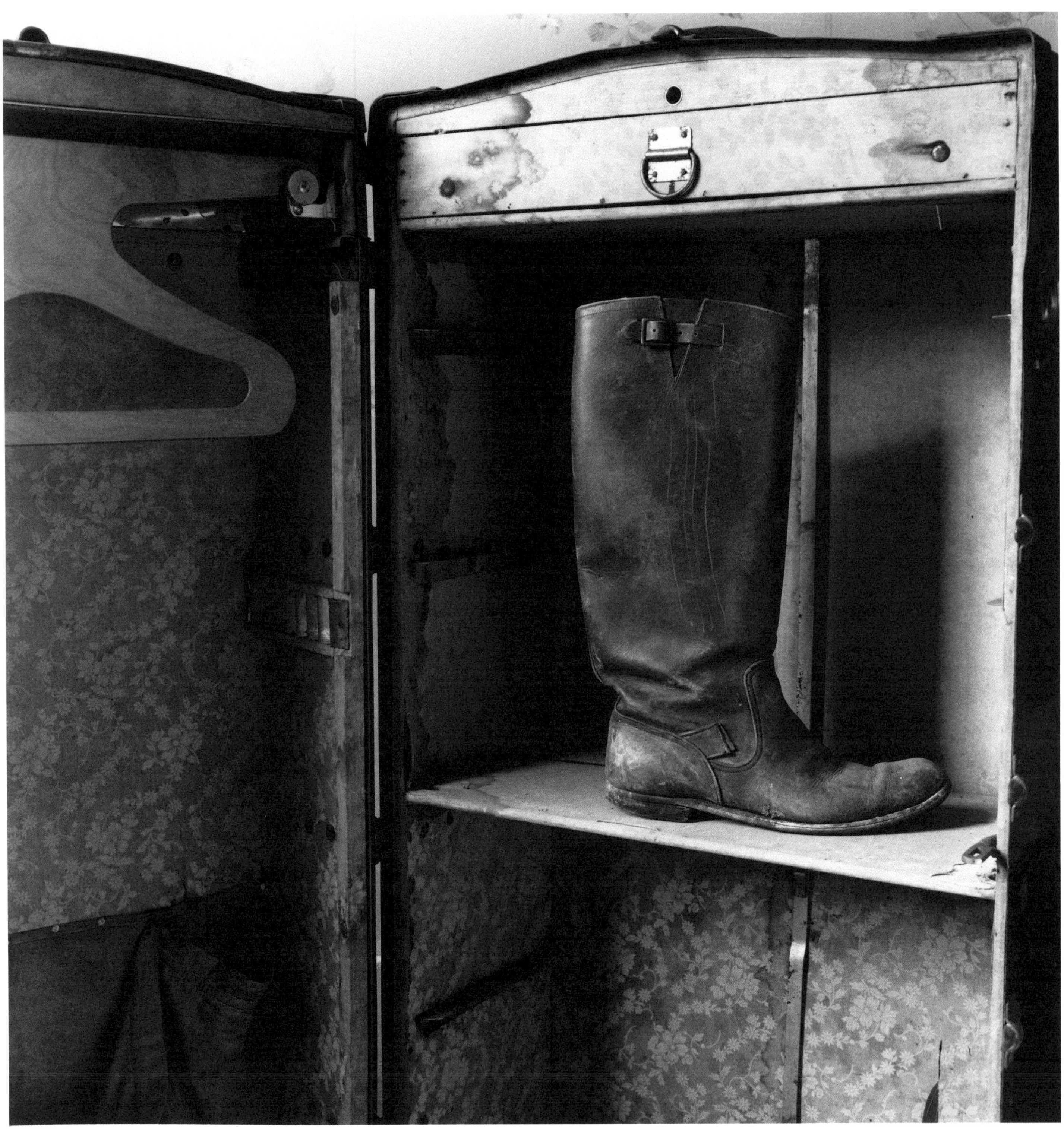

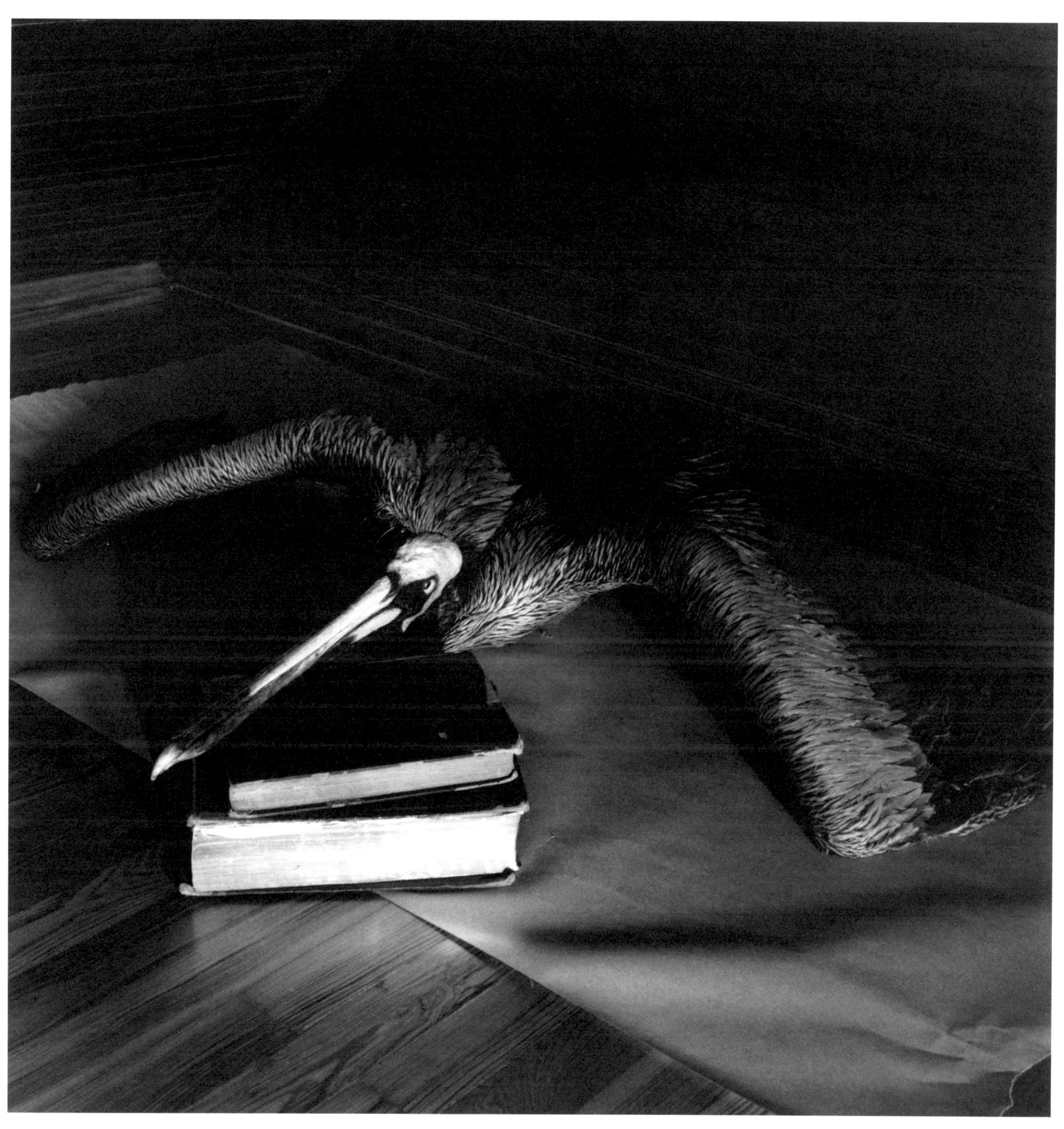

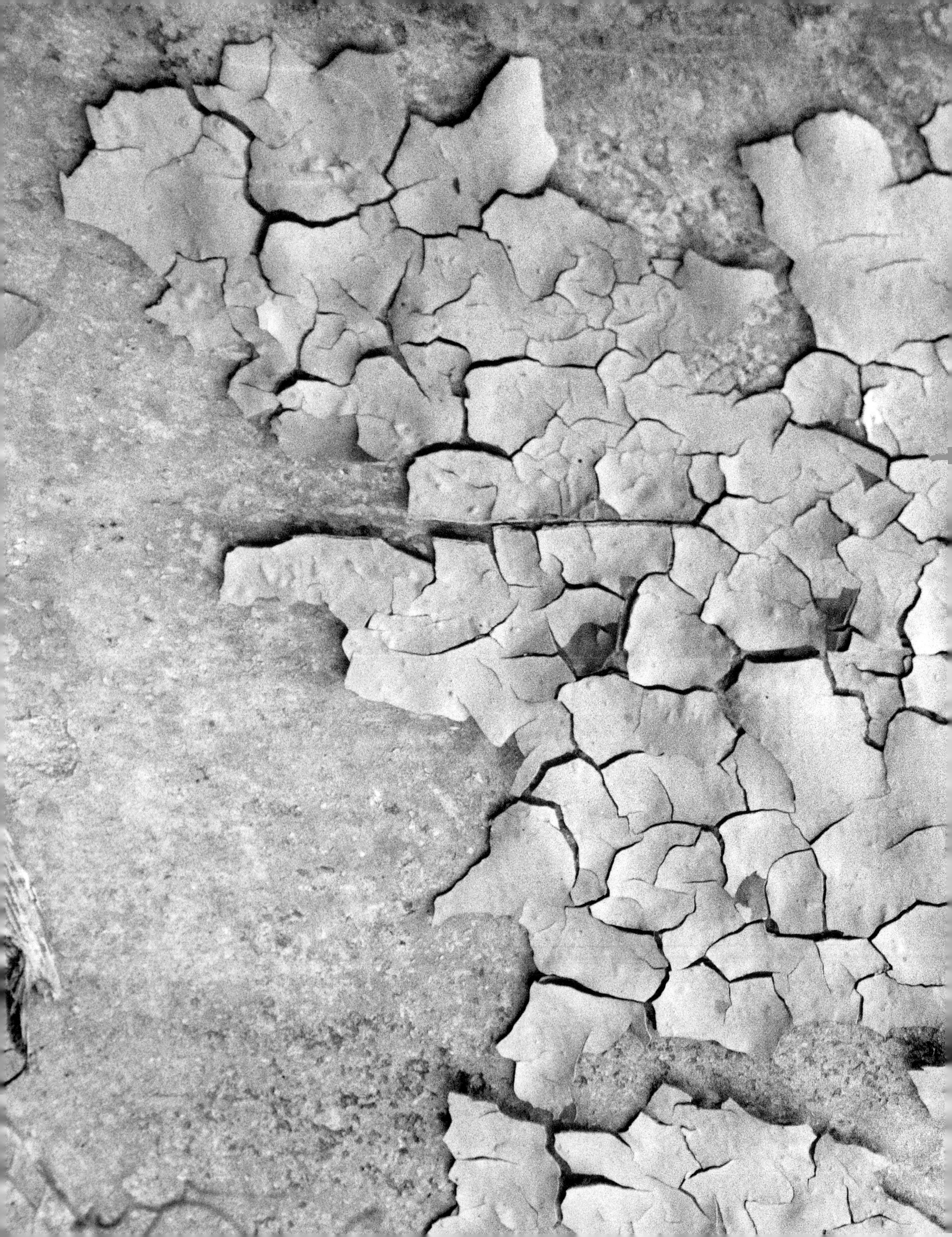

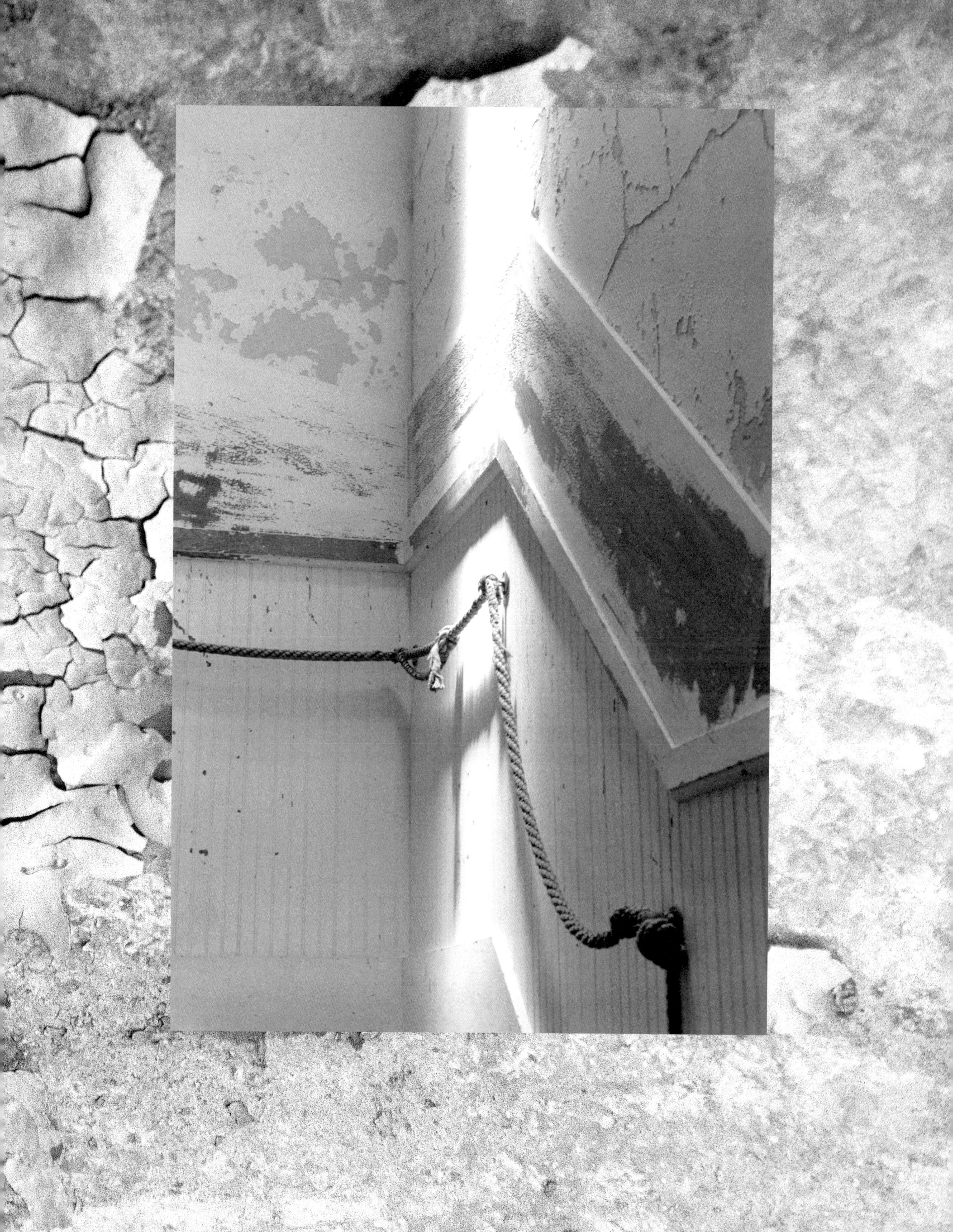

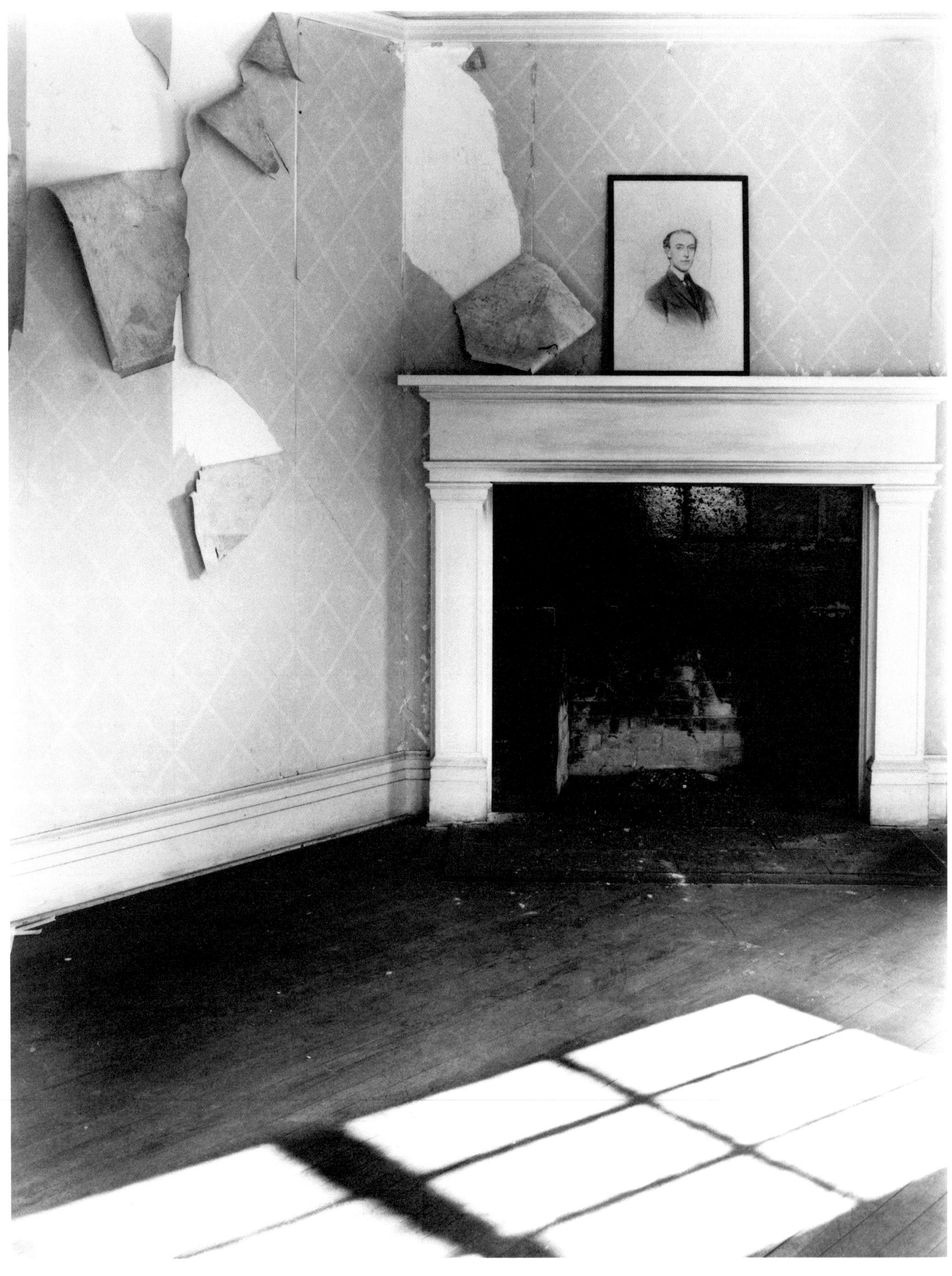

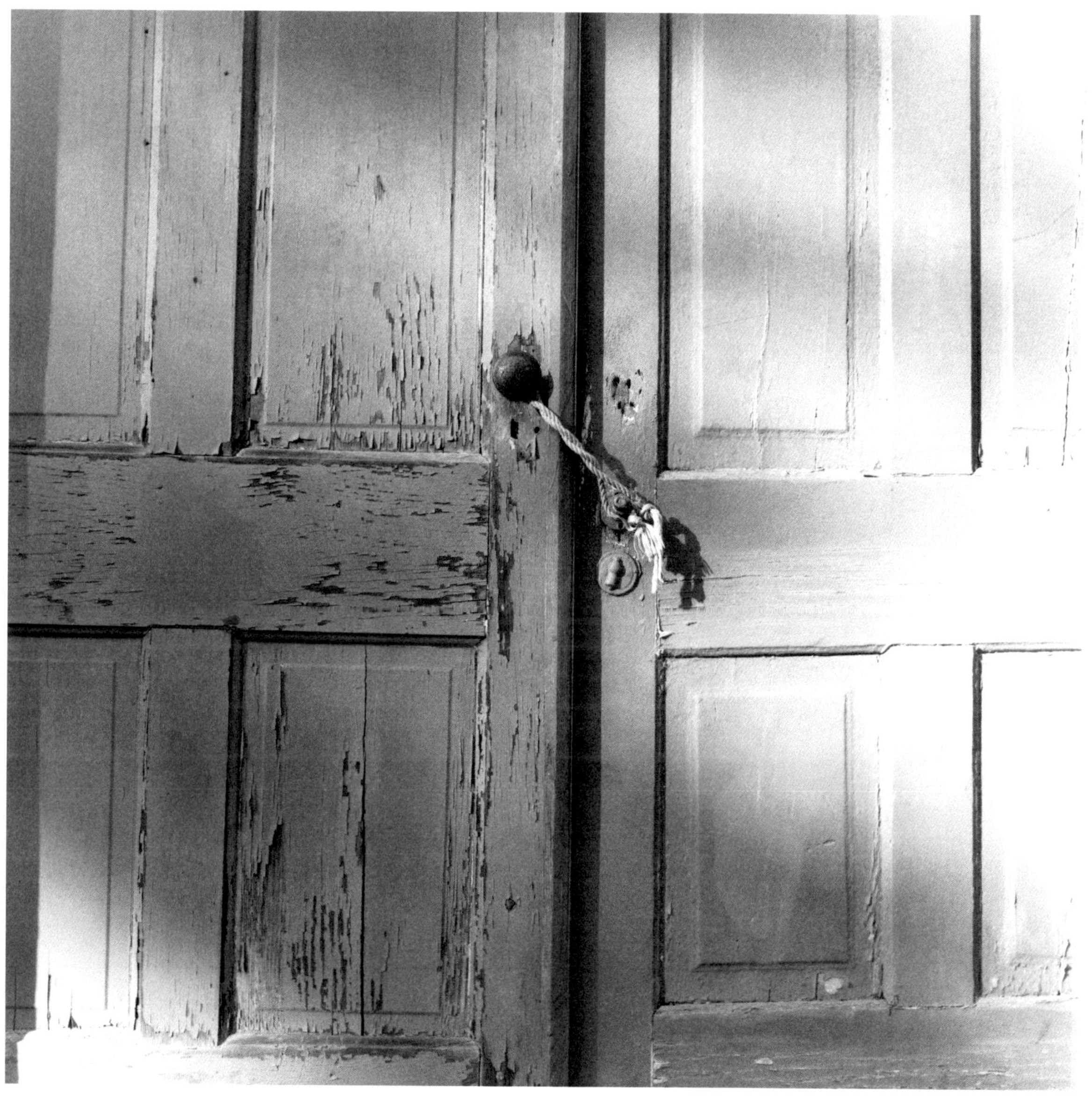

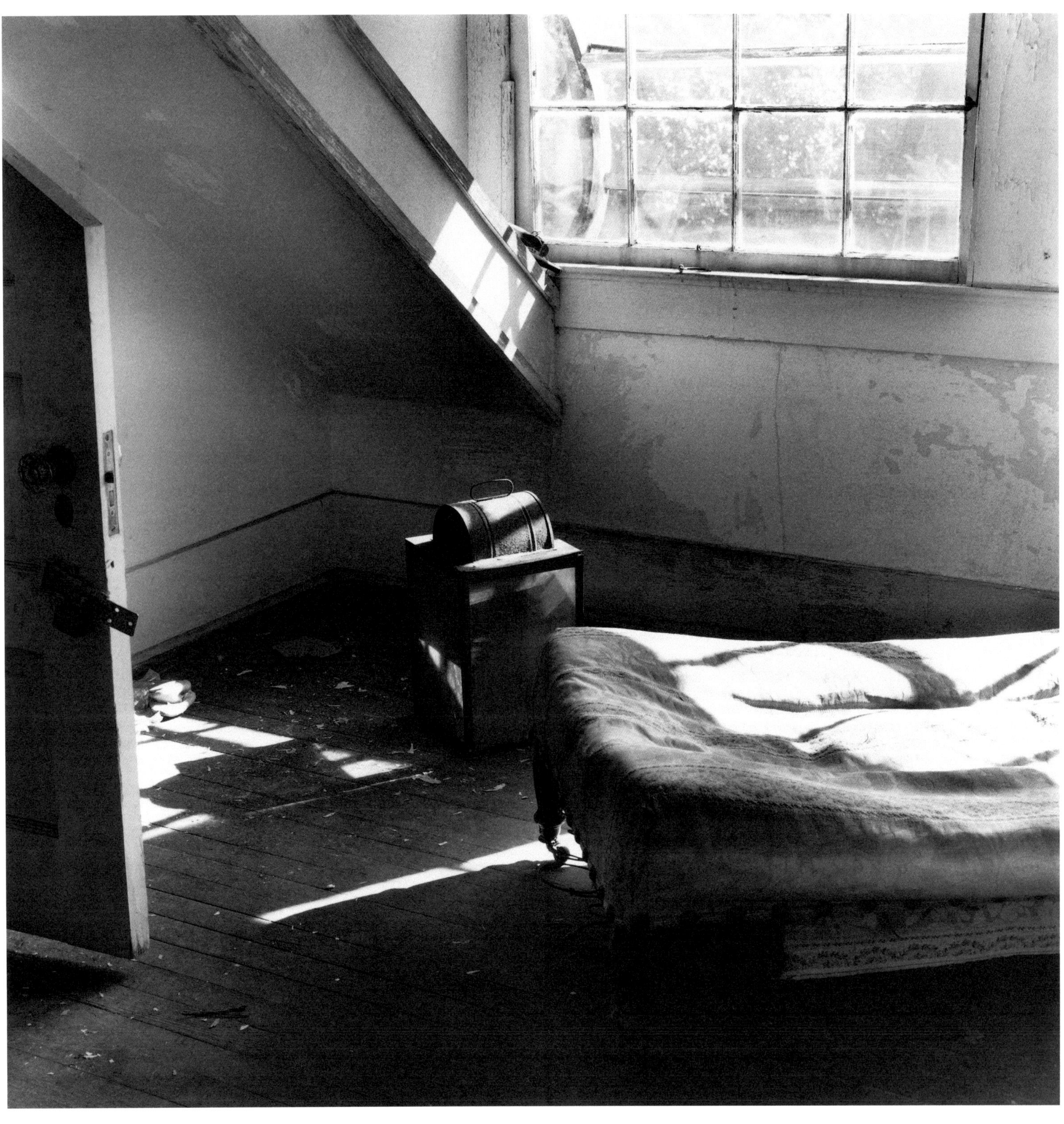

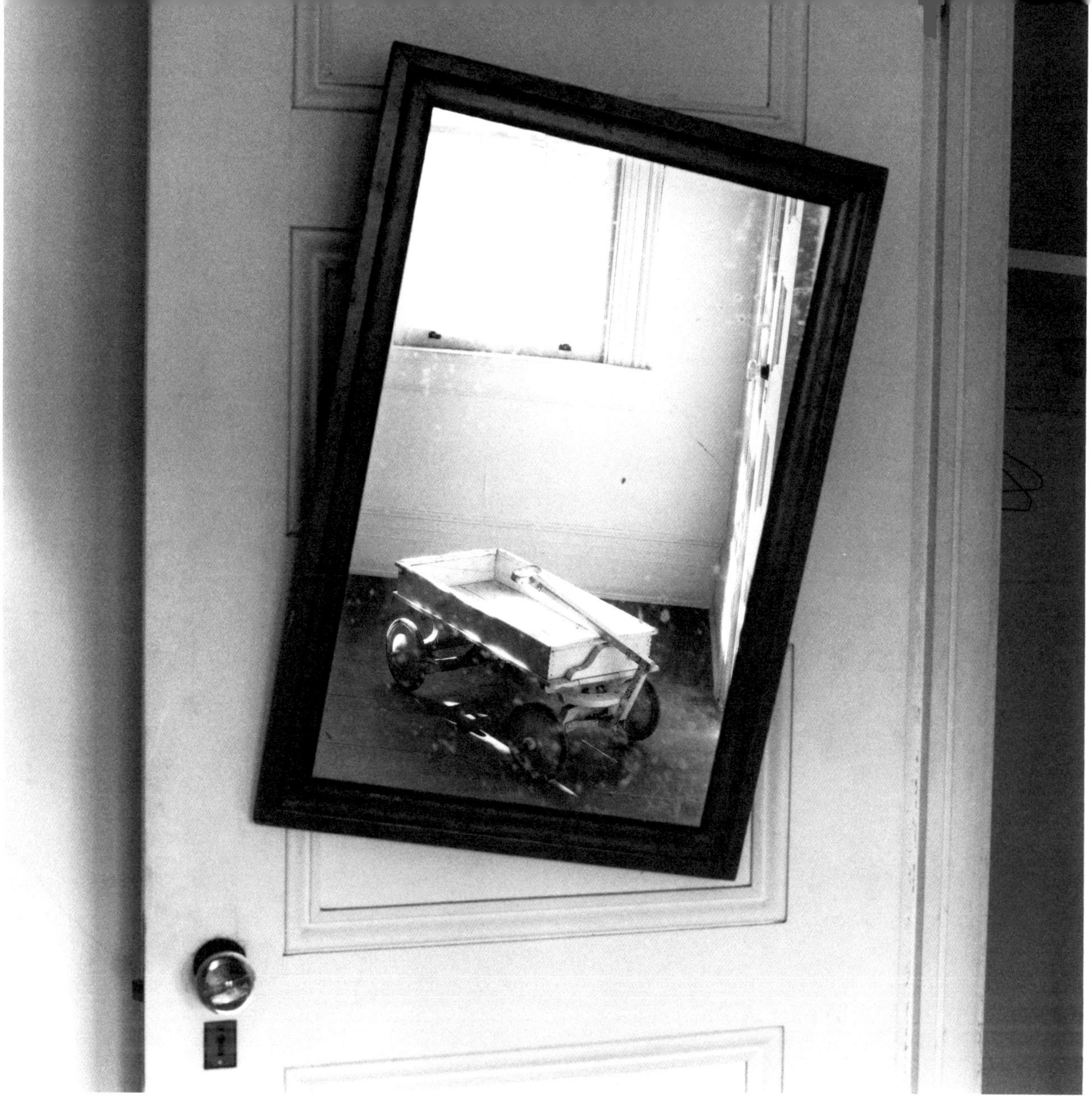

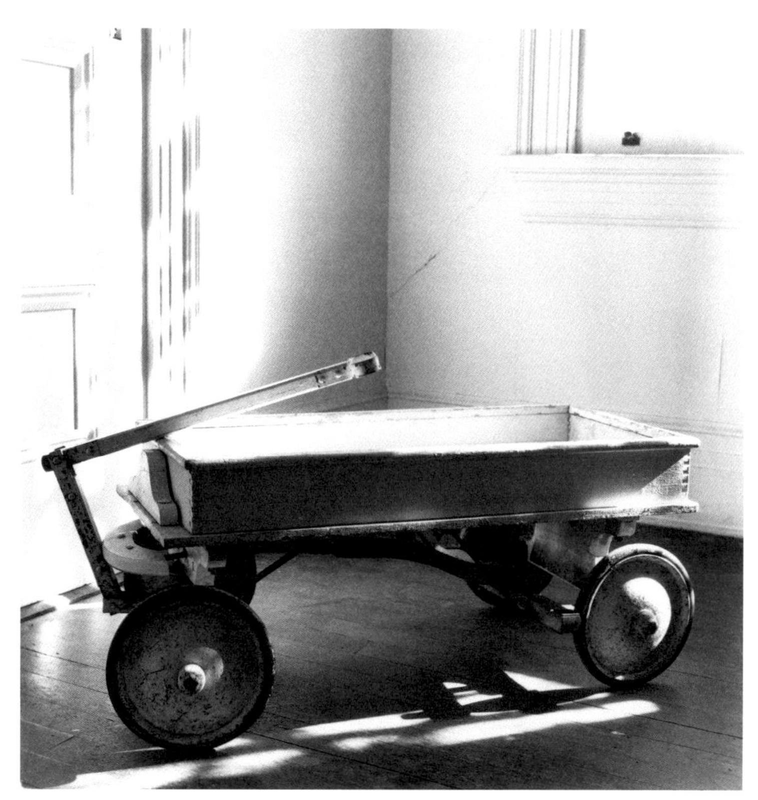

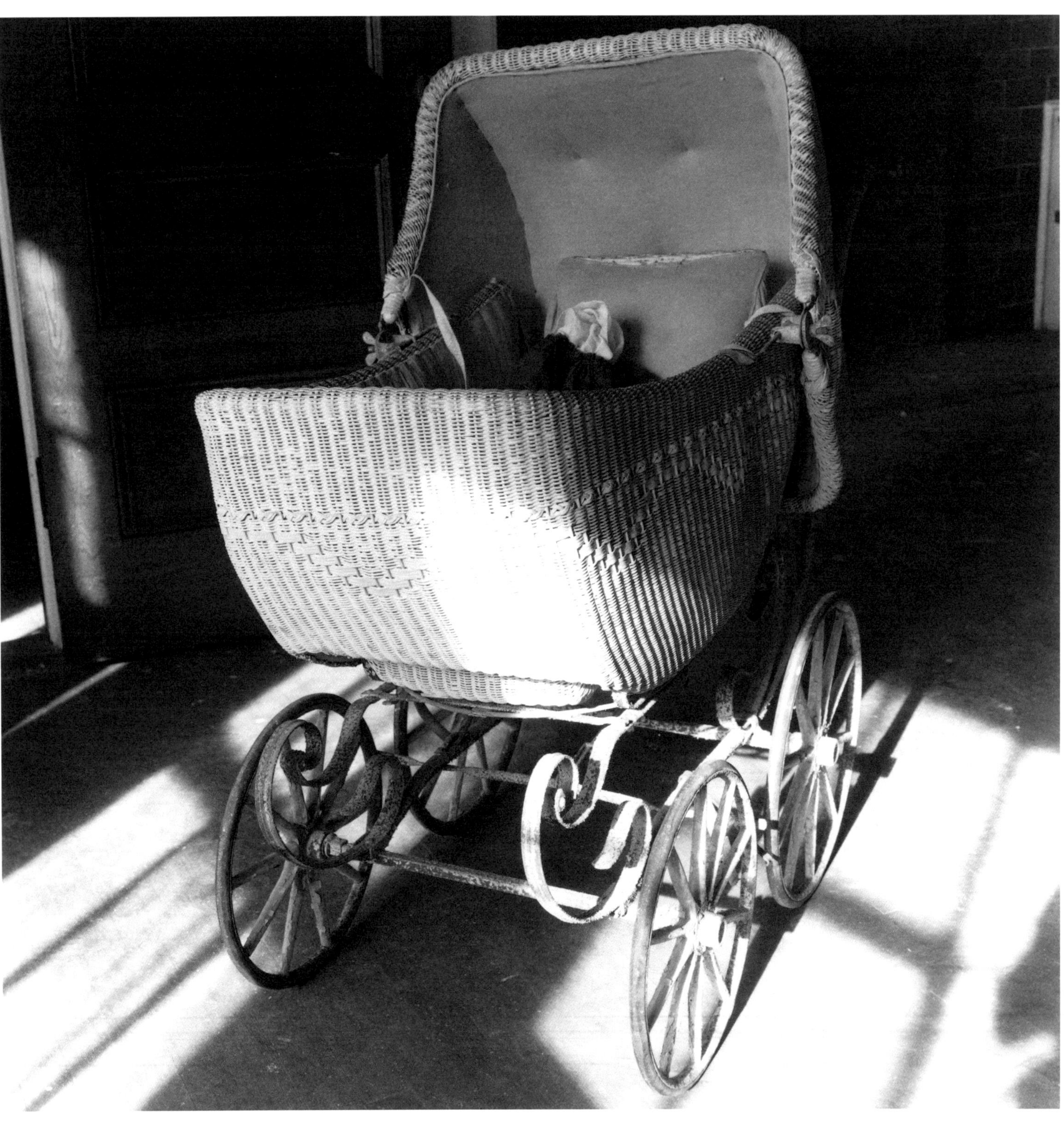

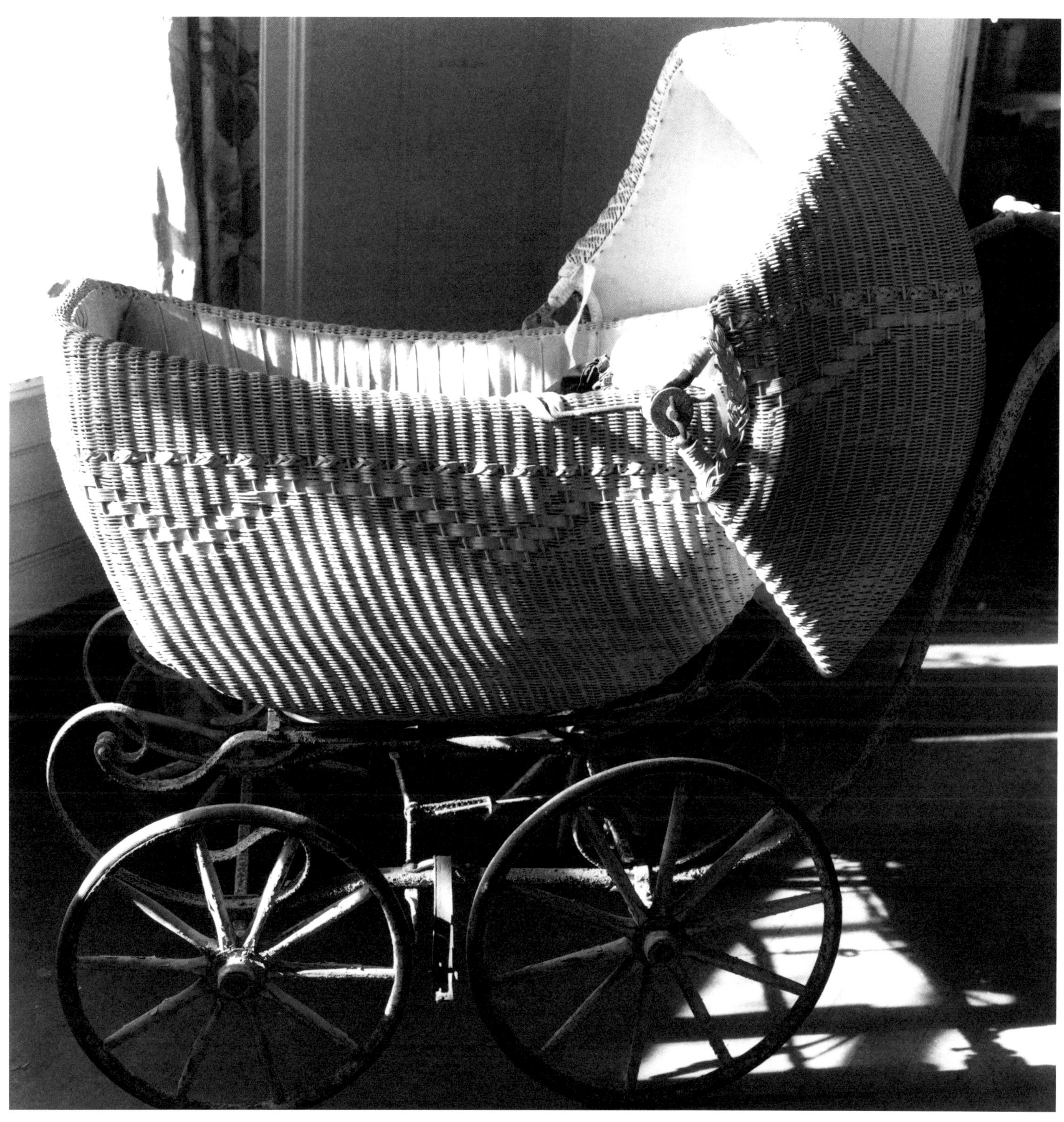

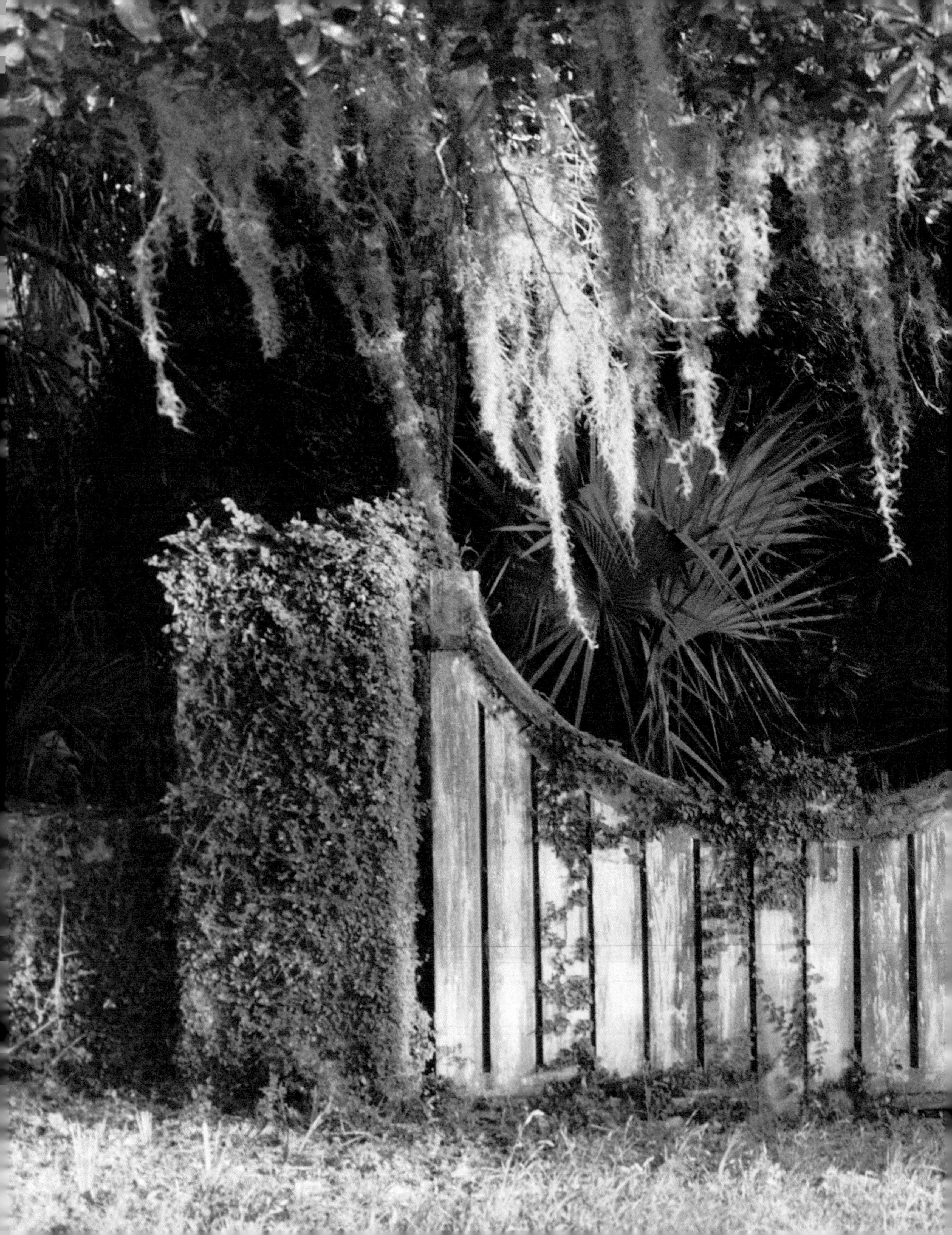

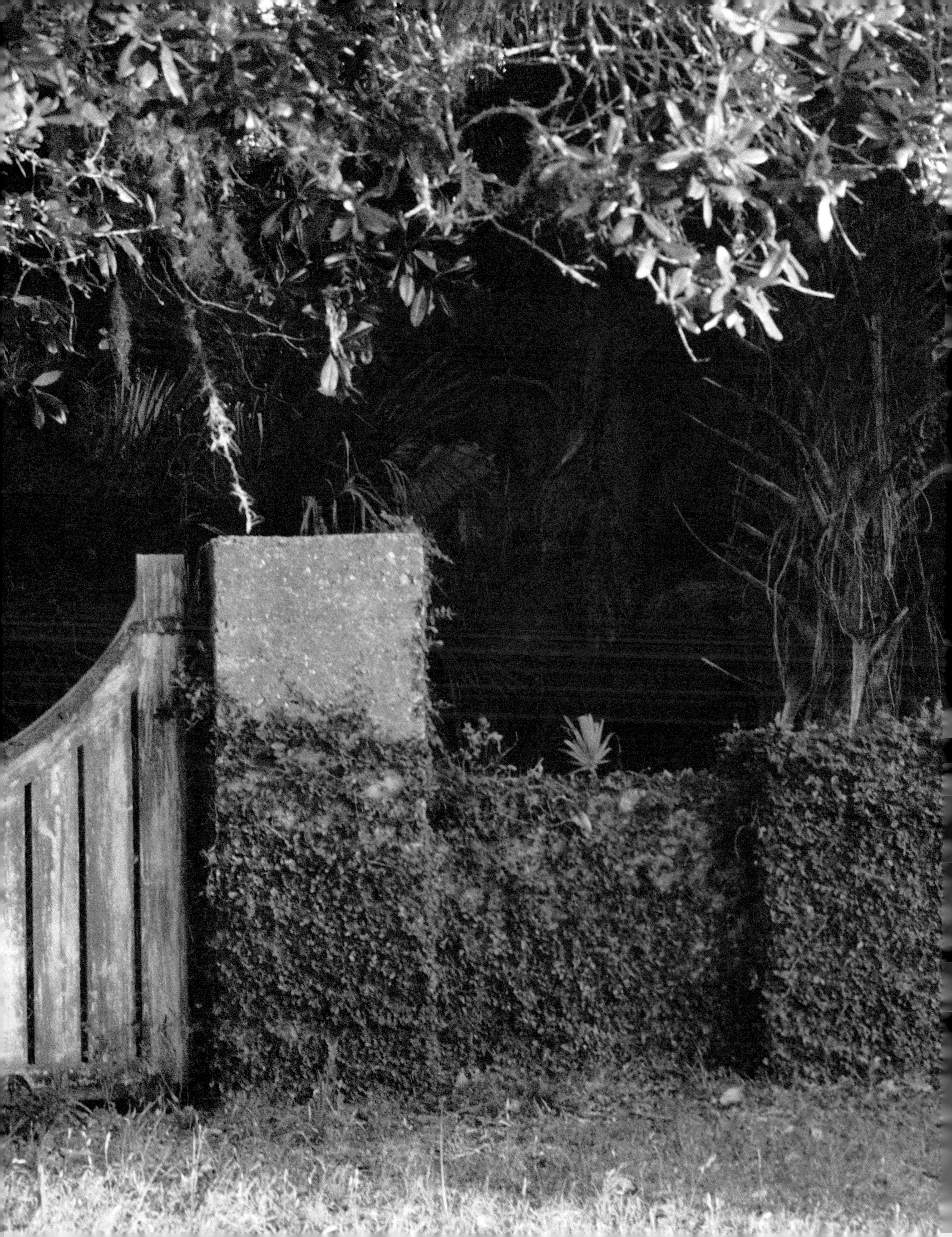

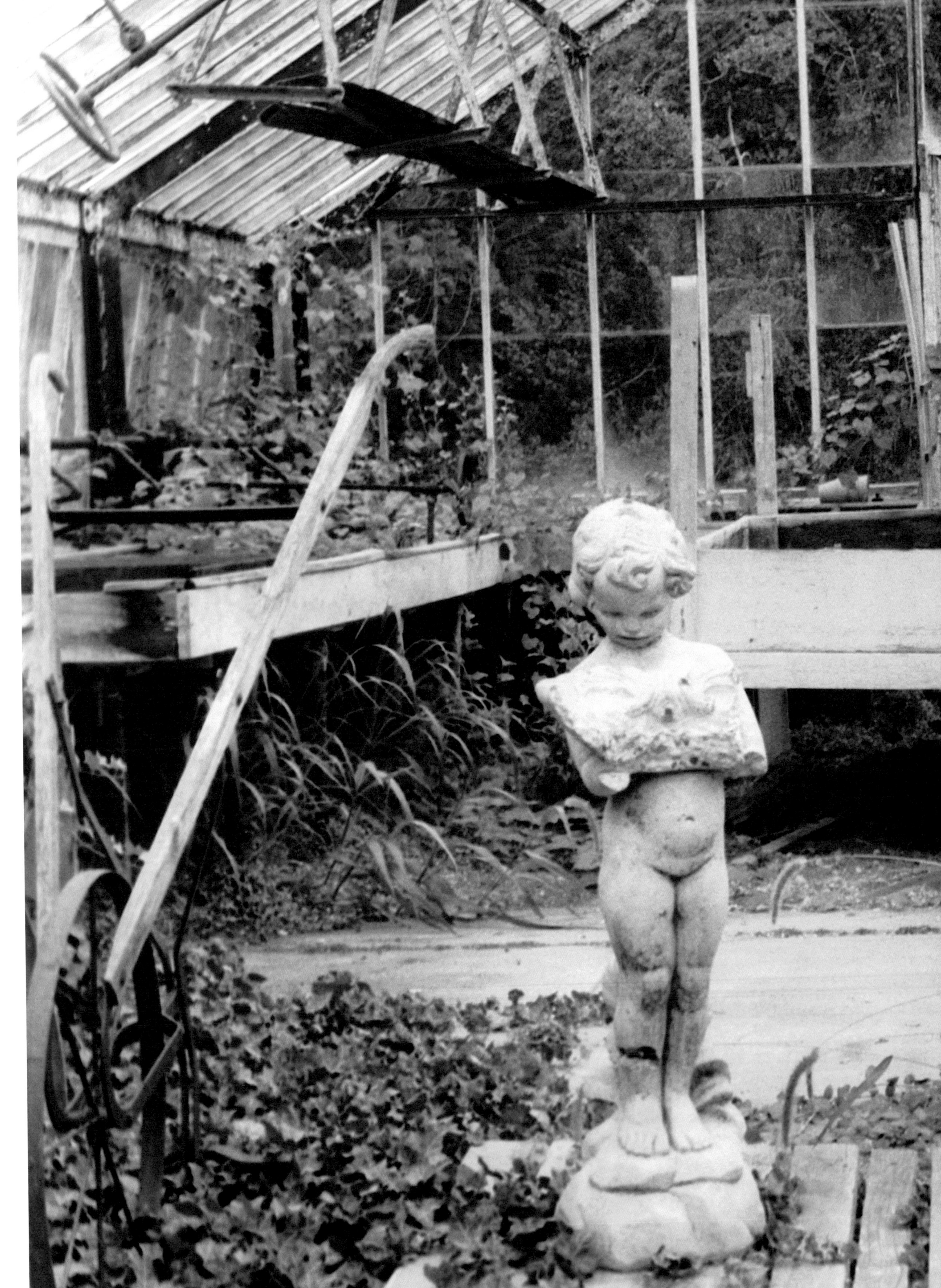

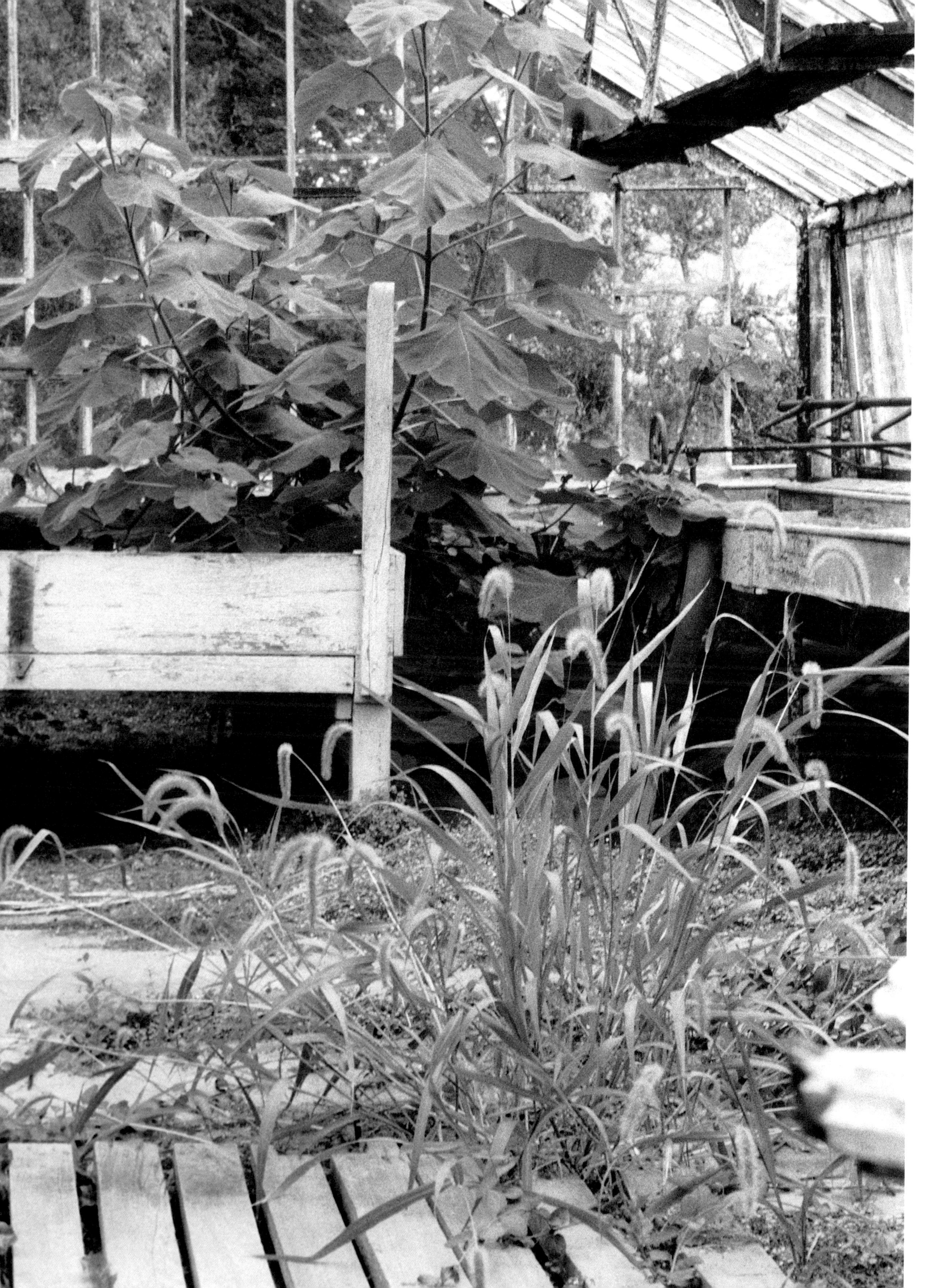

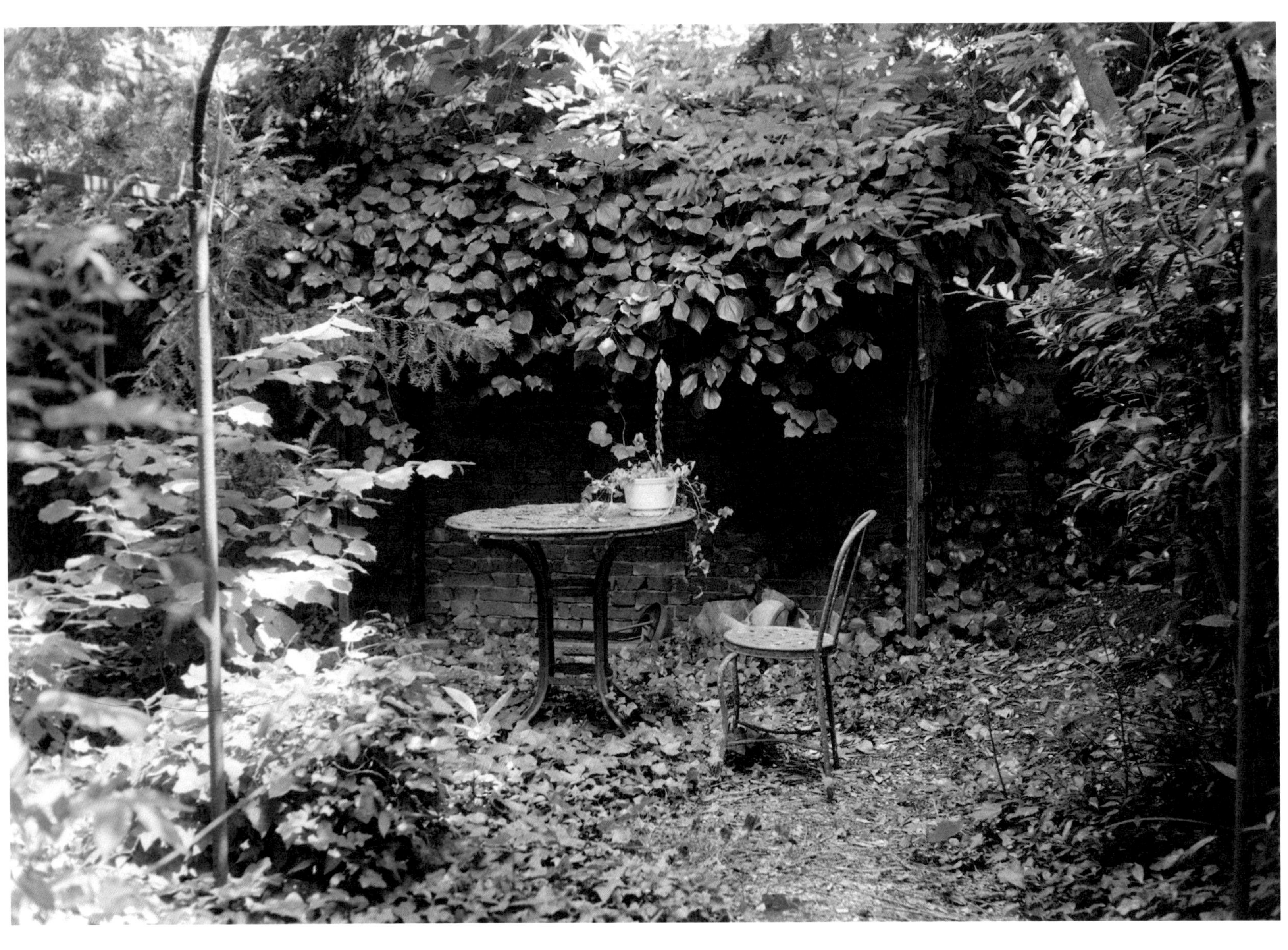

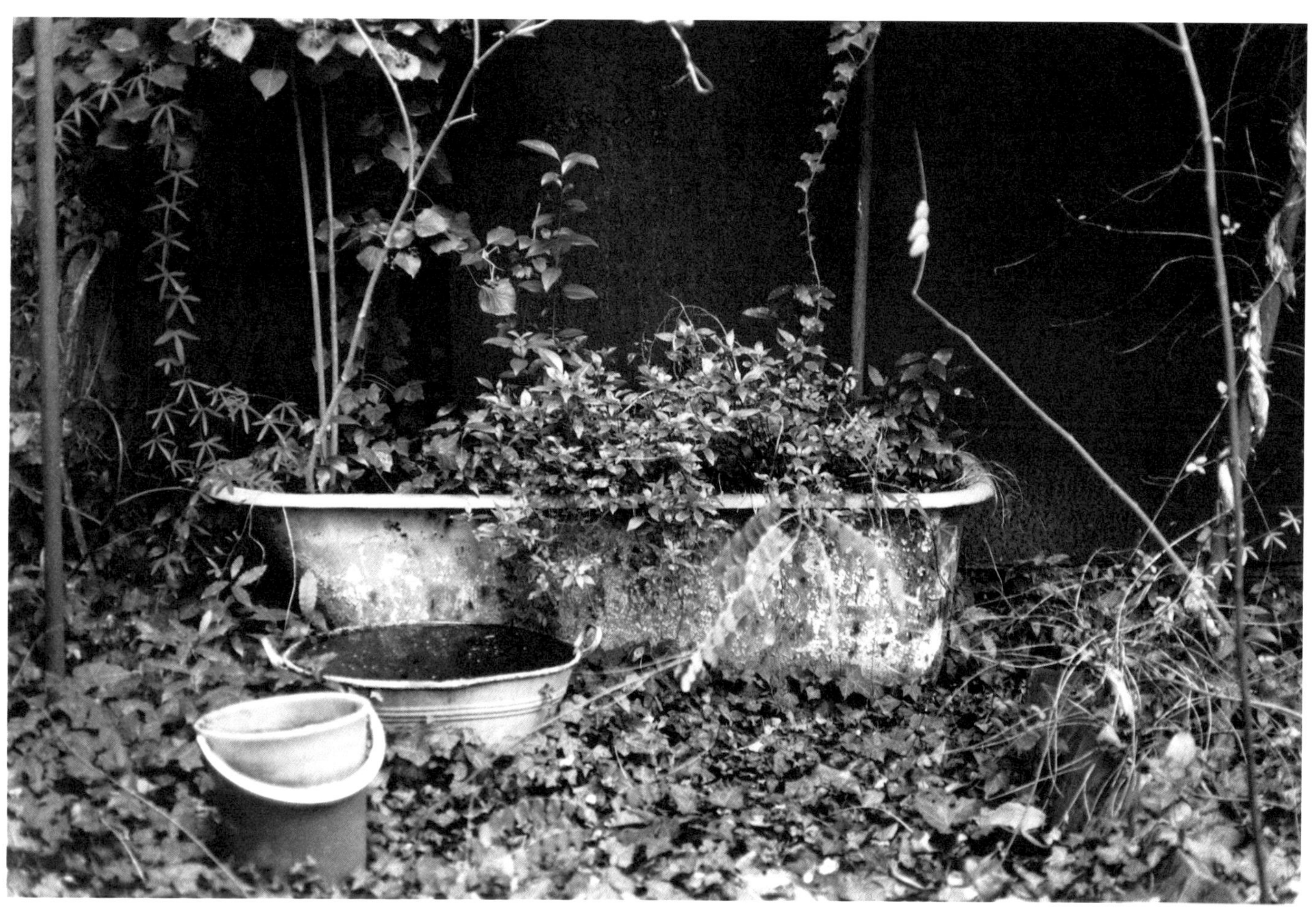

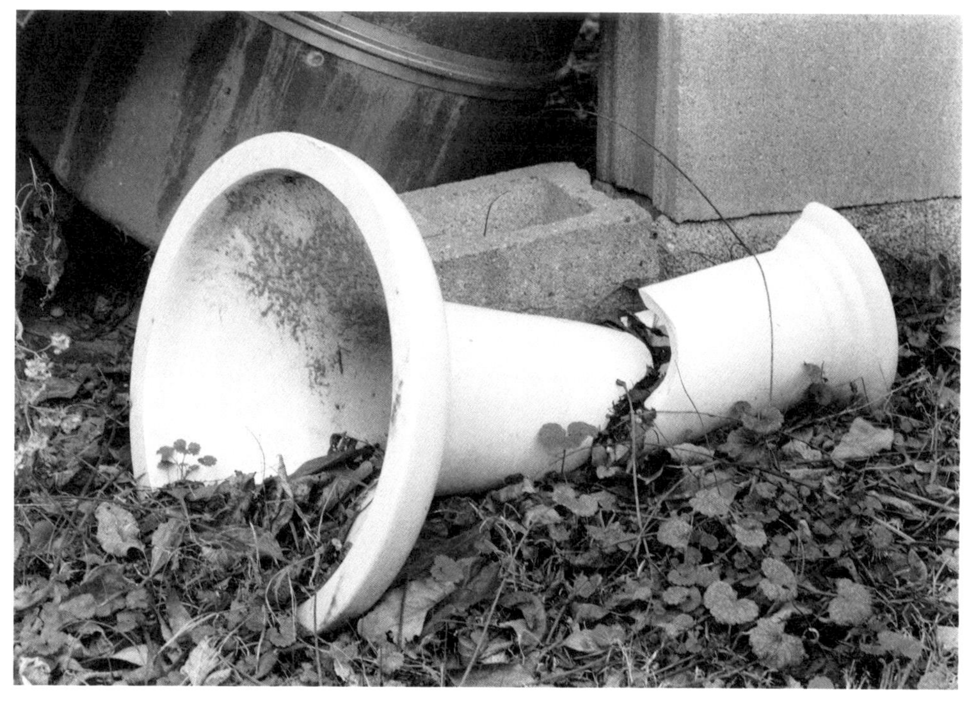

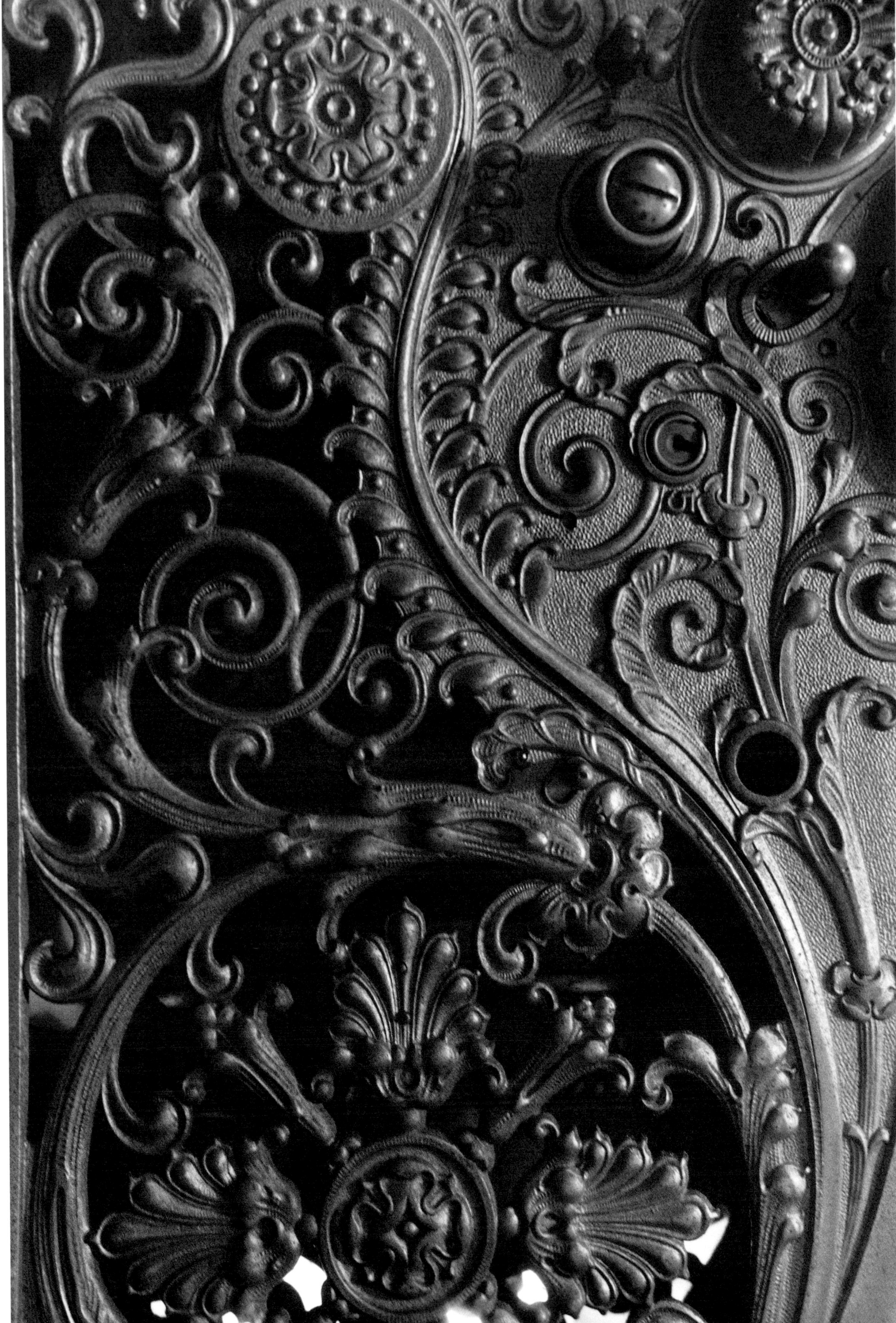

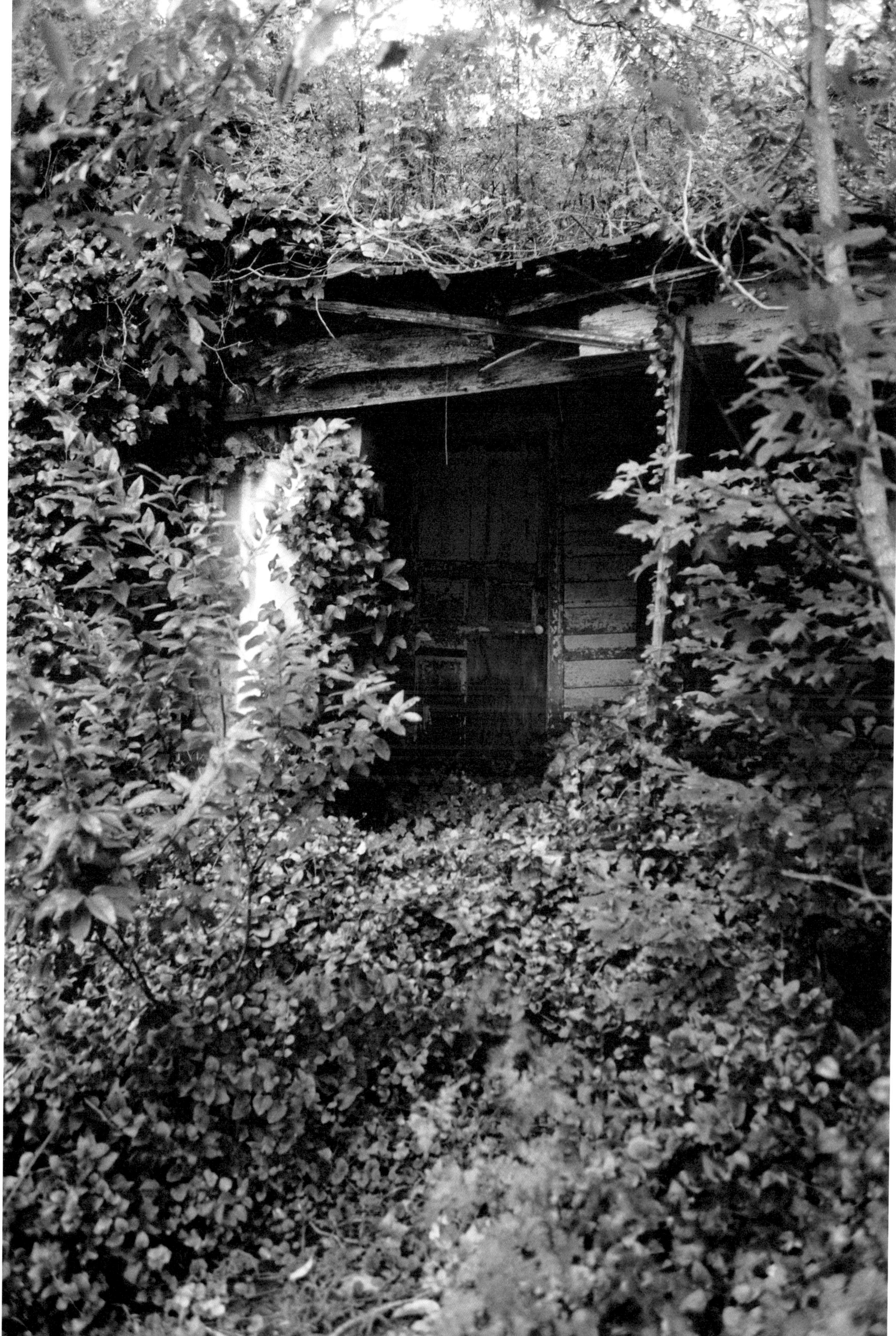

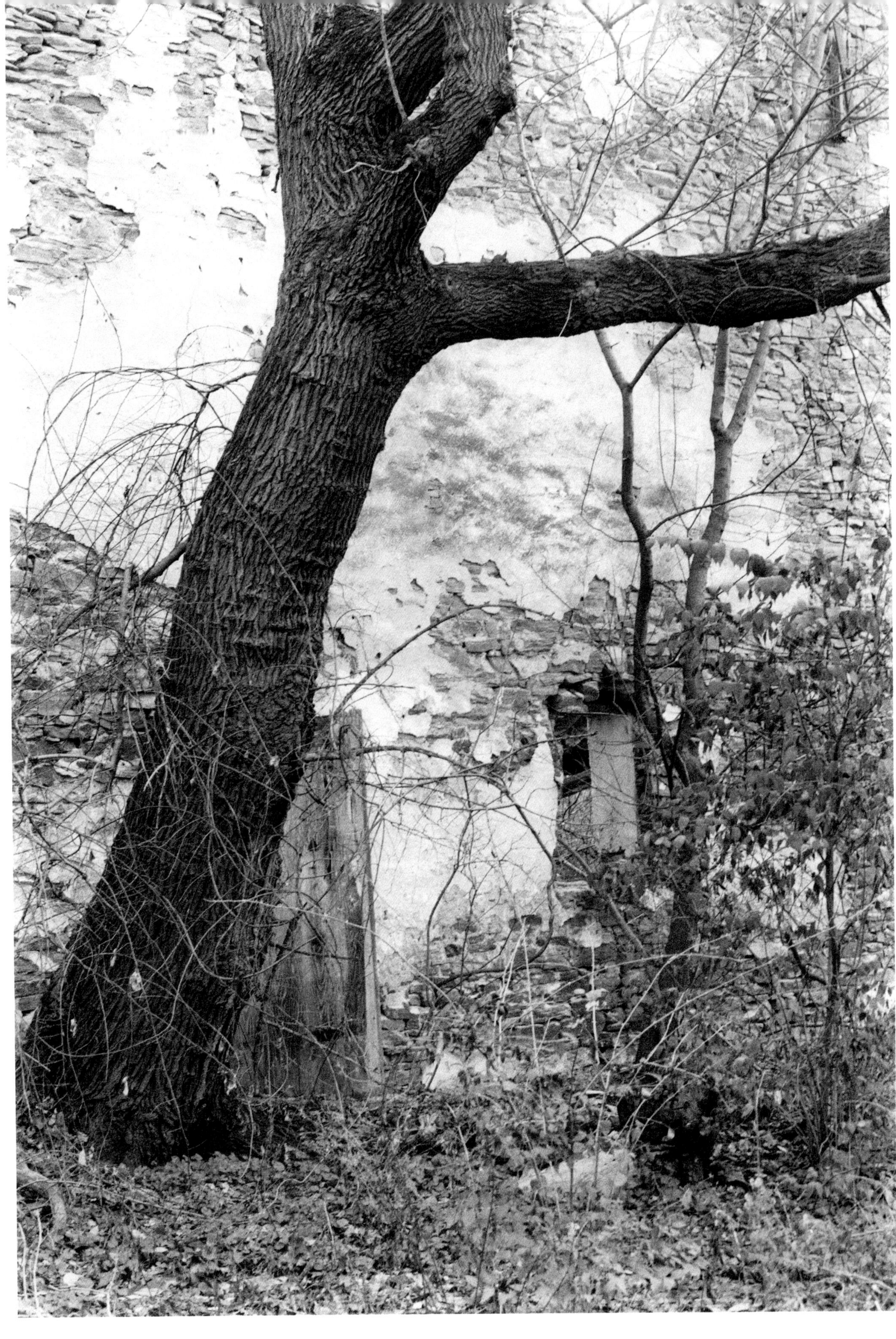

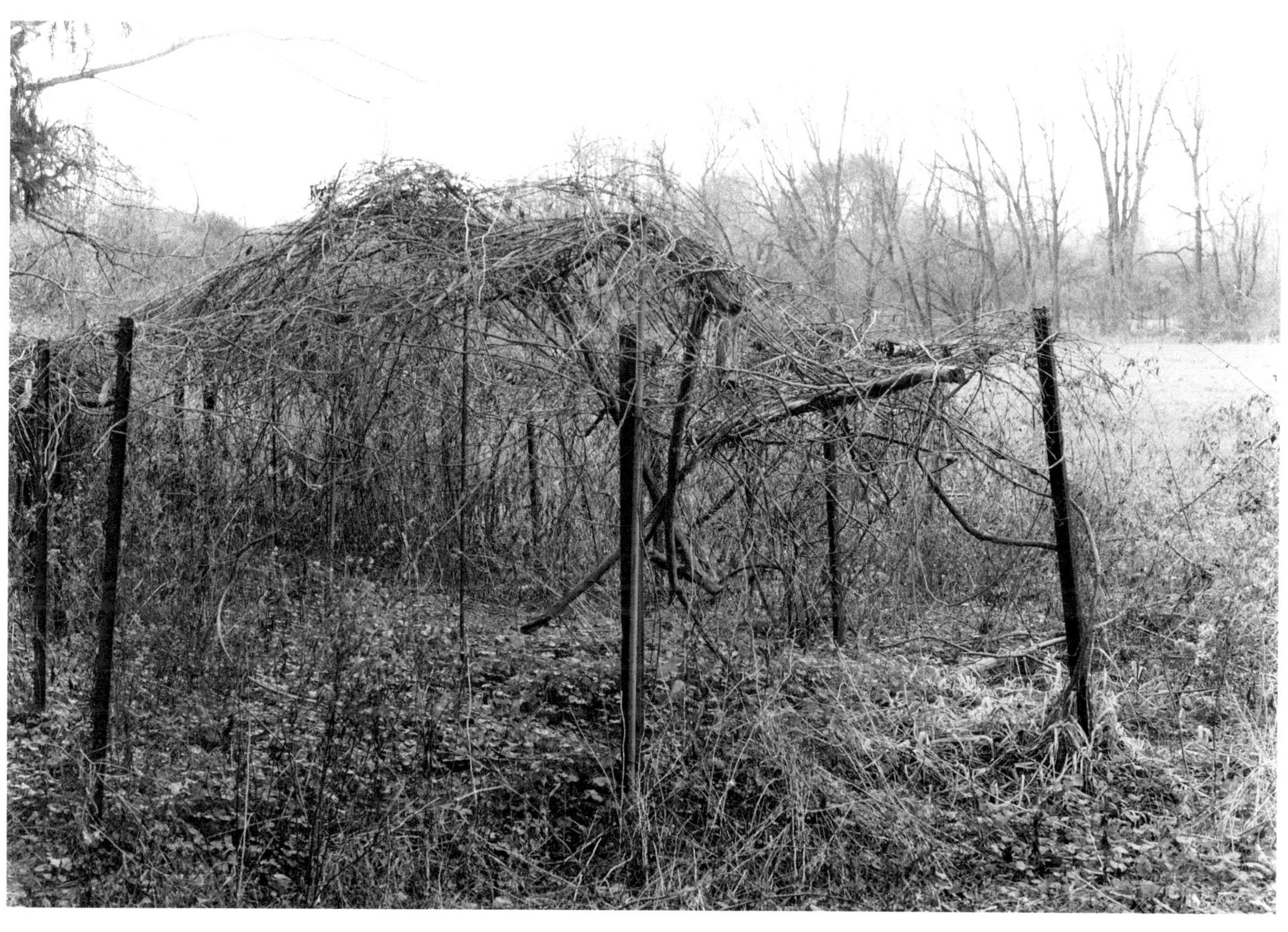

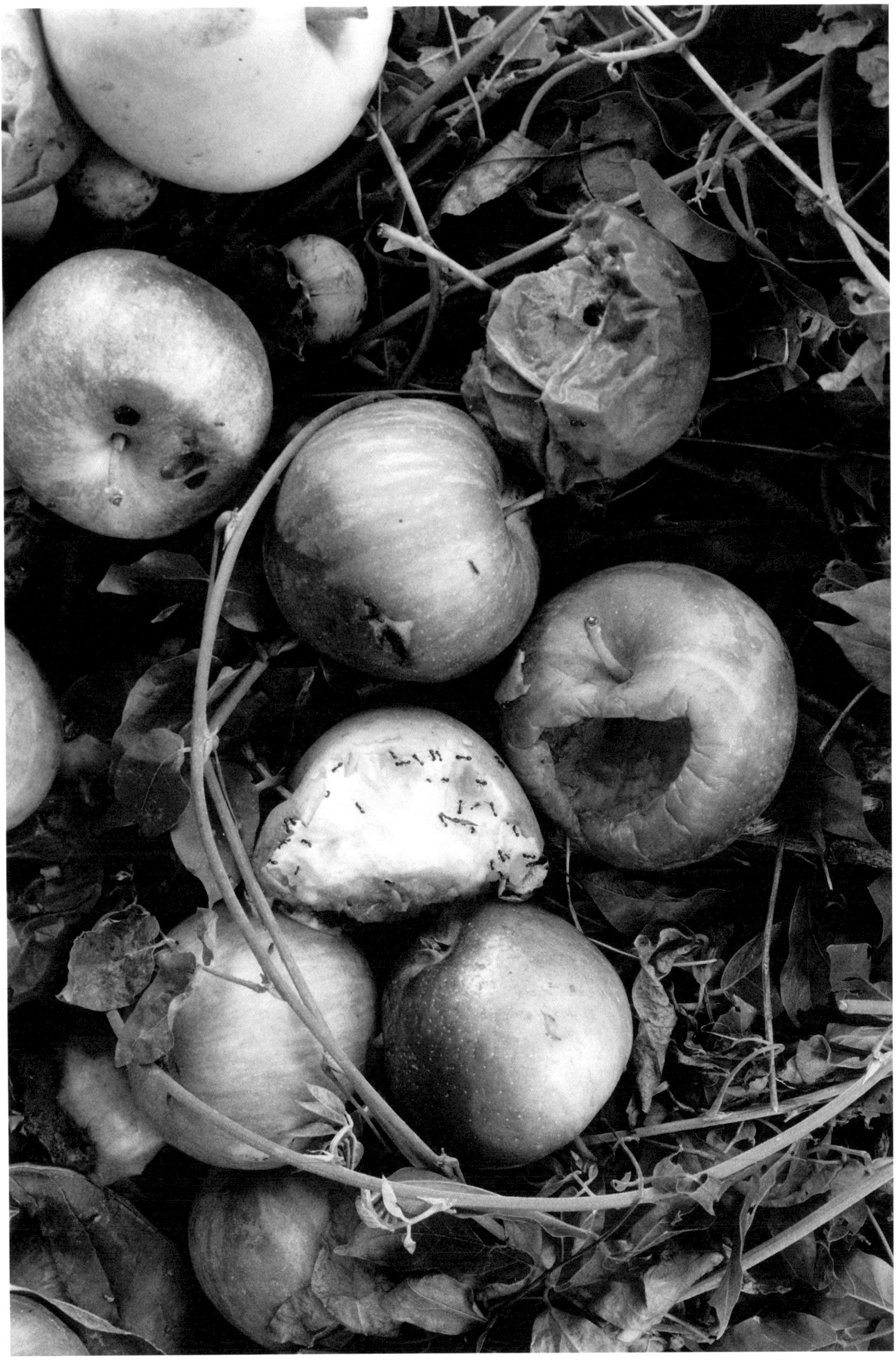

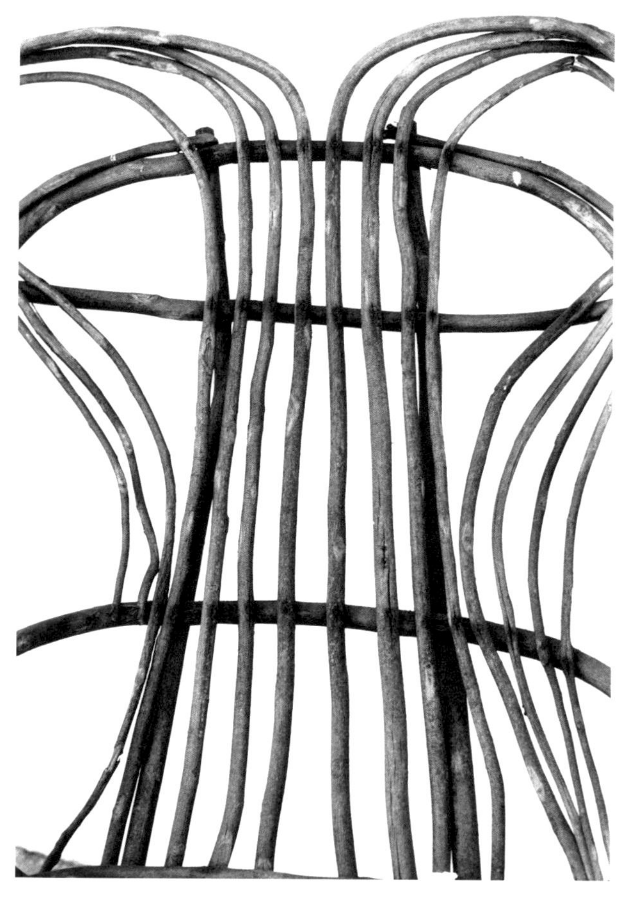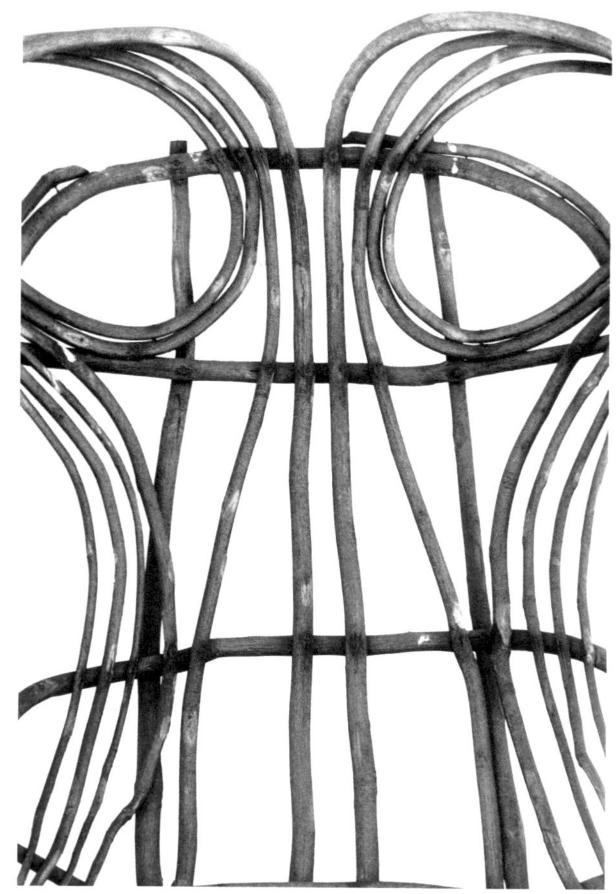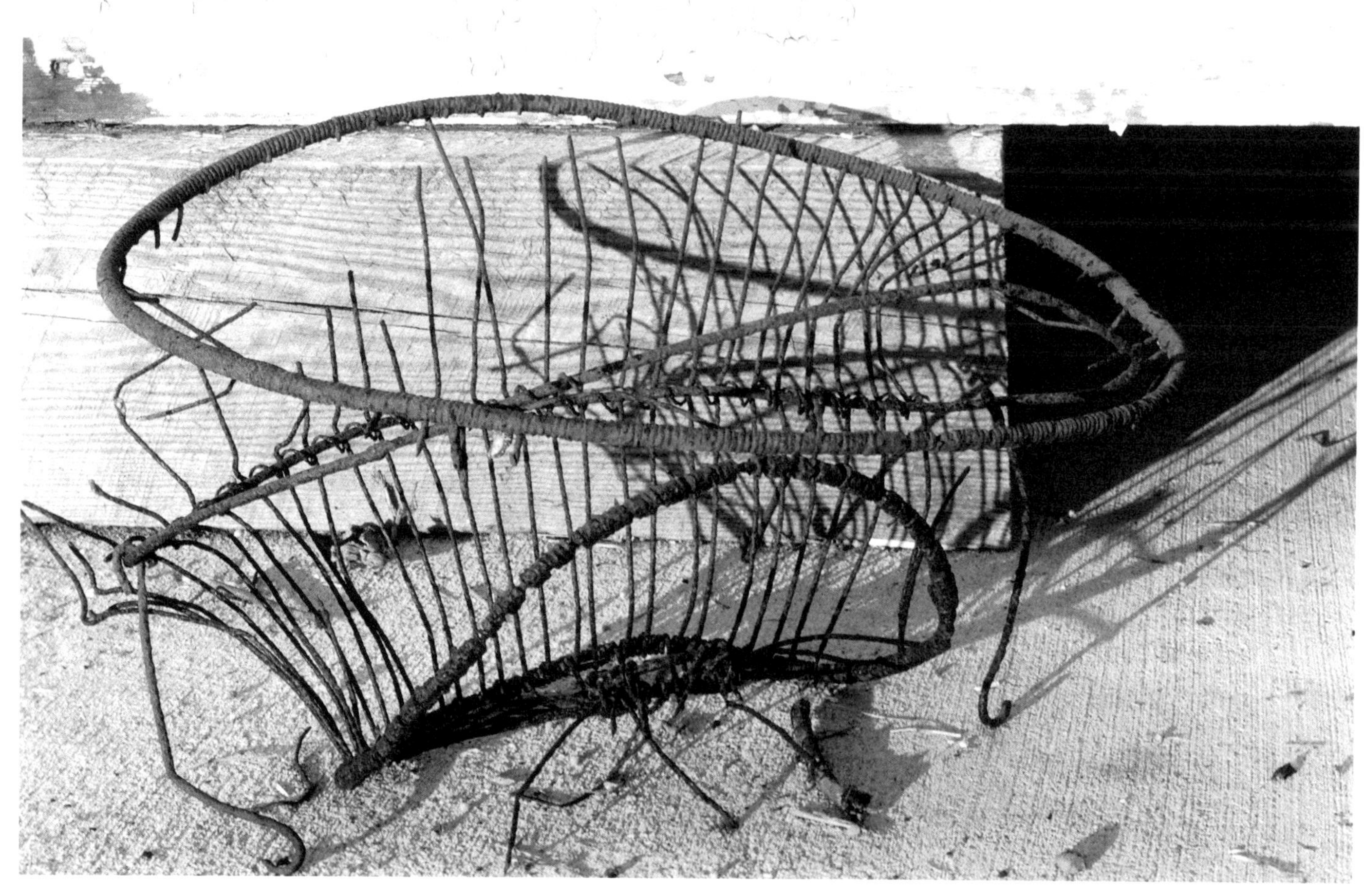

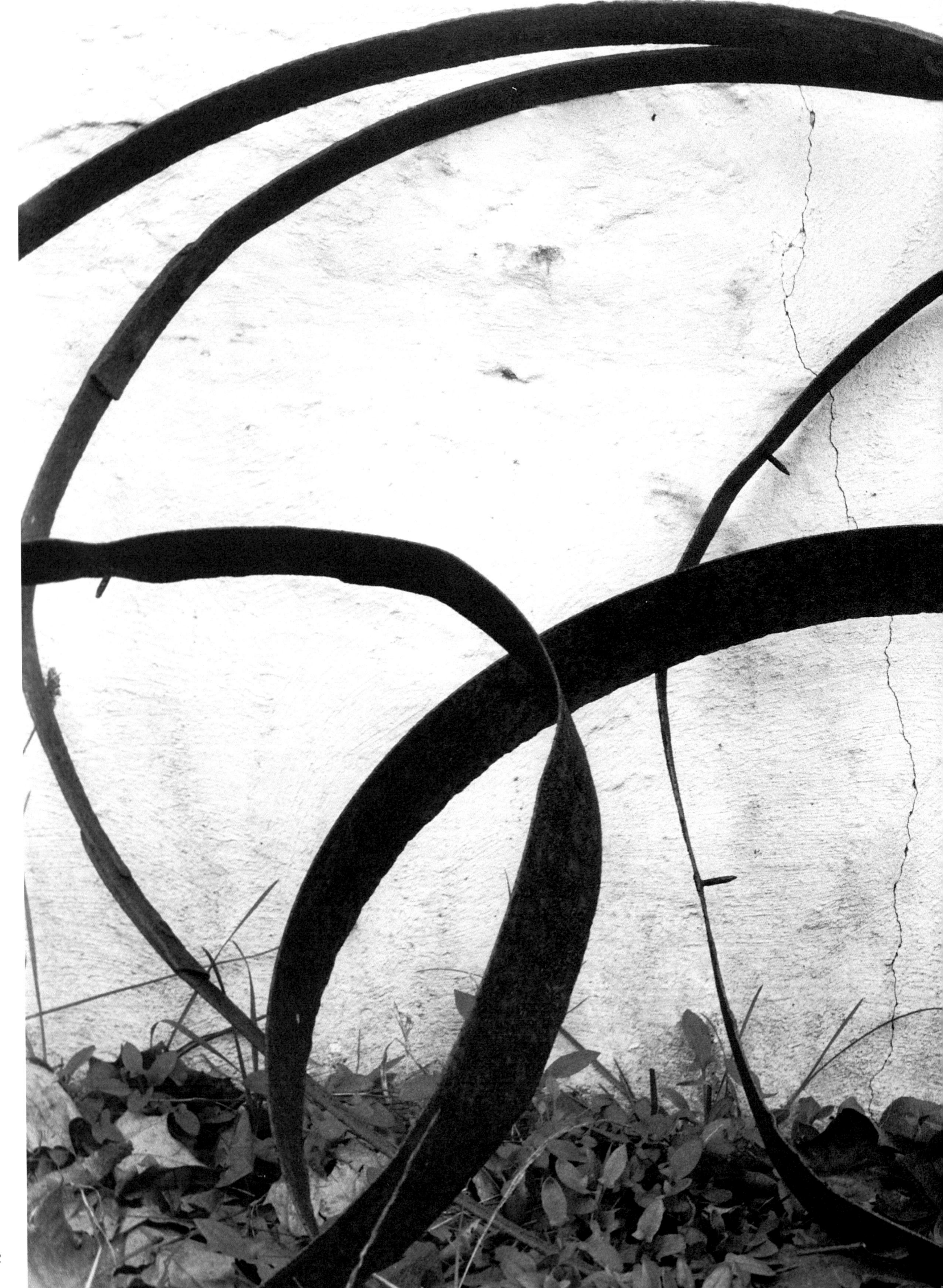

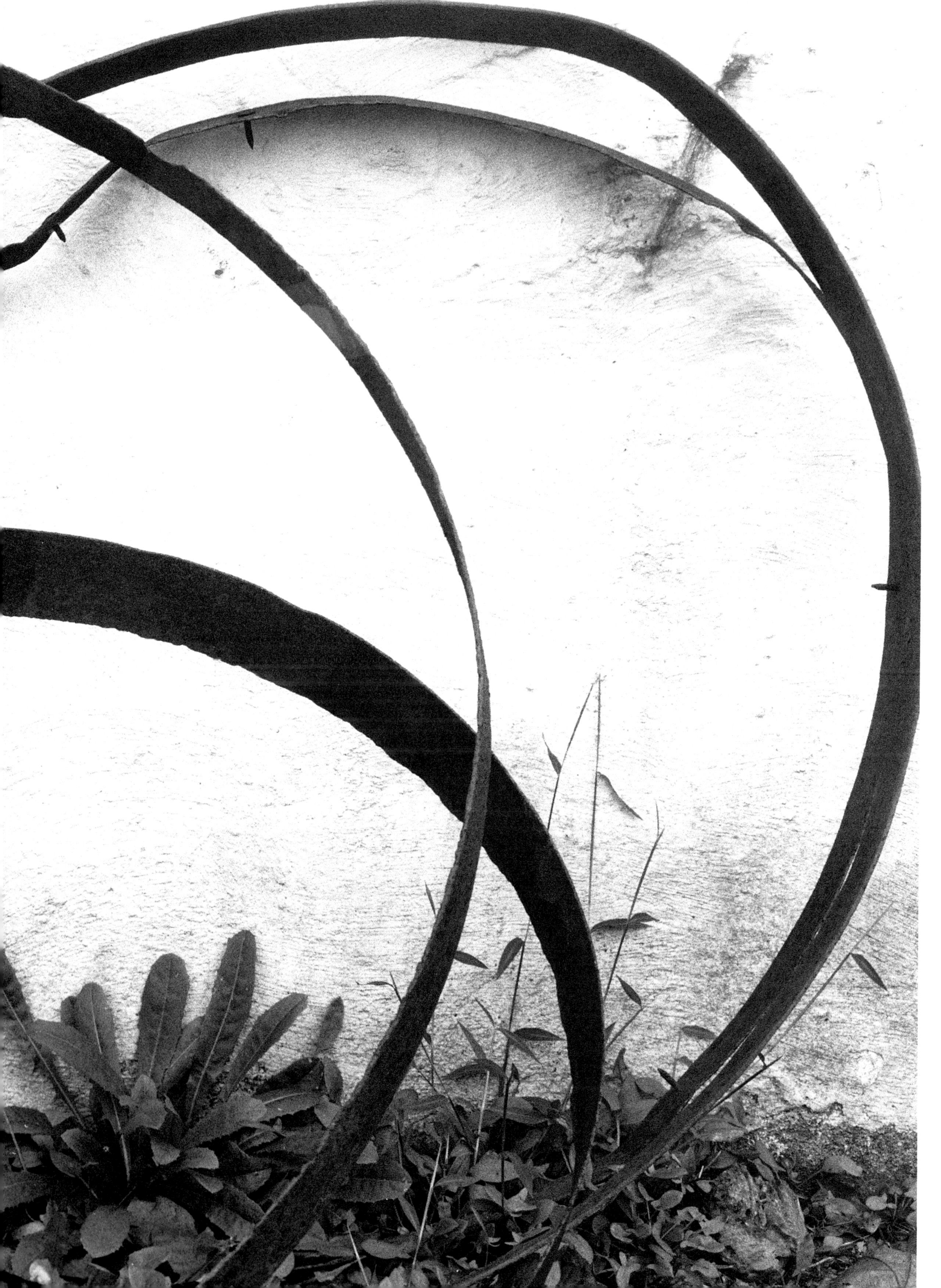

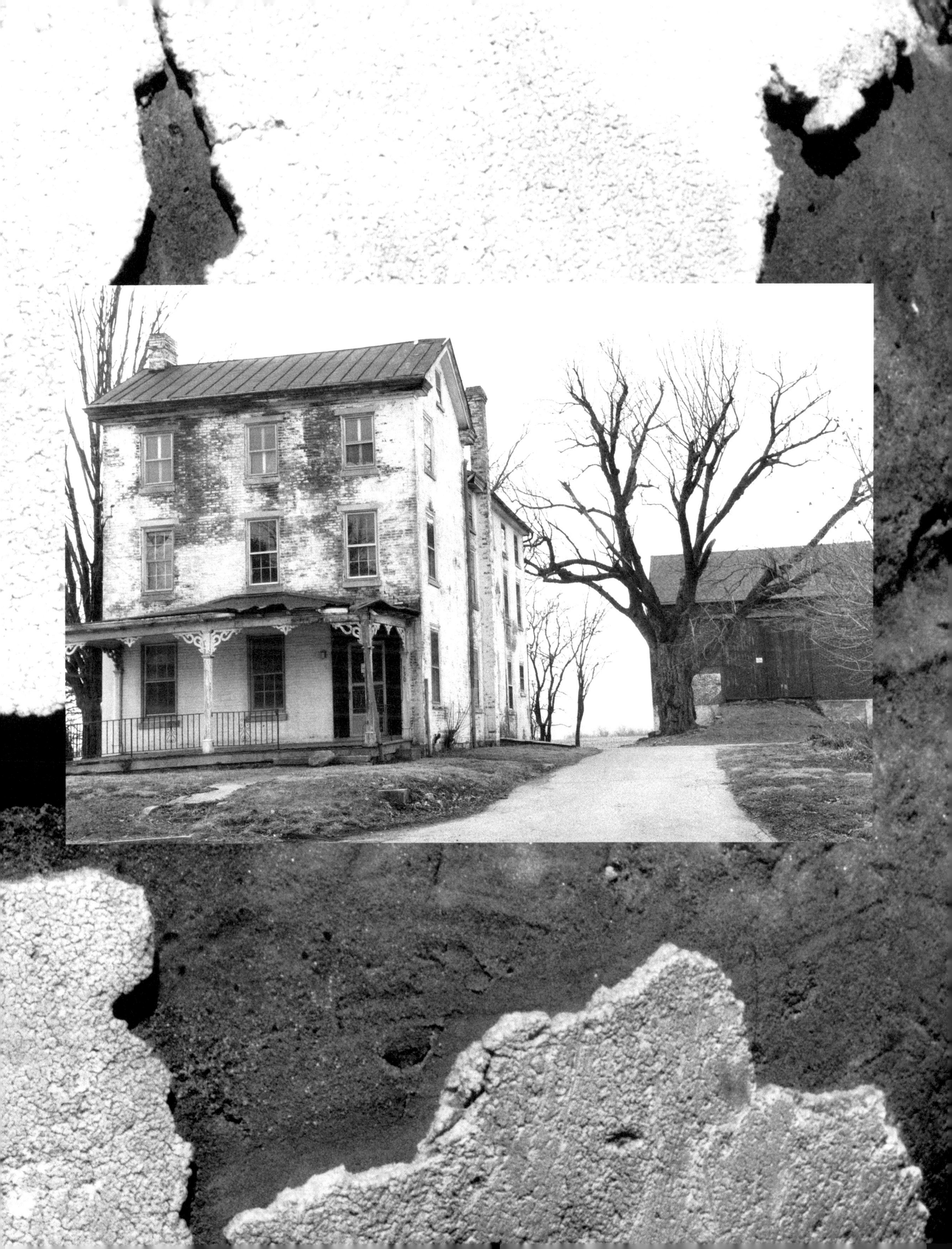

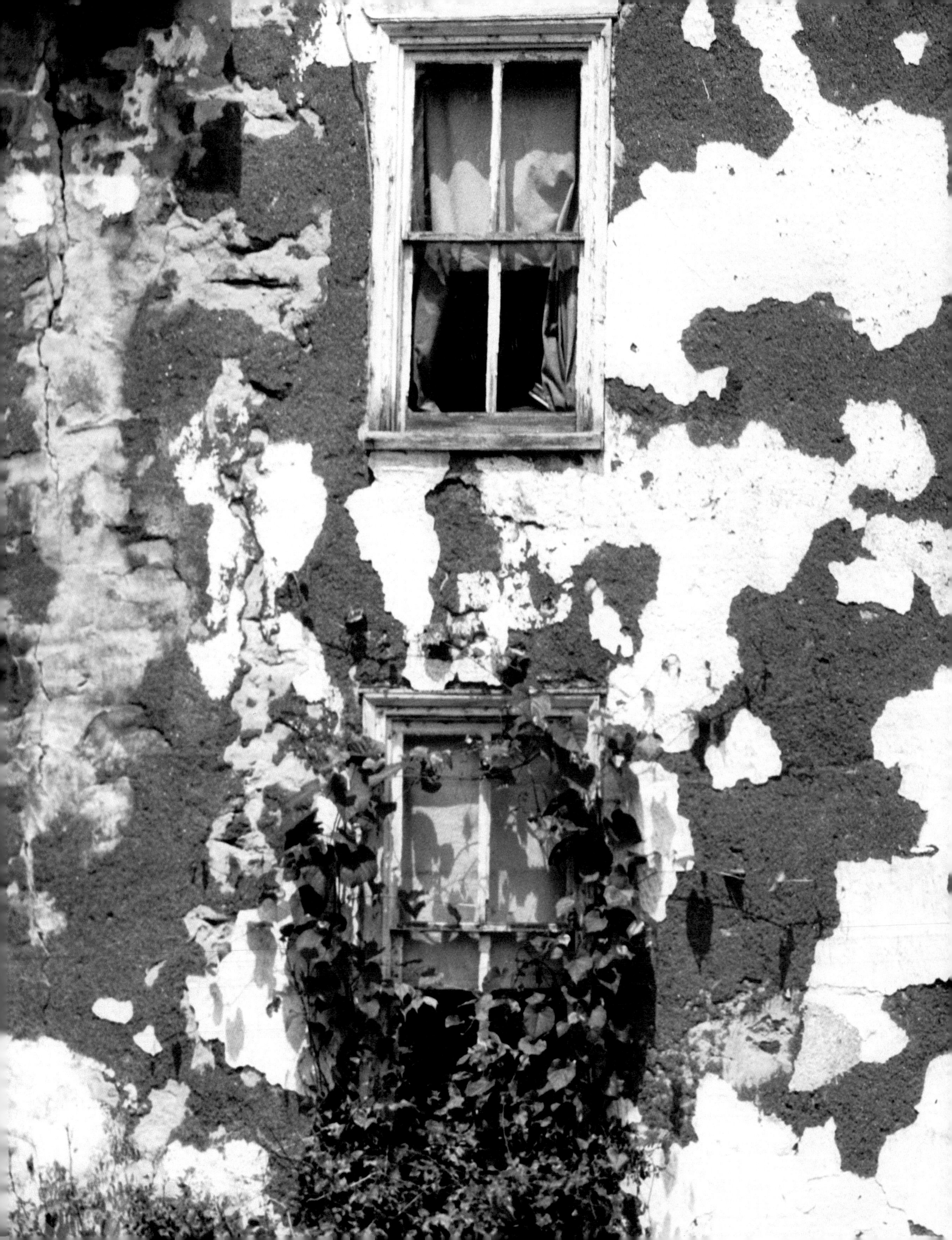

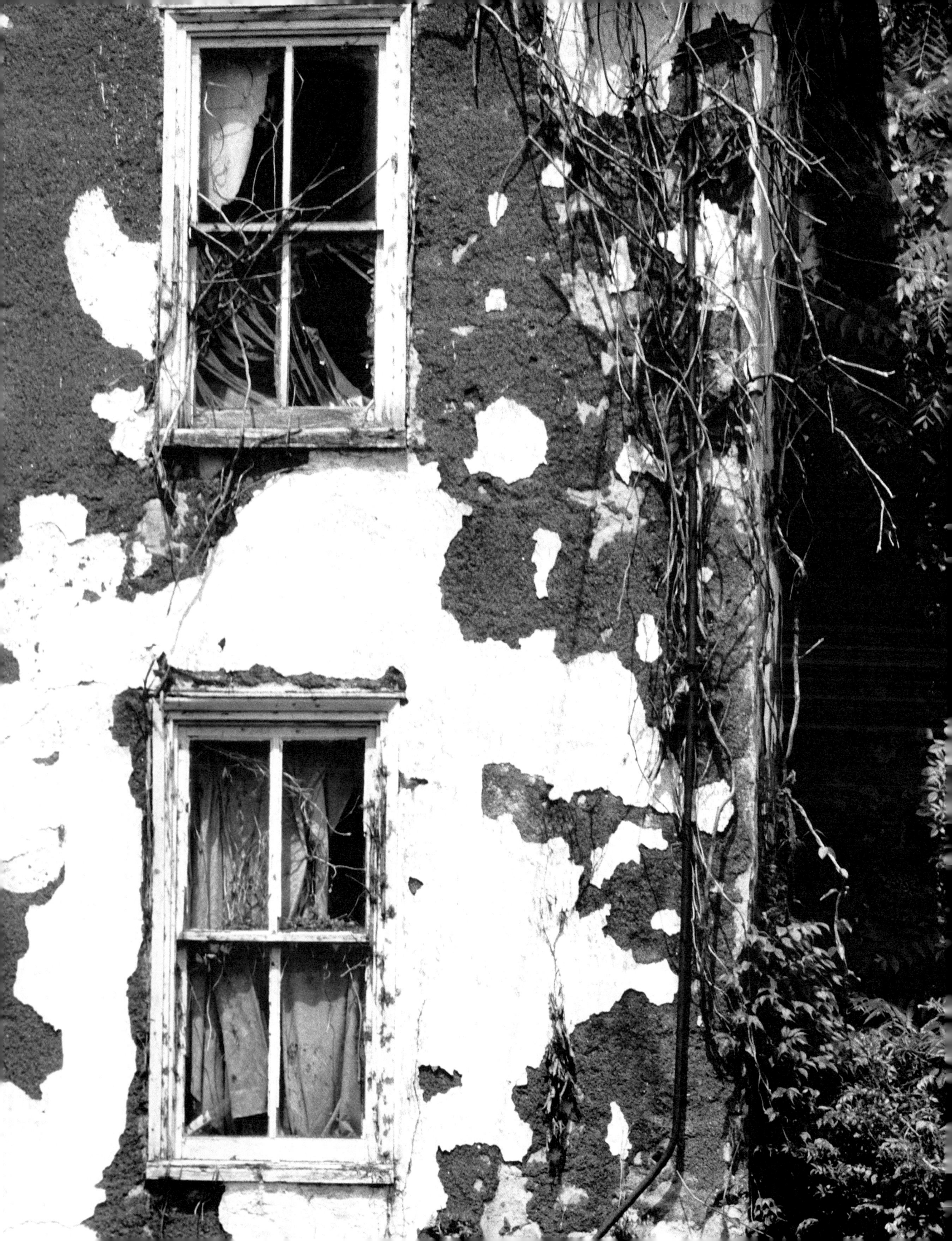

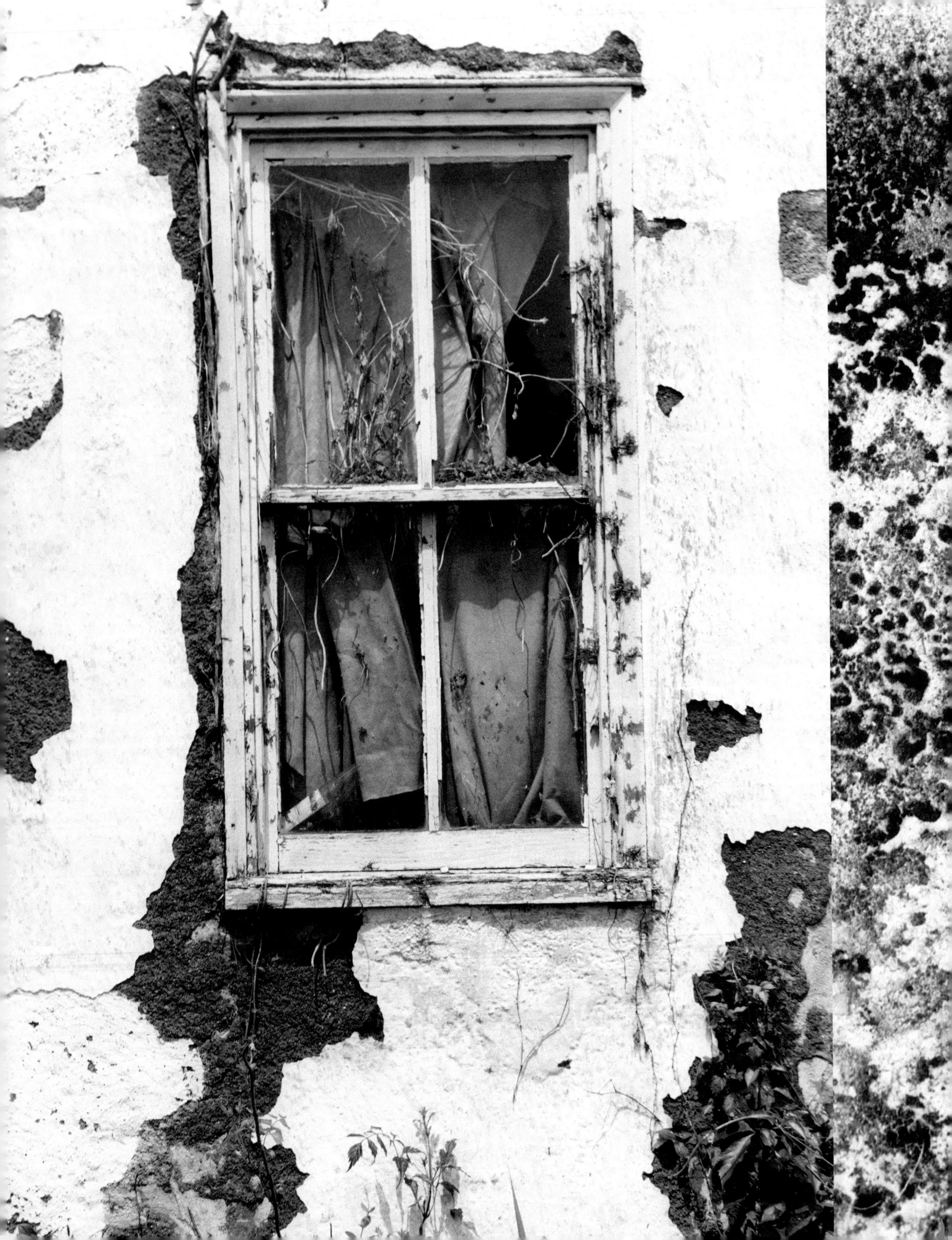

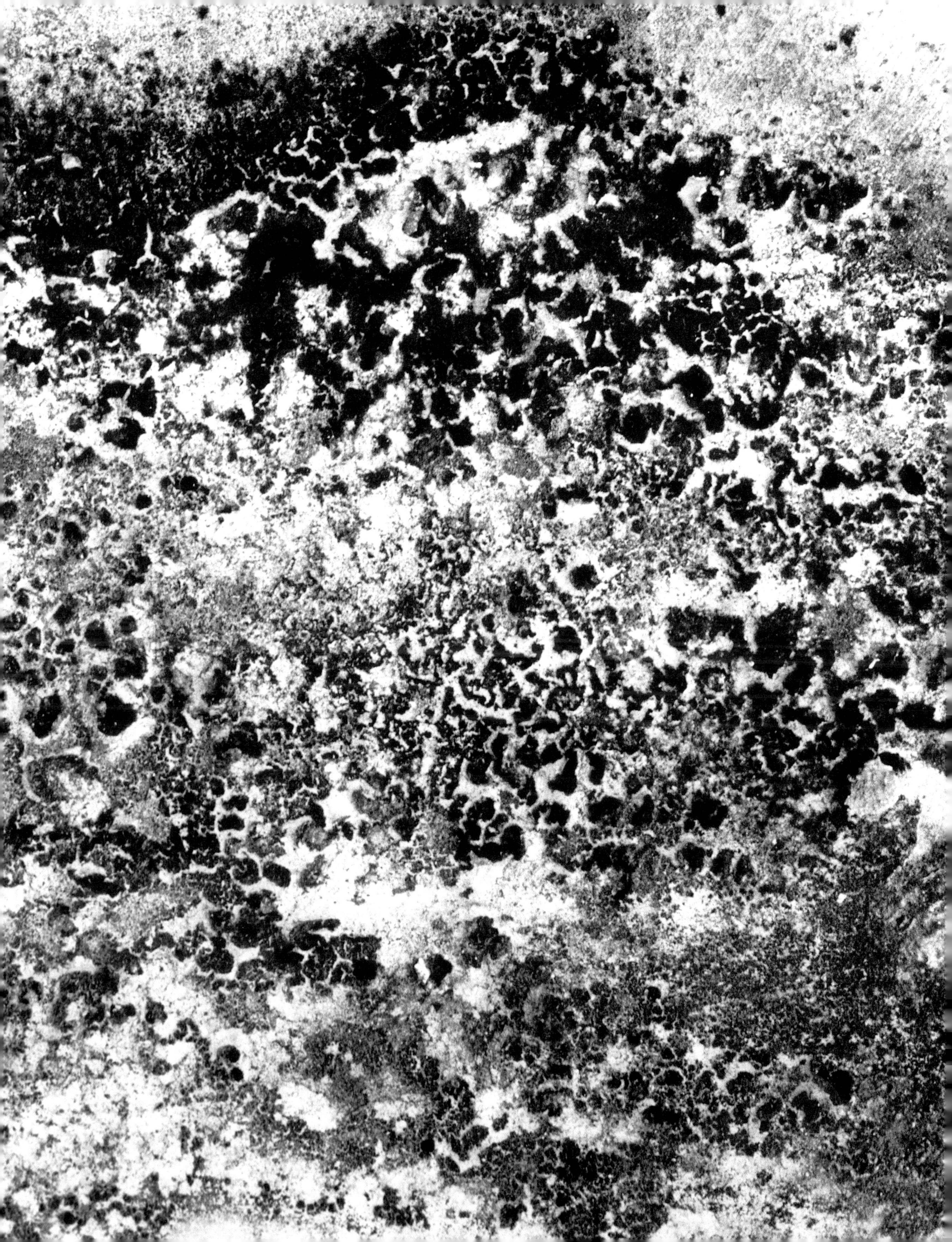

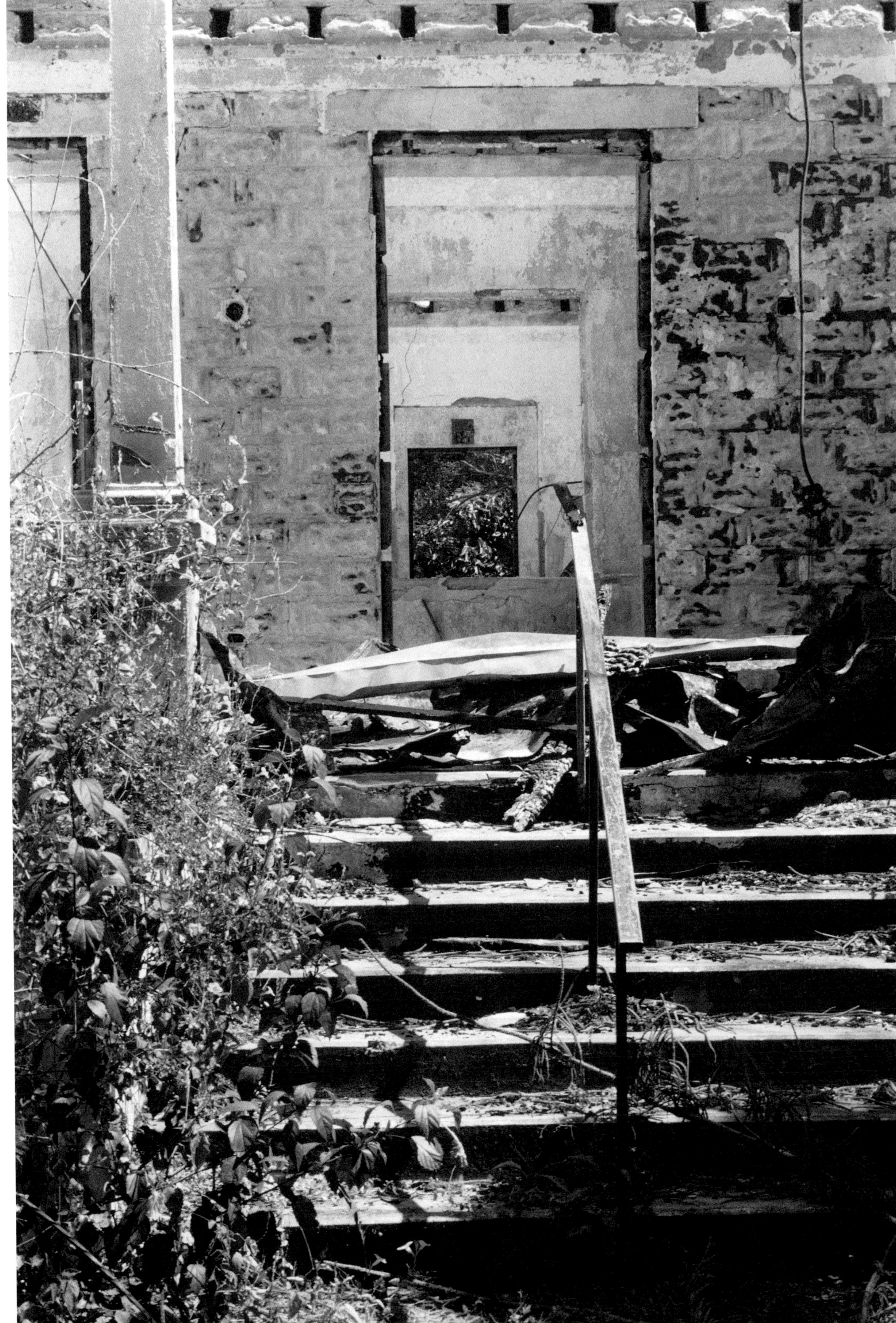

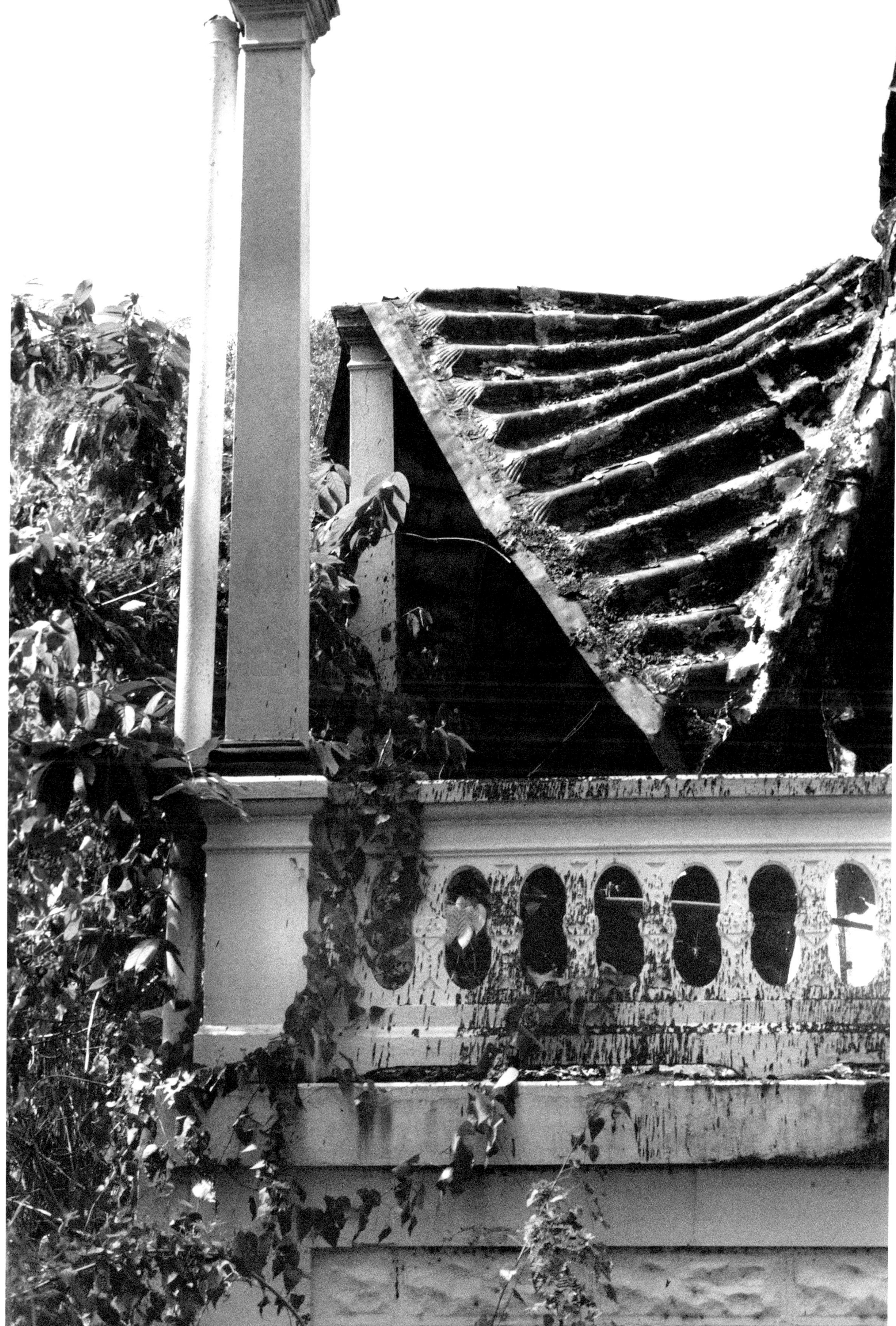

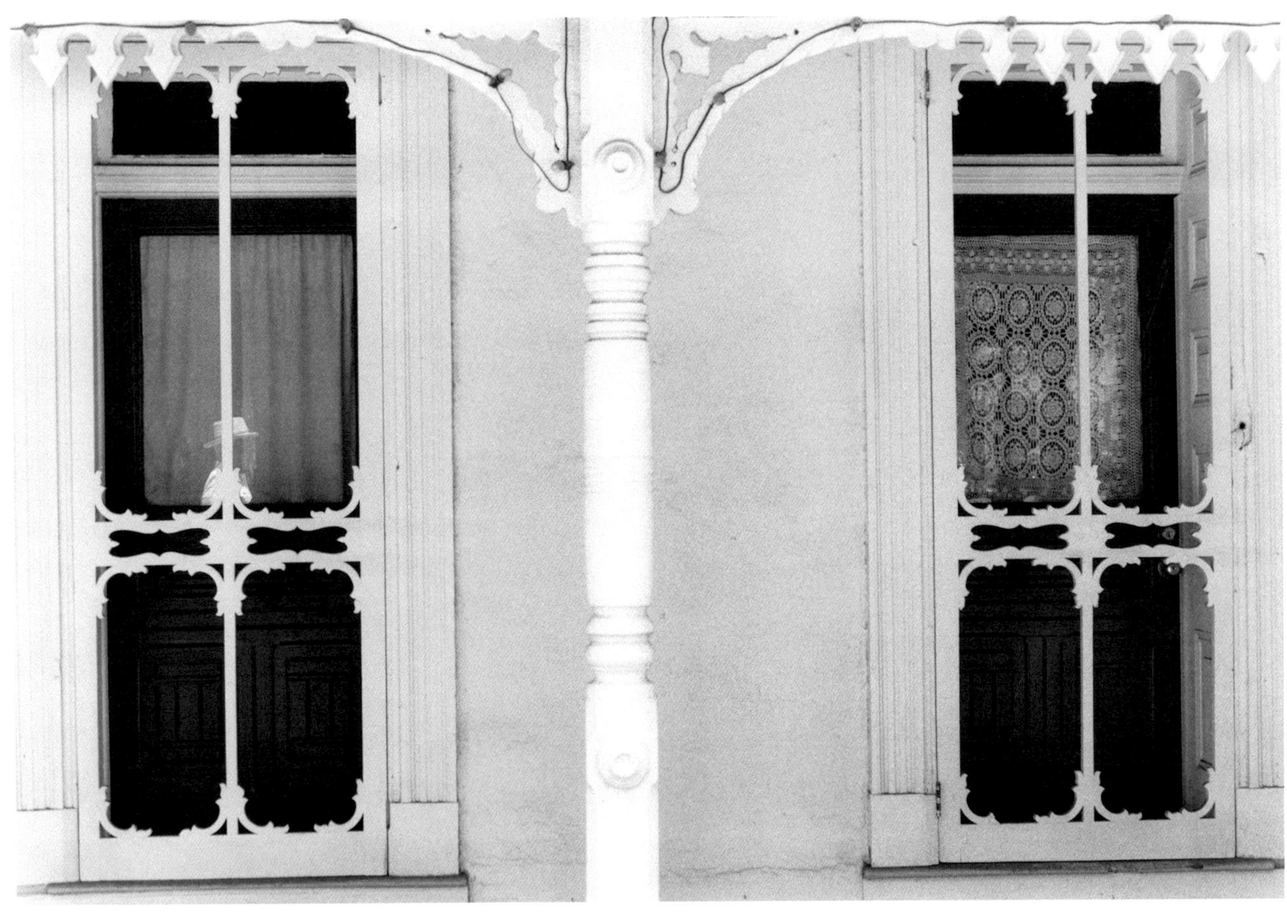

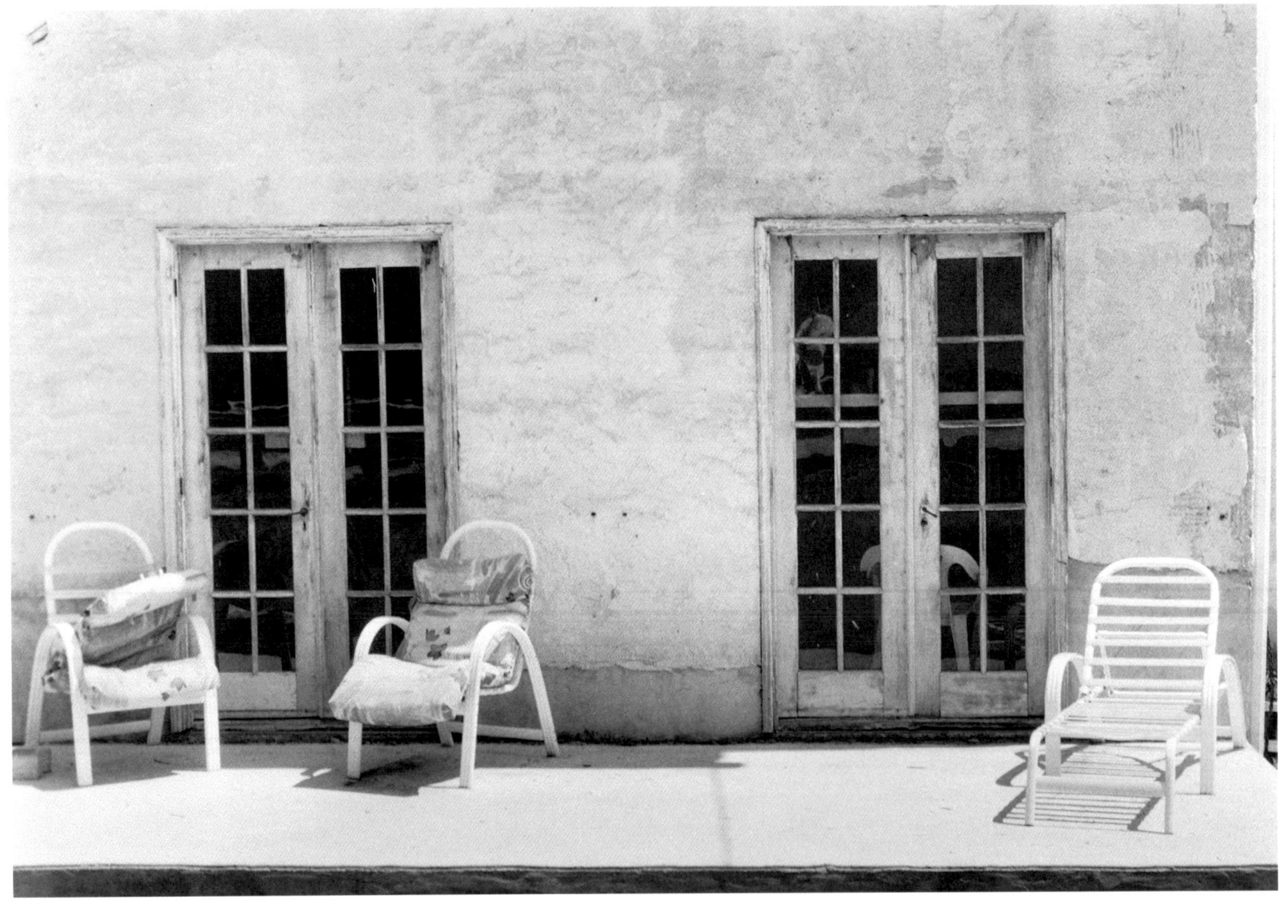

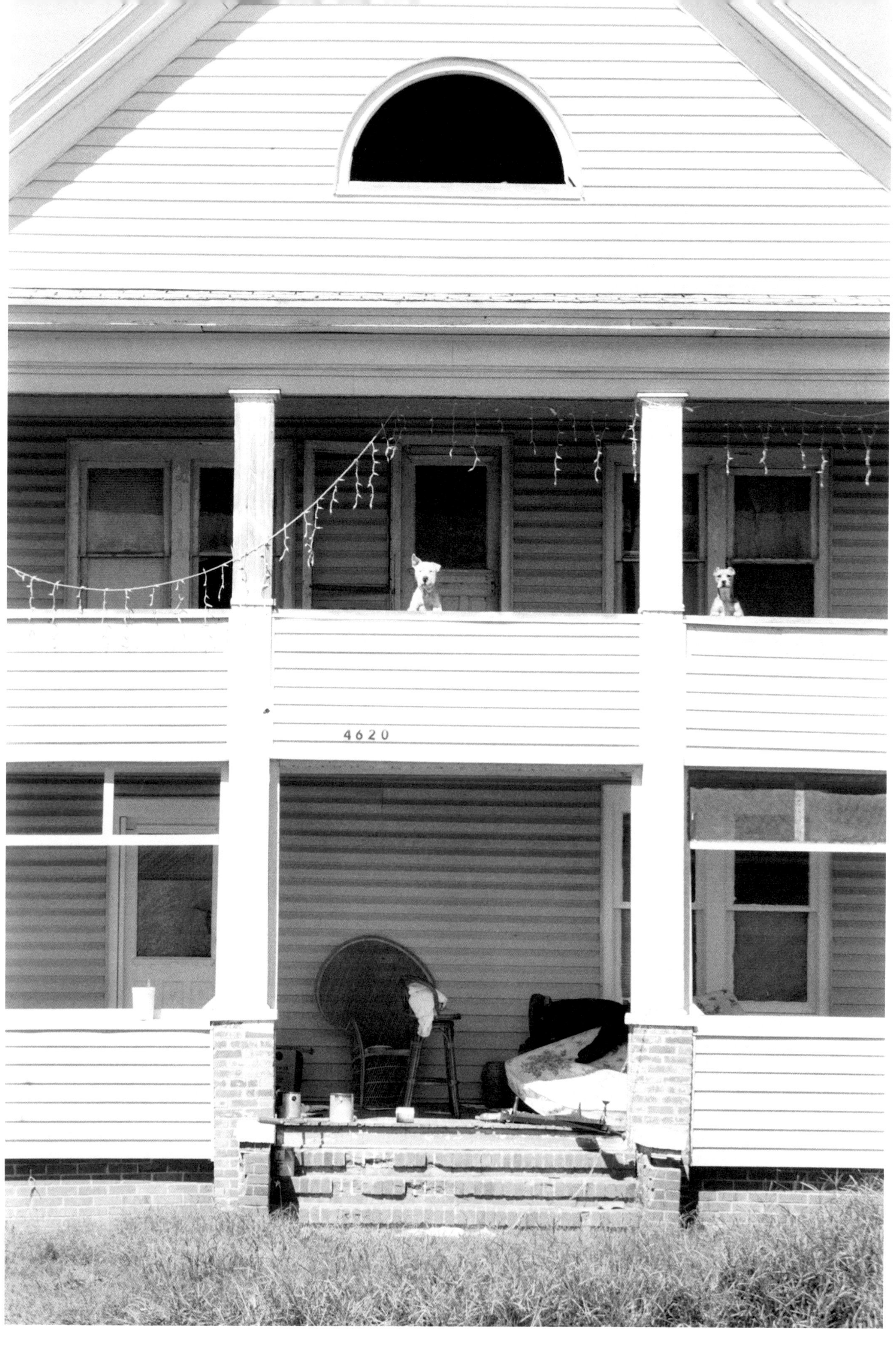

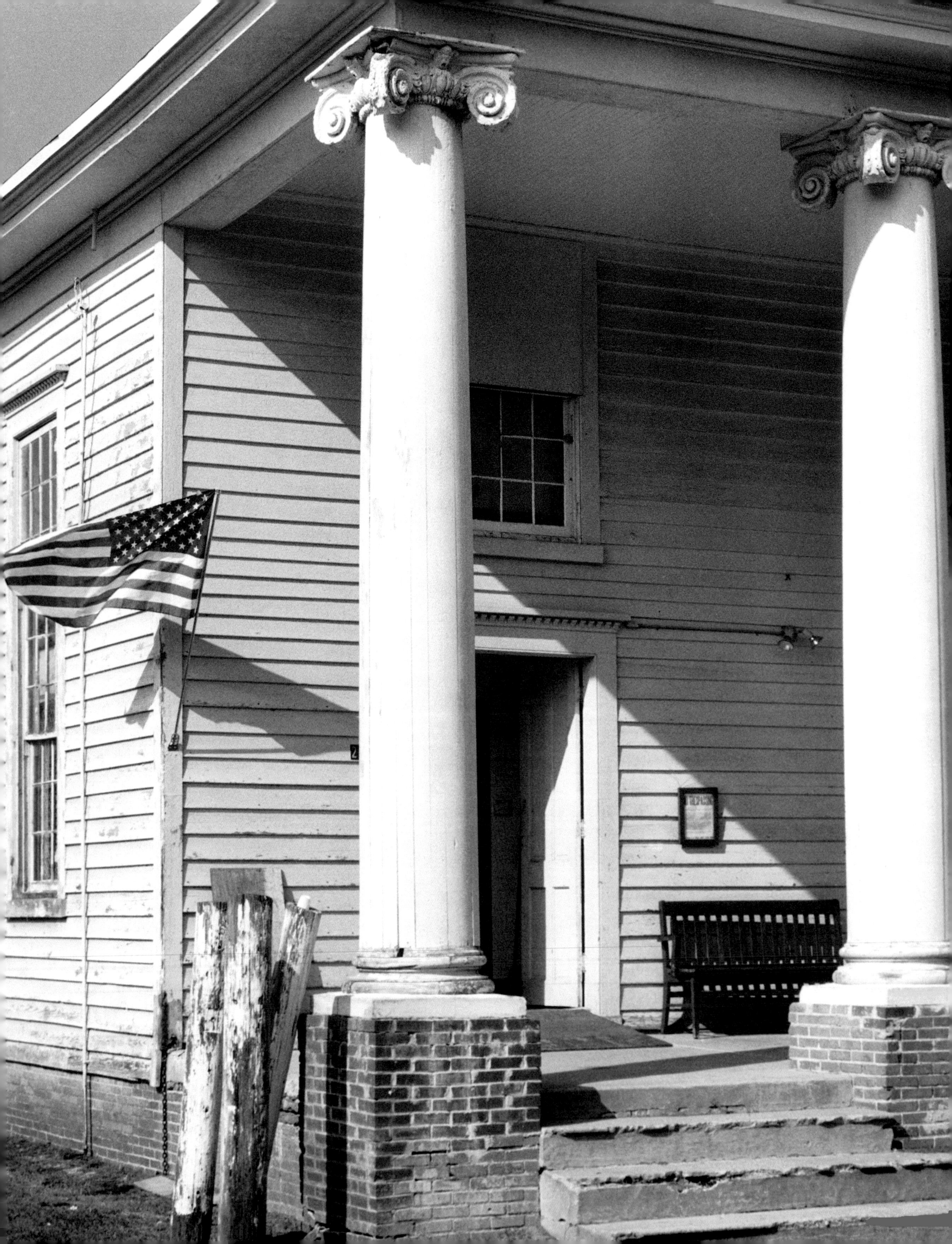

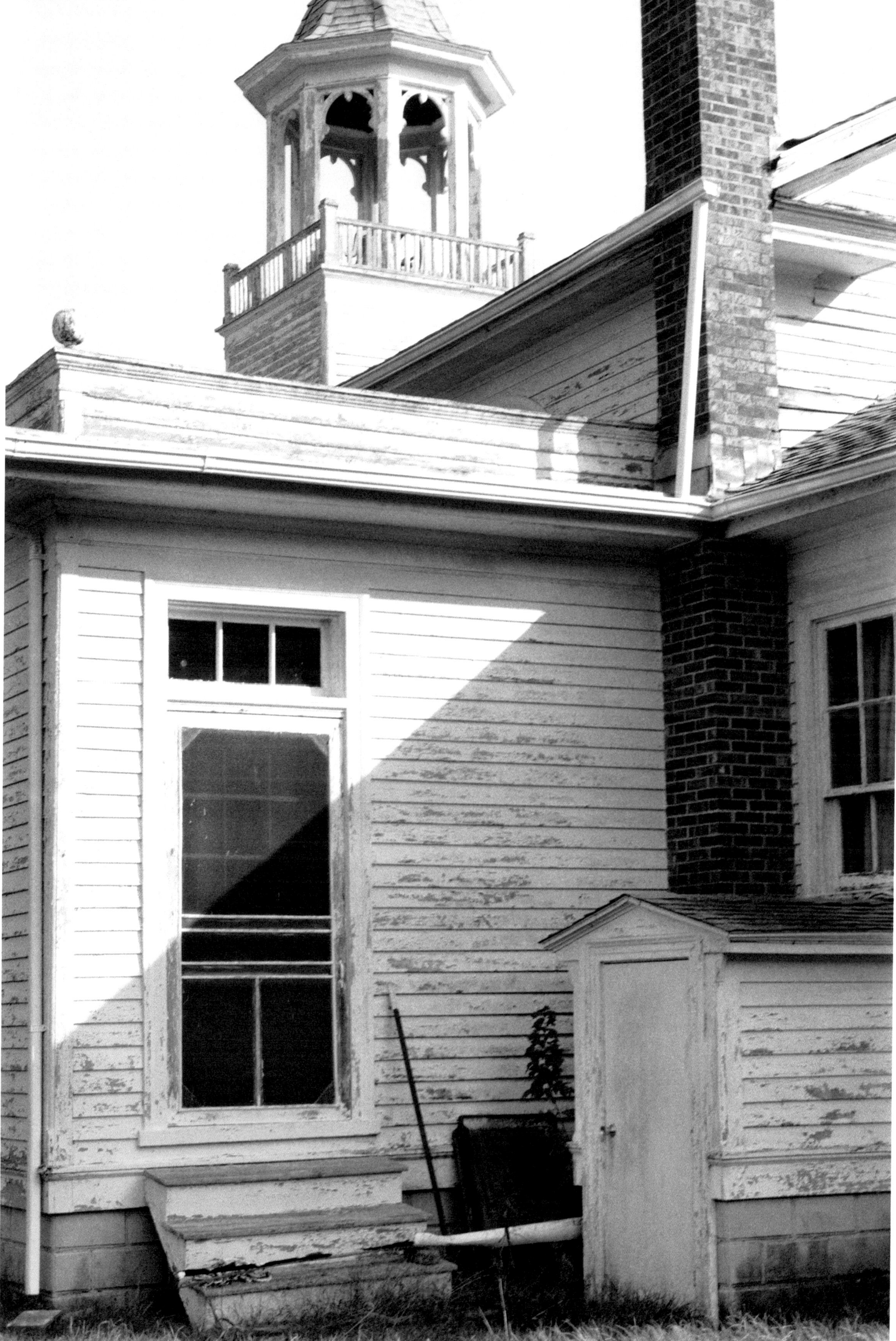

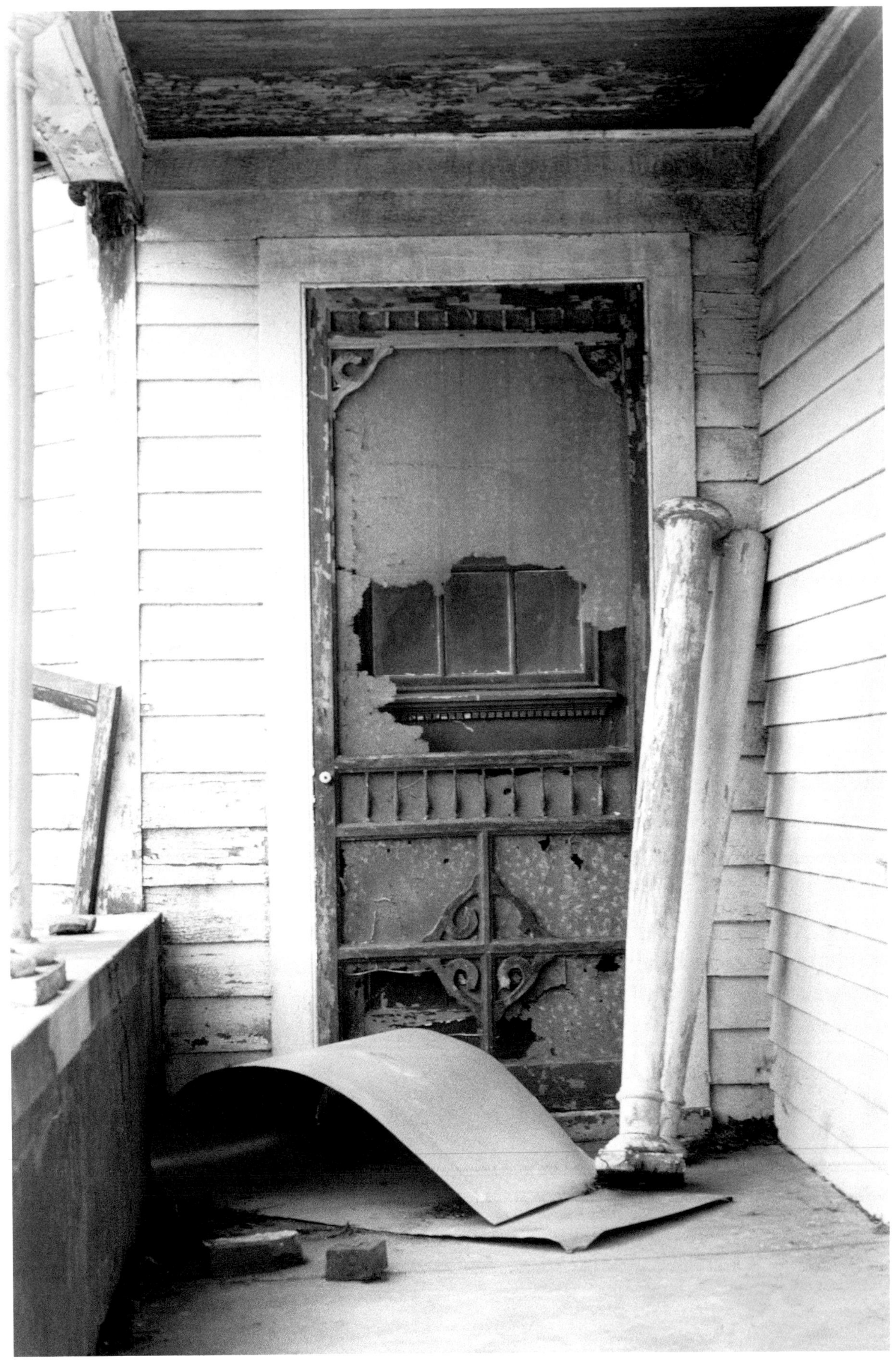

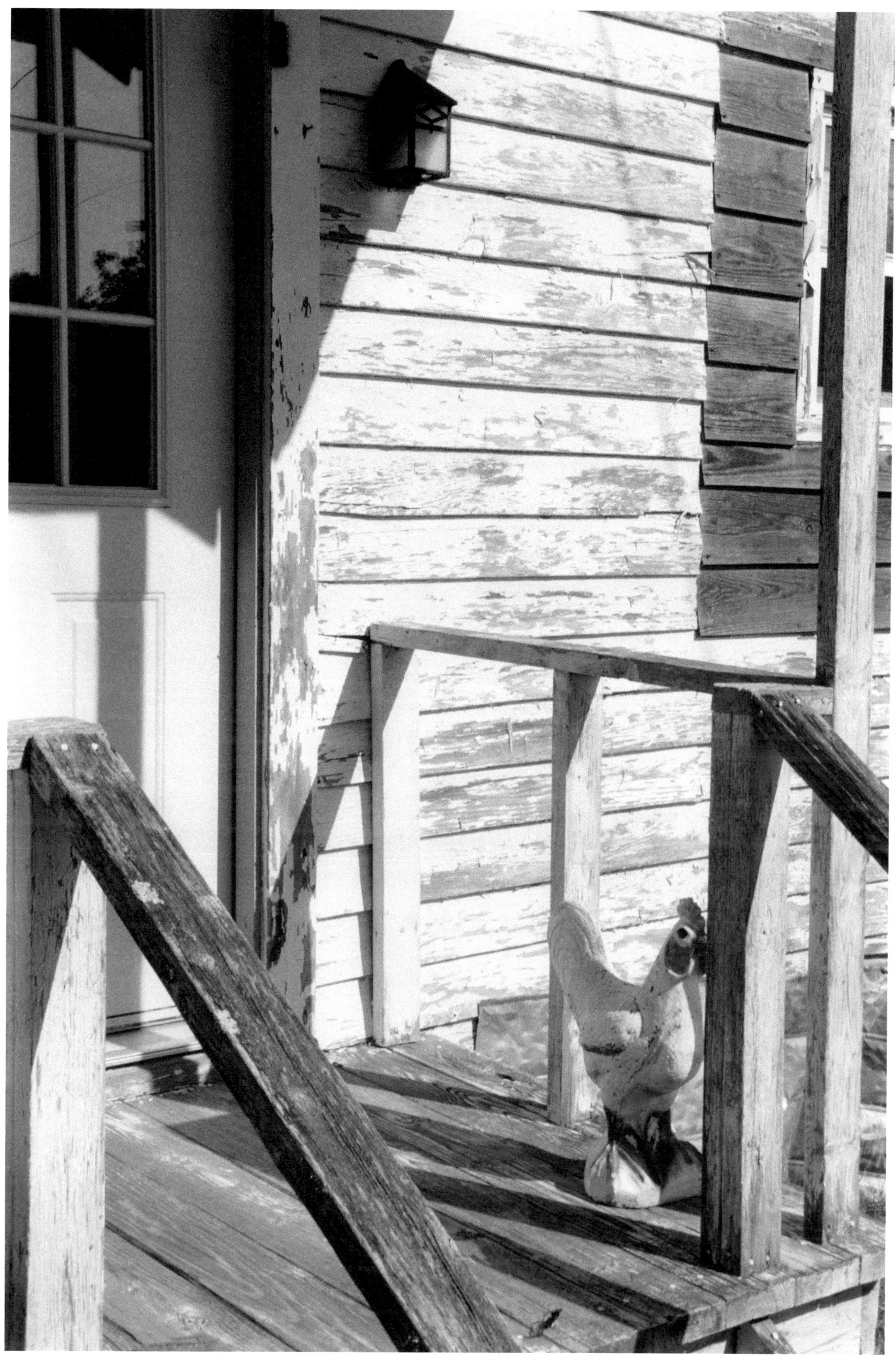

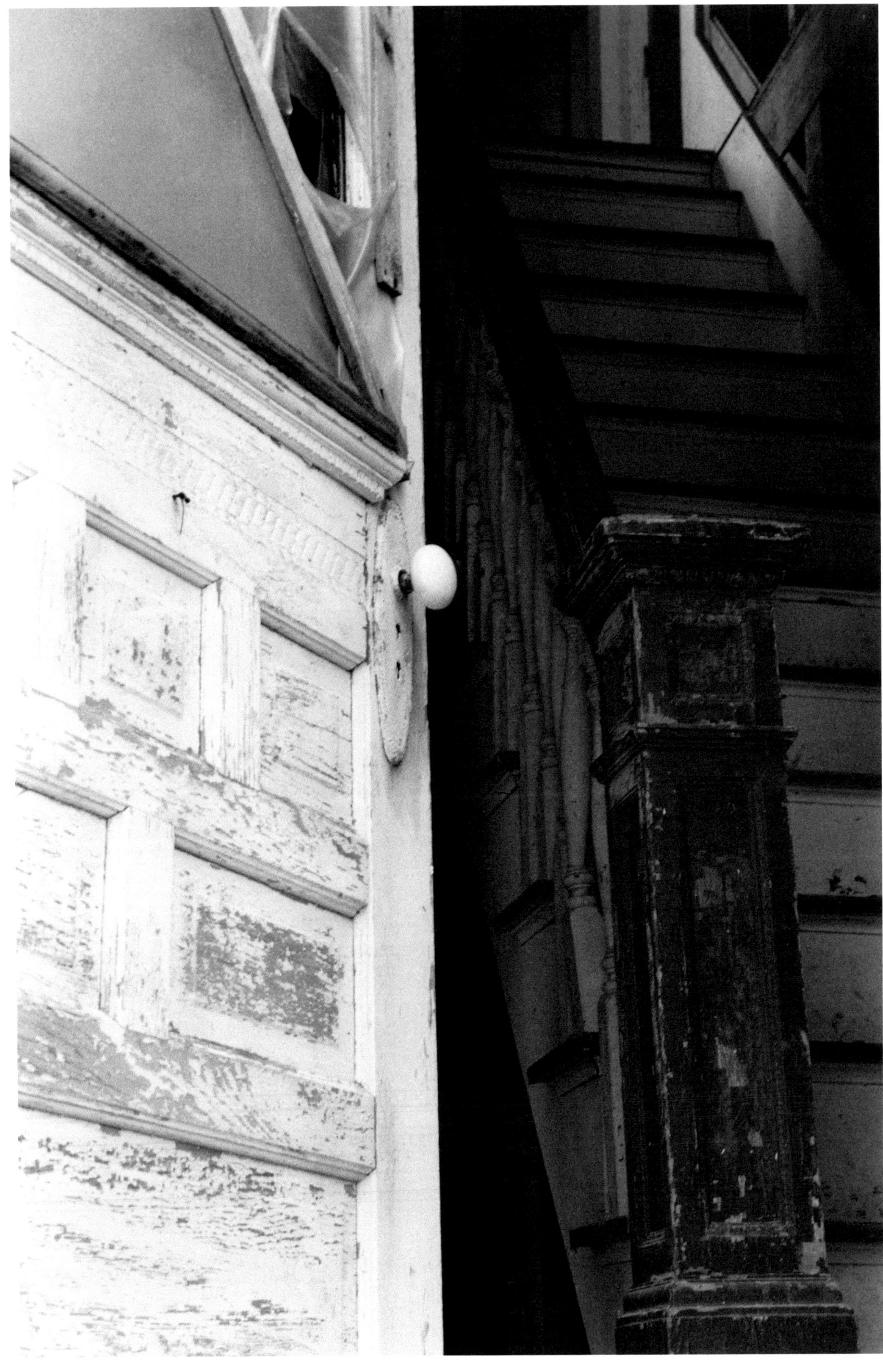

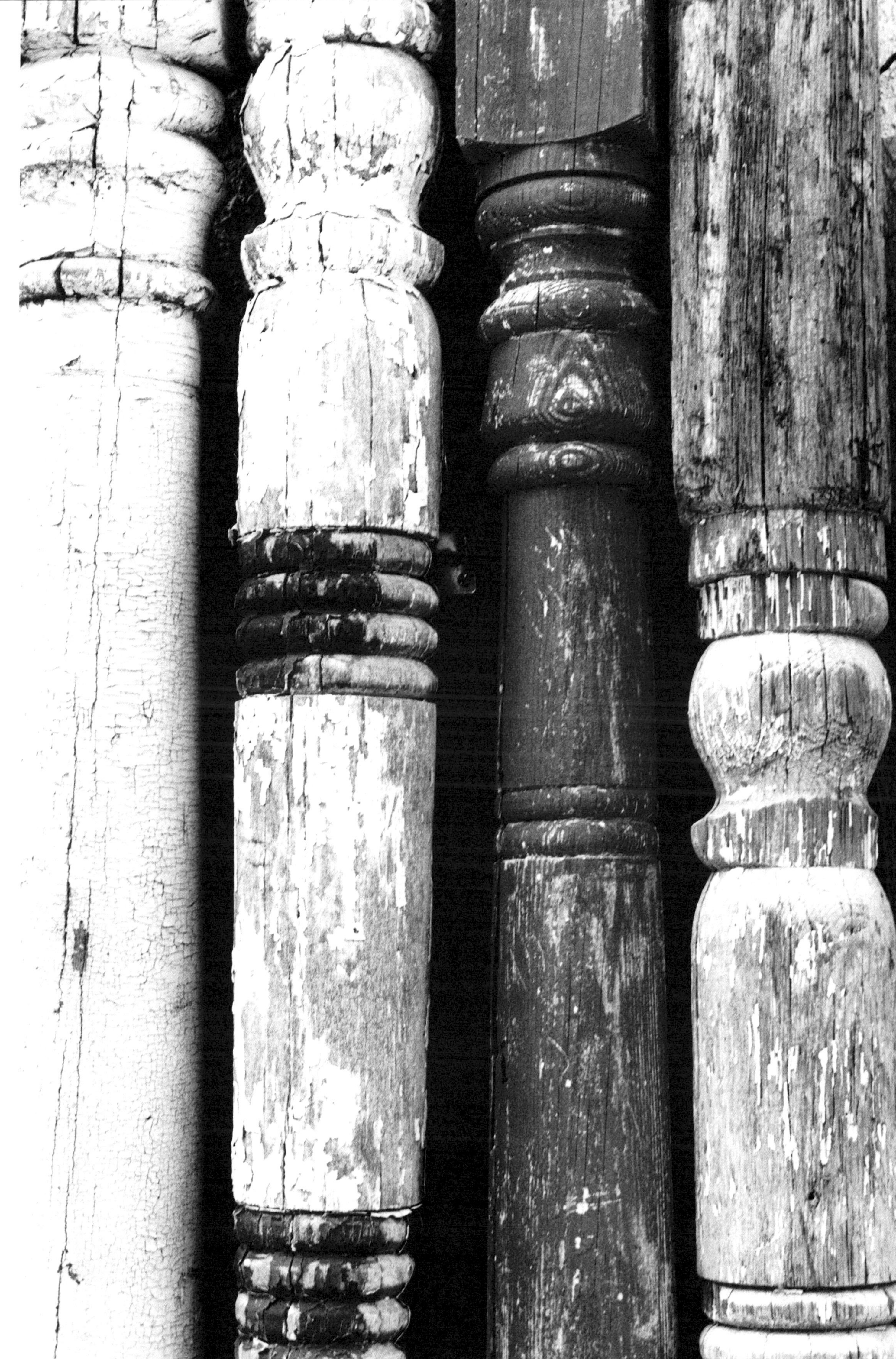

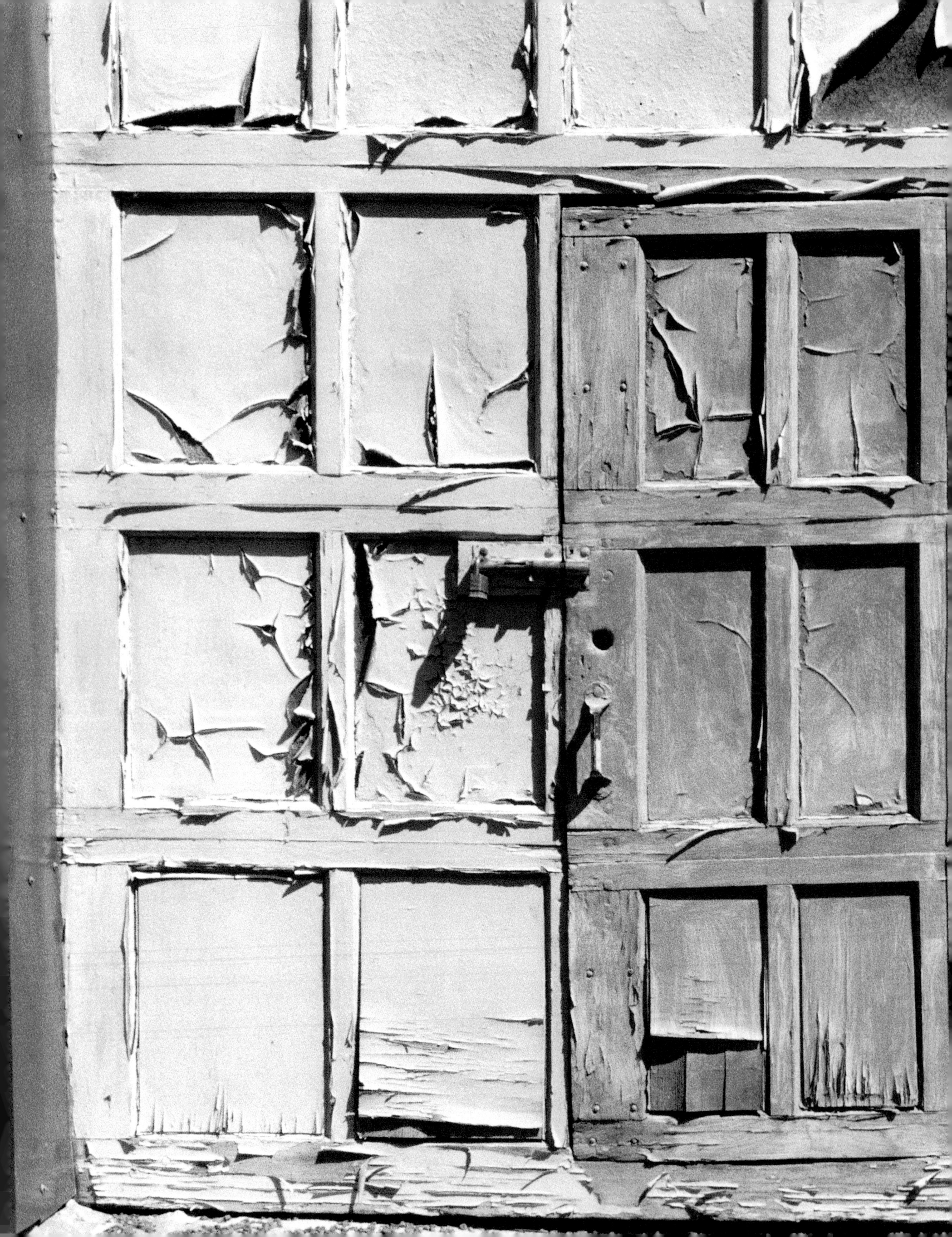

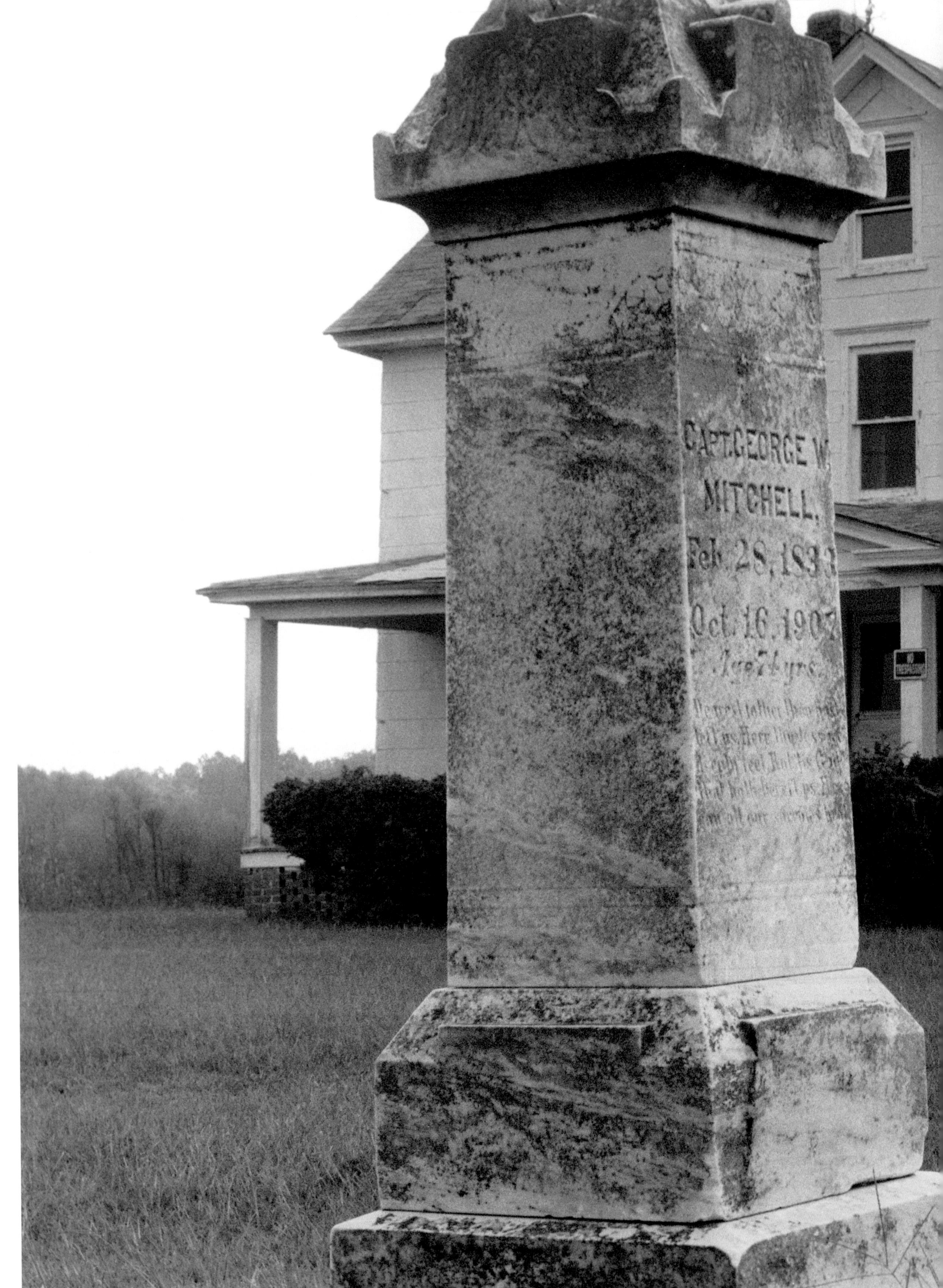

CAPT. GEORGE W.
MITCHELL.
Feb. 28, 1833
Oct. 16, 1907
Age 74 yrs.

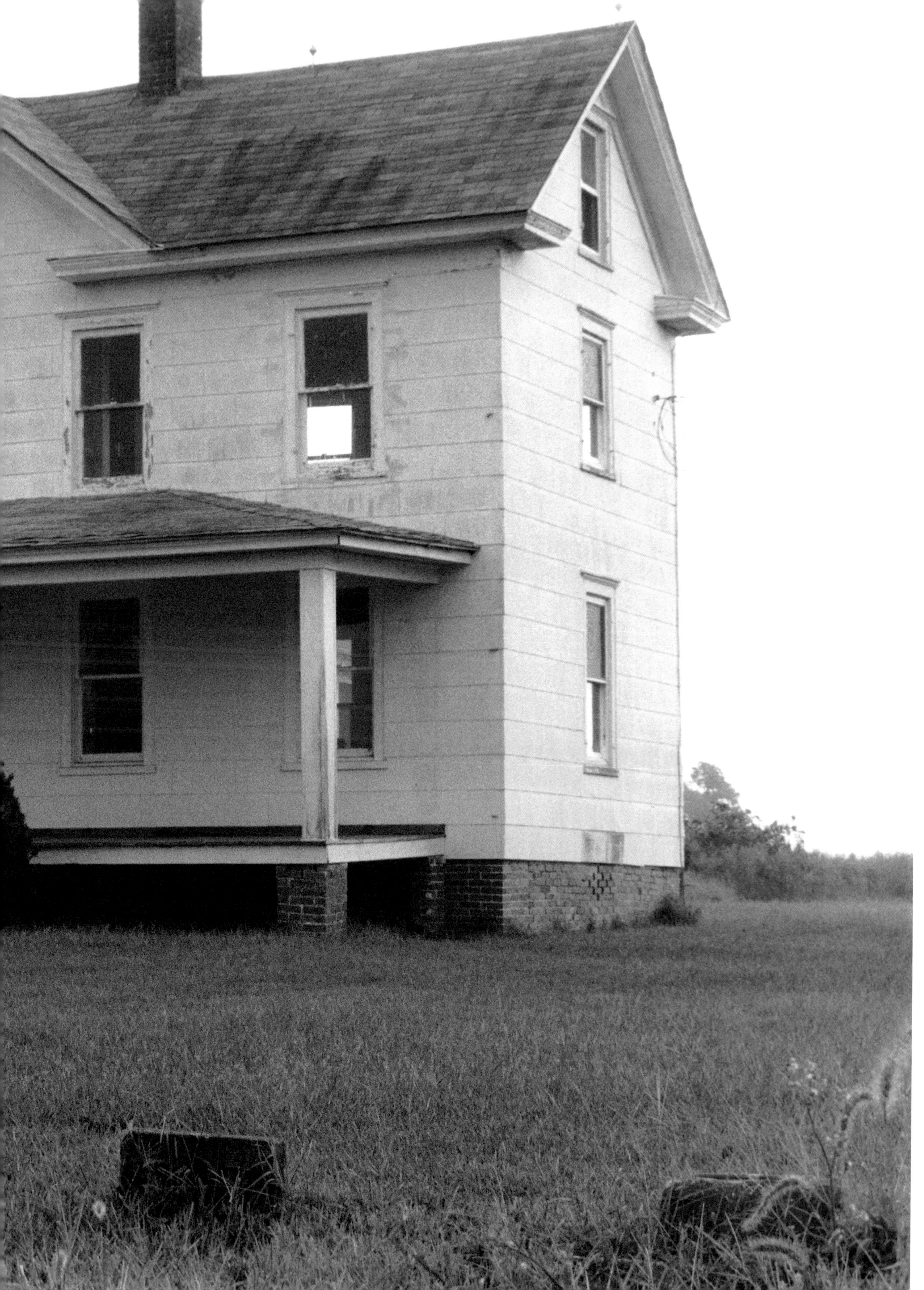

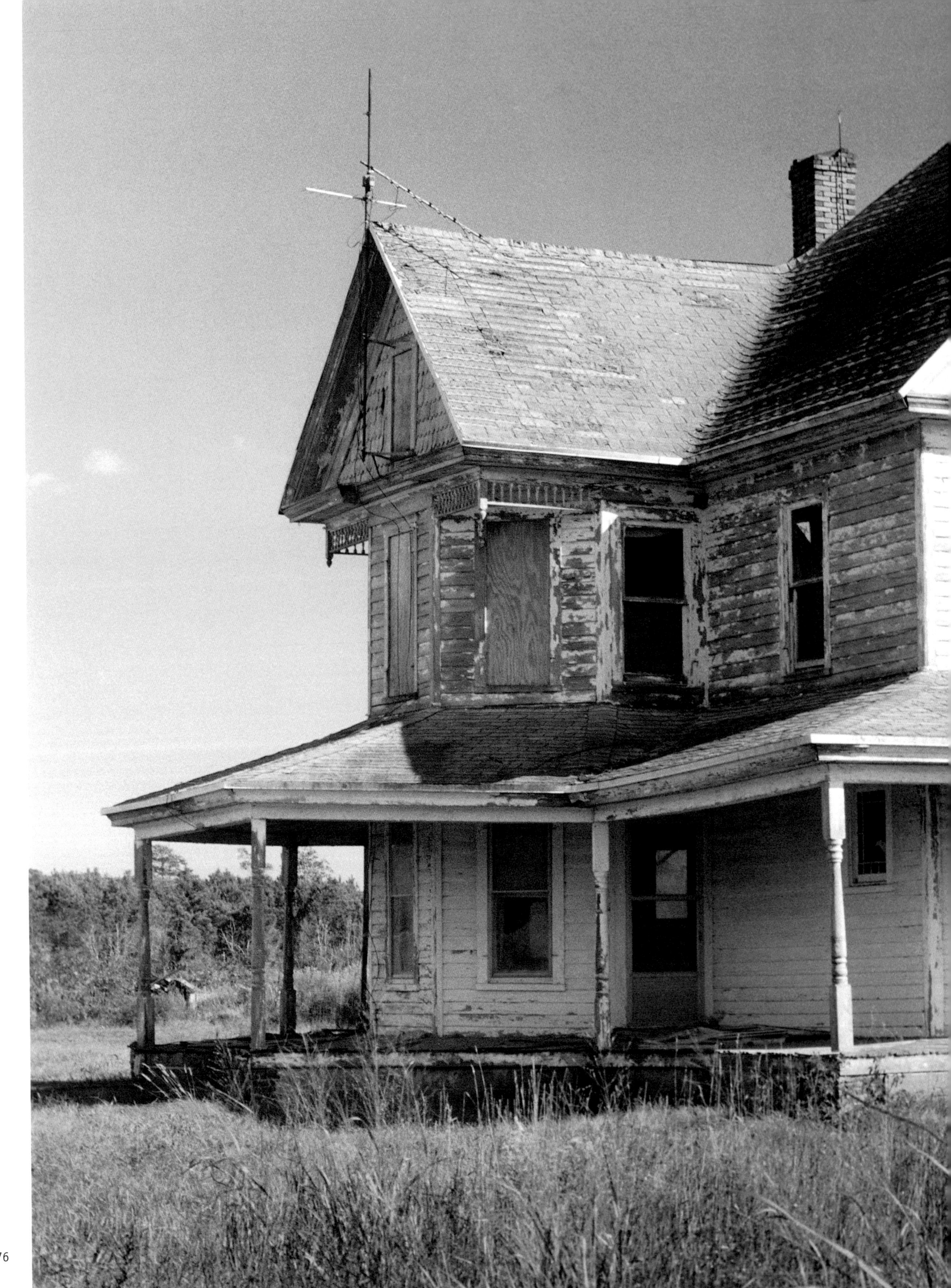

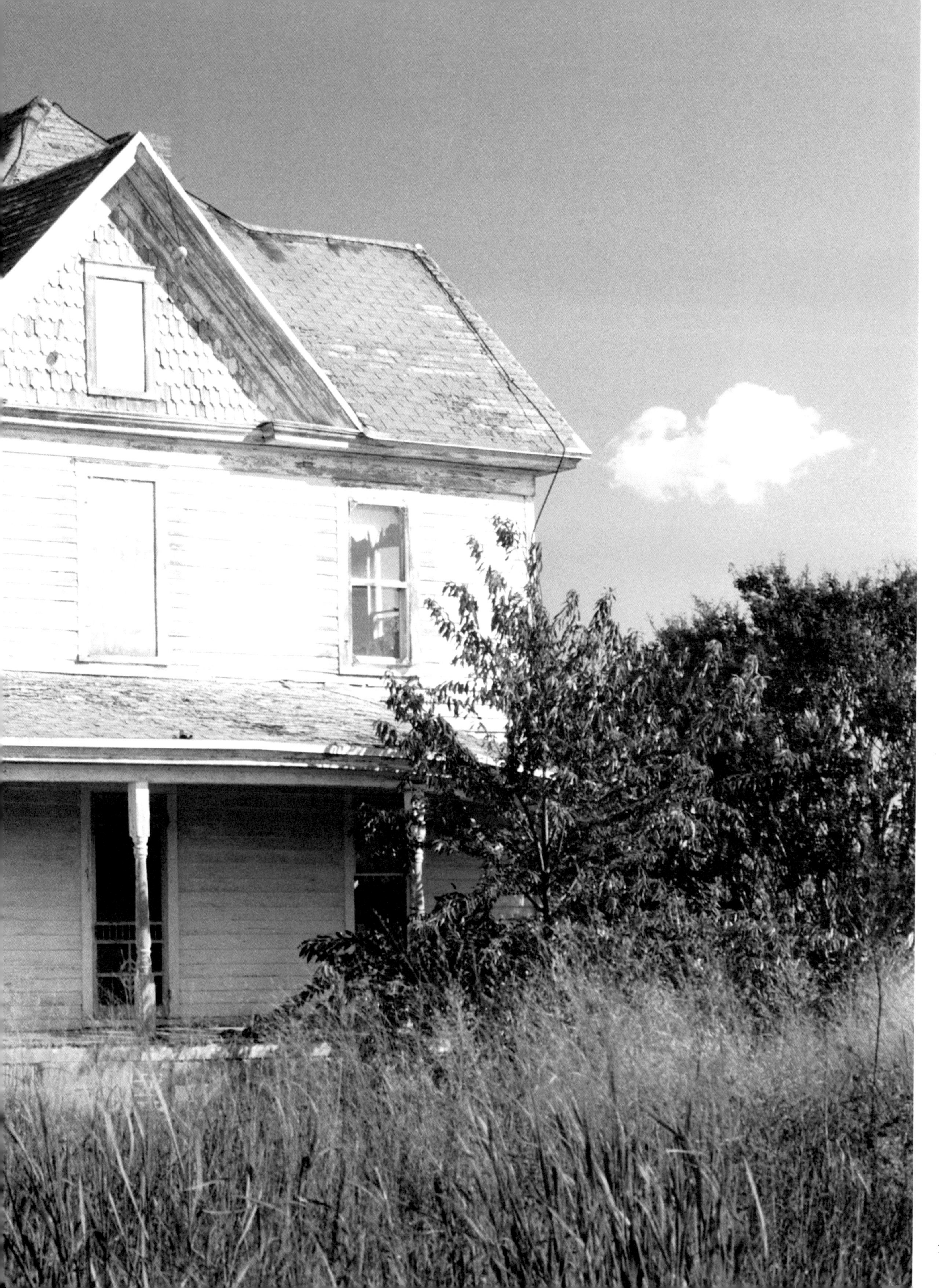

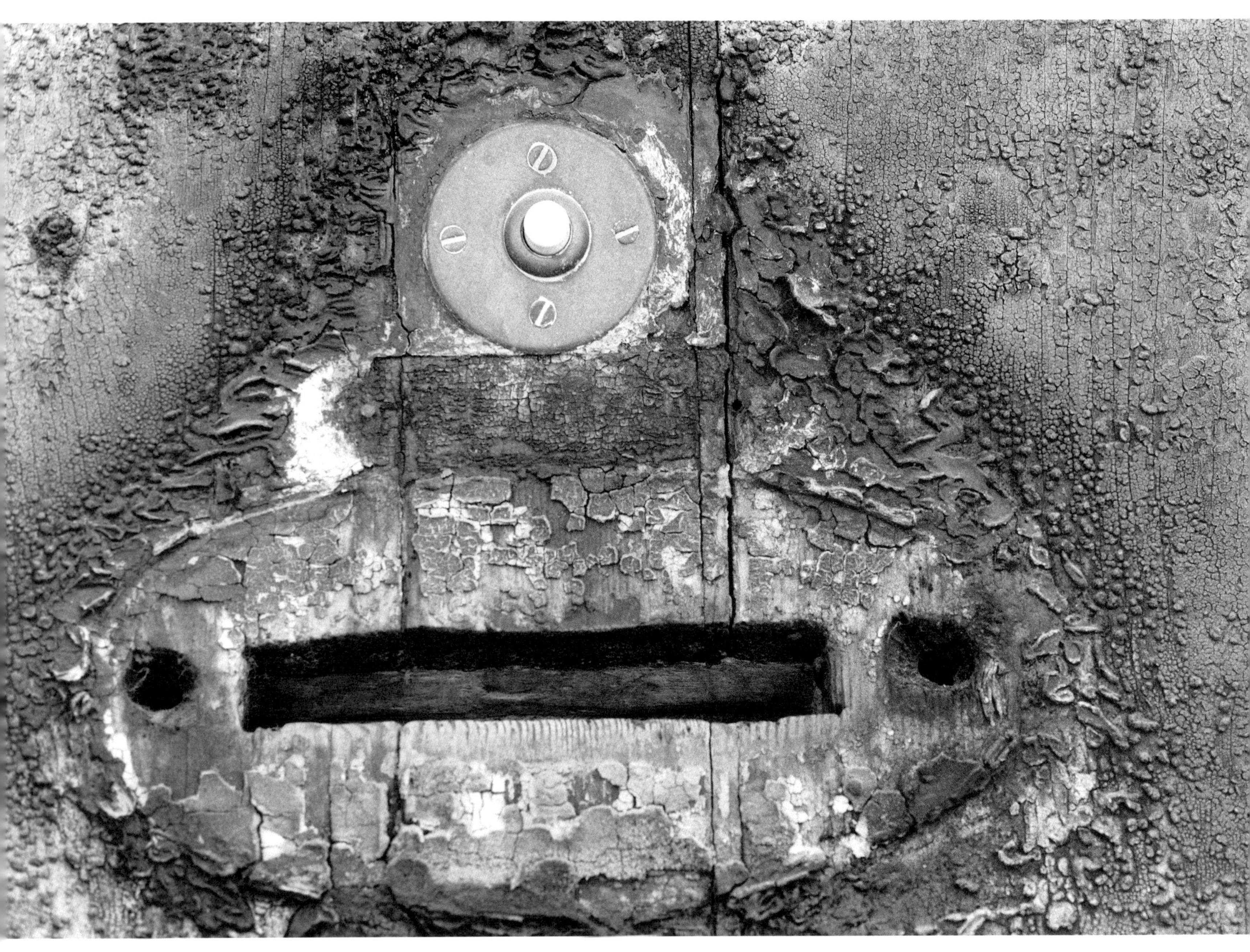

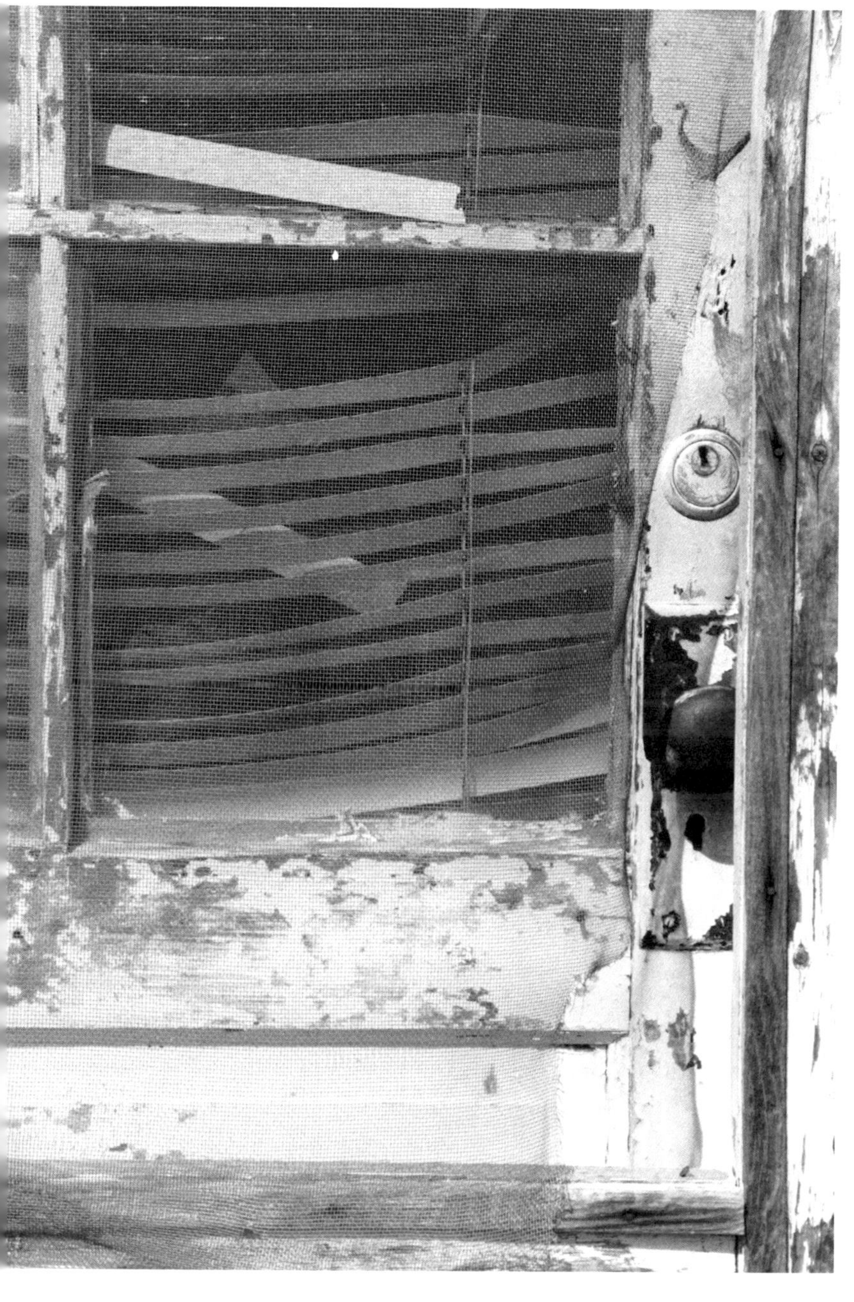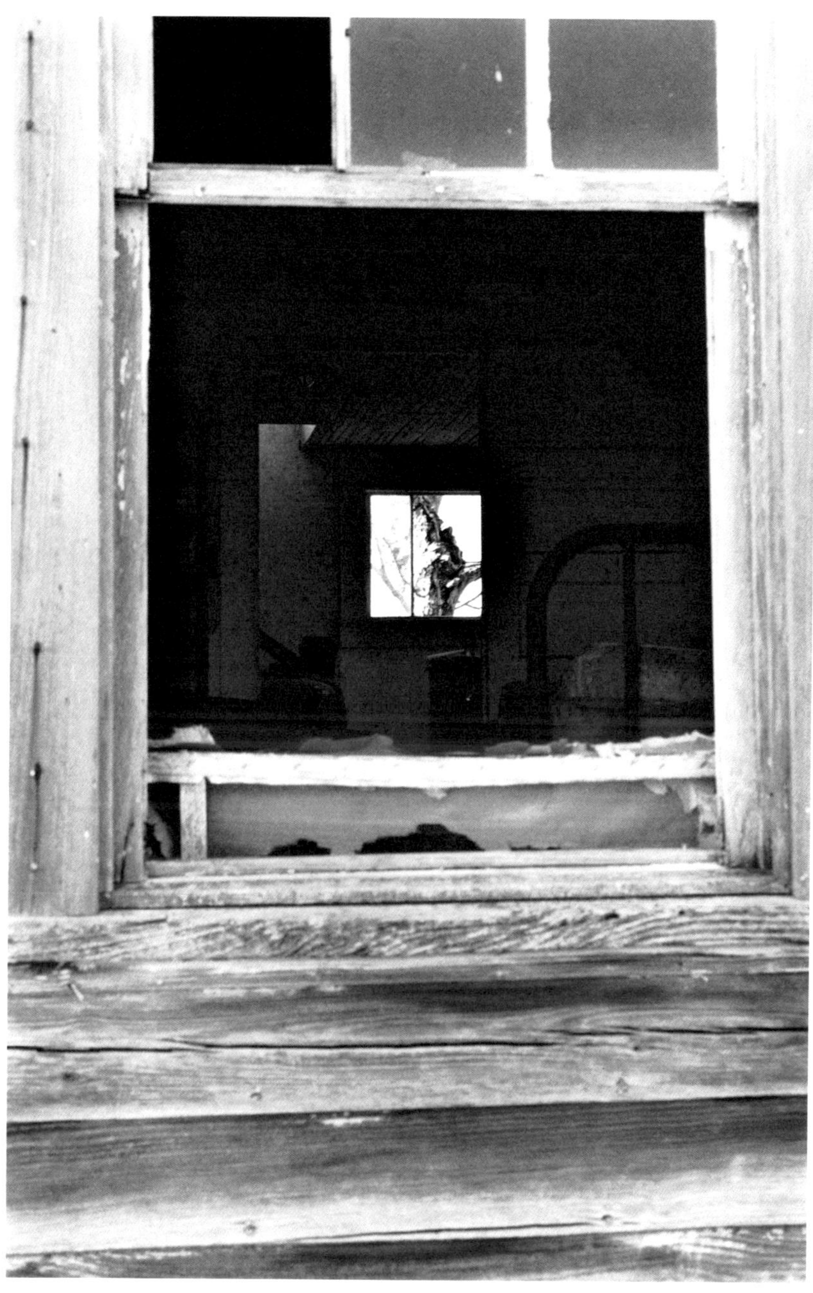

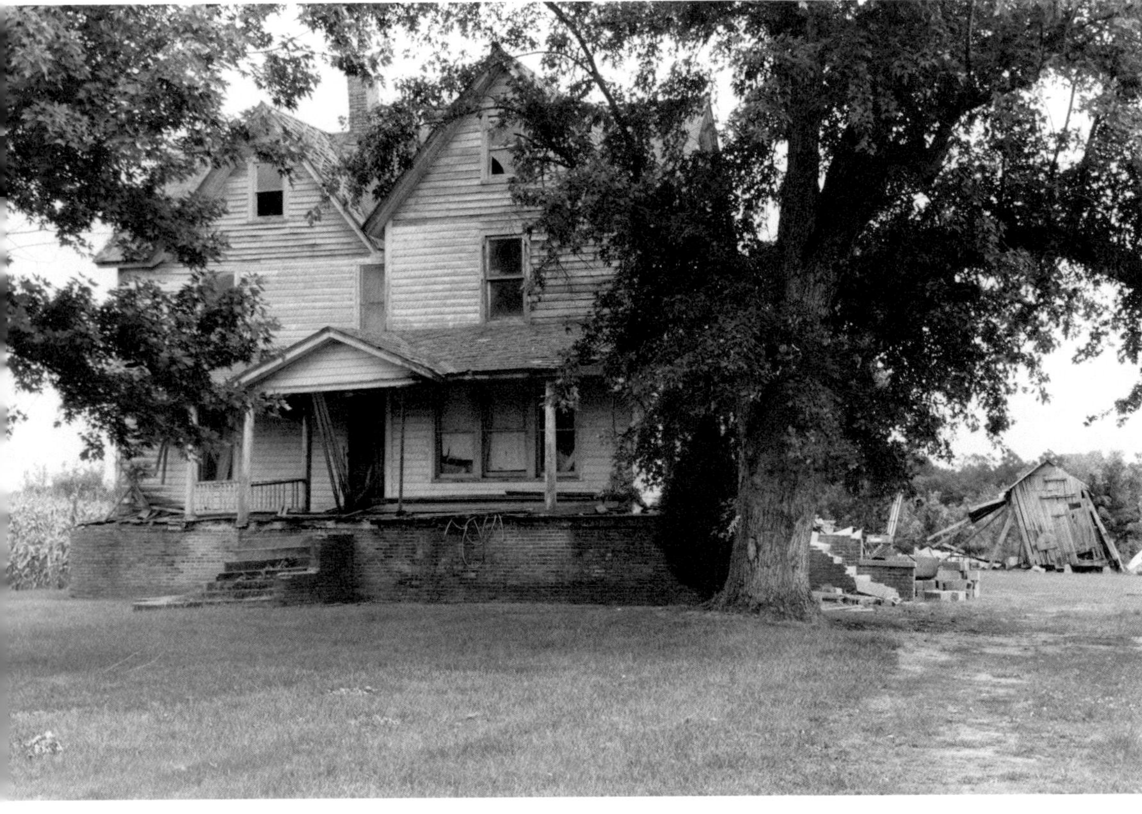

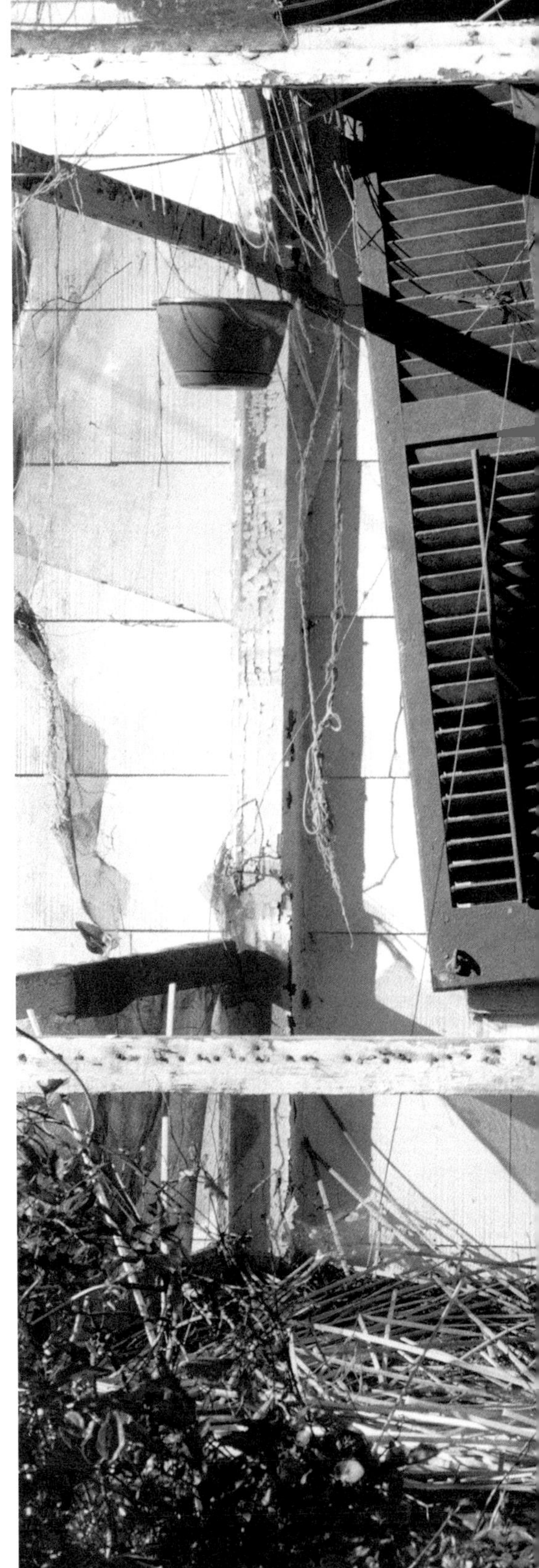

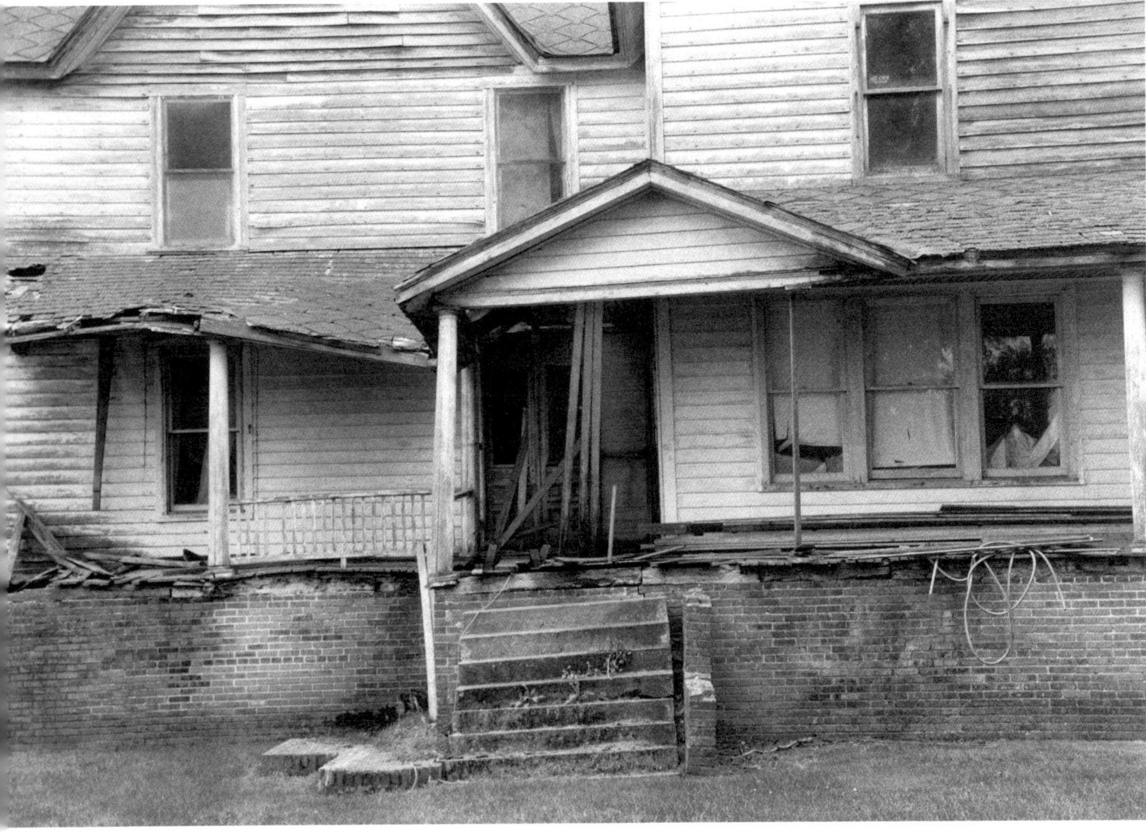

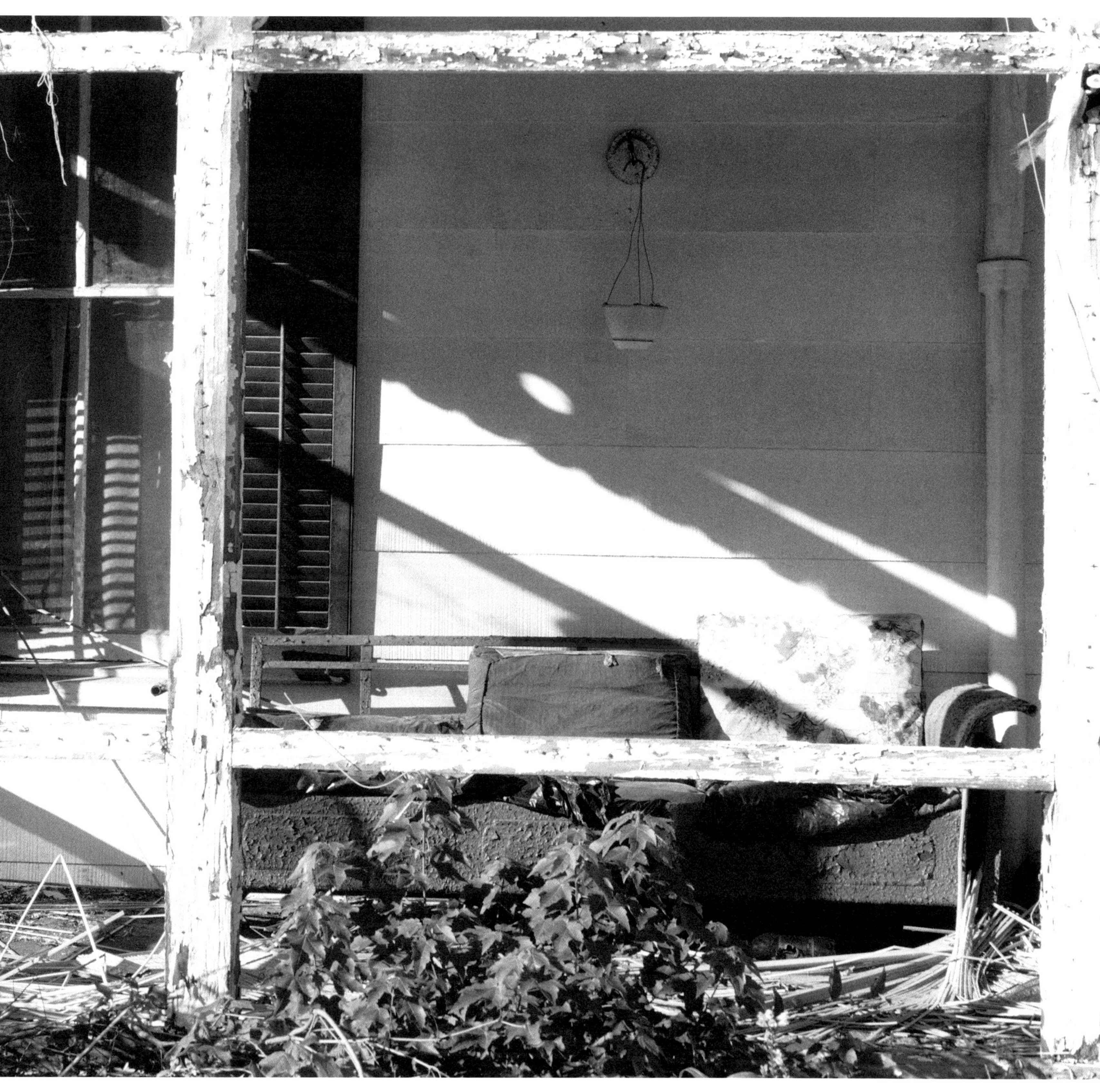

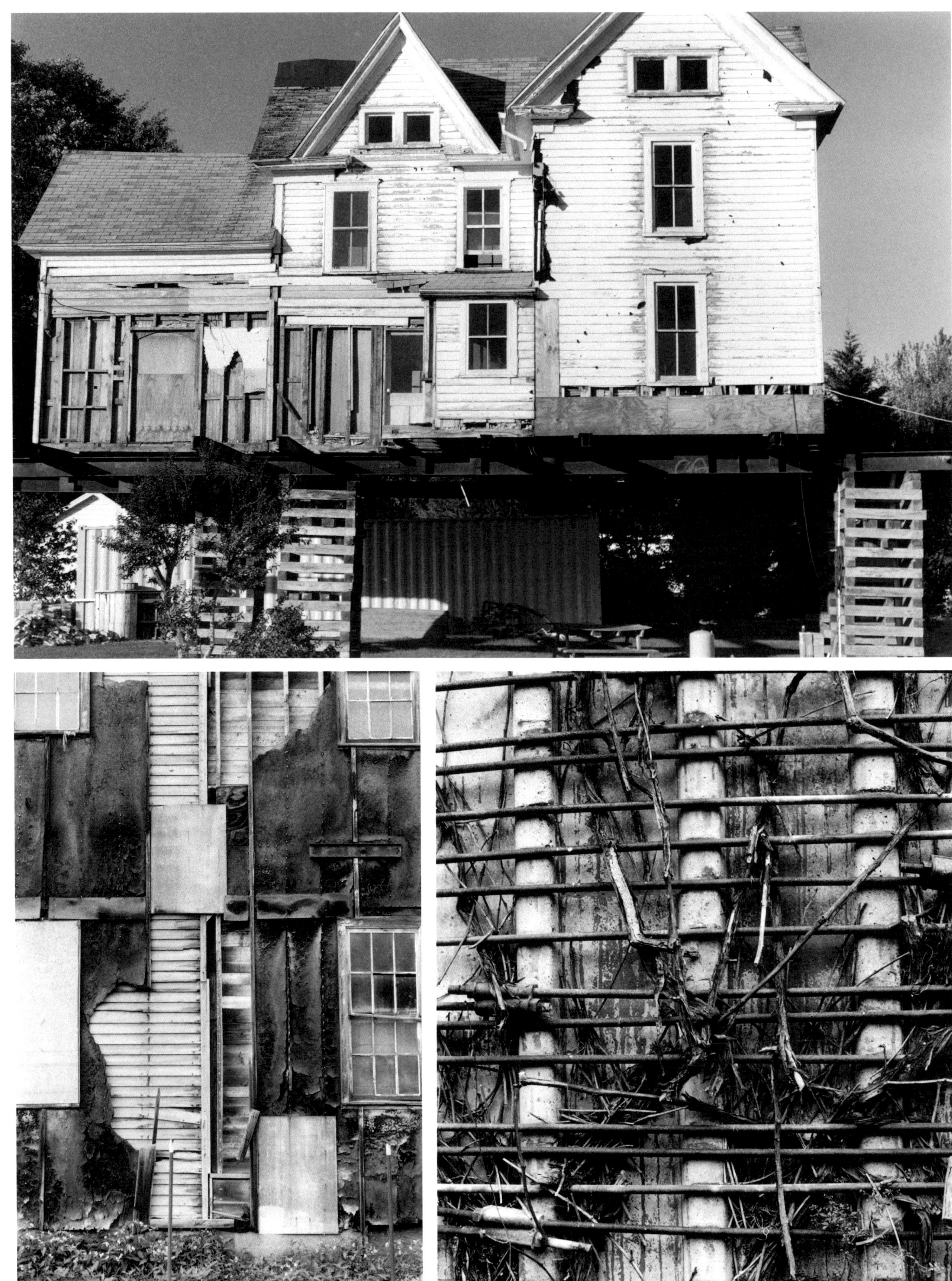

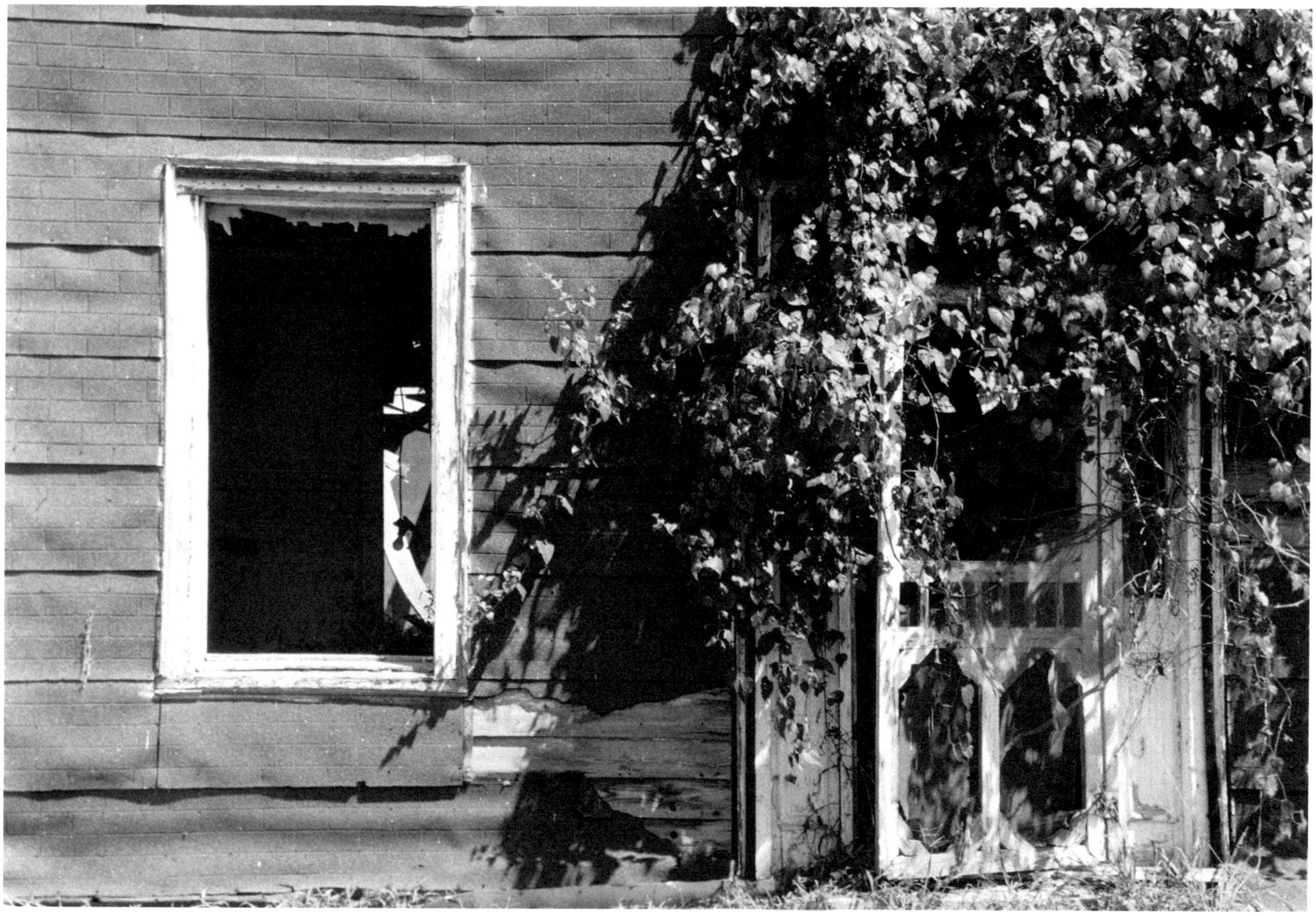

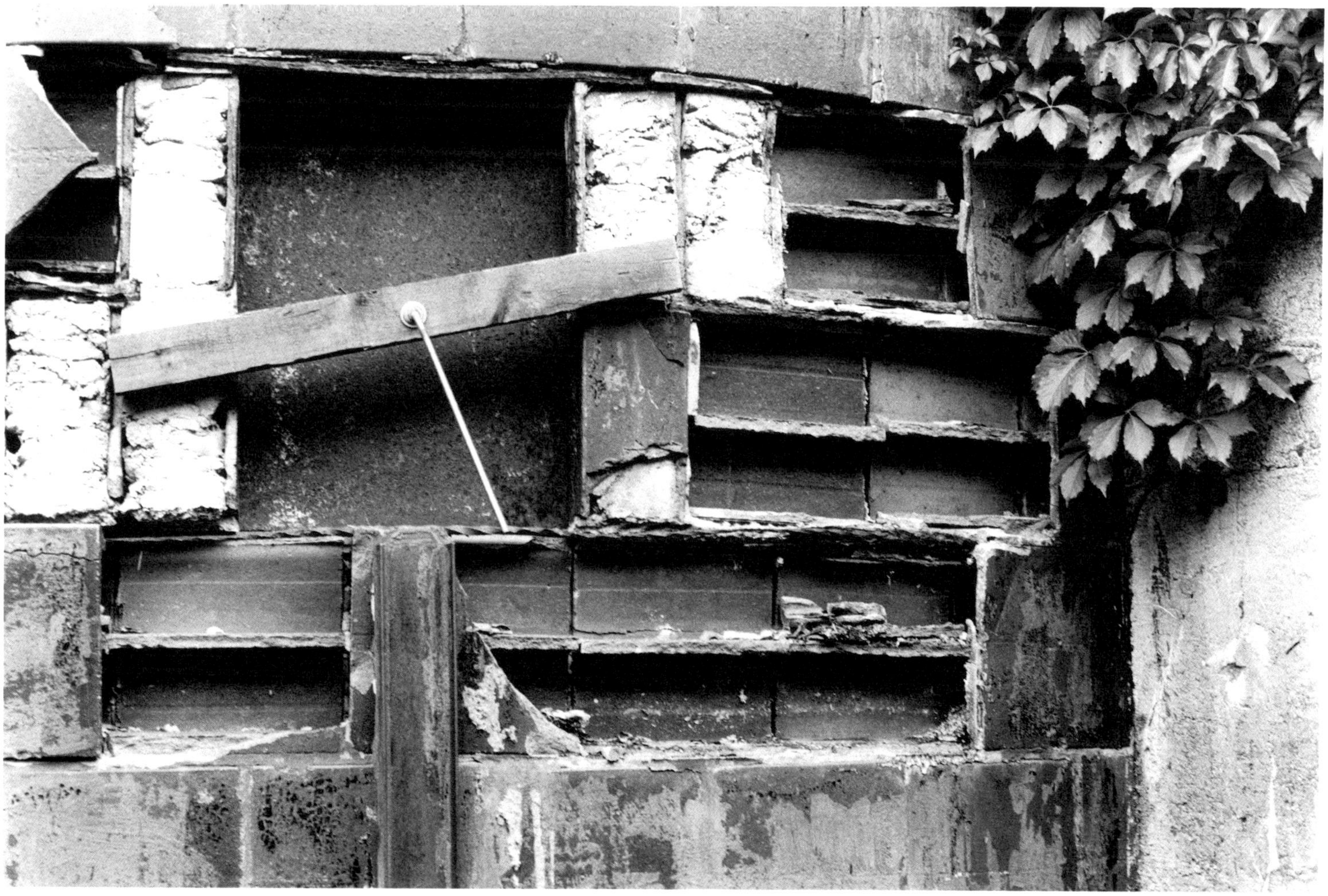

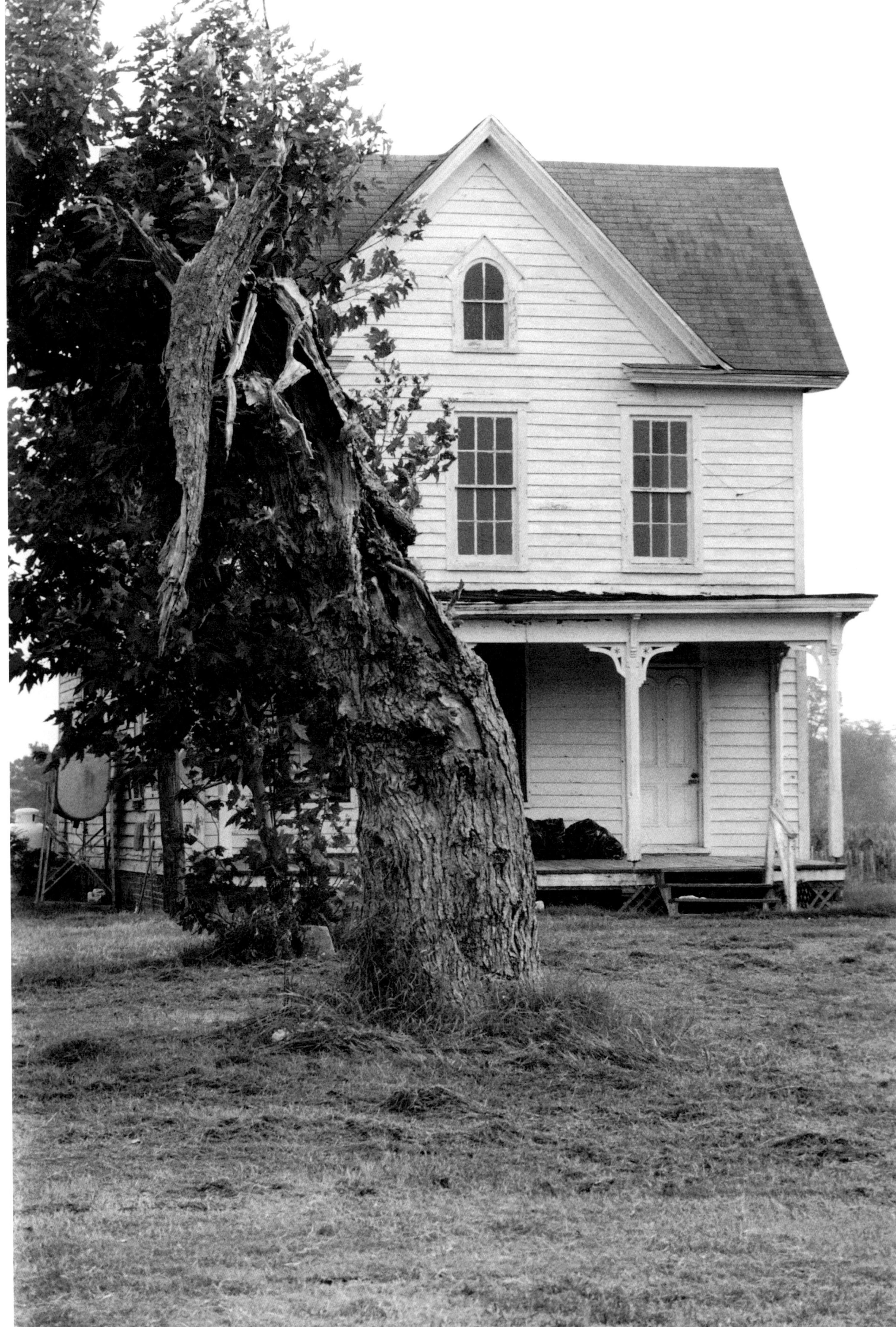

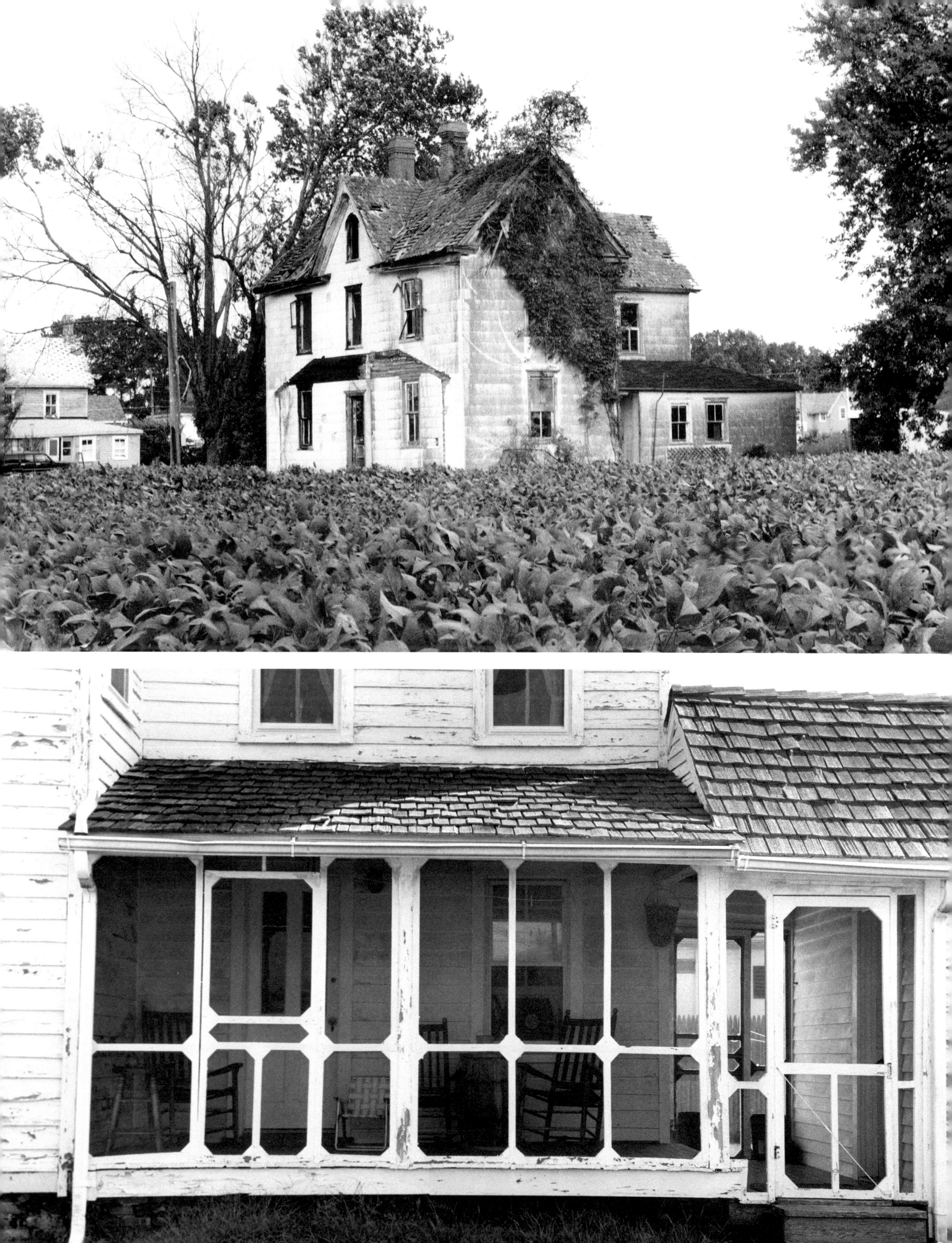

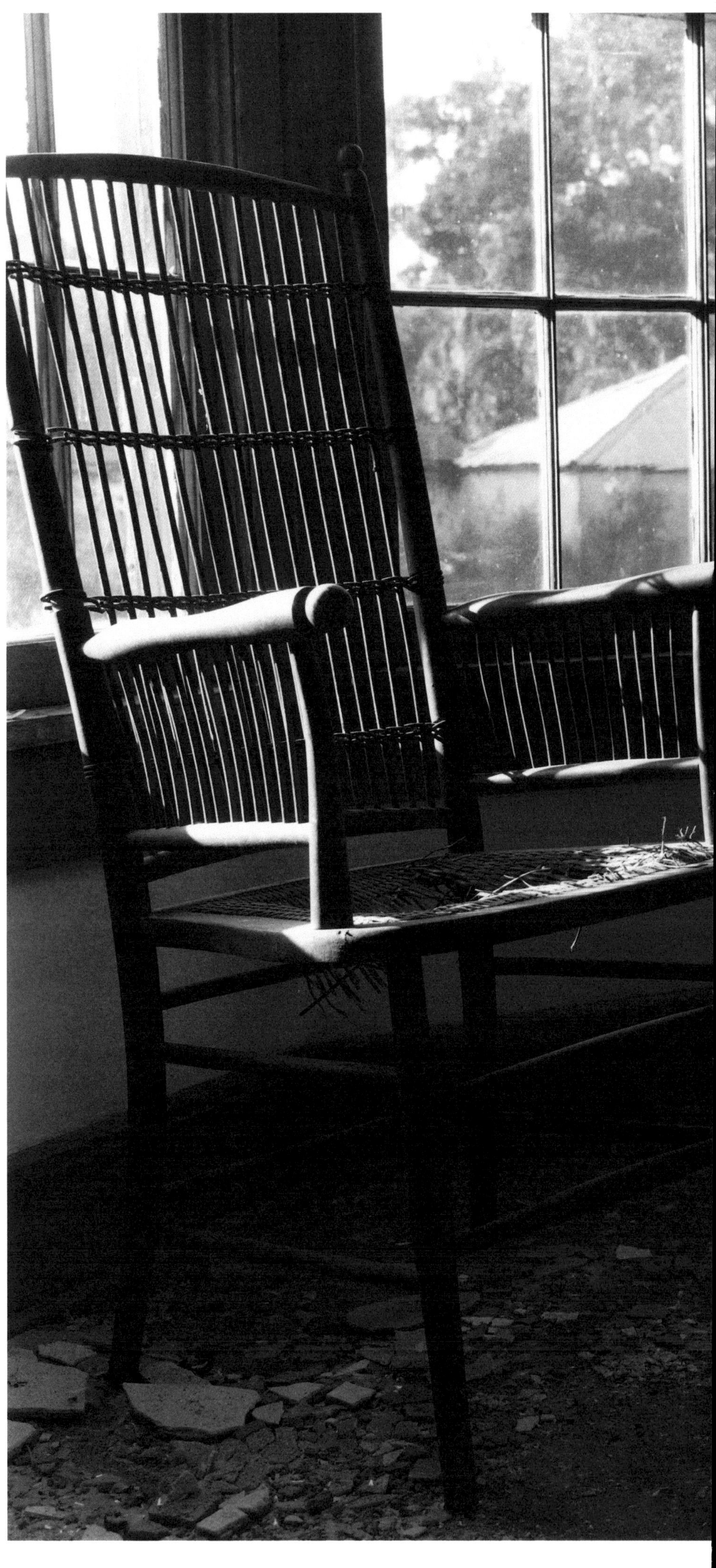

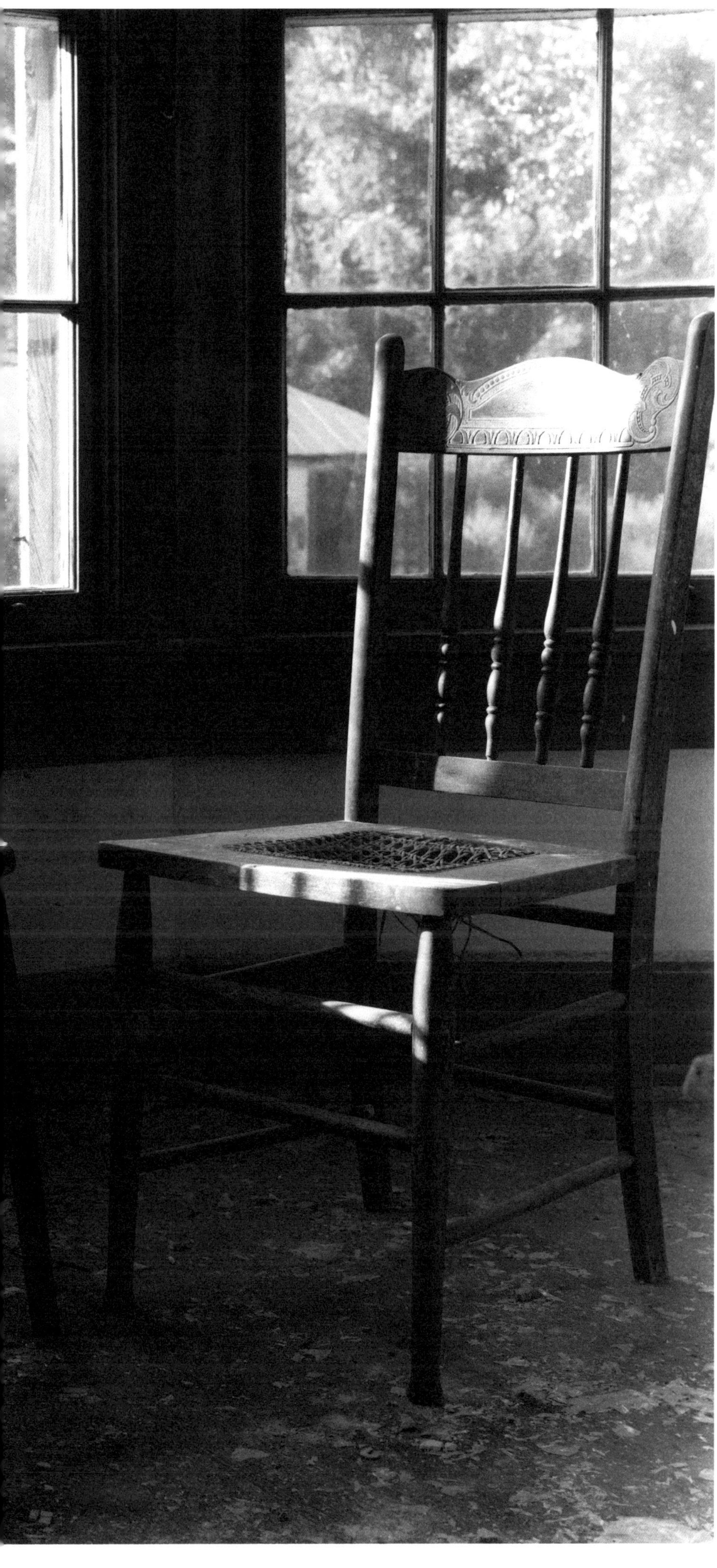

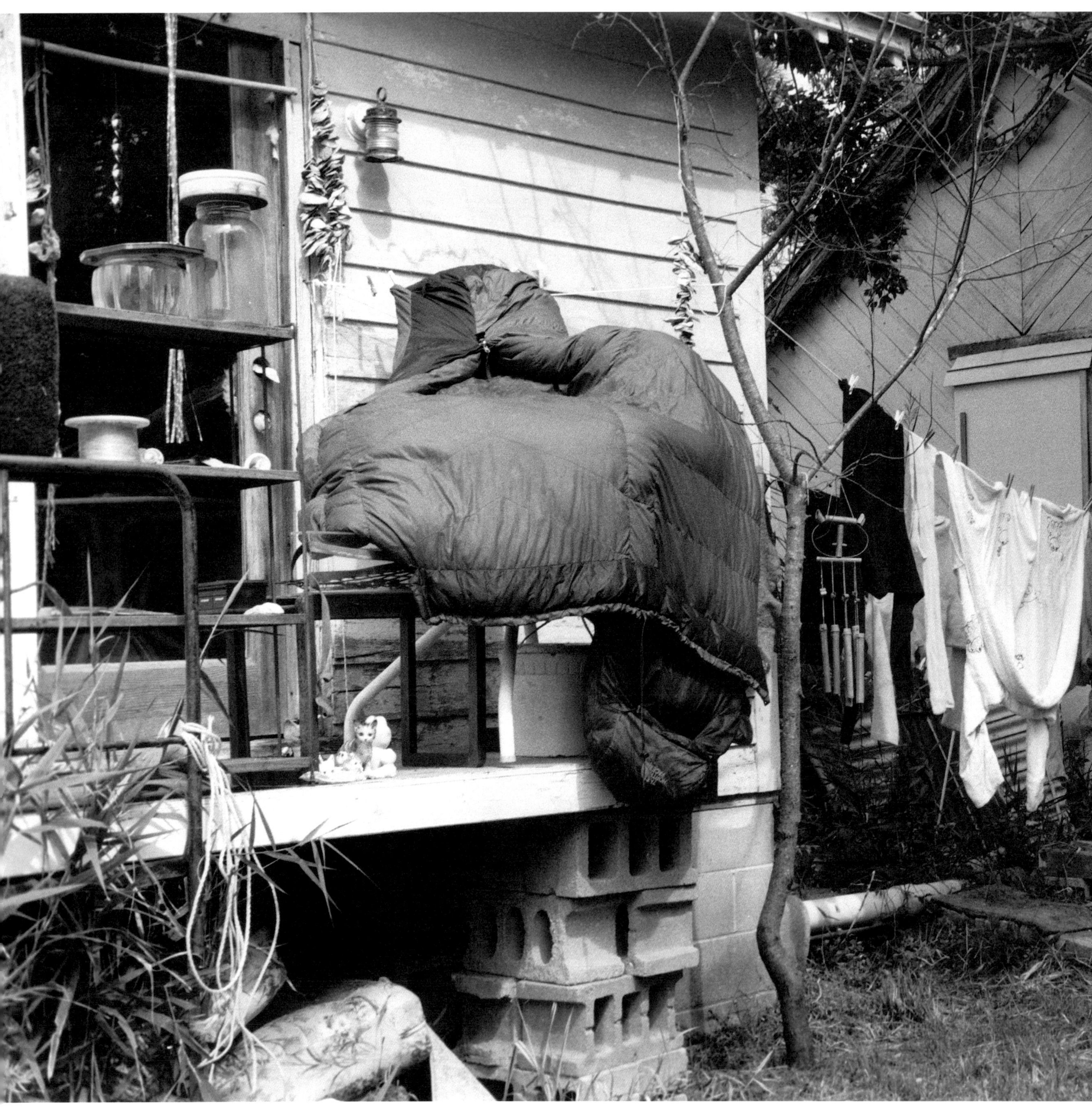

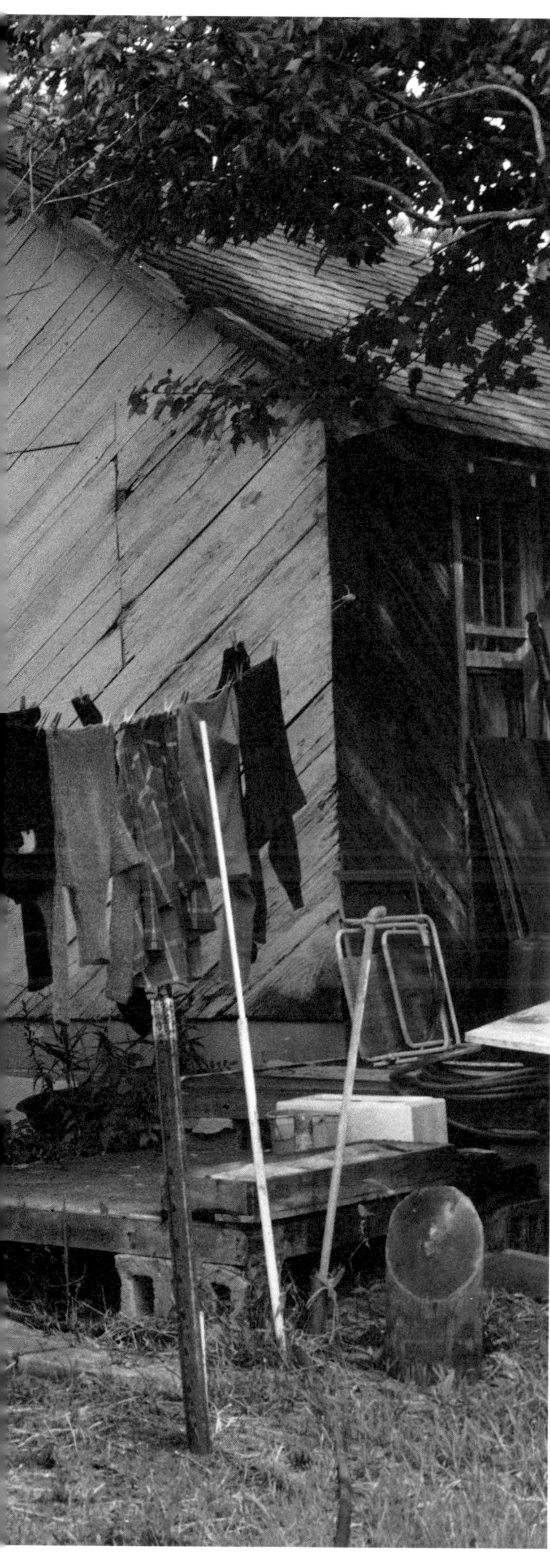

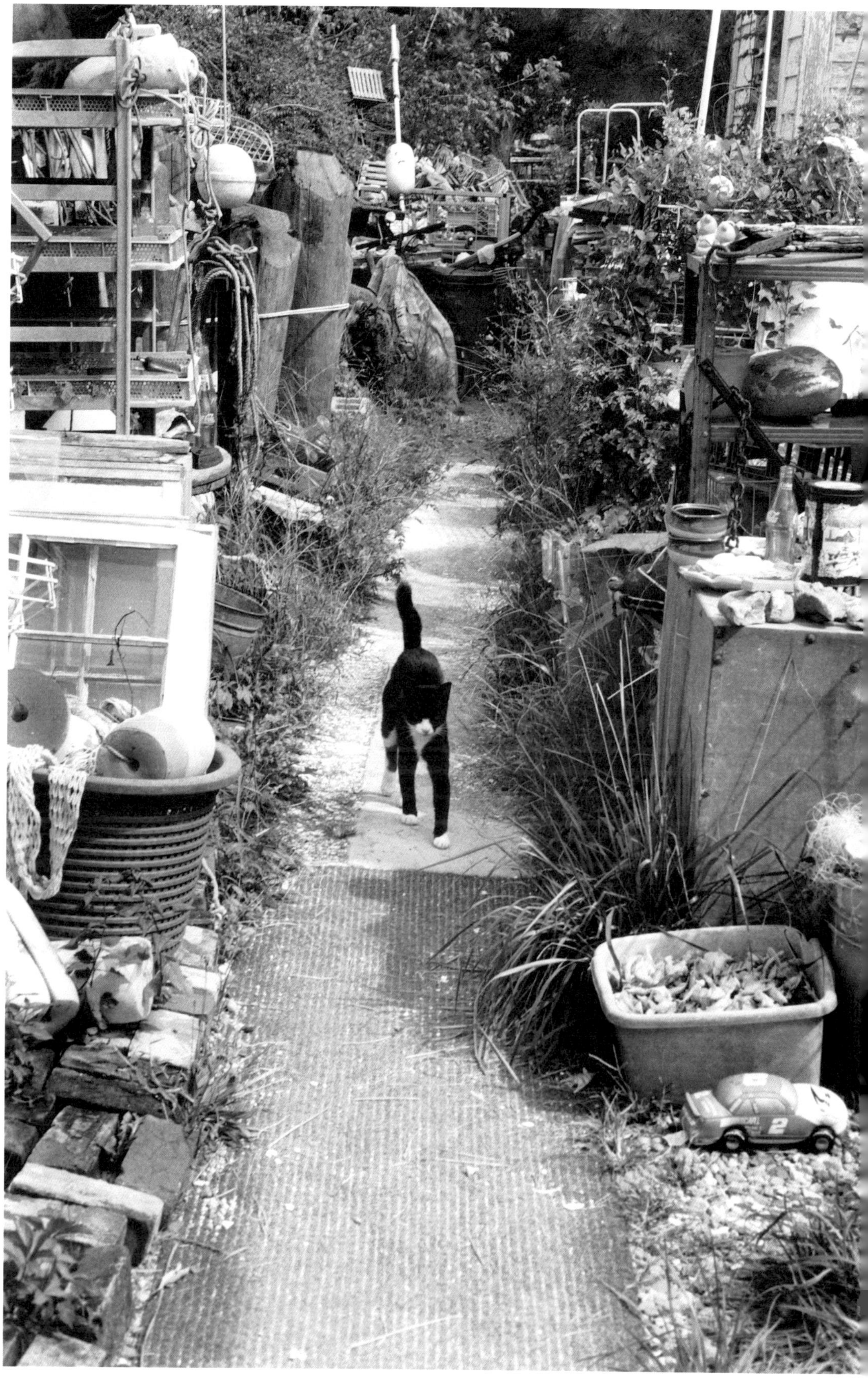

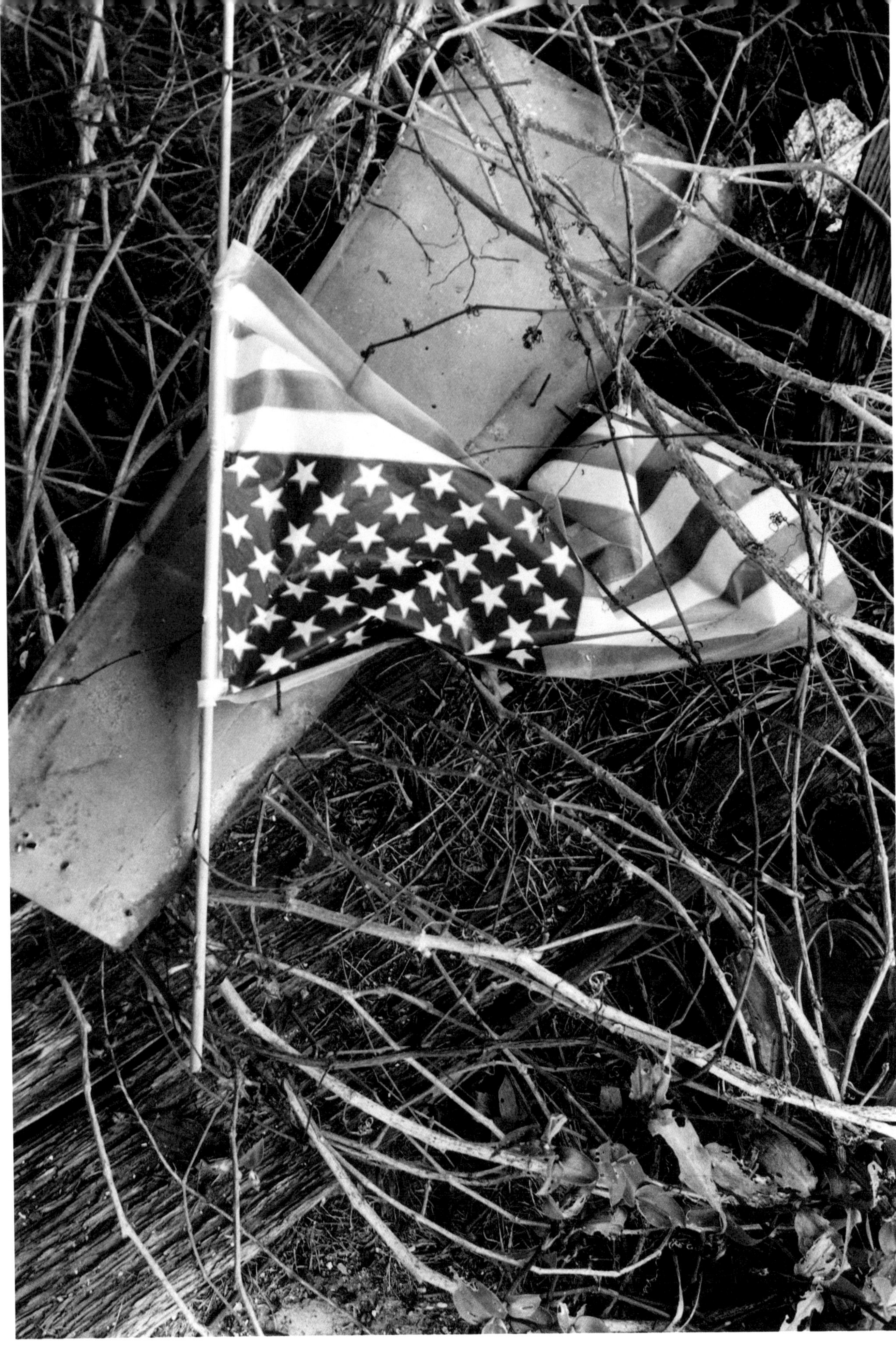

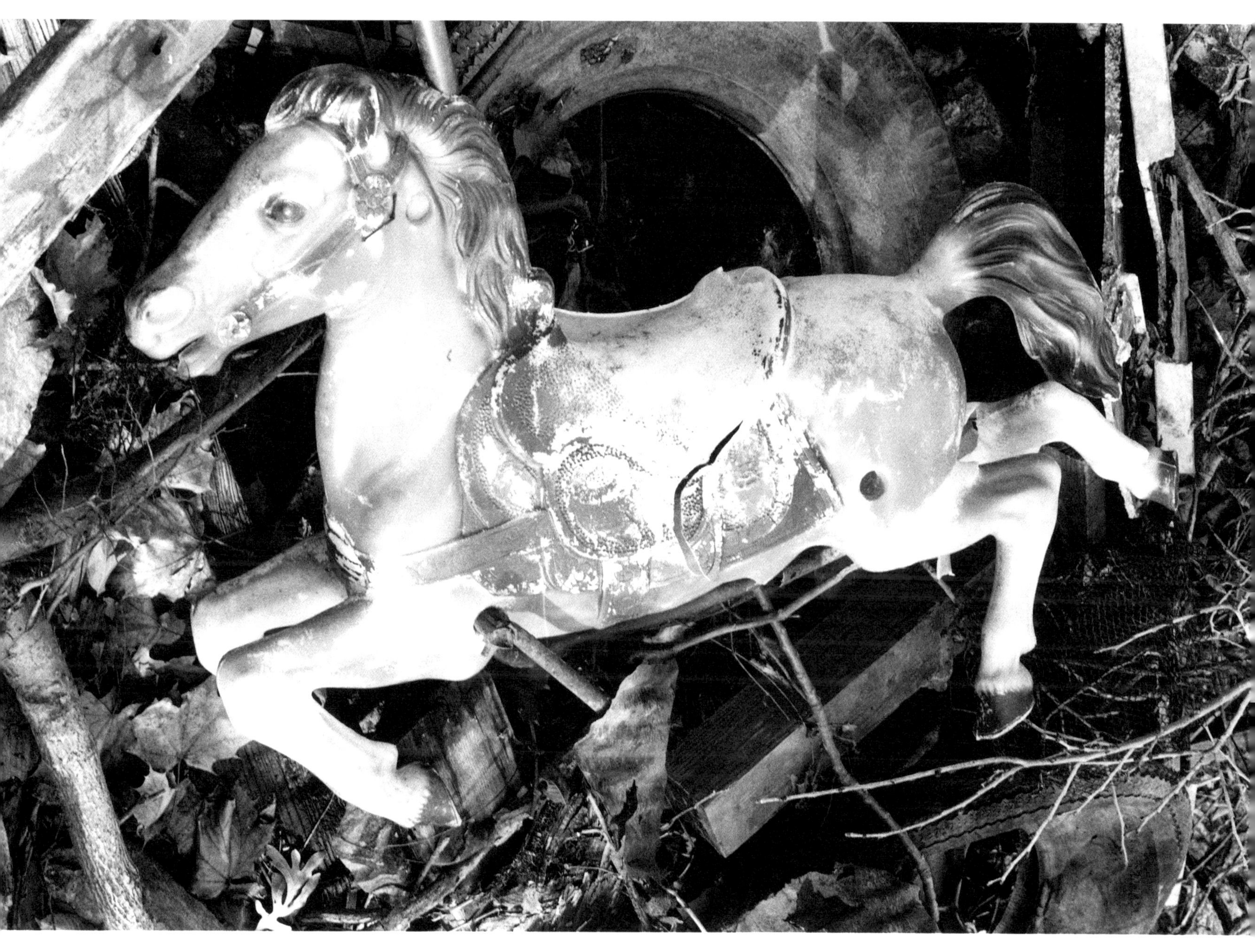

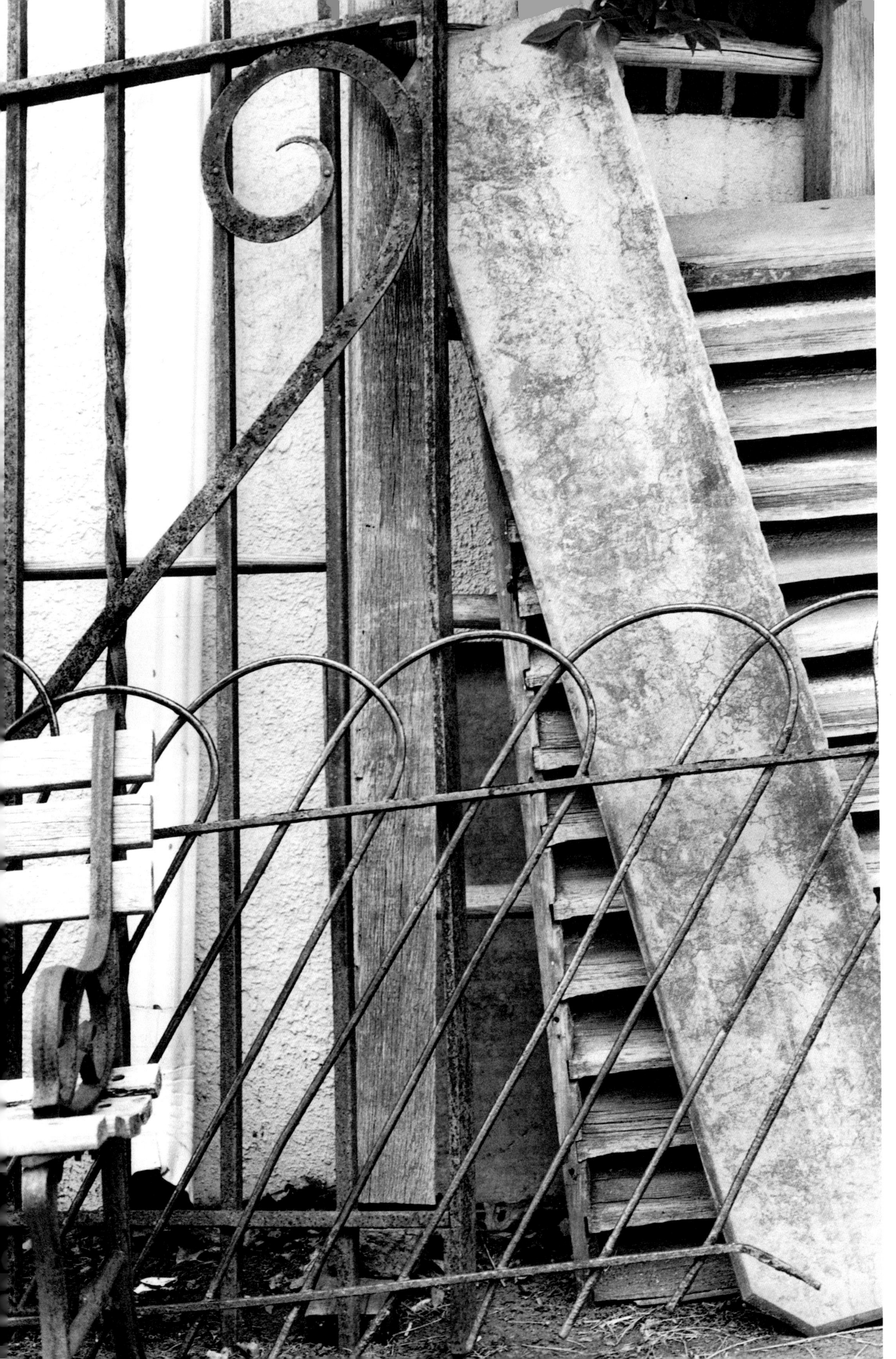

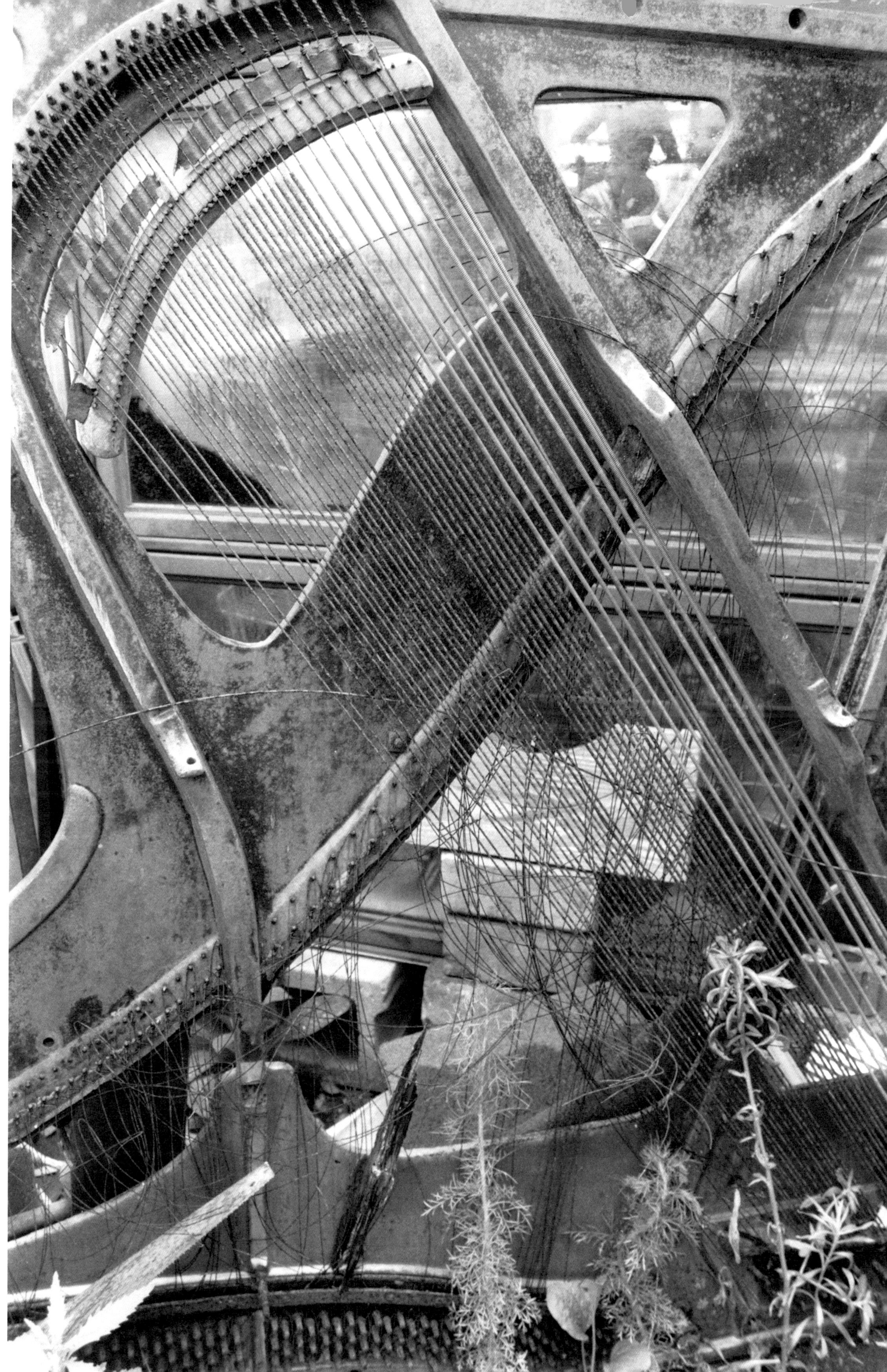

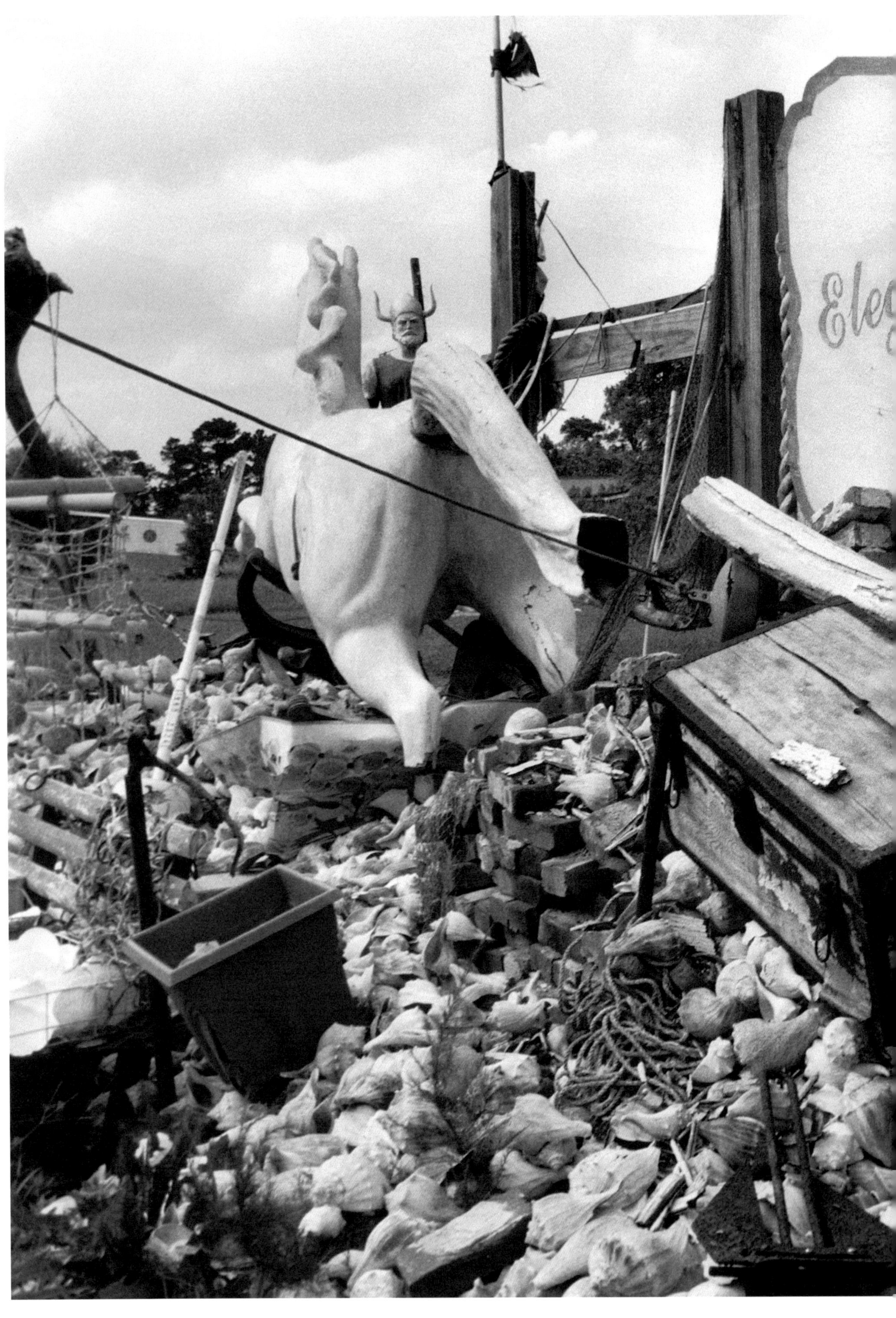

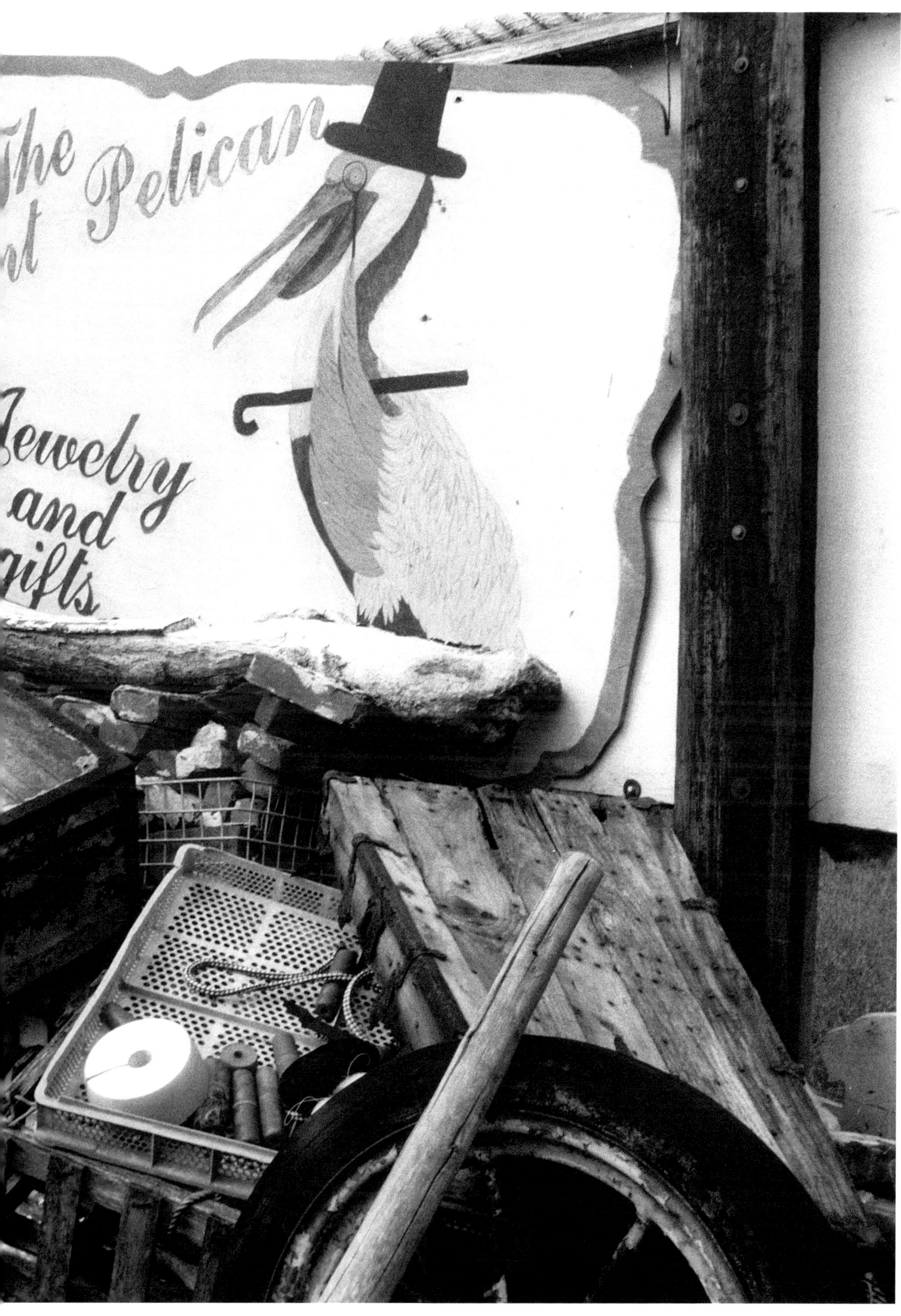
The
t Pelican
Jewelry
and
gifts

For Sale
$5.00
SOLD

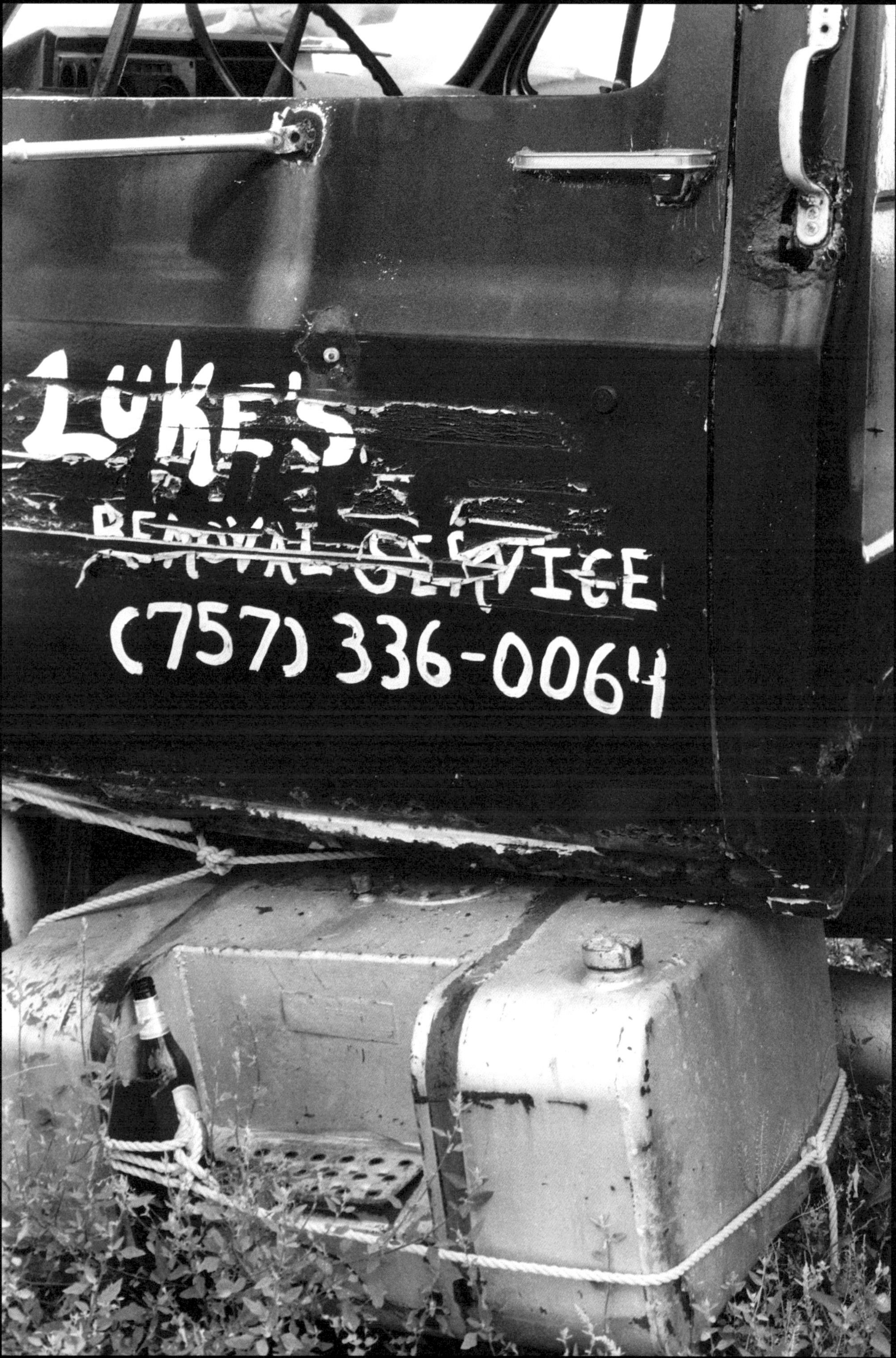

LUKE'S
REMOVAL SERVICE
(757) 336-0064

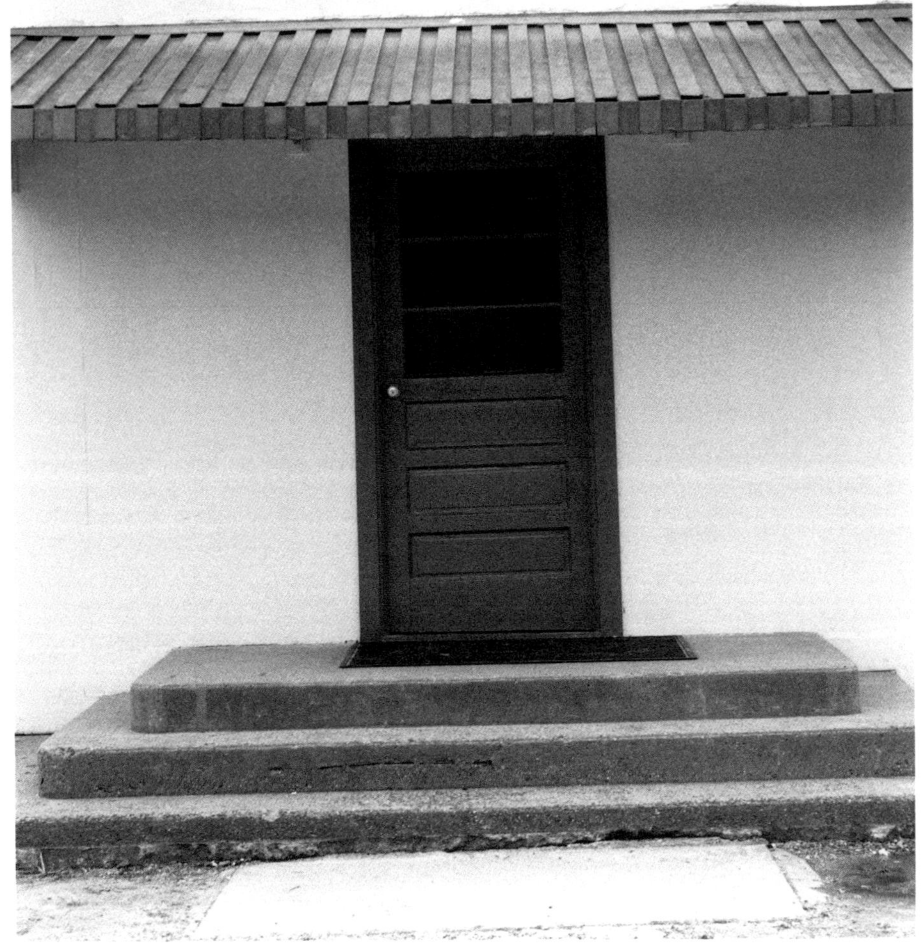

THE
Dream

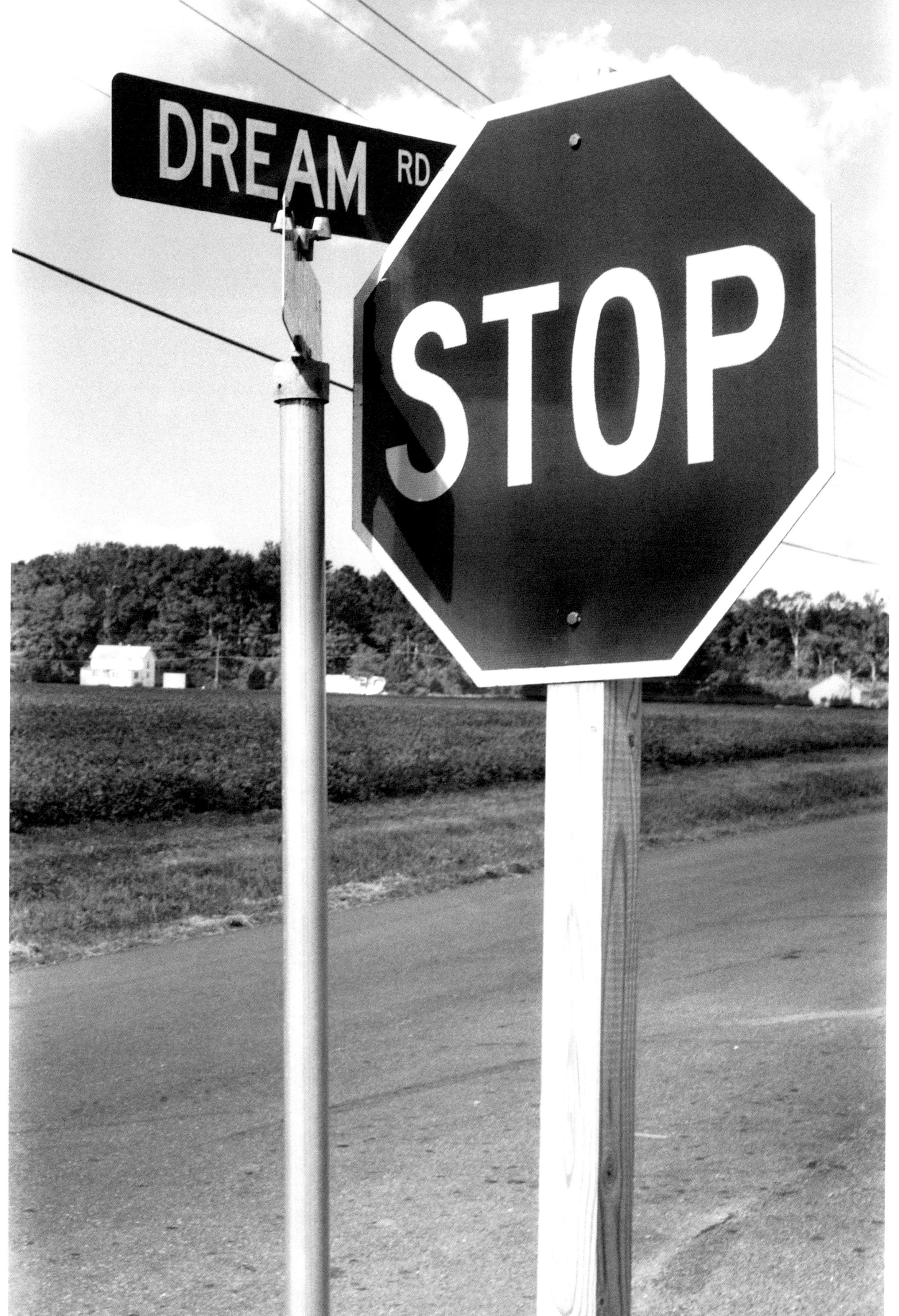

DREAM RD
STOP

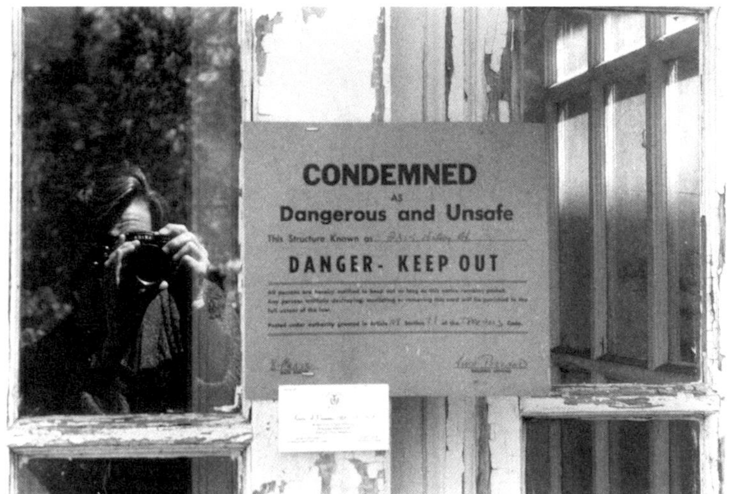

Andrea Baldeck's fascination with photography and travel began with a childhood Brownie camera and a stack of *National Geographics*, and has taken her to the tops of mountains, small islands, ancient cities, and the rivers of Southeast Asia.

A musician and physician, she often squeezes flute and stethoscope into the same bag with the camera on her expeditions.

She pursues the moment, whatever its magnitude, using her craft to create an illusion of permanence from that which is fleeting. Whether plying the Grand Canal or the Mekong, or roaming gardens and fields, Baldeck delights in the micro- and macrocosmic wonders of the visual world.

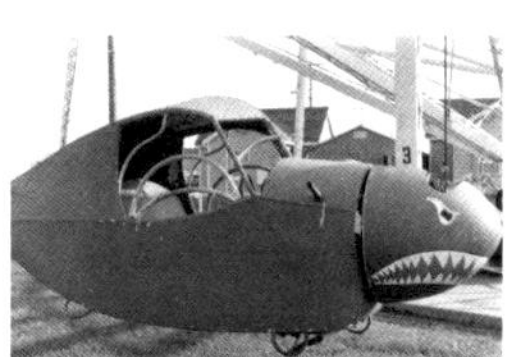

p. 36
Wachapreague, VA

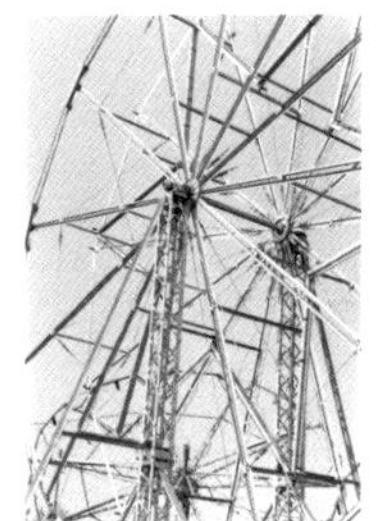

p. 37
Wachapreague, VA

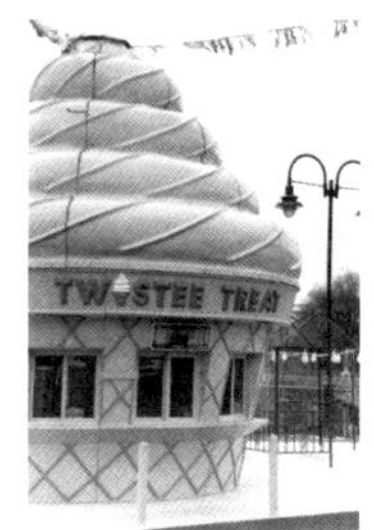

p. 38
Near Collegeville, PA

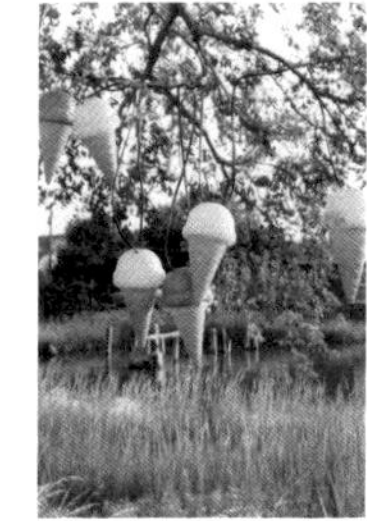

p. 39
Chincoteague, VA

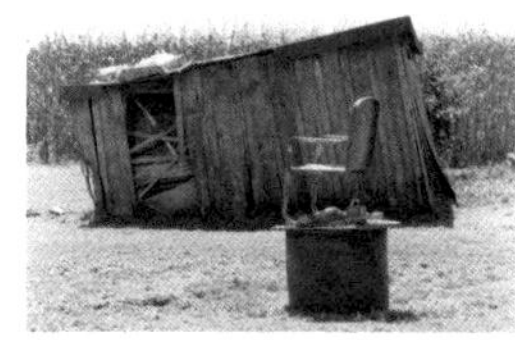

p. 40
Northampton County, VA

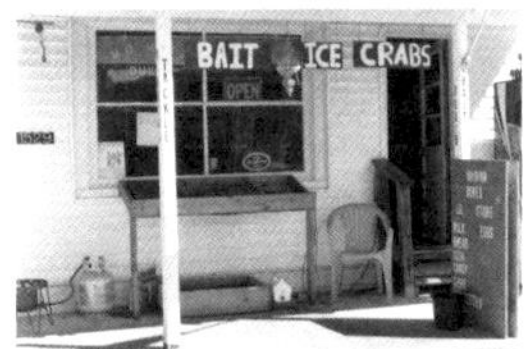

p. 42
Greenbackville, VA

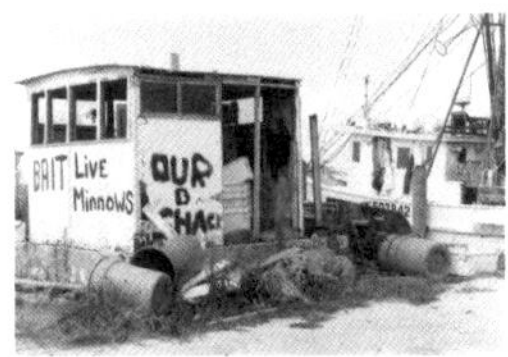

p. 43
Chincoteague, VA

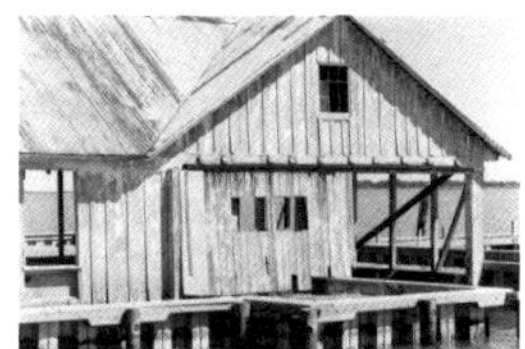

p. 44
Willis Wharf, VA

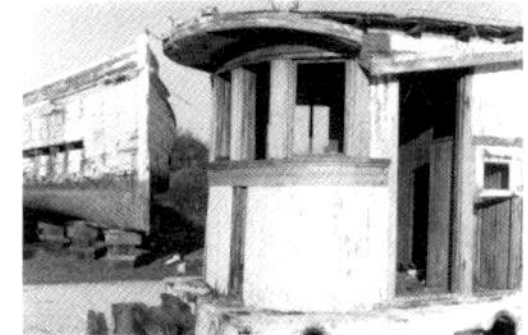

p. 44
Wachapreague, VA

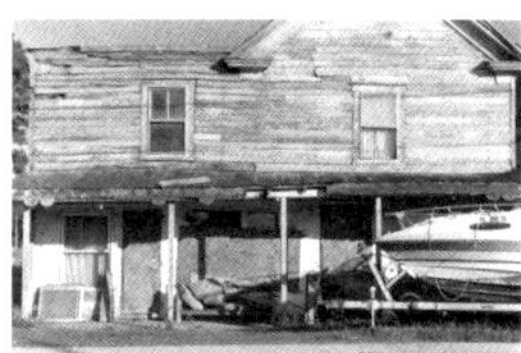

p. 44
Metompkin, VA

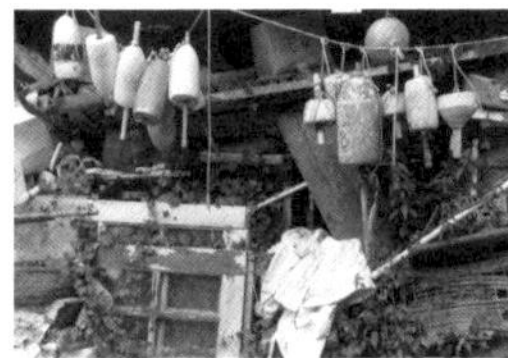

p. 46
Chincoteague, VA

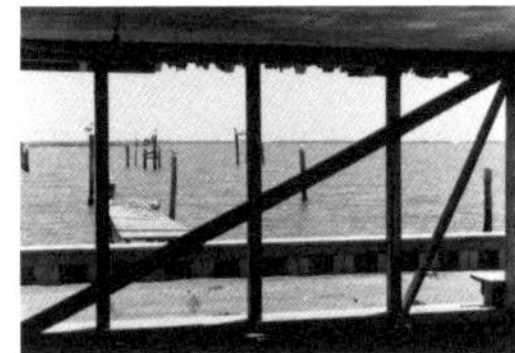

p. 48
Willis Wharf, VA

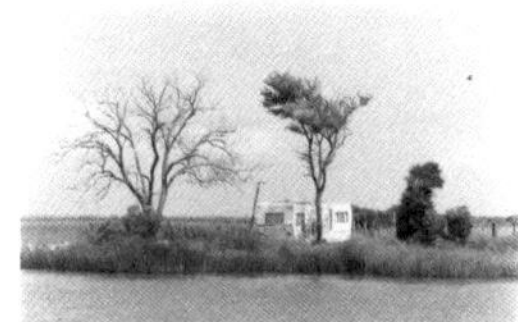

p. 50
Chincoteague, VA

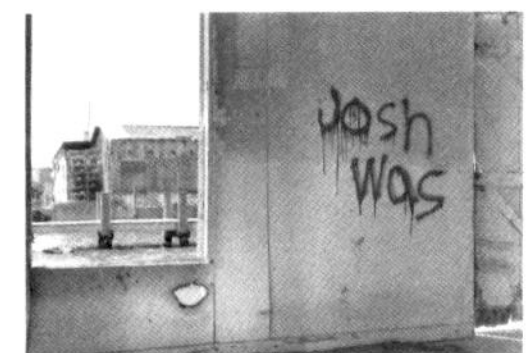

p. 52
Willis Wharf, VA

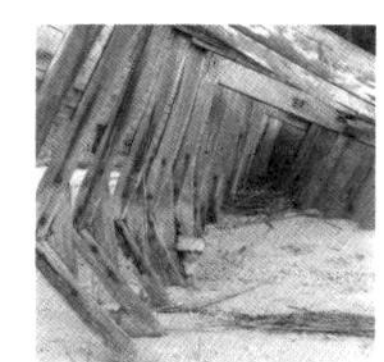

p. 53
Cumberland Island, GA

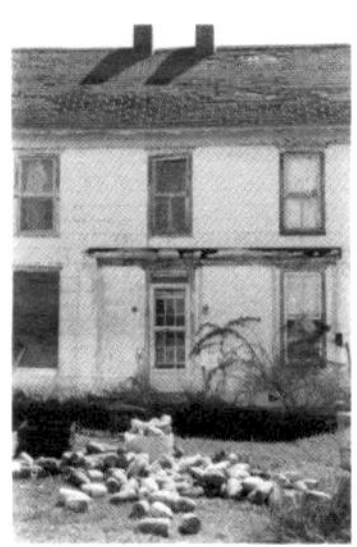

p. 54
Saxis, VA

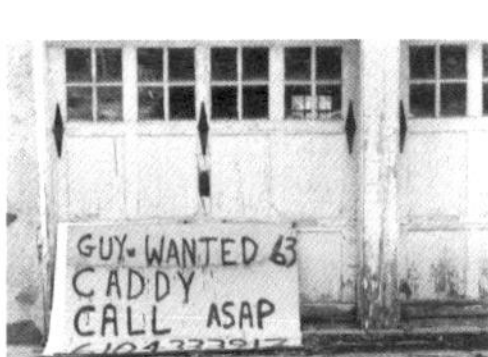

p. 55
Plymouth Meeting, PA

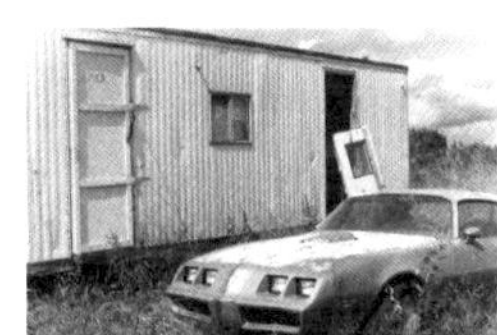

p. 56
Chincoteague, VA

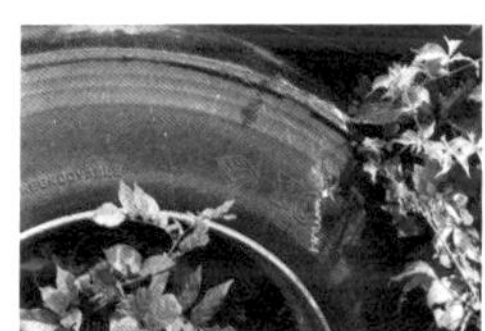

p. 56
Mappsville, VA

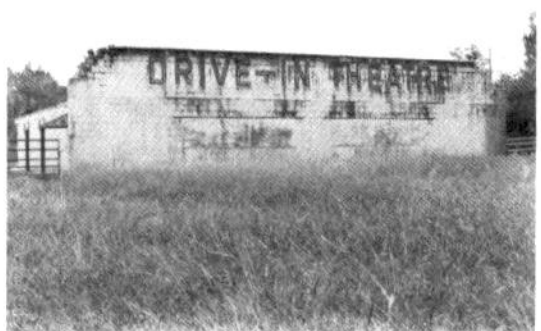

p. 57
Wattsville, VA

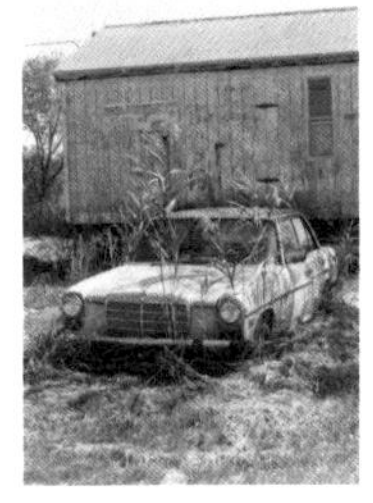

p. 58
Shad Landing, VA

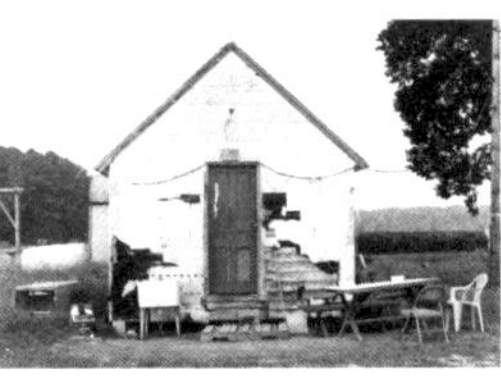

p. 59
Chancetown, VA

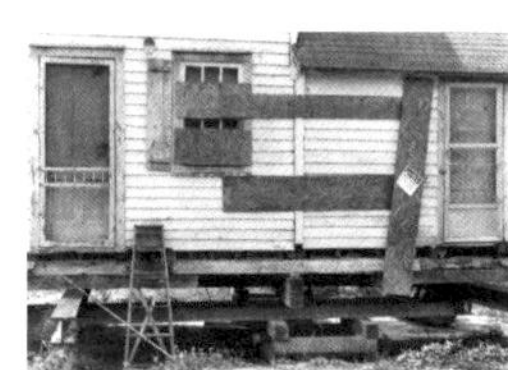

p. 59
Pastoria, VA

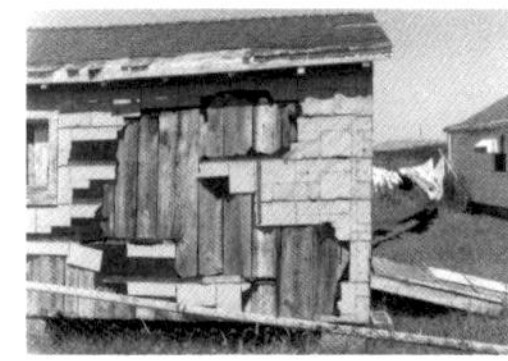

p. 60
Tangier Island, VA

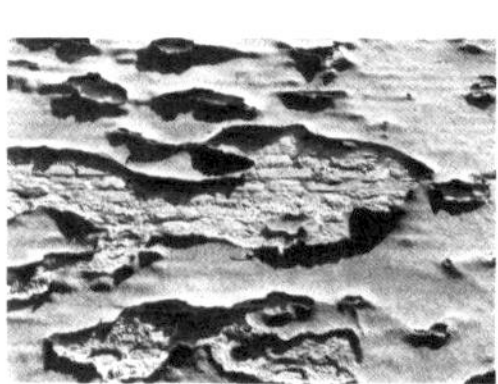

p. 62
Blistered stucco,
Venice, Italy

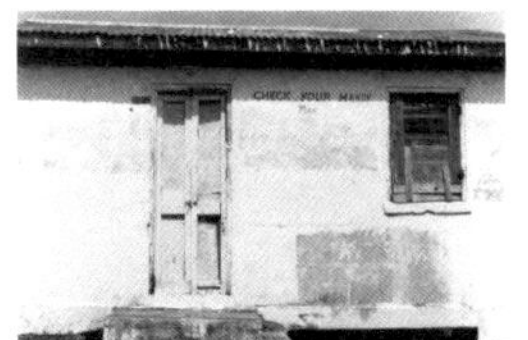

p. 63
Carriacou, Grenada

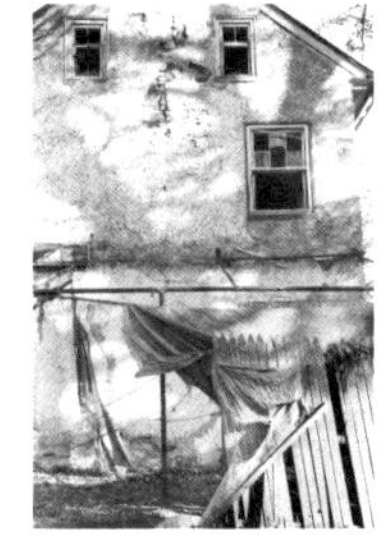

p. 64
Plymouth Meeting, PA

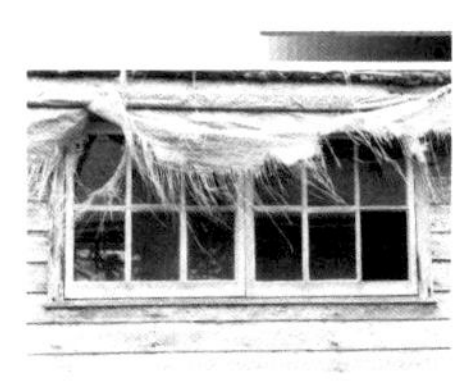

p. 65
Fort Washington, PA

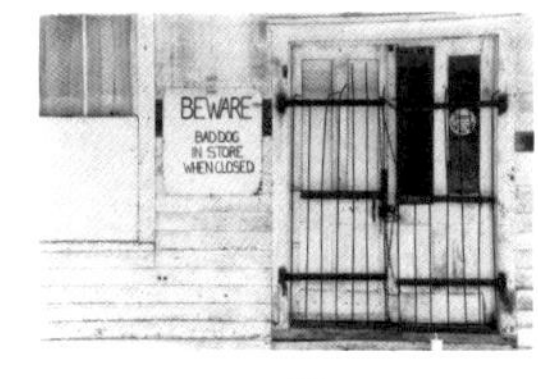

p. 65
Oak Hall, VA

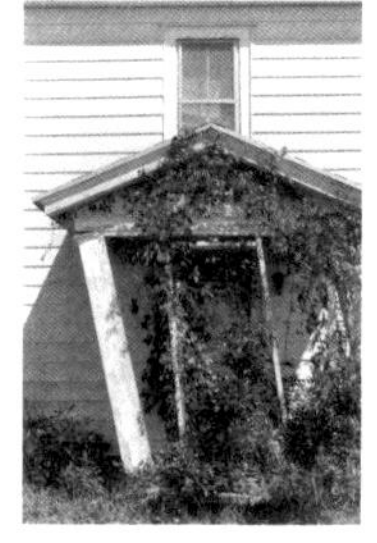

p. 66
Melfa, VA

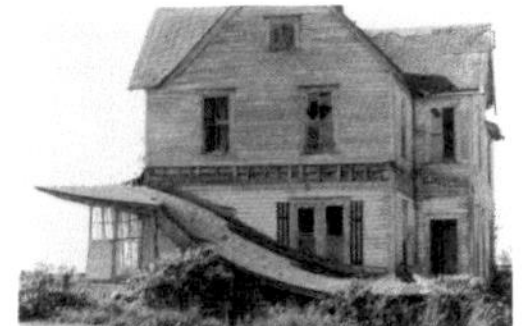

p. 66
Near Assawoman, VA

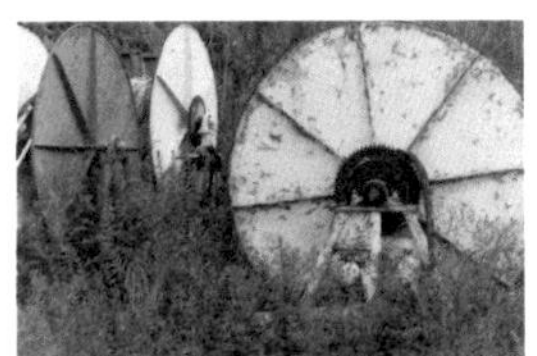

p. 68
Chincoteague, VA

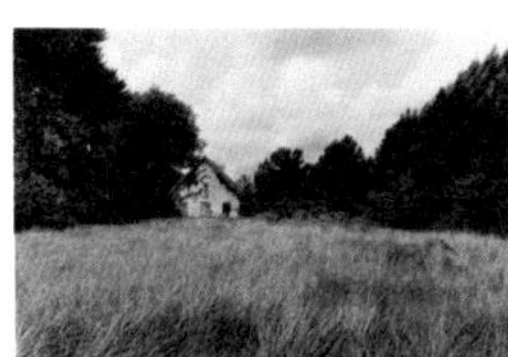

p. 70
Accomack County, VA

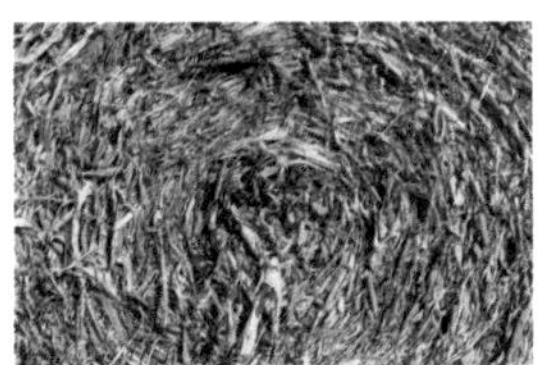

p. 72
Worcester County, MD

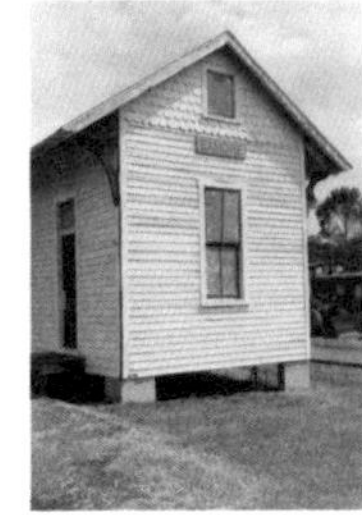

p. 74
Exmore, VA

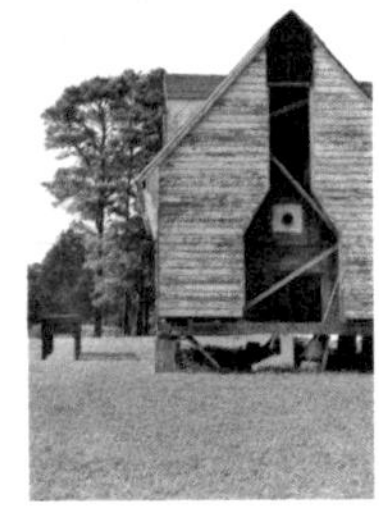

p. 75
Cedar Hall, VA

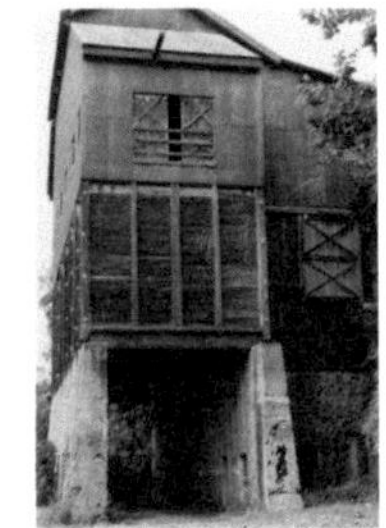

p. 76
Near Lambertville, NJ

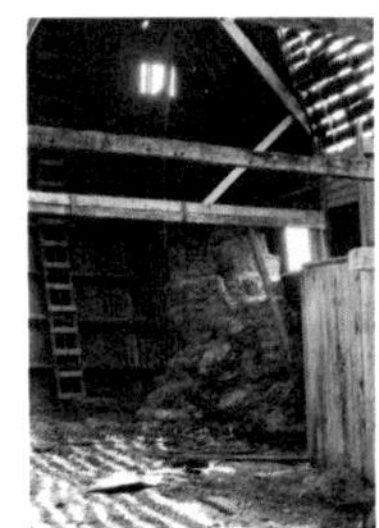

p. 77
Monroe County, NY

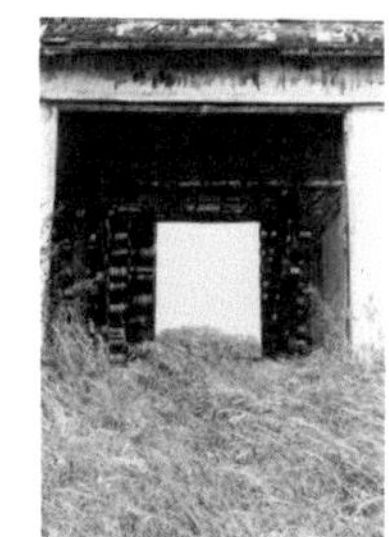

p. 77
Monroe County, NY

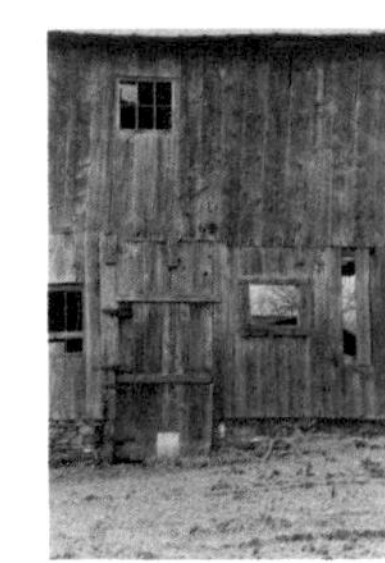

p. 77
Montgomery County, PA

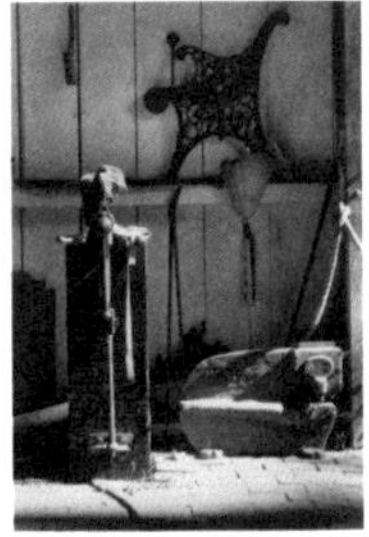

p. 77
Furnacetown, MD

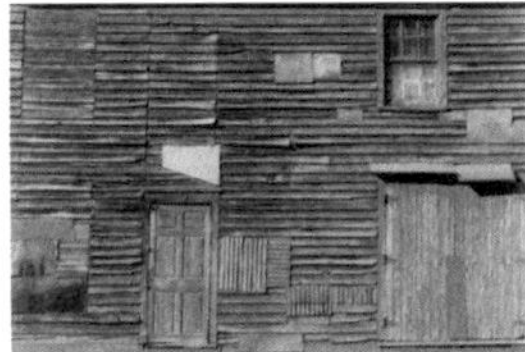

p. 78
Grangeville, VA

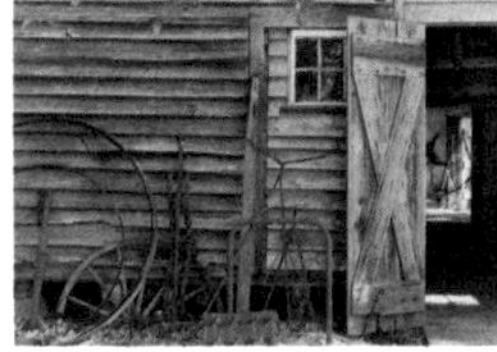

p. 79
Furnacetown, MD

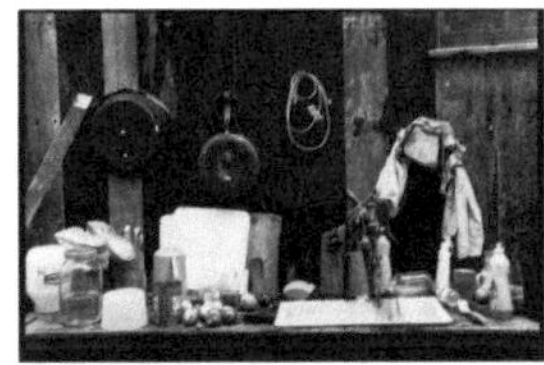

p. 80
Cumberland Island, GA

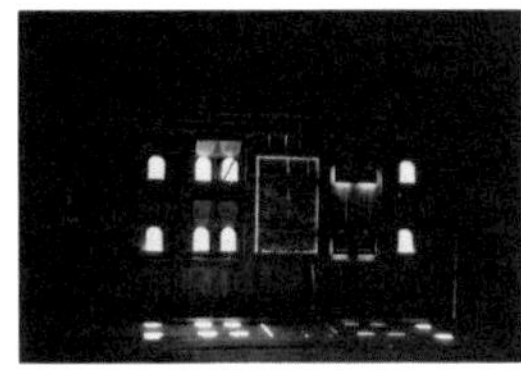

p. 82
Sapelo Island, GA

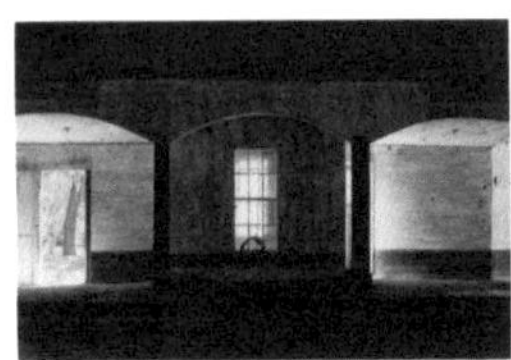

p. 83
Sapelo Island, GA

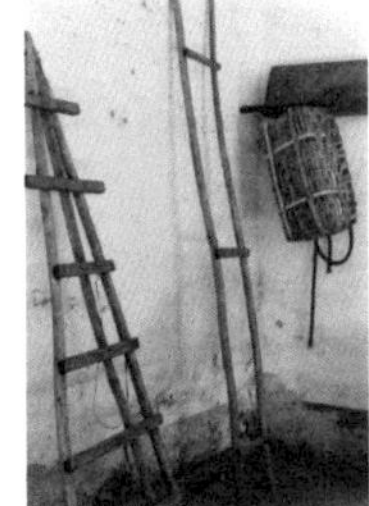

p. 84
Tuscany, Italy

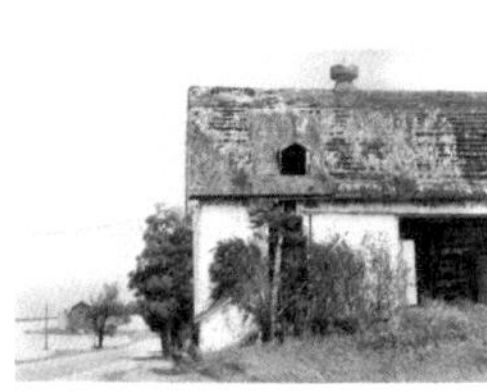

p. 84
Monroe County, NY

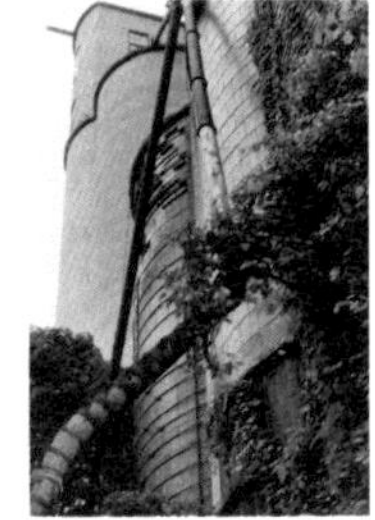

p. 86
Pittsford, NY

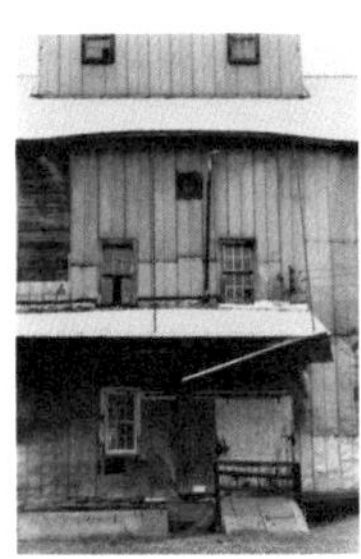

p. 87
Pittsford, NY

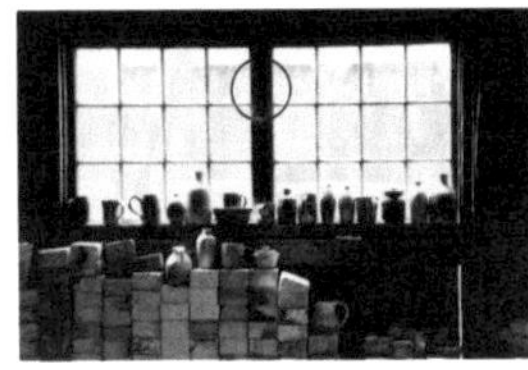

p. 88
Mumford, NY

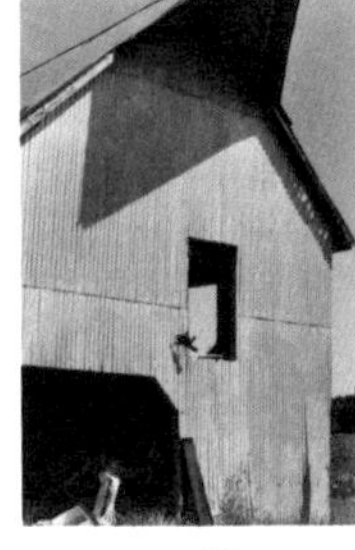

p. 90
Chancetown, VA

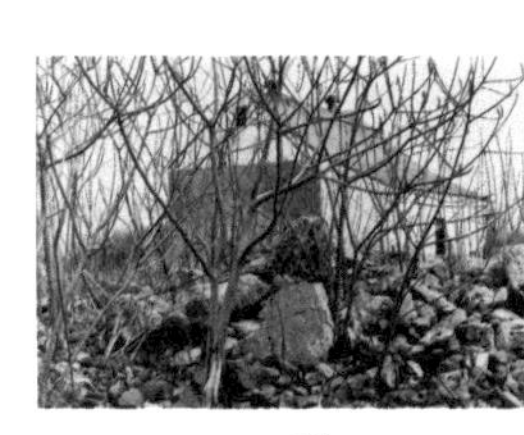

p. 91
Near Collegeville, PA

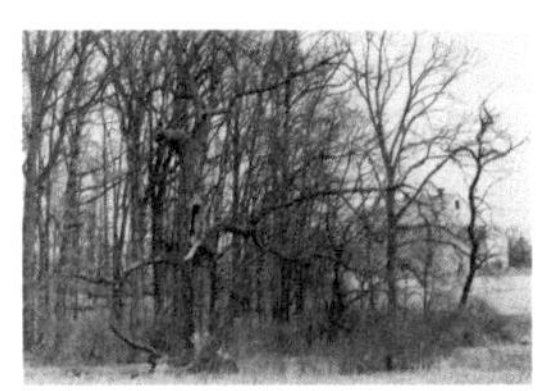

p. 91
Near Collegeville, PA

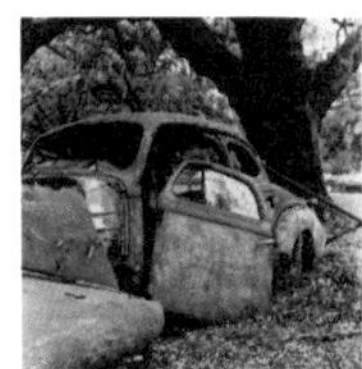

p. 92
Cumberland Island, GA

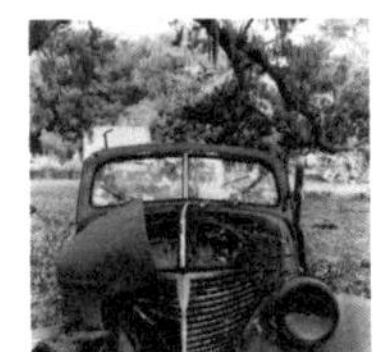

p. 93
Cumberland Island, GA

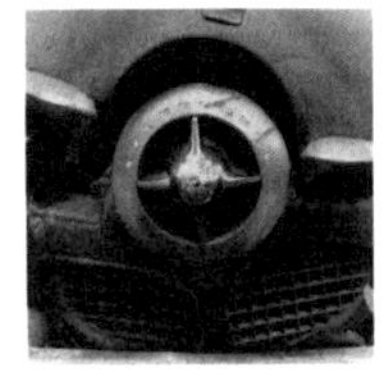

p. 94
Cumberland Island, GA

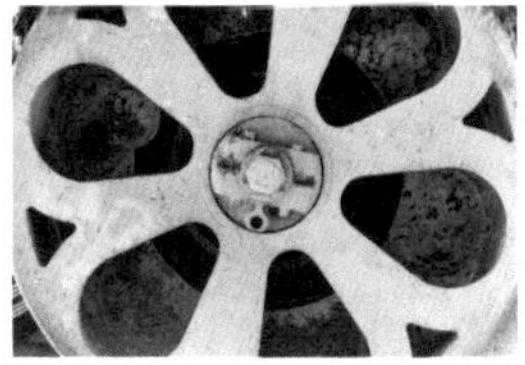

p. 94
Vieques, PR

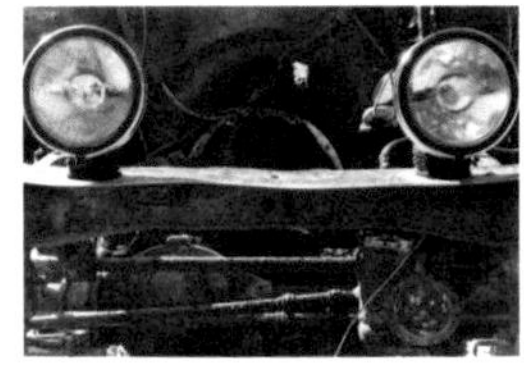

p. 94
Vieques, PR

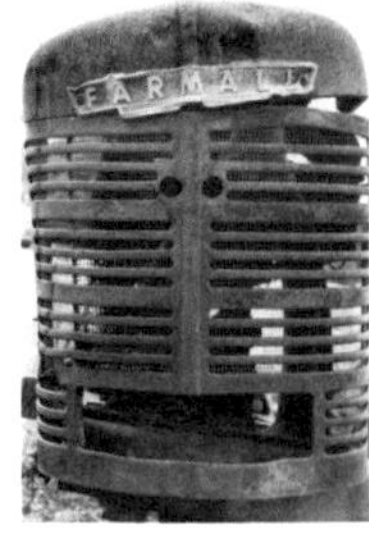

p. 95
Near Collegeville, PA

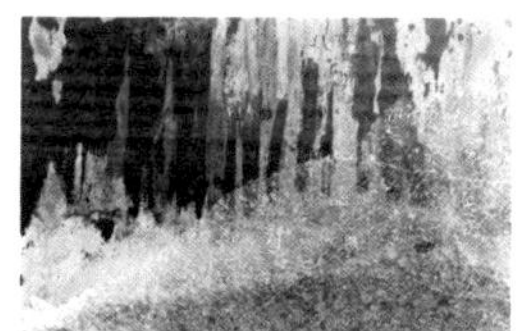

p. 96
Fractured Glass
Blue Bell, PA

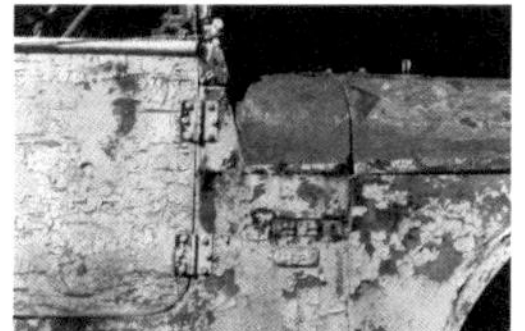

p. 97
Vieques, PR

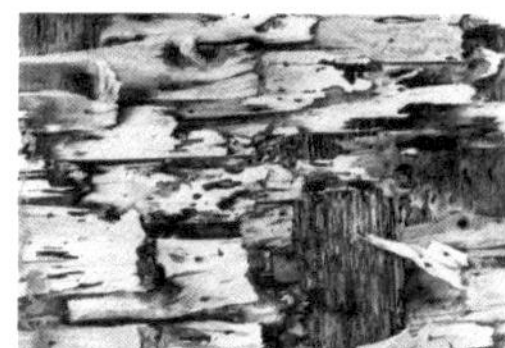

p. 98
Frayed shingles,
Carriacou, Grenada

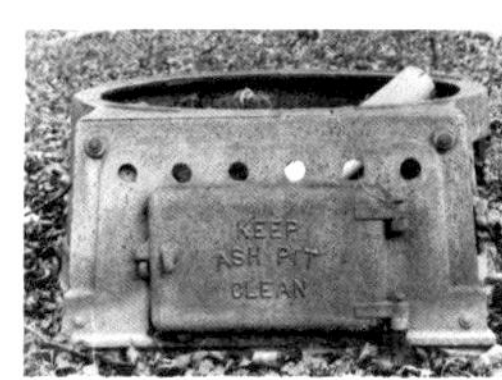

p. 99
Plymouth Meeting, PA

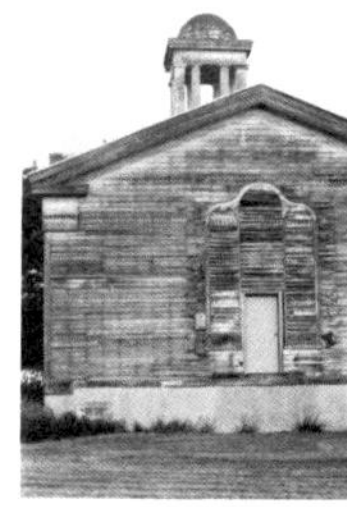

p. 100
Cuylerville, NY

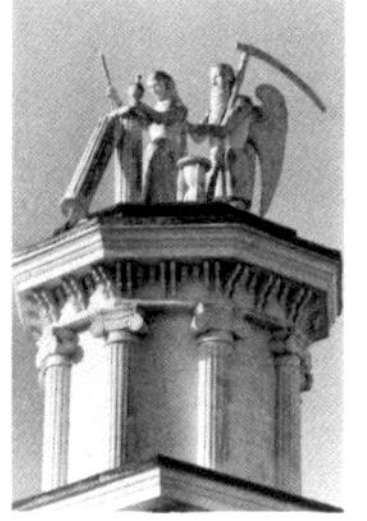

p. 101
Mendocino, CA

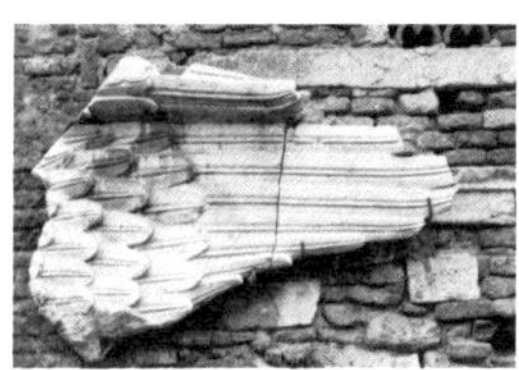

p. 102
Vicenza, Italy

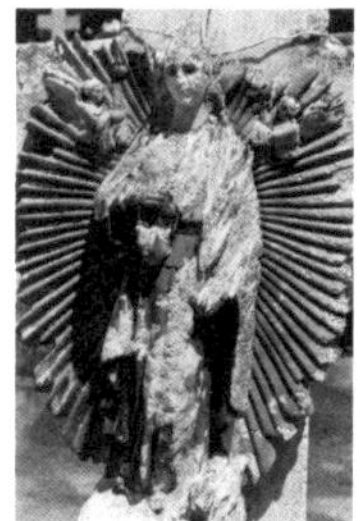

p. 103
Vieques, PR

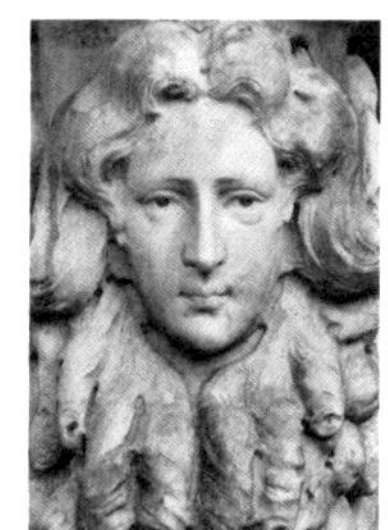

p. 104
Cumberland Island, GA

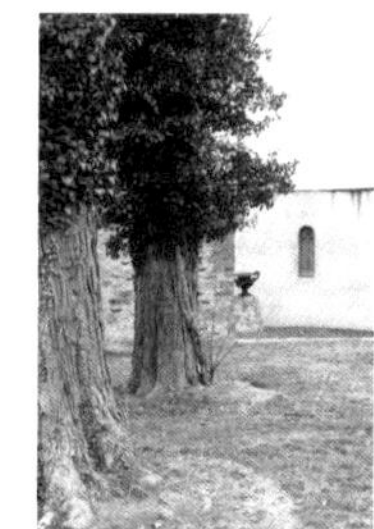

p. 105
Fort Washington, PA

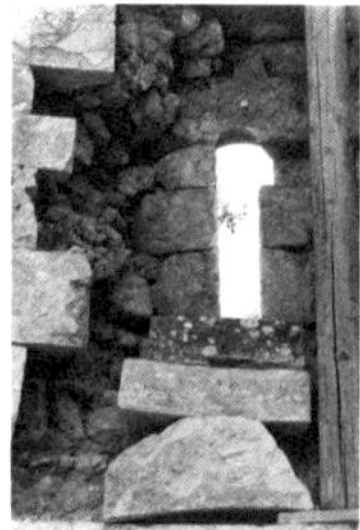

p. 106
Tuscany, Italy

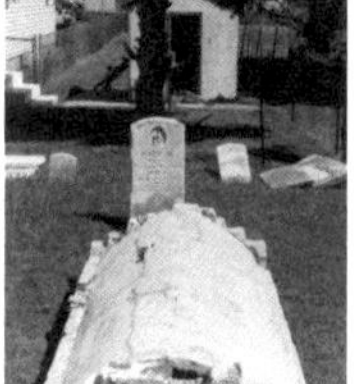

p. 107
Tangier Island, VA

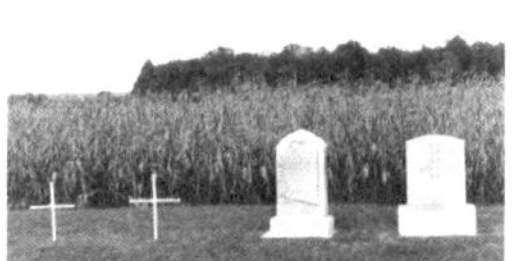

p. 108
Accomack County, VA

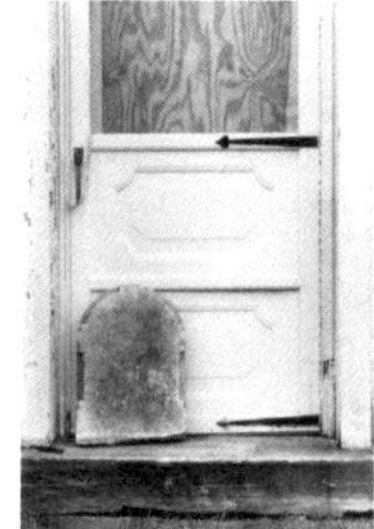

p. 109
Cold Point, PA

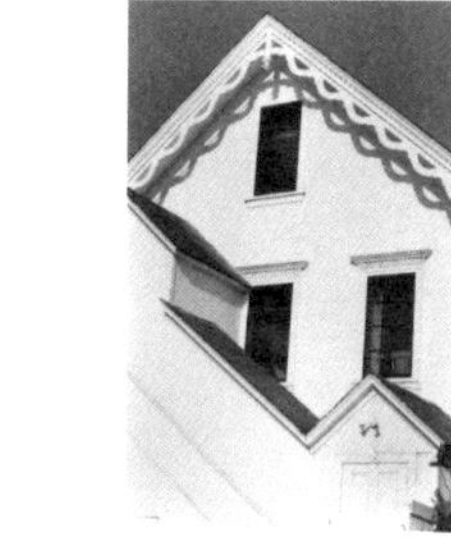

p. 110
Mendocino, CA

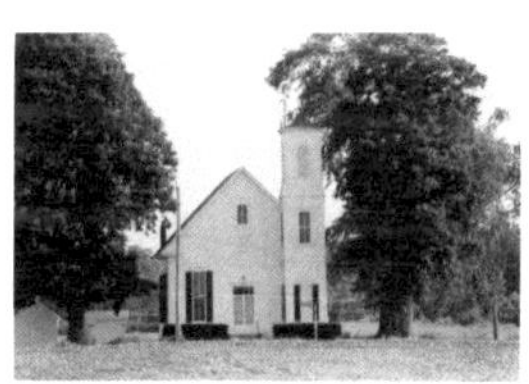

p. 110
Horntown, VA

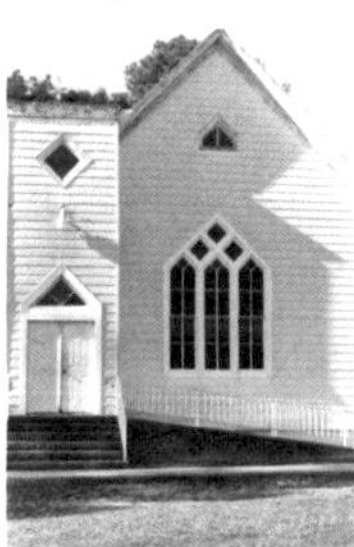

p. 111
Nassawadox, VA

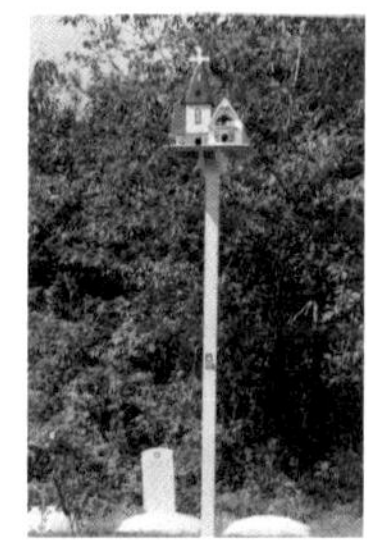

p. 112
Tangier Island, VA

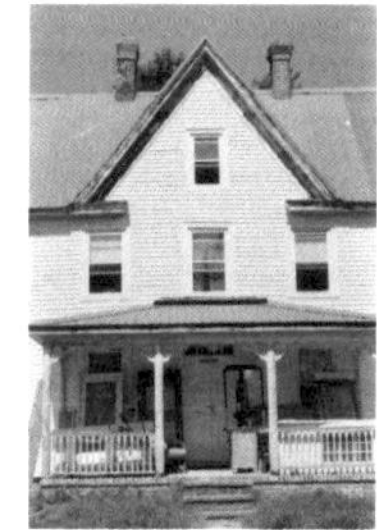

p. 113
Atlantic, VA

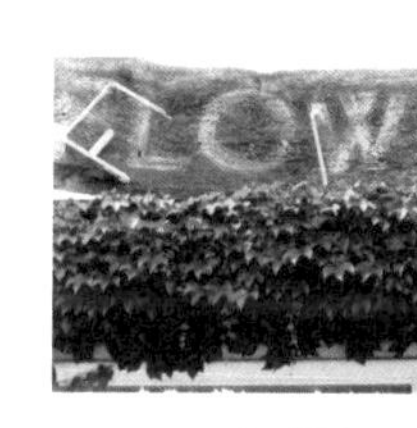

p. 114
Fort Washington, PA

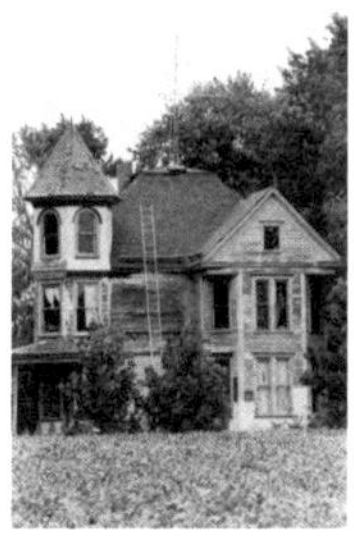

p. 116
Hopeton, VA

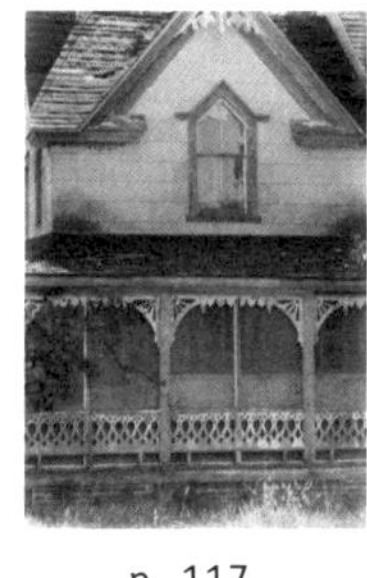

p. 117
Onley, VA

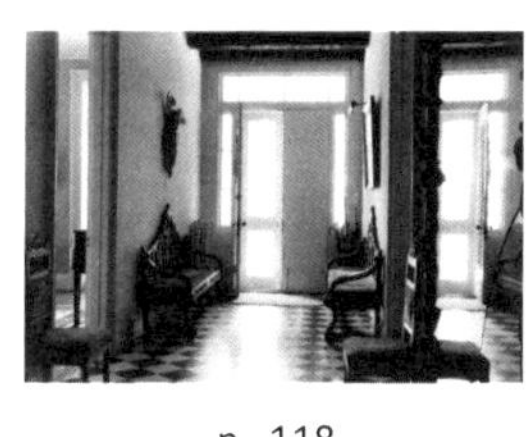

p. 118
Philadelphia, PA

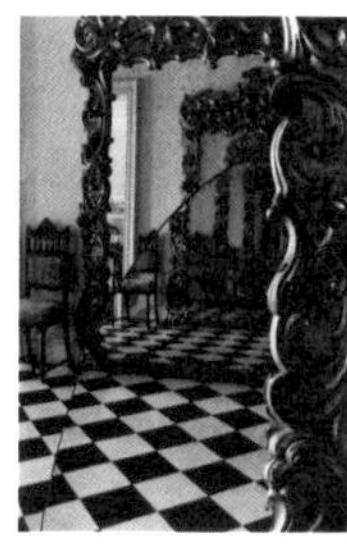

p. 119
Philadelphia, PA

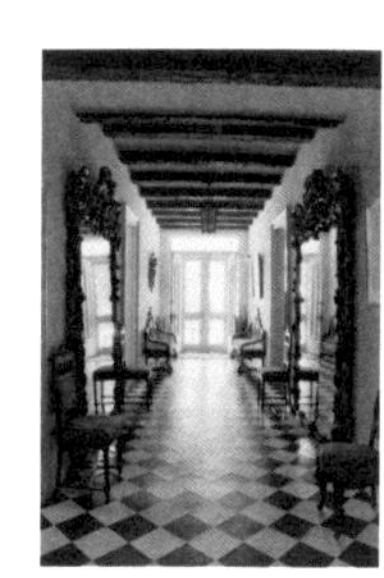

p. 120
Philadelphia, PA

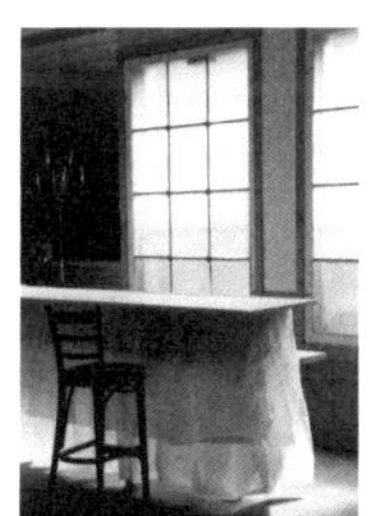

p. 121
Camden, NJ

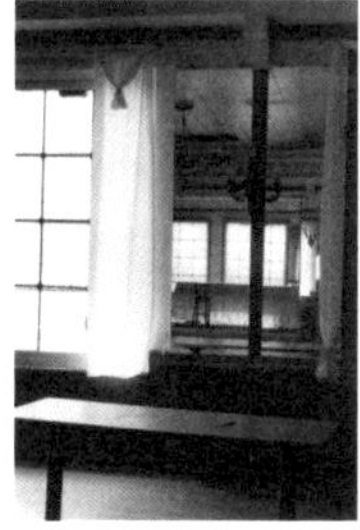

p. 121
Camden, NJ

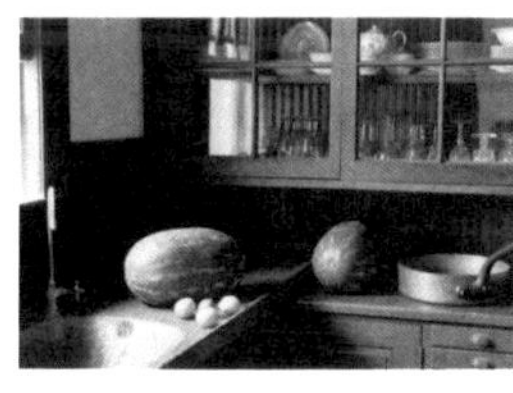

p. 122
Cumberland Island, GA

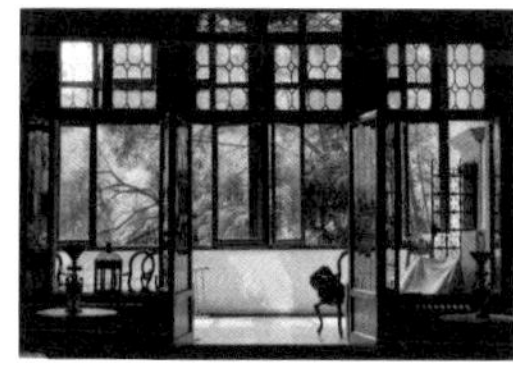

p. 124
Venice, Italy

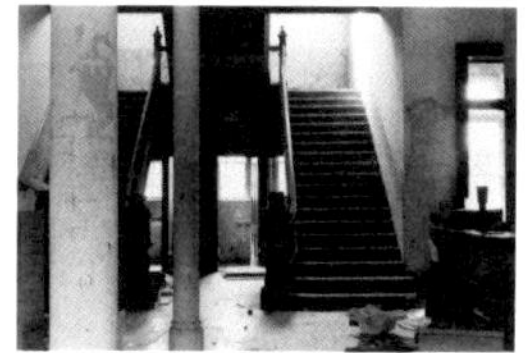

p. 126
Brunswick, GA

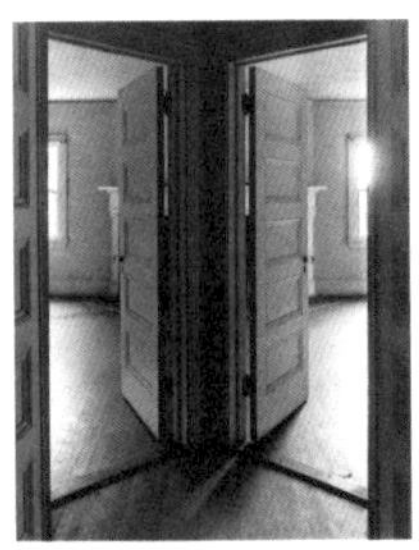

p. 127
Cumberland Island, GA

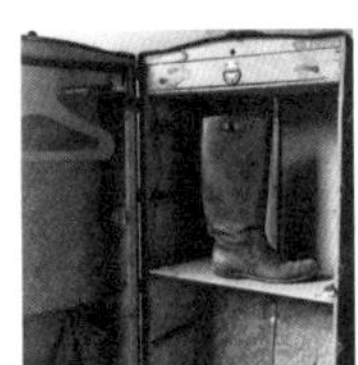

p. 128
Cumberland Island, GA

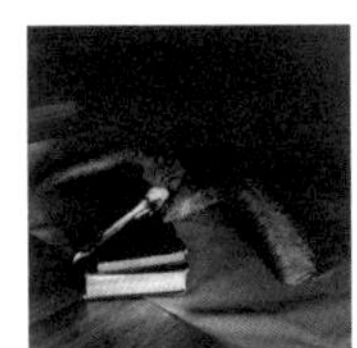

p. 129
Cumberland Island, GA

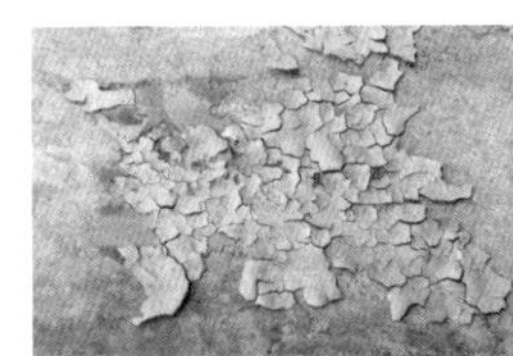

p. 130
Peeling Paint,
Cumberland Island, GA

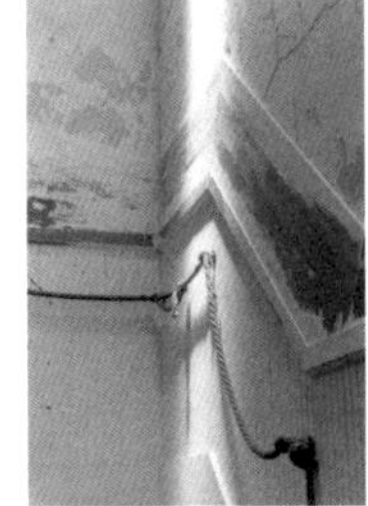

p. 131
Cumberland Island, GA

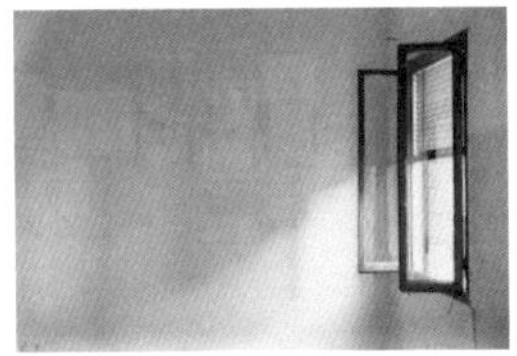

p. 132
Venice, Italy

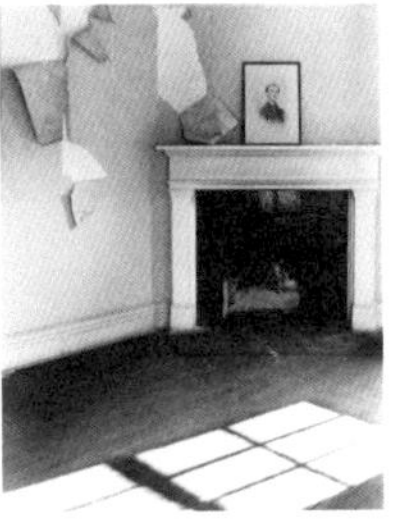

p. 134
Cumberland Island, GA

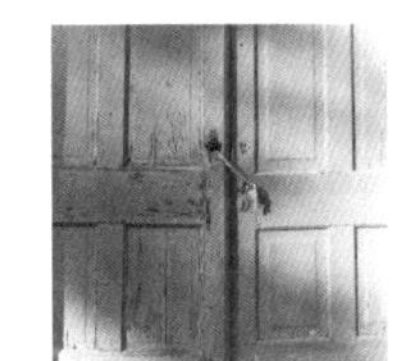

p. 135
Cumberland Island, GA

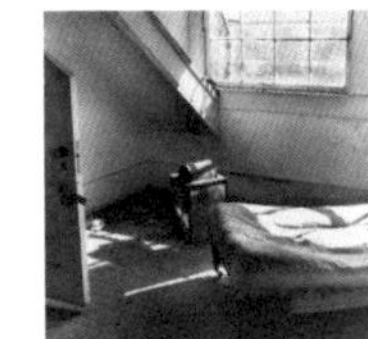

p. 136
Cumberland Island, GA

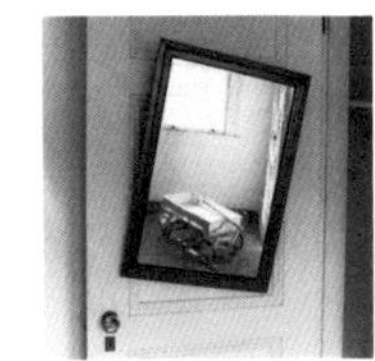

p. 137
Cumberland Island, GA

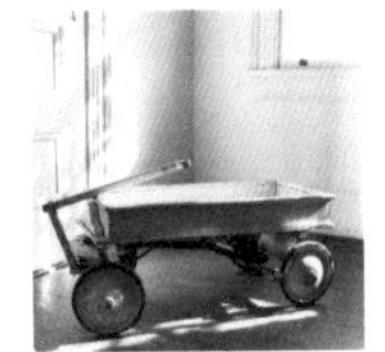

p. 137
Cumberland Island, GA

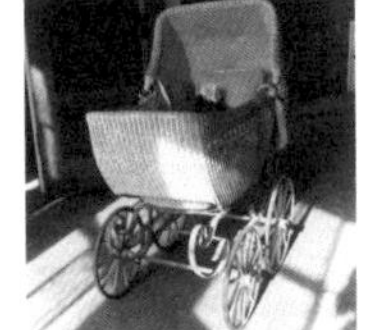

p. 138
Cumberland Island, GA

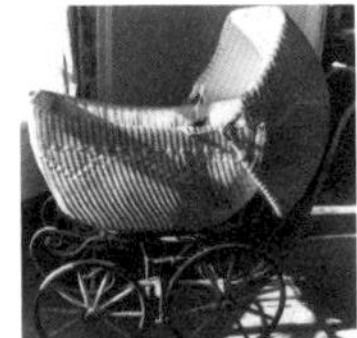

p. 139
Cumberland Island, GA

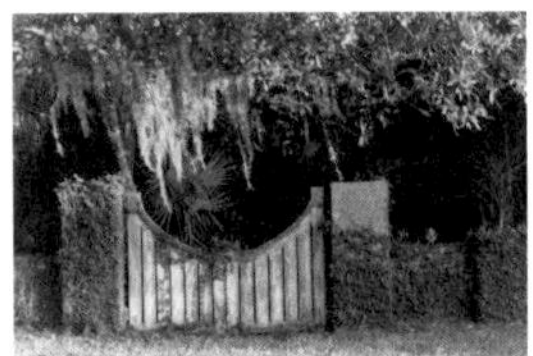

p. 140
Cumberland Island, GA

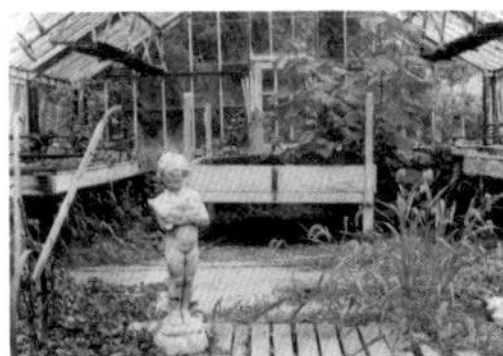

p. 142
Fort Washington, PA

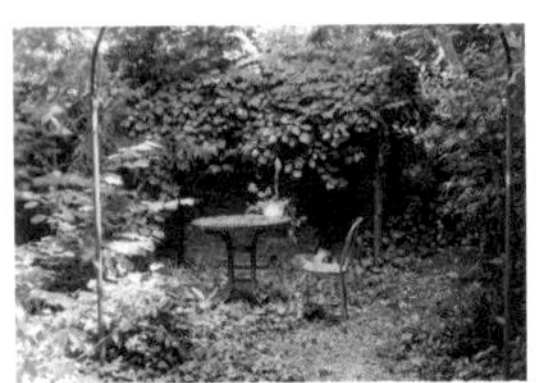

p. 144
Venice, Italy

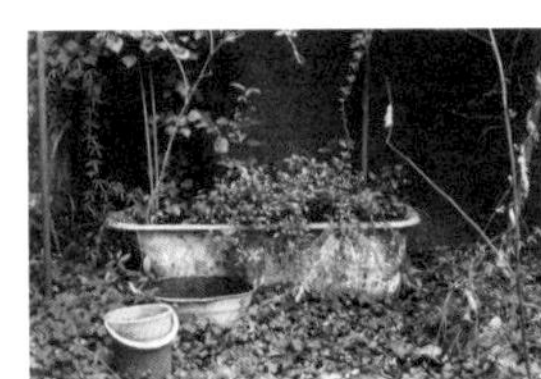

p. 145
Venice, Italy

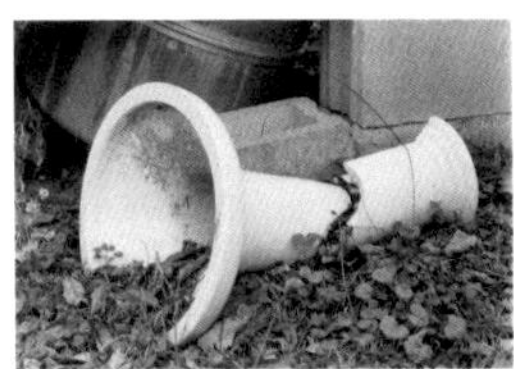

p. 145
Plymouth Meeting, PA

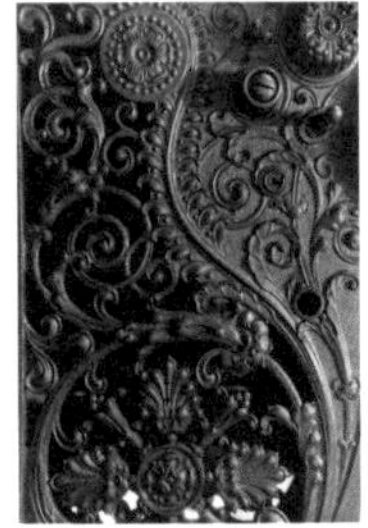
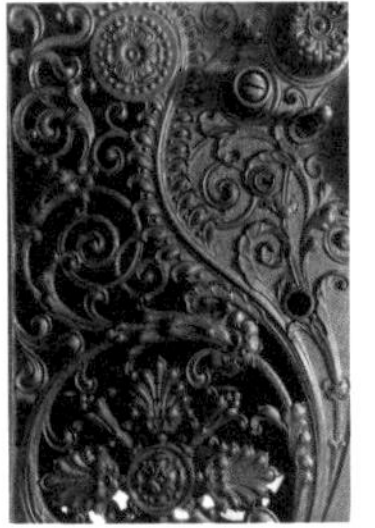

p. 146
Snow Hill, MD

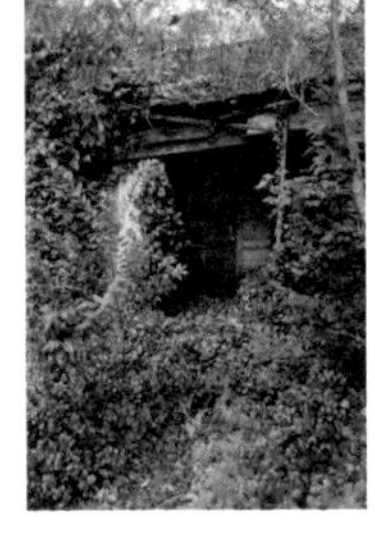

p. 147
Plymouth Meeting, PA

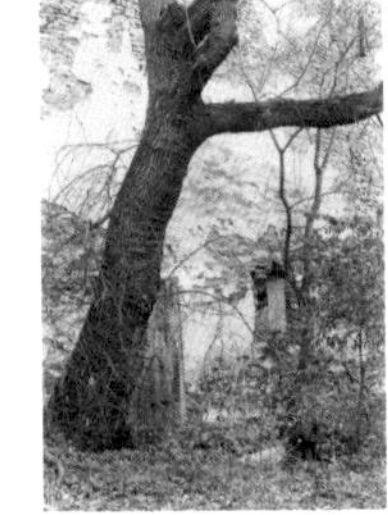

p. 148
Plymouth Meeting, PA

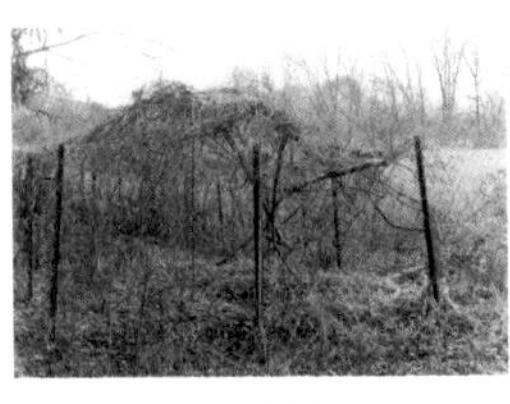

p. 149
Plymouth Meeting, PA

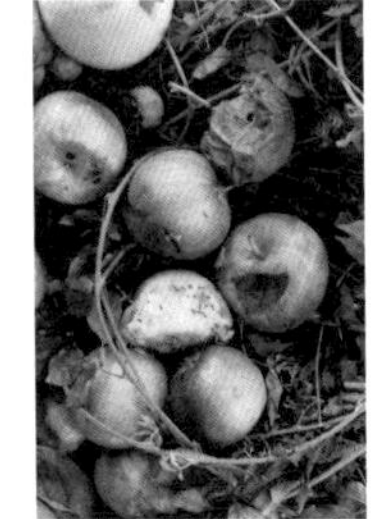

p. 150
Blue Bell, PA

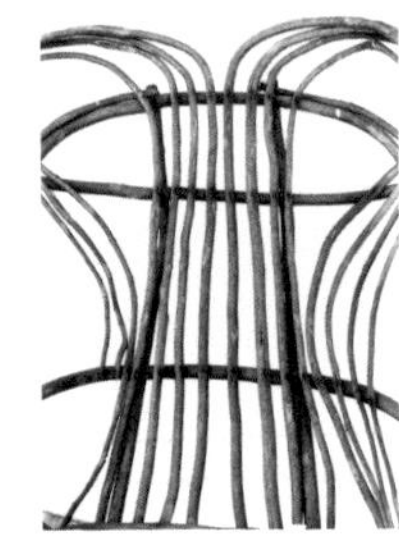

p. 151
Plymouth Meeting, PA

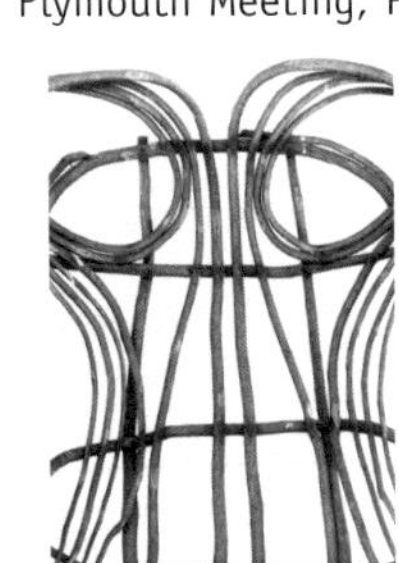

p. 151
Plymouth Meeting, PA

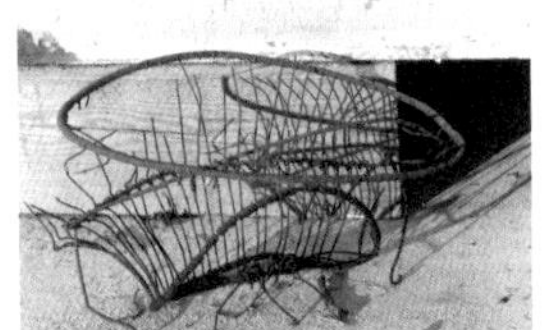

p. 151
Wachapreague, PA

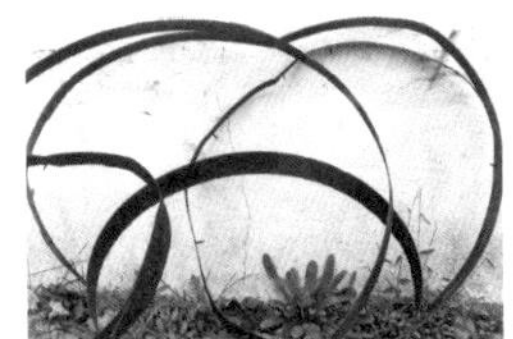

p. 152
Hopewell Village, PA

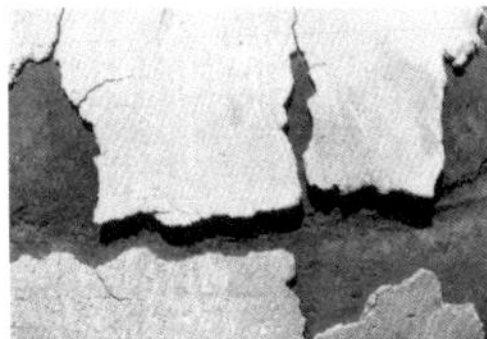

p. 154
Flaking Ship's Paint,
Chincoteague, VA

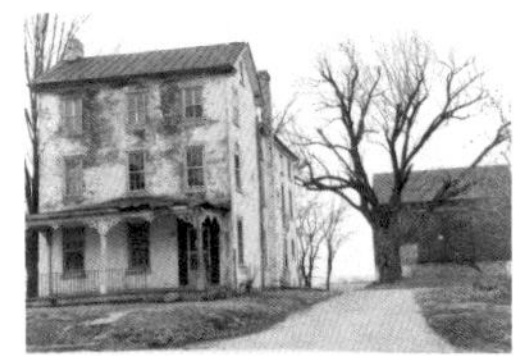

p. 155
Montgomery County, PA

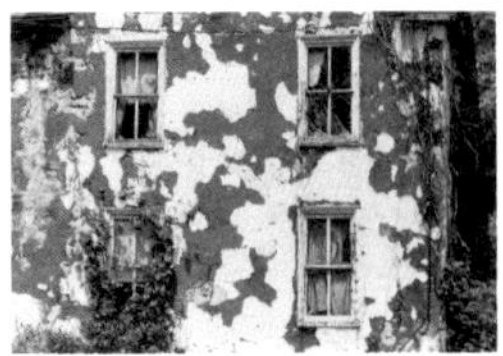

p. 156
Montgomery County, PA

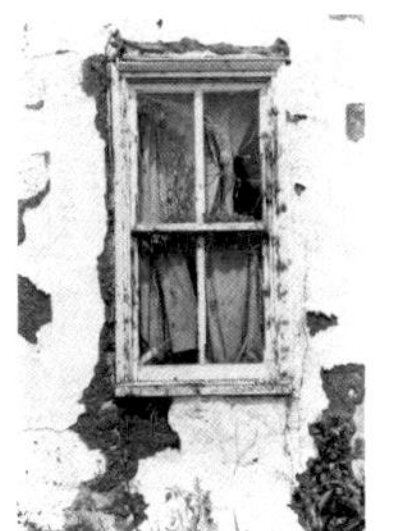

p. 158
Montgomery County, PA

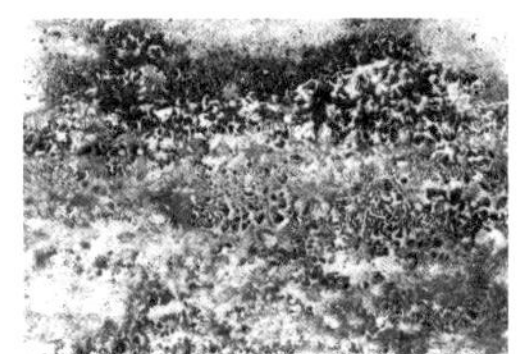

p. 159
Blistered Paint,
Carriacou, Grenada

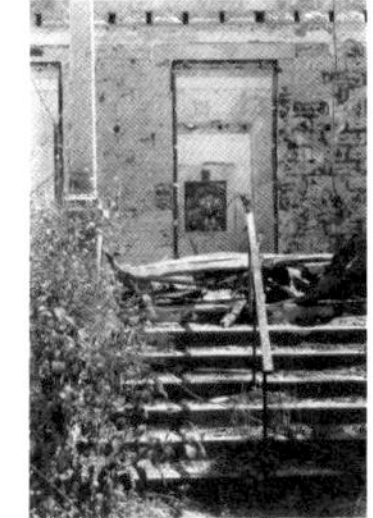

p. 160
Vieques, PR

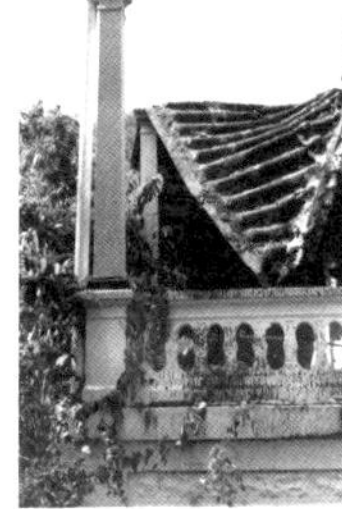

p. 161
Vieques, PR

p. 162
Chincoteague, VA

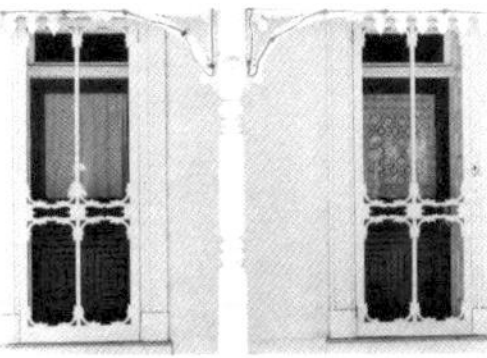

p. 164
Skippack, PA

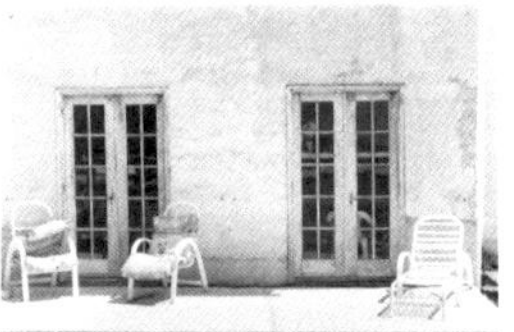

p. 164
Montgomery County, PA

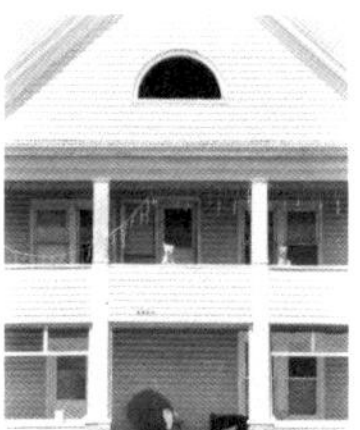

p. 165
Horntown, VA

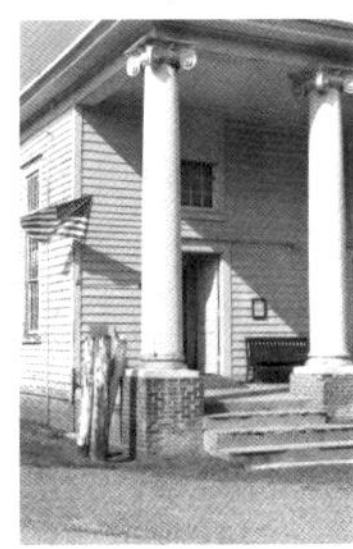

p. 166
Accomac, VA

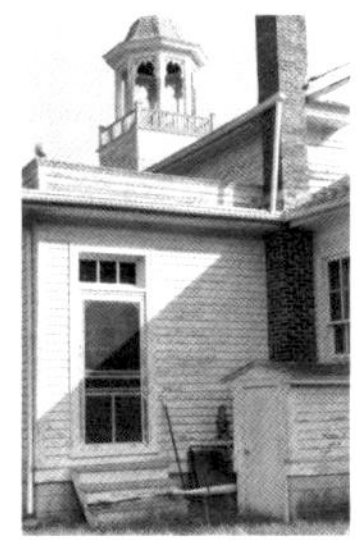

p. 167
Locustville, VA

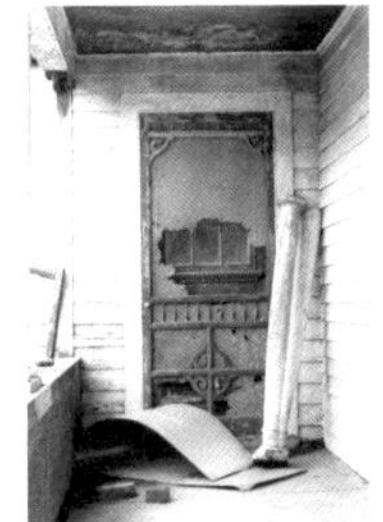

p. 168
Tasley, VA

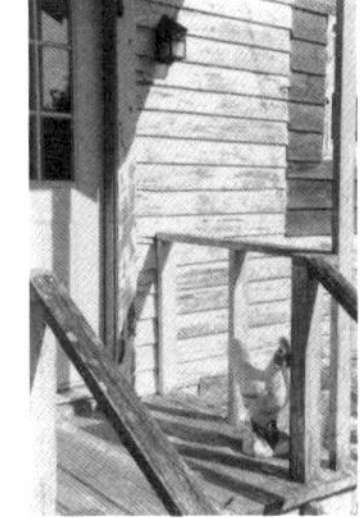

p. 169
Chincoteague, VA

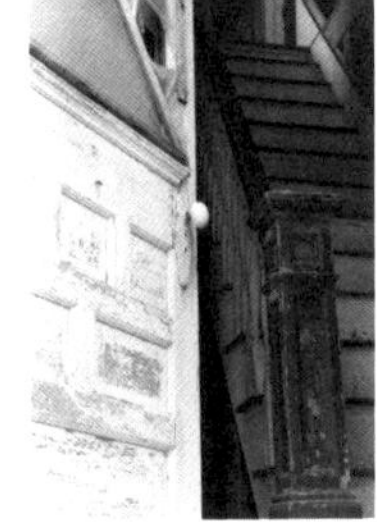

p. 170
Ticktown,VA

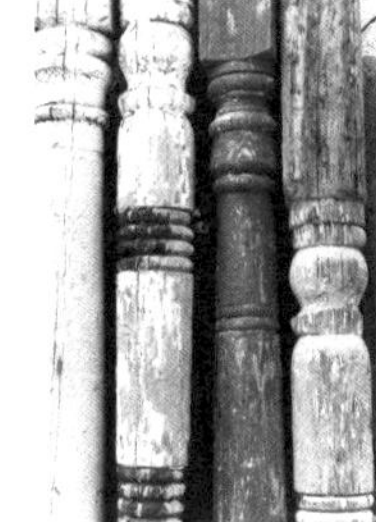

p. 171
Skippack, PA

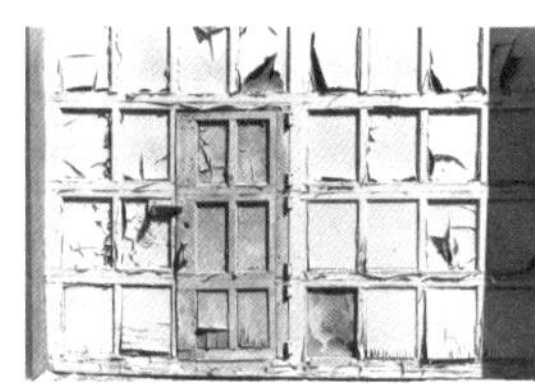

p. 172
Salisbury, MD

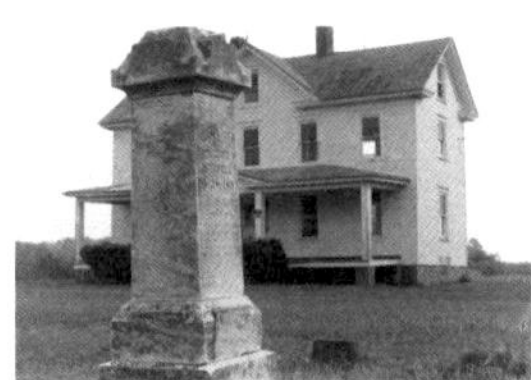

p. 174
Boxiron, MD

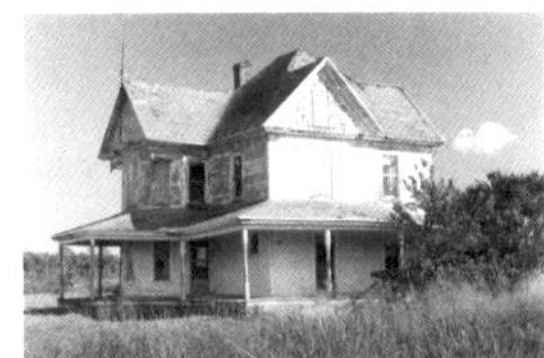

p. 176
Stockton, MD

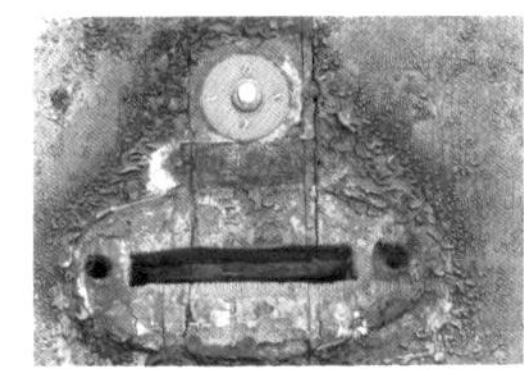

p. 178
Venice, Italy

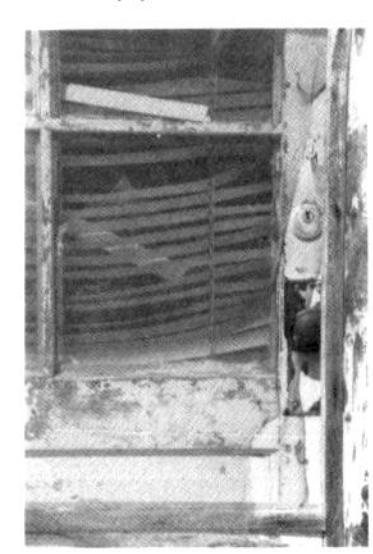

p. 179
Tangier Island, VA

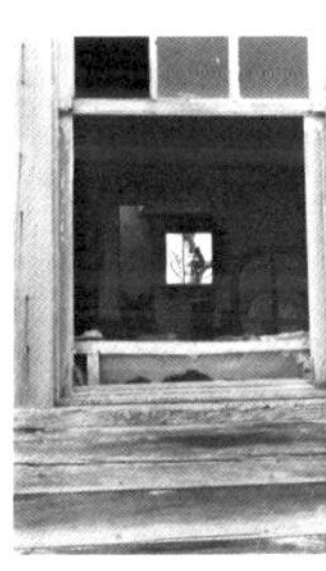

p. 179
Bullbeggar, VA

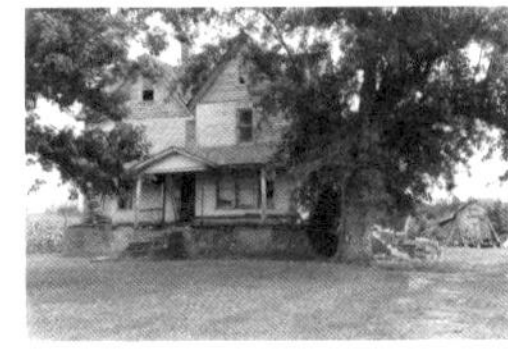

p. 180
Marsh Market, VA

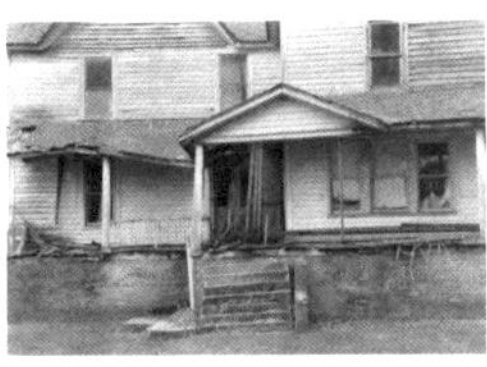

p. 180
Marsh Market, VA

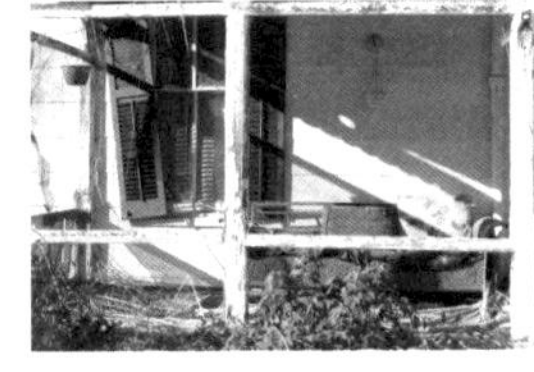

p. 181
Metompkin, VA

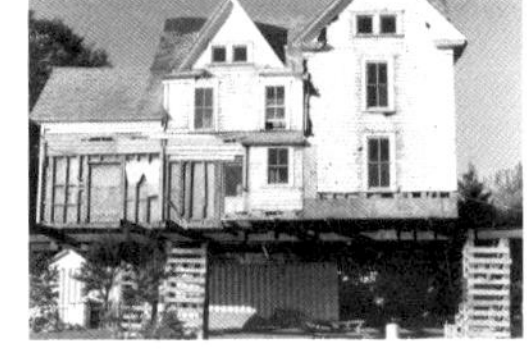

p. 182
Metompkin, VA

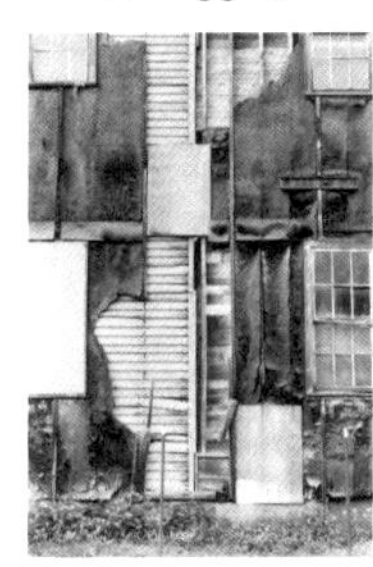

p. 182
Pittsford, NY

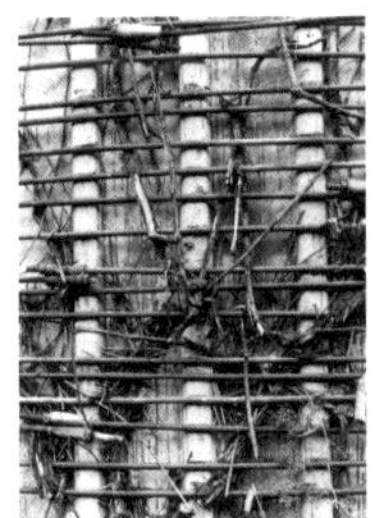

p. 182
Pittsford, NY

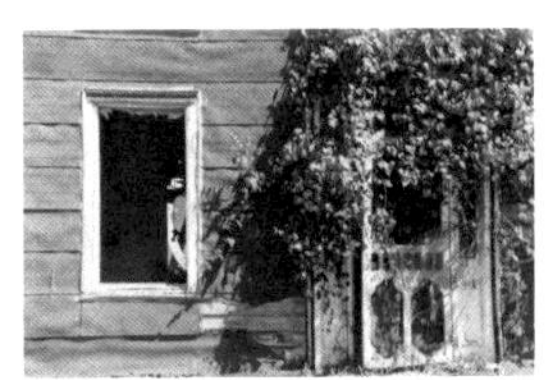

p. 183
Messongo, VA

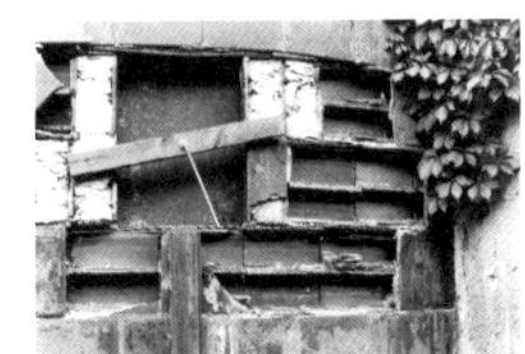

p. 183
Pittsford, NY

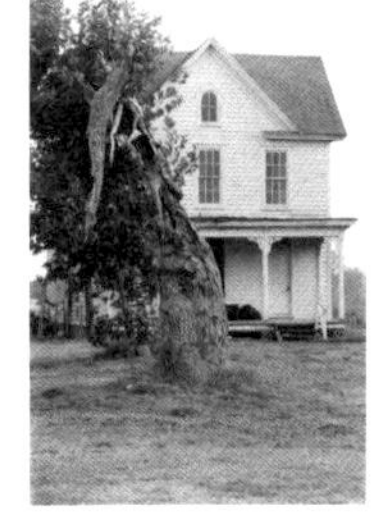

p. 184
Chancetown, VA

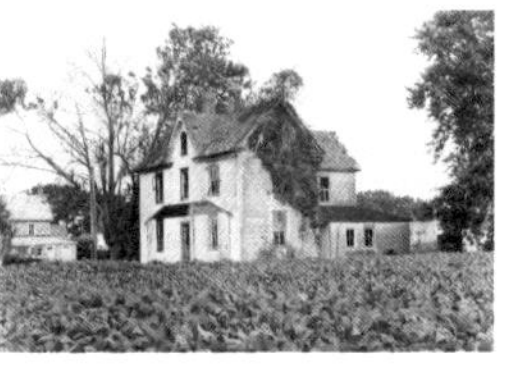

p. 185
Temperanceville, VA

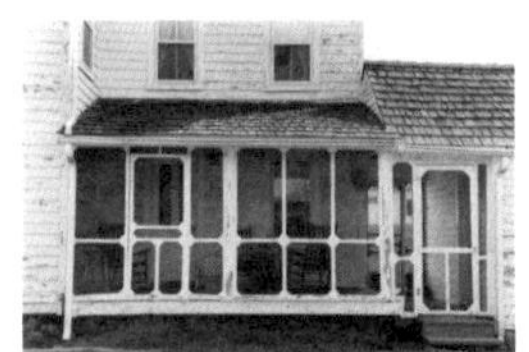

p. 185
Chincoteague, VA

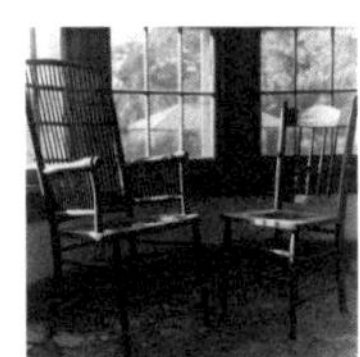

p. 186
Cumberland Island, GA

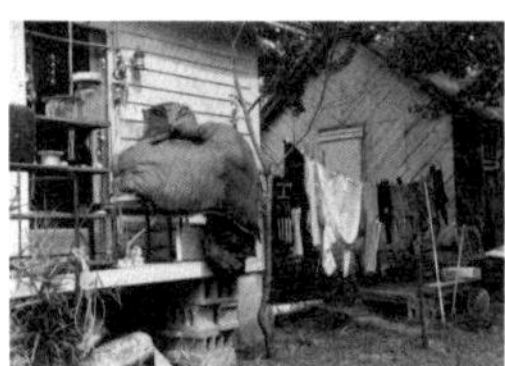

p. 188
Chincoteague, VA

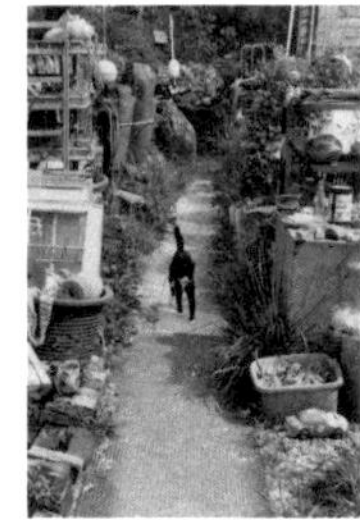

p. 189
Chincoteague, VA

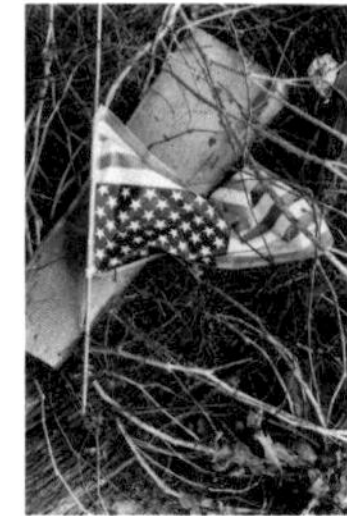

p. 190
Nelsonia, VA

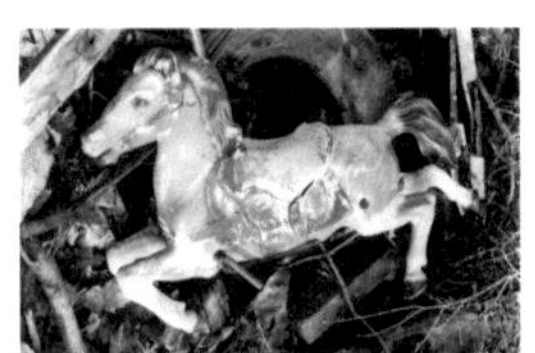

p. 191
Plymouth Meeting, PA

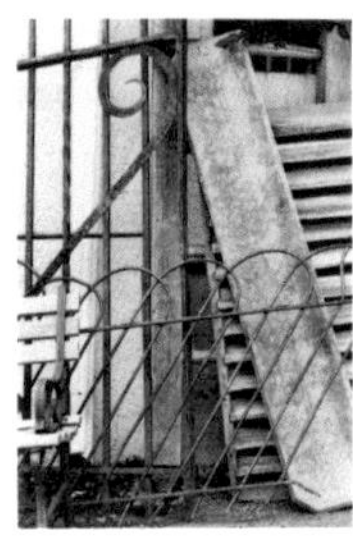

p. 192
Skippack, PA

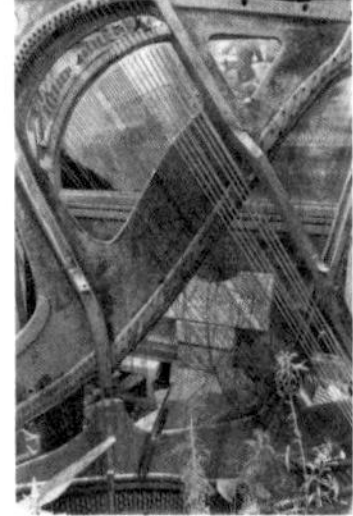

p. 193
Chincoteague, VA

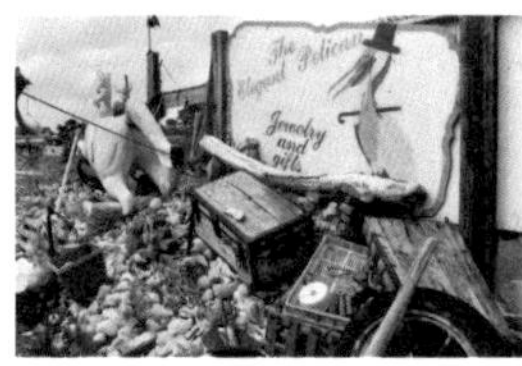

p. 194
Chincoteague, VA

p. 196
Oak Hall, VA

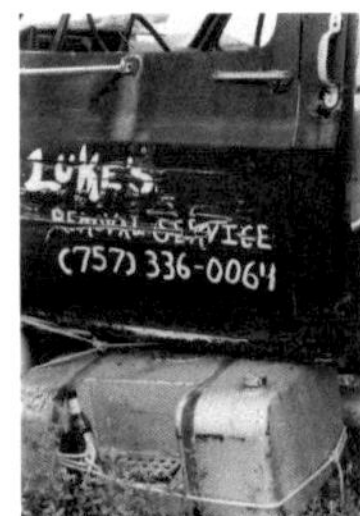

p. 197
Tasley, VA

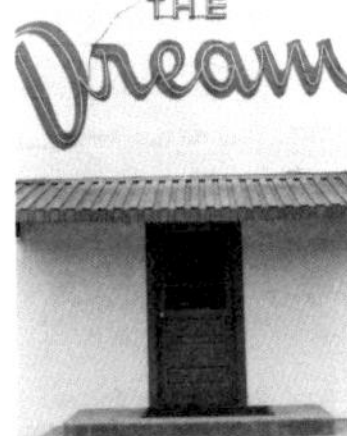

p. 198
Wattsville, VA

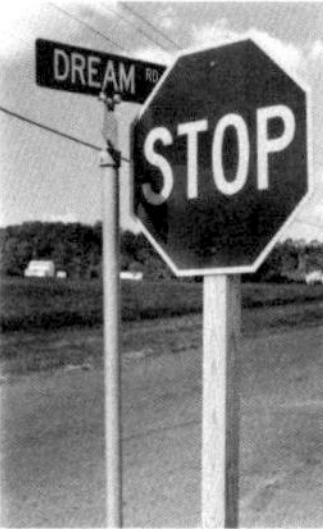

p. 199
Wattsville, VA

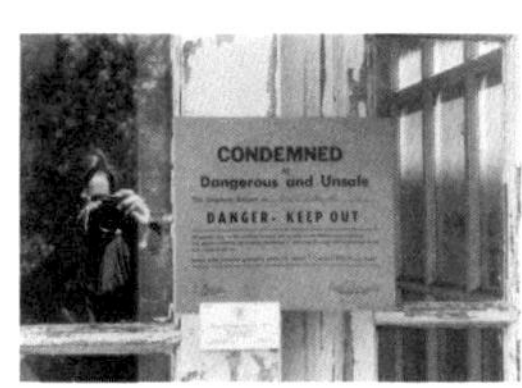

p. 201
Plymouth Meeting, PA

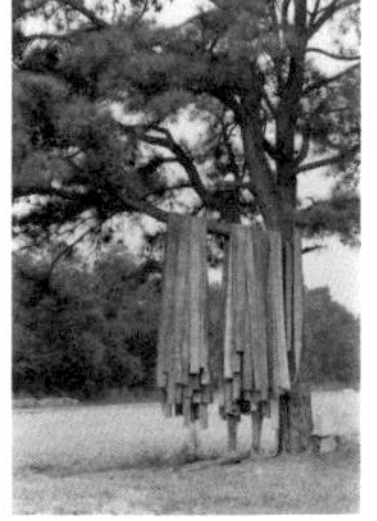

p. 209
Accomack County, VA

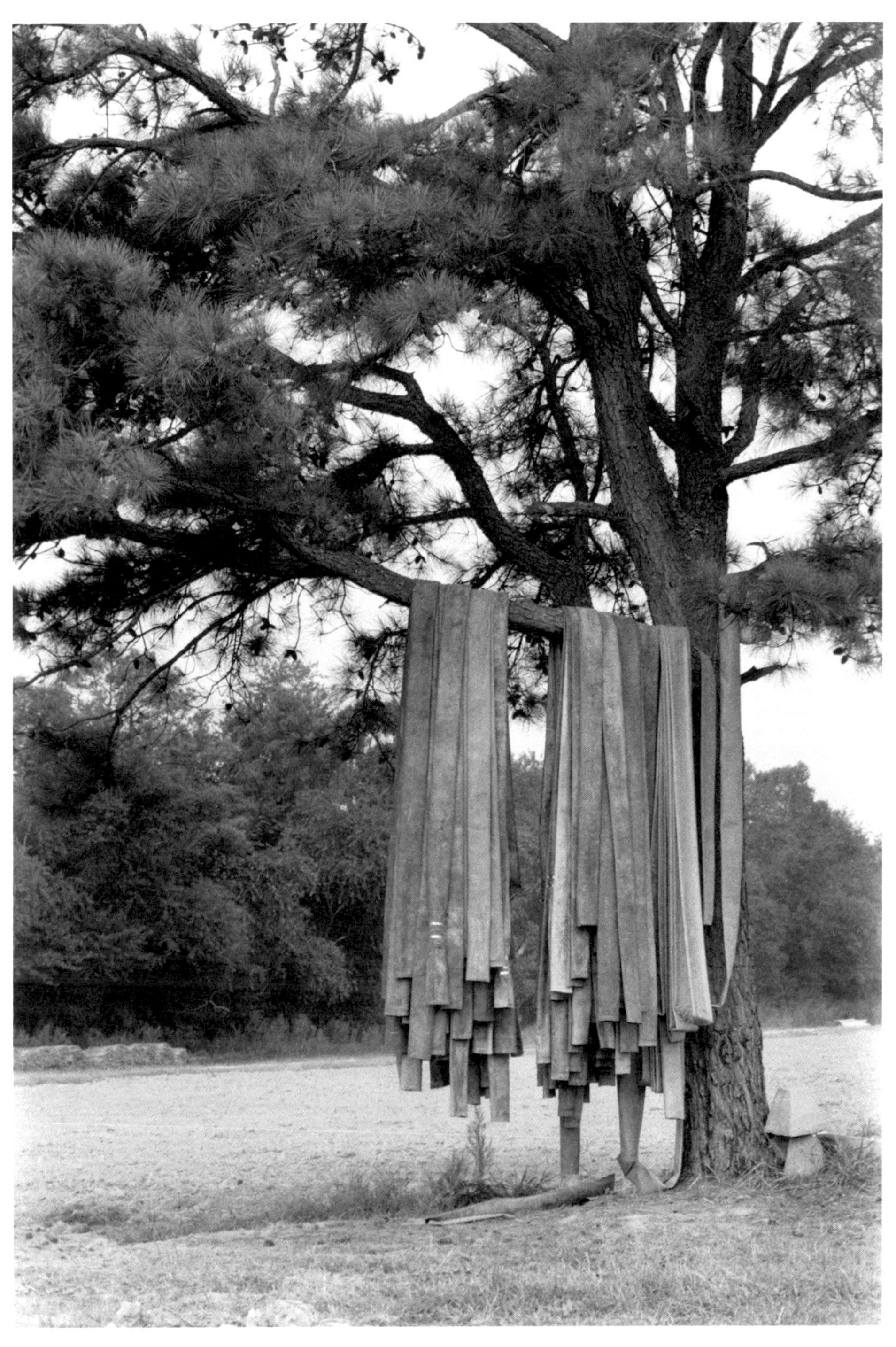

Design and Production of this book were managed by Veronica Miller & Associates, Haverford, Pennsylvania.

Tritone separations and production supervision were provided by Peter Philbin.

This book was printed by Brilliant Studio, Exton, Pennsylvania in an edition of three thousand copies and was bound by Hoster Bindery, inc., Ivyland, Pennsylvania.

Published by the University of Pennsylvania Museum of Archaeology and Anthropology, Philadelphia, Pennsylvania.

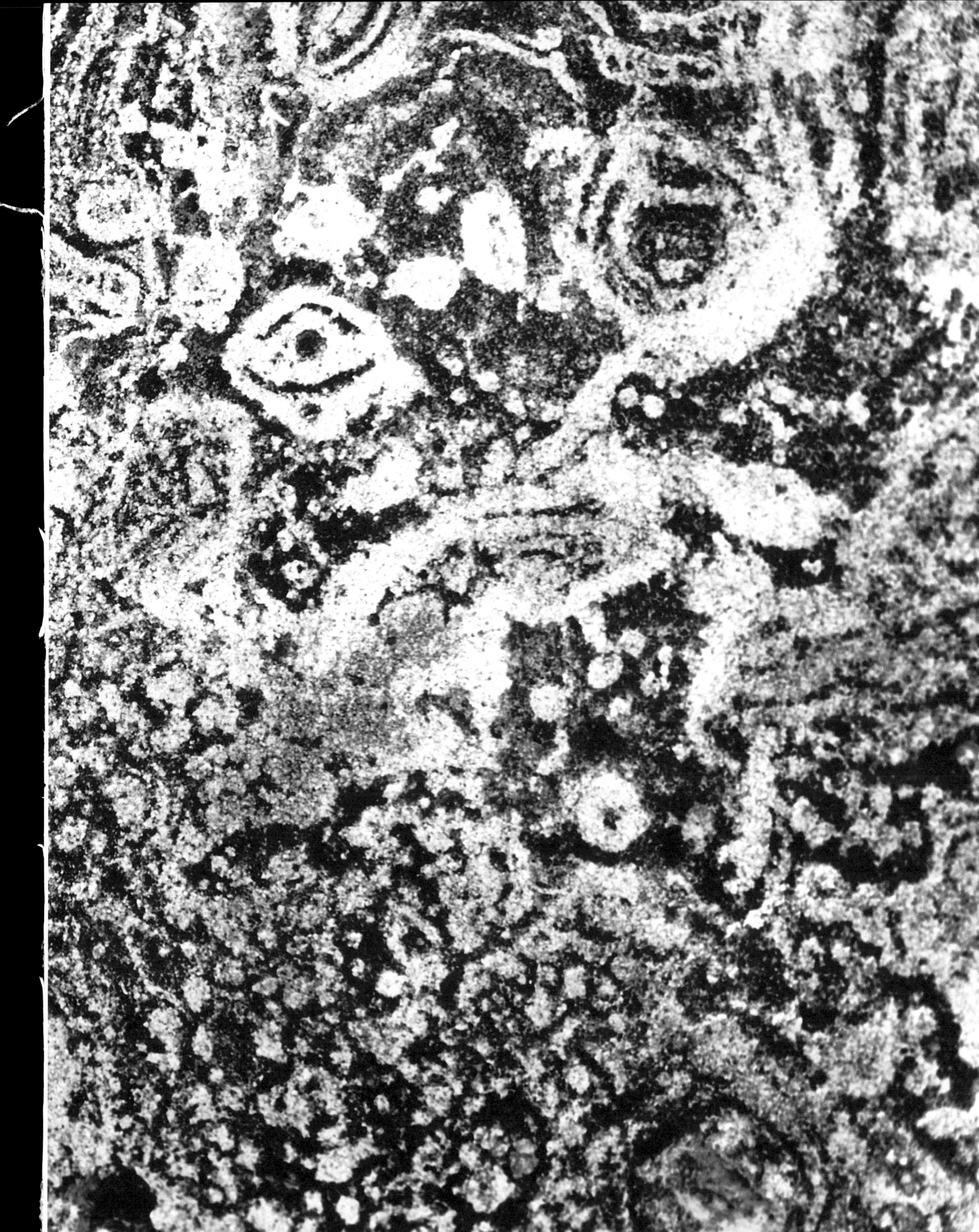

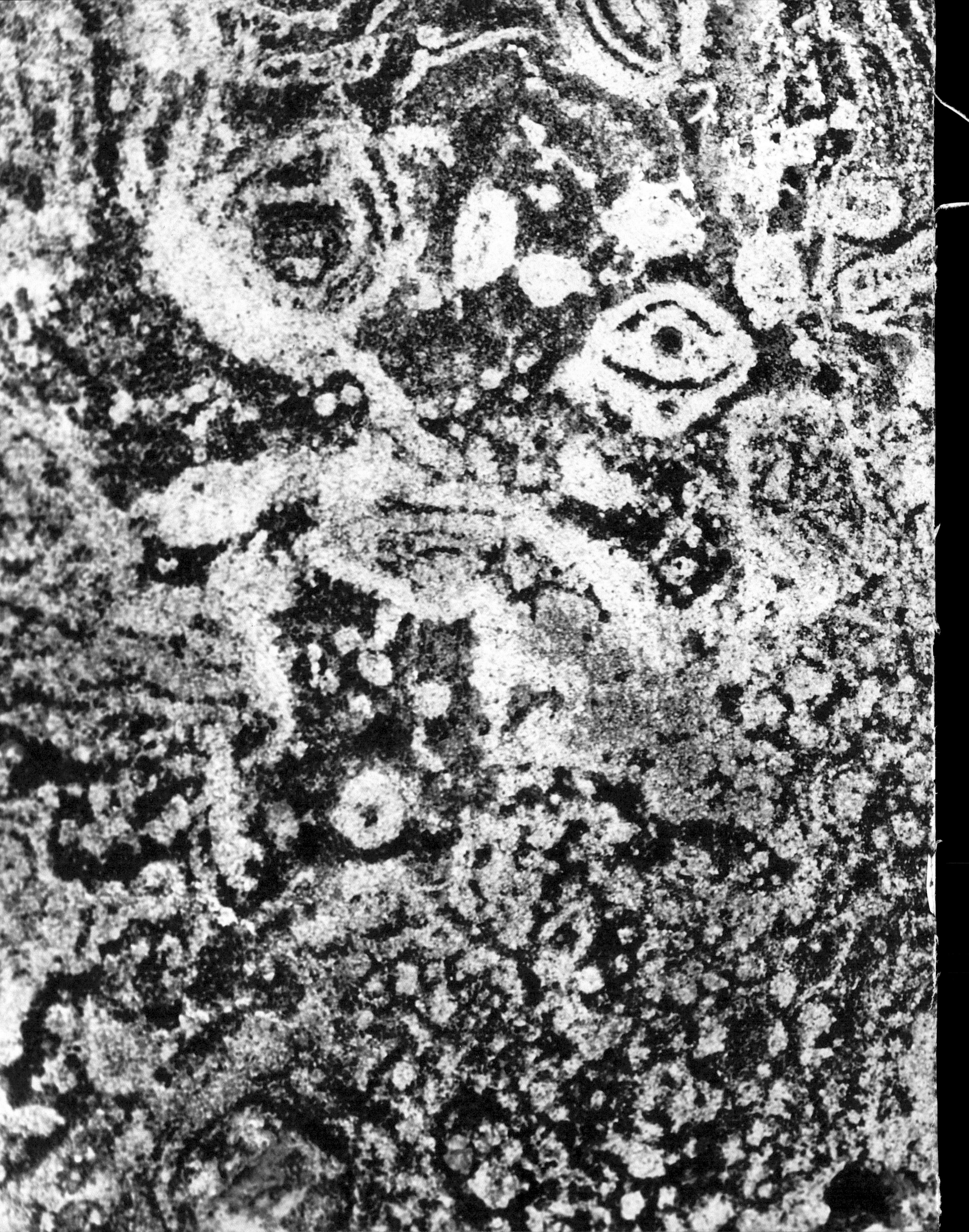